CHURCH AND COMMUNITY CONFLICTS

SOCIETY
OF BIBLICAL
LITERATURE

DISSERTATION SERIES
Michael V. Fox, Old Testament Editor
Mark Allan Powell, New Testament Editor

Number 168
CHURCH AND COMMUNITY CONFLICTS
The Relationships of the Thessalonian,
Corinthian, and Philippian Churches
with Their Wider Civic Communities
by
Craig Steven de Vos

Craig Steven de Vos

CHURCH AND COMMUNITY CONFLICTS
The Relationships of the Thesssalonian,
Corinthian, and Philippian Churches
with Their Wider Civic Communities

Society of Biblical Literature
Dissertation Series

Scholars Press
Atlanta, Georgia

CHURCH AND COMMUNITY CONFLICTS
The Relationships of the Thessalonian,
Corinthian, and Philippian Churches
with Their Wider Civic Communities
by
Craig Steven de Vos

Ph.D., 1997, Flinders University of South Australia
Rev. Dr. Victor C. Pfitzner, Advisor

Library of Congress Cataloging in Publication Data
De Vos, Craig Steven, 1961–
    Church and community conflicts : the relationships of the
Thessalonian, Corinthian, and Philippian churches with their wider
civic communitites / Craig Steven de Vos.
        p.   cm. — (Dissertation series / Society of Biblical
Literature ; no. 168)
    Originally presented as the author's thesis (Ph. D.)—Flinders
University of South Australia, 1997.
    Includes bibliographical references.
    ISBN 0-7885-0563-7 (cloth : alk. paper)
        1. Thessalonikē (Greece)—Church history. 2. Christianity and culture—
Greece—Thessalonikē—History—Early church, ca. 30–600. 3. Corinth
(Greece)—Church history. 4. Christianity and culture—Greece—
Corinth—History—Early church, ca. 30–600. 5. Philippi (Extinct city)—
Church history. 6. Christianity and culture—Greece—Philippi—(Extinct
city)—History—Early church, ca. 30–600. I. Title. II. Series:
Dissertation series (Society of Biblical Literature) ; no. 168.
BR868.T47D48 1999
274.95'01—dc21   99-28036
                                                  CIP

Printed in the United States of America
on acid-free paper

CONTENTS

97800

ACKNOWLEDGMENTS

This study is a slightly modified and revised version of my PhD thesis that was accepted by the Flinders University of South Australia in April 1997. First and foremost, I wish to express my gratitude to my two supervisors, Vic Pfitzner and Alan Cadwallader. Together, they have been a wonderful source of encouragement and wisdom as they continually pushed me to clarify and justify my arguments. Alan's help with *TLG* searches was also much appreciated.

Philip Esler gave considerable advice on how to make my model workable and offered invaluable comments on the overall structure of the thesis. I want to thank John Barclay for his encouragement, his insightful criticism of earlier drafts of chapters four and five, and the opportunity to present my work to a seminar at the University of Glasgow. The continuing conversation I have had with Todd Still on conflict at Thessalonica has been stimulating, and his generous comments on earlier drafts of chapters four and six were greatly appreciated.

I wish to thank Flinders University for giving me an Australian Postgraduate Award. A small grant from the *With Love to the World* Scholarships Committee enabled me to see first-hand the sites of Thessalonica, Corinth, and Philippi, and to spend an invaluable period of research in Scotland. Both awards were greatly appreciated.

Thanks to the support, encouragement, and friendship of Steve Thompson, Stuart Hill, and Margaret Lightbody I remained (relatively) sane. Finally, I must thank my wife, Bronwyn. Although she has not contributed directly to this study, she has been affected by it. She was dragged around ancient ruins in Greece and did her best to seem interested, and she endured the financial burdens, mood swings and social restrictions that such an undertaking involves. Hopefully our life can be more "normal" with its completion!

ABBREVIATIONS

Abbreviations of the works of classical authors and of inscriptions will largely follow those adopted by the *Oxford Classical Dictionary* (2nd ed.), while biblical studies works will largely follow those adopted by the *Journal of Biblical Literature*, except for the following:

ABD	D. N. Freedman (ed.) *The Anchor Bible Dictionary.* 6 vols. New York: Doubleday, 1992.
Arch Rep	*Archaeological Reports*
ASP	American Studies in Papyrology
BAFCS	The Book of Acts in its First Century Setting
BibInt	*Biblical Interpretation*
BIS	Biblical Interpretation Series
BNTC	Black's New Testament Commentary
CSSH	*Comparative Studies in Society and History*
EHR	*Economic History Review*
ESCJ	Studies in Christianity and Judaism/Études sur le christianisme et le judaïsme
ESEC	Emory Studies in Early Christianity
GBS	Guides to Biblical Scholarship
JRASup	Journal of Roman Archaeology Supplement
Kent	J. H. Kent, *Corinth: Results of Excavations. Volume VIII.3: The Inscriptions, 1926-1950.* Princeton, NJ: American School of Classical Studies at Athens, 1966.
Meritt	B. D. Meritt, *Corinth: Results of Excavations. Volume VIII.1: Greek Inscriptions, 1896-1927.* Cambridge, MA: Harvard University Press, 1931.
New Docs	G. H. R. Horsley & S. R. Llewelyn (eds.) *New Documents Illustrating Early Christianity.* 7 vols. Sydney: Macquarie University Press, 1981-95.
PDS	N. Abercrombie, S. Hill & B. S. Turner (eds.) *The Penguin Dictionary of Sociology.* 2nd ed. London: Penguin, 1988.
SIGLM	M. Demitsas, *Sylloge Inscriptionum Graecarum et Latinarum Macedoniae.* 2 vols. Edited by A. N. Oikonomides. Chicago: Ares, 1980 [1896].

Soc An	*Sociological Analysis*
SP	Sacra Pagina Commentary
SNTW	Studies in the New Testament and Its World
TCGNT	B. M. Metzger. *A Textual Commentary on the Greek New Testament.* 2nd ed. Stuttgart: Deutsche Bibelgesellschaft, 1994.
TNTC	Tyndale New Testament Commentary
West	A. B. West, *Corinth: Results of Excavations. Volume VIII.2: Latin Inscriptions, 1896-1927.* Cambridge, MA: Harvard University Press, 1931.

INTRODUCTION

Recently John Barclay observed that "the question of interaction with outsiders is one that has been unduly neglected in sociological studies of early Christianity". He goes on to suggest that in considering this issue, it is necessary to heed the differences between Paul's churches.[1] Indeed, even a cursory reading of Paul's letters suggests that relations between Paul's converts and their wider civic communities varied considerably. Conflictual relations (and suffering) appear to be a significant issue in Philippians and 1 Thessalonians, but they are entirely absent from 1 and 2 Corinthians and Philemon.[2] While there may have been conflict between the churches and the synagogues in Galatia, there is no unambiguous evidence in Paul's letter to the Galatians that conflict with the wider (Hellenistic) civic community was at all a problem, compared to Philippians and 1 Thessalonians.[3]

---

[1] J. M. G. Barclay, "Thessalonica and Corinth: Social Contrasts in Pauline Christianity" *JSNT* 47 (1992) 73.

[2] The arguments for such conflict being significant at Thessalonica and Philippi but not at Corinth will be discussed in chapter 4, 6 and 5 (respectively).

[3] See, for example, 1 Thess 3:1-5 or Phil 1:27-30. The lack of such conflict is recognized by A. J. Goddard & S. A. Cummins ("Ill or Ill-Treated? Conflict and Persecution as the Context of Paul's Original Ministry in Galatia [Galatians 4.12-20]" *JSNT* 52 [1993] 119-20) and P. F. Esler ("Group Boundaries and Intergroup Conflict in Galatians: A New Reading of Galatians 5:13-6:10" in M. G. Brett, ed., *Ethnicity and the Bible* [BIS 19; Leiden: E. J. Brill, 1996] 227-8). J. M. G. Barclay claims that the problem in Galatia was that the Christians lacked a social identity. Consequently, they were tempted to be circumcized and follow the Law and thus to be identified with the Jewish community (*Obeying the Truth: A Study of Paul's Ethics in Galatians* [SNTW; Edinburgh: T. & T. Clark, 1988] 58-72). But this does not necessarily require the churches' context to involve overt conflict with their wider communities and, as already mentioned, there is no clear evidence to suggest such a conflict was a problem.

2   *Church and Community Conflicts*

The situation in Paul's letter to the Romans is unclear. Few commentators ground Paul's statement in Rom 12:14 (εὐλογεῖτε τοὺς διώκοντας [ὑμᾶς], εὐλογεῖτε καὶ μὴ καταρᾶσθε) in a specific historical context. Some scholars link this verse with the reference to θλῖψις ἢ στενοχωρία ἢ διωγμὸς…ἢ μάχαιρα in Rom 8:35 to suggest there was conflict between the Christians and the authorities at Rome.[4] But this is unlikely given Paul's attitude to the State in Rom 13:1-7, and the absence of any specific reference to such conflict in the letter.[5] It is more likely that 12:14, 17-21 refers to Paul's own experience of conflict in Asia Minor and Macedonia, and is intended to prepare his readers for such conflict, should it develop.[6] At the same time, 13:1-7 may be an attempt to prevent conflict developing and hence prejudicing Paul's intended mission at Rome.[7] In other words, at the time he writes, conflict with their wider civic community may not have been an issue for the Christians at Rome.[8] Yet even if there was some conflict, Paul clearly does not perceive it to be a significant issue.

This pattern of varied response concurs with the observation by historians that there was only a limited and sporadic persecution of Christians until well into the second century. The measures that were taken against them were local, temporary and in the nature of police actions. They

---

[4] See, for example, R. Barraclough, "Romans 13:1-7: Application in Context" *Colloquium* 17 (1984) 20.

[5] As with Paul's letter to the Galatians there is no explicit reference to such conflict in his letter to the Romans, compared to, for example, 1 Thess 3:1-5 or Phil 1:27-30. See G. Zerbe, "Paul's Ethic of Nonretaliation and Peace" in W. M. Swartley, ed., *The Love of Enemy and Nonretaliation in the New Testament* (Louisville, KY: W/JK Press, 1992) 187-9. M. D. Nanos has recently argued that 13:1-7 is a call to obey the leaders of the synagogue, and does not refer to the Roman authorities at all (*The Mystery of Romans: The Jewish Context of Paul's Letter* [Minneapolis: Fortress, 1996] 289-336), but I do not find his arguments at all persuasive. He relies heavily on Acts, twists the sense in which ἐξουσίαι is normally used, and on the occasion when the term does refer to authorities (ibid., 303), it is clear from the context that it refers to the Jerusalem government, not the synagogue.

[6] Zerbe, "Nonretaliation", 188-9.

[7] See J. Botha, *Subject to Whose Authority? Multiple Readings of Romans 13* (ESEC 4; Atlanta: Scholars, 1994) 223.

[8] Of course it is possible that if there were some Christians at Rome who had come from a Jewish background, they may have experienced conflict with the authorities before they had become Christians (e.g. in 19, 41 or 49 CE). Such conflicts will be discussed in chapter 2.

were not carried out by imperial edict.[9] Even Nero's punishment of Christians at Rome following the Great Fire of 64 CE was not carried out according to edict, but was a police measure. At the most, this action may have influenced provincial governors and persuaded them to follow suit, but it does not appear to have become a binding legal precedent.[10]

When action was taken in this early period, it followed the normal Roman legal process. This process was accusatorial, such that local enemies would denounce Christians to the governor, but whether or not he acted on the charges lay at his discretion. It has been suggested that in most cases governors acted in response to strong public opinion and from a concern to maintain peace and order. Indeed, Marta Sordi is probably correct in suggesting that "the importance of public opinion in the ancient world is often underestimated, and yet during the first centuries of the Empire it seems often to have been the decisive factor which sparked off the persecution of the Christians".[11]

Given this scenario, the term "persecution" is inappropriate in the first century. It has strong pejorative overtones, implying that such actions were unjustified, unwarranted, even irrational. For example, Oscar Cullmann asserts that "many a persecution of Christians could have been avoided if the State had taken the pains to understand

---

[9] See, for example, A. N. Sherwin-White, "The Early Persecutions and Roman Law Again" *JTS* 3 (1952) 200-1; G. E. M. de Ste. Croix, "Why Were the Early Christians Persecuted?" *Past & Present* 26 (1963) 6-7; W. H. C. Frend, *Martyrdom and Persecution in the Early Church: A Study of a Conflict from the Maccabees to Donatus* (New York: New York University Press, 1967) 165-7; M. Sordi, *The Christians and the Roman Empire* (London: Routledge, 1994) 196; G. W. Bowersock, *Martyrdom and Rome* (Cambridge: Cambridge University Press, 1995) 41; cf. A. Yarbro-Collins, *Crisis and Catharsis: The Power of the Apocalypse* (Philadelphia: Westminster, 1984) 69-73, 100; G. Theissen, *Social Reality and the Early Christians: Theology, Ethics and the World of the New Testament* (Minneapolis: Fortress, 1992) 285; P. Oakes, "Philippians: From People to Letter" (unpublished DPhil dissertation, University of Oxford, 1995) 121.

[10] See, for example, Sherwin-White, "Early Persecutions", 209; de Ste. Croix, "Early Christians", 8, 14; Frend, *Martyrdom*, 165-7; S. Benko, *Pagan Rome and the Early Christians* (Bloomington: Indiana University Press, 1984) 7-9; Sordi, *The Christians*, 35; cf. Yarbro-Collins, *Crisis*, 100.

[11] Sordi, *The Christians*, 194; cf. See de Ste. Croix, "Early Christians", 15-16; Sherwin-White, "Early Persecutions", 209; Benko, *Pagan Rome*, 7; Yarbro-Collins, *Crisis*, 70, 100.

their attitude and convince itself of their loyalty".[12] But Cullmann is guilty of a similar attitude to that of which he accuses the Roman authorities. He displays an inability or unwillingness to understand the problem from the non-Christian side. In the period of the early first century, when the actions taken against Christians followed normal legal processes and were local and sporadic, the issue is clearly one of conflict, not persecution.

Some scholars have suggested that such conflict was, at least in part, politically motivated because the Christians were suspected of disloyalty on account of their secret meetings and rites.[13] But such suspicions would not necessarily have led to strong public opinion. More significantly, it is difficult to understand why magistrates would choose not to take action if this was a major factor.[14] Consequently, A. N. Sherwin-White argued that actions were primarily taken against the Christians because they were thought to have engaged in immoral acts (*flagitia*), such as incest and cannibalism. G. E. M. de Ste. Croix convincingly challenged this argument. In so doing, he demonstrated that the main issue in such conflict was the refusal of Christians to worship the gods of the state.[15] Consequently, it is now widely accepted that his argument is correct.[16] In other

---

[12] O. Cullmann, *The State in the New Testament* (New York: Scribners, 1956) 55.

[13] See de Ste. Croix, "Early Christians", 16; Frend, *Martyrdom*, 168.

[14] A similar argument is suggested by Sordi (*The Christians*, 194).

[15] The exchanges between A. N. Sherwin-White ("Early Persecutions"; "Why Were the Early Christians Persecuted? — An Amendment" *Past & Present* 27 [1964] 23-7) and G. E. M. de Ste. Croix ("Early Christians"; "Why Were the Early Christians Persecuted? — A Rejoinder" *Past & Present* 27 [1964] 28-33) are almost legendary. Sherwin-White's argument misconstrues some of the evidence, while de Ste. Croix's makes much better sense of it because the Gnostics were never subject to the same actions as those taken against Christians and they did offer worship to the gods and the Emperor, and that those who renounced Christianity and offered worship were generally spared — something that could not have happened if they were guilty of *flagitia*.

[16] See, for example, R. Macmullen, *Christianizing the Roman Empire AD 100-400* (New Haven, CT: Yale University Press, 1984) 19; Benko, *Pagan Rome*, 4; Sordi, *The Christians*, 30; Bowersock, *Martyrdom*, 4; cf. Yarbro-Collins, *Crisis*, 70, 73; Theissen, *Social Reality*, 281; Oakes, "Philippians", 114-17; chapter 10 of T. D. Still, "Θλῖψις in Thessalonica: A Study of the Conflict Relations of Paul and the Thessalonian Christians with Outsiders" (unpublished PhD dissertation, University of Glasgow, 1996).

words, the first Christians experienced conflict with their wider society primarily for rejecting the gods of the state. While this is certainly the most likely cause or charge, it does not really *explain* why such conflicts took place, and it certainly does not explain why they were only limited, local and sporadic.

Some scholars have suggested that such conflict was sporadic because Christians and Christianity were insignificant and hence not noticed by the authorities.[17] Admittedly, the insignificance of Christianity on the broad scale may account for the absence of a general edict until much later. Yet it sheds no light on the presence or absence of conflict in individual cities in the early first century. Gerd Theissen has argued that actions were taken against the earliest Christians because Christianity conferred a sense of status and power on ordinary people and gave them an "'aristocratic' sense of their own value and dignity". This, he suggests, was not tolerated by the ruling elite.[18] But his argument also fails to account for popular opinion and for the sporadic nature of the actions that were taken against the earliest Christians.

Some scholars have interpreted the link between conflict and the rejection of the traditional gods and cults via the sociology of deviance.[19] Such an approach is better since it takes greater cognisance of the social implications of religious behavior and may well explain the problem of adverse popular opinion at the local level. But if Christians were branded deviants because of their refusal to worship the traditional gods, and this was seen as a threat to the community, why were actions against Christians still only sporadic and limited?

To date, no one has really attempted to account for this problem. Therefore, in a general sense, this study will seek to explain why the conflict between the earliest Christians and their wider civic communities was sporadic. More specifically it will attempt to explain *why some of Paul's churches experienced conflict with their wider civic communities but others did not.*

---

[17] So Sherwin-White, "Early Persecutions", 201; Frend, *Martyrdom*, 166; Benko, *Pagan Rome*, 8.

[18] Theissen, *Social Reality*, 280-1.

[19] See Todd Still,"Θλîψις"; cf. Theissen, *Social Reality*, 281.

Since the aim of this study is to *explain* this phenomenon, it will be necessary to employ a social-scientific methodology.[20] Traditional historical criticism is unable to explain social phenomena since it can really only identify them. At best it can only answer "what"-type questions (such as "what was the cause of conflict"). In order to explain phenomena, that is, to answer "why"-type questions, theories and models are required.[21] A social-scientific method generally involves two stages: the *gathering and organization of data*, based on a preliminary hypothesis or model, followed by *interpretation*, where the data is analyzed according to the preliminary model.[22] However, for a model to be appropriate for studying Paul's churches it must be "constructed on the basis of research and data pertaining to

---

[20] The use of social-scientific methodology in Biblical criticism is now quite well established, even if it still encounters some resistance. However, I do not think it is necessary for me to defend the legitimacy of this methodology here when this has already been accomplished admirably by others. See, for example, P. F. Esler, *Community and Gospel in Luke-Acts: The Social and Political Motivation of Lukan Theology* (SNTSMS 57; Cambridge: Cambridge University Press, 1987) 12-16; idem., "Introduction: Models, Context and Kerygma in New Testament Interpretation" in P. F. Esler, ed., *Modelling Early Christianity* (London: Routledge, 1995) 1-20; J. H. Elliott, *What is Social-Scientific Criticism?* (GBS; Minneapolis: Fortress, 1993) 87-100.

[21] See R. Stark, "Jewish Conversion and the Rise of Christianity: Rethinking the Received Wisdom" *SBLSP* (1986) 315; Elliott, *Criticism*, 12, 40. Elliott defines a theory as "an organized and interactive body of generalizations based on empirical evidence that purport to explain a set of phenomena" and a model as "an abstract selective representation of the relationships among social phenomena used to conceptualize, analyze, and interpret the patterns of social relations, and to compare and contrast one system of social relations with another". Models "operationalize particular theories" (*Criticism*, 132, 135; cf. *PDS* sv "Model").

[22] In any case, all historical investigation uses models, although usually tacitly, implicitly or unconsciously. Indeed, they determine the sort of information that is examined and deemed relevant. They also determine the manner in which that information is interpreted. See T. F. Carney, *The Shape of the Past: Models and Antiquity* (Lawrence, KS: Coronado, 1975) 5; Elliott, *Criticism*, 41-3, 56. Therefore, by making my particular model explicit I am being more honest about the selective nature of my data collection, and about the premises on which it is based. Compare, for example, Carney, *Shape*, 5-6; P. F. Esler, *The First Christians in Their Social World: Social-Scientific Approaches to New Testament Interpretation* (London: Routledge, 1994) 12.

the geographical, social, and cultural region" in which they were located.[23]

Therefore, in part one of this study, I will begin by constructing a preliminary social-scientific model for explaining differences in the incidence of conflict within different societies and cultures (chapter one). The validity of this preliminary model will be tested against data from the first century Greco-Roman world (chapters two and three). Then it will be modified, where appropriate, so that there is a good degree of fit. Once this preliminary model has been modified, so that it is specific for the world of Paul's churches, the nature of these churches, their civic communities, and the relationships between them, will be explored (chapters four to six). The data collected via this exploration will, of course, be shaped by the demands and the purpose of the specific model. Finally, then, the material from these three cities and churches will be brought together and the model will be used as a means of explaining the observed differences in the relationships between these Christian and civic communities (chapter seven).

Rather than examine all of Paul's churches and their cities, I will examine the contexts of the churches at Thessalonica, Corinth and Philippi. These three have been selected because each of these churches was founded by Paul himself within a fairly close chronological and geographical proximity.[24] By using these three churches it is possible to establish certain controls, that is, by ruling out some potential causal factors at the beginning, it is easier to determine the particular combination of factors that is significant.

In particular, since the Thessalonian, Corinthian and Philippian churches were all founded by Paul within a short time-span, it is reasonable to assume that the apparent differences in their relationships with their wider civic communities cannot be attributed to them having received a fundamentally different version of the gospel.[25] Although

---

[23] Elliott, *Criticism*, 49.

[24] For a considerable part of the first century CE, both Achaia and Macedonia were linked and administered by the same governor. See, for example, F. Papazoglou, "Macedonia under the Romans" in M. B. Sakellariou, ed., *Macedonia: 4000 Years of Greek History and Civilization* (Athens: Ektodike Athenon, 1983) 196.

[25] This statement is consistent with the "coherence-contingency" model that has been used by J. C. Beker (e.g. "Recasting Pauline Theology: The Coherence-Contingency Scheme as Interpretive Model" in

Paul's basic message may not have diverged greatly in each city, it is of course possible, indeed likely, that his message was appropriated differently by the three groups of Christians. Therefore, I am not ruling theological differences out as a contributing factor to the different relationships. But by establishing this control I am trying to ensure that the theological differences relate to the individual churches themselves. I am suggesting that any theological differences between them are the result of different pre-existing norms, values, beliefs, attitudes, and experiences inherent to those churches themselves.[26] Indeed, underlying the model that will be used in this study is the presupposition that the differences in relationships between various Pauline churches and their wider communities, and hence the incidence of conflict, will be the result of different attitudes, beliefs, social-structures and other socio-cultural factors.[27]

On the other hand, Paul did not found the church at Rome. Therefore, we cannot be sure that the Christians had not been instructed with a fundamentally different gospel that affected their relationships with their wider civic community. Furthermore, since it is not clear that Paul wrote his letter to the Galatians to one particular church (and even if he did, we do not know to which particular church), the sort of data collection required for the specific model that will be constructed in this study would not be possible. Therefore, the study will seek to explain the different incidence of conflict in the relationships of the Thessalonian, Corinthian and Philippian churches with their wider civic communities.

J. M. Bassler, ed., *Pauline Theology, Volume I.* [Minneapolis: Fortress, 1991] 15-24), which has gained support from many scholars. However, it is not necessarily dependent on it.

[26] Regarding the theological divergence of Paul's churches and the links between this divergence and their experiences and underlying world-views see Barclay, "Contrasts", 49-74.

[27] In any case, it is a fundamental presupposition of social-scientific criticism that "the study of 'religion' in the Bible and its environment requires a study of social structures and relations" (Elliott, *Criticism*, 57). This will be discussed further in chapter 2.

PART ONE

CONFLICT IN
GRECO-ROMAN CITIES

Chapter One

THE DEVELOPMENT OF CONFLICT

"Conflict" is best understood as a process, not an event. It involves an escalating sequence of responses between two disputants, and is shaped by their relationship and their respective interpretations of each other's motives and actions. By definition it presupposes some relationship between the disputants.[1] There are several stages through which conflict progresses. First, the process begins with the recognition of differences in attitudes, norms, values or beliefs between different people or groups. Second, these differences come to be considered intolerable and in need of "resolution".[2] It is at this point that conflict-proper commences, regardless of whether it involves coercion (open hostility) or non-coercive engagement (negotiation, dialogue).[3] Normally a "trigger" is

---

[1] L. A. Coser, *The Functions of Social Conflict* (London: Routledge & Kegan Paul, 1956) 59; A. G. Woodhead, "Conflict in Ancient Society" in J. W. Allison, ed., *Conflict, Antithesis, and the Ancient Historian* (Columbus: Ohio State University Press, 1990) 5; M. H. Ross, *The Culture of Conflict: Interpretations and Interests in Comparative Perspective* (New Haven, CT: Yale University Press, 1993) 17, 182; *contra* J. N. Porter & R. Taplin, *Conflict and Conflict Resolution* (Lanham, MD: University Press of America, 1987) 3. Disputants may be either individuals or groups. Ian Robertson defines a *group* as "a collection of people interacting together in an orderly way on the basis of shared expectations about each other's behavior" (*Sociology* [3rd ed.; New York: Worth, 1987] 92). By interacting with other people, a group develops a structure, boundaries, norms and roles. (ibid., 168).

[2] At this point I am not using the term "resolution" in the technical sense of conflict resolution, but in the sense of "to take action". The point is that there is a step from recognizing a difference to feeling the need to take action to deal with that difference (by whatever means).

[3] D. Landis & J. Boucher, "Themes and Models of Conflict" in J. Boucher *et al*, eds., *Ethnic Conflict: International Perspectives* (Newbury Park, CA: SAGE, 1987) 27-8. They are, however, critical of this model claiming that it does not explain how personal conflicts become group conflicts (ibid., 30). This will be clearer when the "socialization" and the nature of *Gemeinschaft*-type community are discussed. Besides, this is

needed for a transition from the first stage to the second. In other words, the move from recognizing a difference to regarding it as something needing to be "resolved" requires some incident or event that causes the particular difference to be seen as a threat to the identity or existence of one's particular group.[4]

This particular model explains how conflicts develop. Although this is a useful starting point, the aim of this study is to explain differences in the development of conflict so the use of theories and models concerned with why conflict does or does not develop is required. John Elliott notes that models are used to explain social phenomena "at varying levels of abstraction or scope, from person-to-person relations to entire social systems".[5] In this chapter, the model that will be developed will be a composite one, operating at three levels of abstraction. The first, at a very high level of abstraction, is a particular sociological theory: the "Culture of Conflict" theory. The second, at a somewhat lower level of abstraction, is the macro-sociological model of the "pre-industrial" society, while the third level involves the use of Mediterranean Cultural Anthropology, as outlined by Bruce Malina.[6]

---

an analytical classification, not an explanation, and should be treated as such. That the model is drawn from the study of ethnic conflict need not lessen its relevance. In the context of conflicts in the ancient city, especially involving Christian groups, it may actually be more useful.

[4] Ibid., 27.

[5] Elliott, *Criticism*, 46-7; cf. B. J. Malina, *The New Testament World: Insights from Cultural Anthropology* (rev. ed.; Louisville, KY: W/JK Press, 1993) 18-19. A "level of abstraction" refers to the levels or degrees of generalization or specificity at which the model may relate to the social structure under investigation. In this case, the most concrete level may be the specific city or community. Increasing levels of abstraction may then be Greco-Roman culture, Mediterranean culture, advanced agrarian society, pre-industrial society and so on.

[6] In developing this model I will draw on models and theories that operate from the three sociological perspectives: structural functionalism, conflict and symbolic interactionism. Overall, my approach will tend more to the structural functionalist perspective. It is often suggested that this perspective functions like a still picture or snap-shot, compared to the conflict perspective that functions like a slow-motion camera (e.g. Malina, *World*, 21-3). Since the nature of the sources — Paul's letters to Thessalonica, Corinth and Philippi — are, in many ways, like still pictures and we cannot be certain that we know what preceded or followed them, a functionalist perspective seems most useful. Furthermore, I do not believe that the structural functionalist, conflict and symbolic interactionist perspectives are necessarily mutually exclusive. While conflict is inevitable, in most cases those

I. WHAT CAUSES CONFLICT?

The most recent, and potentially the most useful, explanation of the development of conflict is the "Culture of Conflict" theory of Marc Howard Ross. He defines "culture" as "a society's particular constellation of norms, practices and institutions", and adds that culture "defines what people value". Thus, the "Culture of Conflict" explains what people fight about, with whom they fight and the way they fight.[7] While conflict appears to be fought out around a particular issue, the interpretations of the issue by the disputants are equally important. Thus, Ross' theory suggests that conflict involves two aspects: psychocultural dispositions and structural factors. Psychocultural dispositions determine how disputants interpret their social world, how they are likely to react to particular events and behaviors, and what intensity of feeling these events and behaviors are likely to arouse.[8] Social-structural factors, such as patterns of relationship, determine the targets of these reactions.[9]

Psychocultural dispositions comprise the interpretations disputants give to their social world and the values they assign to aspects of it. Ross points out that the main determinant of psychocultural dispositions is the pattern of primary socialization. This, he claims, determines how people "process events and the emotions, perceptions, and cognitions the events evoke".[10] Nevertheless, Ross acknowledges that in most cases more immediate manifestations of psychocultural dispositions, such as particular norms, will be more crucial.[11]

This calls for an explanation of socialization and the way it influences people's interpretations of, and emotional attachment to, aspects of their social world. But such an explanation is not possible without an understanding of the sociology of knowledge. The central idea of this is, according to Peter Berger and Thomas Luckmann, that the human

---

involved probably maintain a commitment to the social institutions.

[7] Ross, *Culture*, 2, 21. Ross' theory has great potential for explaining conflict in the ancient world since it has been developed in relation to modern pre-industrial societies. See also, J. Rex, *Social Conflict: A Conceptual and Theoretical Analysis* (London: Longman, 1981) 12. On the sociological definition of "culture" see *PDS* sv "Culture".

[8] Ross, *Culture*, 2, 9-10, 65, 68.

[9] Ibid., 2, 9, 13, 35.

[10] Ibid., 10. He also links with this other forms of social learning, such as modelling by significant others (ibid., 177).

[11] Ibid., 10, 61-2, 198-9.

"world" (comprised of norms, values, beliefs and customs) is socially-constructed. This social world is created by a process of externalization and objectivation (by which it comes to exist in its own right, independent of its creators), in which people participate by internalization.[12] Socialization is the process of internalizing this socially constructed world. Through this process, individuals identify with the norms, values, beliefs and customs of their particular social world, or society, and are shaped by them. Yet the individual does not simply learn these elements, or their meanings, but appropriates them and makes them her/his own. This appropriation is not a matter of absorption alone. It is undertaken actively.[13] And like the process which creates this social world that is internalized, socialization also takes place socially.[14] It is successful to the degree that these elements come to be taken for granted as the way the world is and how it operates.[15] Since socialization is a process, it is never complete but continues throughout an individual's lifetime.[16] Nor is total socialization possible. At best, there is a "high degree of objective/subjective symmetry".[17] This degree of symmetry is inversely proportional to the social complexity of a given society.[18]

Thus, socialization appears to be very successful in societies that fit the *Gemeinschaft* or "community" type expounded by Ferdinand Tönnies.[19] A *Gemeinschaft* is characterized by relationships that are intimate and face-to-

---

[12] P. L. Berger & T. Luckmann, *The Social Construction of Reality* (Harmondsworth: Penguin, 1966) 13; P. L. Berger, *The Sacred Canopy: Elements of a Sociological Theory of Religion* (New York: Doubleday, 1967) 3-8; cf. S. R. F. Price, *Rituals and Power: The Roman Imperial Cult in Asia Minor* (Cambridge: Cambridge University Press, 1984) 11.

[13] Berger, *Sacred Canopy*, 14-18.

[14] Ibid., 14-16.

[15] Berger, *Sacred Canopy*, 24; Berger & Luckmann, *Construction*, 37; Esler, *First Christians*, 7-8.

[16] Berger, *Sacred Canopy*, 15-16.

[17] Berger, *Sacred Canopy*, 15; cf. Berger & Luckmann, *Construction*, 183.

[18] Berger & Luckmann, *Construction*, 183.

[19] By "type", I am referring to a Weberian ideal-type, a model which involves the observation of the essential features of a social phenomenon and the extrapolation of these features to form an abstract benchmark against which examples from the real world may be compared. See Carney, *Shape*, 13; Robertson, *Sociology*, 178; Esler, *Community*, 7-8; M. Waters & R. Crook, *Sociology One: Principles of Sociological Analysis for Australians* (2nd ed.; Melbourne: Longman Cheshire, 1990) 360.

face, involve reciprocity, paternal authority, mutual assistance (often via guilds and associations), concord and group loyalty.[20] They arise through close contact, shared work and experiences. In effect, each *Gemeinschaft* appears to resemble an extended household.[21] As such it has an innate unity which presupposes shared customs, beliefs, *mores*, a traditional religion, a common understanding of good and evil, and common friends and enemies.[22]

On the other hand, the *Gesellschaft*, or "association", is characterized by impersonal relationships, individualism rather than group loyalty, and relationships that are contractual and commercial, fostered for the sake of specific goals. As such it represents a co-existence of independent people, and reciprocity, when it does occur, is equal in kind. The relationships resemble those of a business or corporation, rather than a household. Its unity is attained by agreement, planning or contract.[23]

Tönnies' *Gemeinschaft-Gesellschaft* typology laid the foundation for most of the later sociological work on the nature of community life.[24] His typology is useful, because it suggests that for a society that shares many characteristics of the *Gemeinschaft*-type, socialization would be highly successful leading to an innate commitment to the societal norms, values, beliefs and customs. Therefore, in a *Gemeinschaft*-type society, the socially constructed world is more likely to be taken for granted. And this is a feature of both pre-industrial and Mediterranean societies.[25]

---

[20] F. Tönnies, *Community and Society: Gemeinschaft and Gesellschaft* (East Lansing: Michigan State University Press, 1957) 37-40, 46-8; cf. Robertson, *Sociology*, 109-10; Waters & Crook, *Sociology*, 64; S. L. Dyson, *Community and Society in Roman Italy* (Baltimore: Johns Hopkins University Press, 1992) 12.

[21] Tönnies, *Community*, 42-3, 62-4.

[22] Tönnies, *Community*, 34, 49-50; cf. Dyson, *Community*, 12.

[23] Tönnies, *Community*, 34, 49, 59, 64-5; cf. Robertson, *Sociology*, 109-10; Waters & Crook, *Sociology*, 64; Dyson, *Community*, 12.

[24] This is despite the fact that Tönnies' work itself has been largely ignored by modern scholars because of his prejudiced and primitivist ideals. See Waters & Crook, *Sociology*, 64. As an ideal-type, however, it is useful in analysing pre-industrial societies. See Dyson, *Community*, 11-12.

[25] See, for example, G. Sjoberg, *The Preindustrial City: Past and Present* (New York: Free Press, 1960) 227; Carney, *Shape*, 92-3; Malina, *World*, 30.

Furthermore, when socialization is highly successful, people do not generally conceive of themselves in a individual sense, but in a social one. They exhibit a strong attachment to, and identification with, the dominant structures, values and beliefs of their social world. In such cases, all their social interactions reinforce their subjective appropriation of this world. Under such circumstances genuine individualism is not really a possibility.[26] Indeed, Mediterranean society seems to be much more socially oriented than our own and, in social anthropological terms, such people are said to have a "dyadic personality" and to be "embedded".[27]

Nevertheless, as socialization is never complete or total, social control mechanisms are also required. While the former functions to induce a common commitment to the important elements of the socially constructed world, the latter seek to restrict divergences from this world to an acceptable level.[28] Where both function effectively, the validity of the socially constructed world and its social control mechanisms are largely taken for granted unless a problem arises which the particular definition of reality is unable to accommodate.[29]

When such problems do occur it calls for legitimation — what Berger describes as "reality-maintenance".[30] Normally, the socially constructed world legitimates itself, but other means are needed whenever the taken-for-granted quality of the socially constructed world is threatened. Usually this entails the use of myths, legends, proverbs and maxims.[31] Esler points out that legitimation becomes important in "any social order where the prevailing arrangements are under threat from dissenters".[32] Since this world is socially

---

[26] Berger & Luckmann, *Construction*, 184, 190.

[27] According to Malina, dyadic personality "is characteristic of individuals who perceive themselves and form their self-image in terms of what others perceive and feed back to them...Every individual is perceived as embedded in some other" (*World*, 67-8). Besides, as Malina notes, individualism is a rarity among world cultures and perhaps completely absent from the ancient world of the NT (ibid., 66-7).

[28] Berger, *Sacred Canopy*, 29. An example of social control is the legal system.

[29] Berger & Luckmann, *Construction*, 58.

[30] Berger, *Sacred Canopy*, 29-31; Esler, *Community*, 16-17.

[31] Berger & Luckmann, *Construction*, 112-13; Berger, *Sacred Canopy*, 30-1; cf. H. C. Kee, *Knowing the Truth: A Sociological Approach to New Testament Interpretation* (Minneapolis: Fortress, 1989), 52-3.

[32] Esler, *First Christians*, 9; cf. Berger, *Sacred Canopy*, 42. Esler also notes that legitimations are common among revitalization

constructed, its maintenance also requires a social group. Berger calls this its *plausibility structure*. The larger this plausibility structure is, the stronger will be the socially constructed world on which it rests. If any group defects, the plausibility structure is weakened and the need for legitimation is greater.[33] Consequently, challenges or threats to the norms, beliefs, values and customs of a society elicit attempts to explain and justify those elements under threat. When this threat is posed by another group, the differences in norms, values and beliefs form the basis of conflict. In terms of the conflict process, legitimation would appear to be a non-coercive means of engaging in conflict.

In the case of those whose social world is under threat, this threat would evoke legitimations to justify the present order, and probably lead to attempts to discredit, repress or destroy the deviant definition of reality. But legitimation would be especially important in the case of a break-away group, since many of its members would retain some commitment to, and identification with, the old system of beliefs and norms. They would also be likely to experience pressure to conform, even repression, which could cause doubts, wavering or acquiescence.[34]

movements such as revolutions, revivals and sects (*Community*, 17).

[33] Berger, *Sacred Canopy*, 45-6; cf. B. Holmberg, *Sociology and the New Testament: An Appraisal* (Minneapolis: Fortress, 1990) 141.

[34] Esler, *Community*, 17; idem, *First Christians*, 14; cf. Berger & Luckmann, *Construction*, 124-5. When a new minority group arises, with its own body of traditions, norms, values and customs, this poses a threat to the taken-for-grantedness of the dominant world view. Repression by the custodians of that social world is to be expected. For such a group, the most common form of legitimation is the appeal to the past, especially in traditional societies, and the attempt to show that what appears to be new is actually old. See Esler, *Community*, 19; Berger & Luckmann, *Construction*, 120-1. Similar is the labelling theory of deviancy, which claims that a deviant is a person so labelled by others, especially the dominant population or "official agents of a politically organized society", not because of some inherent difference. See J. P. Gibbs, "Conceptions of Deviant Behavior: The Old and New" in D. H. Kelly, ed., *Deviant Behavior: A Text-Reader in the Sociology of Deviance* (3rd ed.; New York: St.Martin's Press, 1989) 16-19; cf. Kelly's introduction on page 3. On this understanding of deviance as labelling, and it relevance to first century Mediterranean society see B. J. Malina & J. H. Neyrey, "Conflict in Luke-Acts: Labelling and Deviance Theory", in J. H. Neyrey, ed., *The Social World of Luke-Acts: Models for Interpretation* (Peabody, MA: Hendrickson, 1991) 110-20; J. M. G. Barclay, "Deviance and Apostasy: Some Applications of Deviance Theory to First-Century Judaism and Christianity", in P. F. Esler, ed.,

In the face of such pressure a member of a deviant group must order his/her social life to avoid this pressure. This would normally mean dissociating from former friends and acquaintances who remain with the older plausibility structure, and bonding more closely with the new one which maintains her/his new definition of reality.[35] Such a deviant definition of reality usually is better tolerated among foreigners or outsiders, and friendly relations may still be maintained with them, than when members of one's own plausibility structure defect.[36]

In joining a social group with a divergent definition of reality, a person must undergo a process of resocialization. However, it is unlikely that this process will be as successful as primary socialization, for the new norms, values and beliefs may be imperfectly internalized such that they do not lead to identification. That is, they do not necessarily become the individual's reality. Instead, this "internalization" can be associated with a degree of detachment, even manipulation, by deliberately putting on the new beliefs, values and norms when in the company of the members of the new group.[37] Another way of seeing this is via the sociological concept of marginality. This refers to a situation where "a person's membership in two groups poses a contradiction or cross pressure such that a person's status is lowered by his or her membership in the other group". Generally, people will

---

Modelling Early Christianity: Social-Scientific Studies of the New Testament in Its Context (London: Routledge, 1995), 115-25; Still, "Θλῖψις", 68-94. While the understanding of "conflict" that will be used in this study follows a deviance rather than a challenge-response approach, deviance theory itself is not particularly useful for my purpose. For while it describes the process of conflict (similarly to the conflict process described in the introduction to this chapter) it fails to adequately explain why some who break a society's norms are labelled as deviants but others are not (cf. Malina & Neyrey, "Conflict", 100-2; Barclay, "Deviance", 115-16).

[35] Berger, *Sacred Canopy*, 49-51; cf. L. M. White, "Finding the Ties that Bind: Issues from Social Description" *Semeia* 56 (1992) 20.

[36] Berger & Luckmann, *Construction*, 140; Esler, *Community*, 21-2.

[37] Berger & Luckmann, *Construction*, 192. This is helpful in explaining why apparently conflicting values, beliefs and norms may be found operating within one particular group. See R. L. Rohrbaugh, "'Social Location of Thought' as a Heuristic Construct in New Testament Studies" *JSNT* 30 (1987) 109-10.

endeavor to resolve a marginal position, often by assimilation to one group or the other.[38]

This, however, has begun to touch on matters related to social structural factors. What the discussion of socialization, as the main determinant of the psychocultural dispositions of conflict, has shown is that the commitment to common norms, values and beliefs engendered in a society will determine what conflicts will be about. Ross points out that care should be taken against presuming that individual and group interests can be equated.[39] Yet, when socialization is successful, as in the case of the *Gemeinschaft*-type society, such as a pre-industrial city or Mediterranean society in general, this is less of a problem.

Overall, Ross' "Culture of Conflict" theory contends that the psychocultural dispositions of a society determine how it interprets and responds to events and behaviors, while social structural factors indicate who will be the targets of conflict. This may be seen clearly in the Mediterranean world in relation to the pattern of challenge and response. Honor appears to be the pivotal social value of Mediterranean society, and thus a major psychocultural disposition. It is acquired through the "game" of challenge and response. However, "the interaction over honor, the challenge-response game, *can take place only between social equals*" and non-kin.[40] In other words, the target of the conflict is determined by a social-structural factor.

Since conflict, by definition, presupposes some relationship between the disputants, the social-structural factors must concern the nature and patterns of relationships. Drawing on the work of Talcott Parsons, John Rex argues

---

[38] Stark, "Jewish Conversion", 317. A similar idea is found in deviance theory. Kelly claims that "unless some personal gain can be realized, such as the enhancement of one's prestige or status in the eyes of others, most persons will reject a deviant label imputed to them" ("Introduction", 7-8); cf. Coser, *Functions*, 51. A person belonging to two different groups, with different norms, who tries to follow the norms and expectations of each while with members of that group, will be able to sustain this "duality of action" only to the extent that the two groups have few links with each other (L. M. White, "Social Networks: Theoretical Orientation and Historical Applications" *Semeia* 56 [1992] 28-9).

[39] Ross, *Culture*, 48.

[40] Malina, *World*, 34-7, 41; cf. P. F. Esler, "Making and Breaking an Agreement Mediterranean Style: A New Reading of Galatians 2:1-14" *BibInt* 3 (1995) 289-90.

that an individual's behavior is influenced by his/her need for the action or approval of another.[41] In most relationships, however, both of these motivations would be present, a fact which could potentially increase or decrease the possibility of conflict. This becomes quite apparent when the pattern of relationships is considered from the perspective of roles.

Sociologically, a *role* is defined as a "set of expected behavior patterns, obligations and privileges", and operates via a number of specific norms.[42] Every person occupies a series of roles, each of which is defined and organized relative to its complementary role — that definition described as the *role expectation*. Each role and its complementary roles forms a *role-set*.[43] In the case of a *Gemeinschaft*-type society, roles would generally be very clearly defined and relatively fixed. As we would expect, roles also appear to be quite firmly fixed in both pre-industrial and Mediterranean societies.[44]

Yet, to successfully perform each of multiple roles, sociologists contend that they must be separated from each other temporally and spatially.[45] Inadequate performance of a role or roles is a major cause of conflict, since roles govern relationships and drawn on key societal norms and values. This conflict may be manifest as either Simple or Multiple Role Conflict.[46]

Simple Role Conflict occurs when a person fails to fulfil a role to the expectations of that role set. In other words, the

---

[41] Rex, *Social Conflict*, 4; cf. Porter & Taplin, *Conflict*, 5-6. The same could also be said of groups.

[42] See Robertson, *Sociology*, 91; Waters & Crook, *Sociology*, 33.

[43] Robertson, *Sociology*, 92; Waters & Crook, *Sociology*, 33.

[44] On pre-industrial cities see Sjoberg, *Preindustrial*, 84, 88; Carney, *Shape*, 101, 126; on Mediterranean society see Malina, *World*, 31, 48-9, 107; H. Moxnes, "Patron-Client Relations and the New Community in Luke-Acts" in J. H. Neyrey, ed., *The Social World of Luke-Acts: Models for Interpretation* (Peabody, MA: Hendrickson, 1991) 245. In particular, Malina suggests that in Mediterranean society conformity is valued, authoritarianism is a norm, subordinates expect to be ordered around while those in power expect to act paternalistically and to receive special privileges (*World*, 82-3).

[45] See Waters & Crook, *Sociology*, 33-4.

[46] Theoretically, there are also Role Set Conflicts, where the "different members of a role set have different expectations of the complementary role". That is, the conflict concerns role expectations within the role set (Waters & Crook, *Sociology*, 35). Since roles in pre-industrial and Mediterranean societies were well defined and quite fixed, role set conflicts would not have been common and can therefore be ignored.

performance does not match what both the incumbent of the role and the incumbent of the complementary role expect from that particular role. Such conflicts are normally resolved by modifying the role expectation, by sanctions, or by terminating the relationship.[47] Multiple Role Conflict occurs when the temporal and spatial separation of an individual's various roles is inadequate. This lack of separation leads to a clash of role expectations for the incumbent and increased pressure from the various complementary role incumbents for adequate role fulfilment. These conflicts are resolved by rigidly compartmentalizing roles, by negotiation and modification of role expectations, or by withdrawal from one or more roles.[48] Such conflicts would be common in Mediterranean society since roles were not distinct.[49]

In each case, the conflict occurs between the members of the role set. Thus, while socialization might engender commitment to a variety of norms and values and thus determine that poor role performance will initiate a conflict process, the structure of the role set determines that the conflict will occur between the various role incumbents.

Another structural factor that determines who will be involved in a conflict is the pattern of social networks. *Social networks* are defined as relational webs connecting people directly and through these connections to other people indirectly. Networks are not groups, because not all the members of a network interact with each other. They can also provide people with access to other groups to which they themselves do not belong.[50]

People generally use their social networks to seek advice or support when in difficulty, to find work, or to advance their careers.[51] The idea of networks can be summed up by the old adage, "it's who you know, not what you know that counts". Social networks are particularly important in Mediterranean society, given its collectivist orientation and the importance of patronal relationships.[52] Clearly, networks are related to roles and role-fulfilment, since the way that a

---

[47] Waters & Crook, *Sociology*, 35; cf. Robertson, *Sociology*, 92.

[48] Waters & Crook, *Sociology*, 35.

[49] See Moxnes, "Patron-Client", 245.

[50] Robertson, *Sociology*, 174; cf. B. N. Adams, "Interaction Theory and the Social Network" *Sociometry* 30 (1967) 64-5.

[51] Robertson, *Sociology*, 174-5.

[52] See Carney, *Shape*, 94; Moxnes, "Patron-Client", 242-6; Malina, *World*, 101-2.

person fulfils a given role depends on the pattern of, and the various weightings attached to, different ties. Some ties are deliberately fostered, some happen by chance, and others are simply "givens".[53]

The relational ties within networks can be either reinforcing or cross-cutting. Reinforcing ties occur when an individual's kin and neighborhood ties, and ties associated with social groups, and political affiliations, overlap such that the same people are involved in each case. On the other hand, cross-cutting ties occur when an individual's ties are shared between a variety of different people.[54] Given that different social status groups are generally segregated in preindustrial and Mediterranean societies, reinforcing ties would tend to be more common.[55]

This has important implications for conflict. Ross' "Culture of Conflict" theory postulates that social structural factors will determine who will be the targets of conflict, and this is most clearly seen in terms of roles and networks. Generally, the disputants will be the role set incumbents, and conflict will be based upon role performance. The pattern of network ties, in terms of the kinds of bonds and their degree of overlap, also influence the way in which roles are fulfilled and thus how various norms, beliefs and values are manifest as conflict.[56]

---

[53] White, "Social Networks", 23-5; J. K. Chow, *Patronage and Power: A Study of Social Networks in Corinth* (JSNTSup 75; Sheffield: JSOT Press, 1992) 34. Modern network analyses attempt quantitative studies, which are not possible historically, given the lack of data. Instead, what is important is the quality and strength of relations. See Chow, *Patronage*, 36; White, "Social Networks", 29-30.

[54] Ross, *Culture*, 39.

[55] See Sjoberg, *Preindustrial*, 95-101; Carney, *Shape*, 85-6, 94; Malina, *World*, 92; R. L. Rohrbaugh, "The Pre-Industrial City in Luke-Acts: Urban Social Relations", in J. H. Neyrey, ed., *The Social World of Luke-Acts: Models for Interpretation* (Peabody, MA: Hendrickson, 1991) 133-4.

[56] "Conflict" is not necessarily reactive, but may be proactive. The latter is particularly evident in the Mediterranean practice of challenge and response in order to acquire honor, as mentioned above. In this study, however, the particular conflict under investigation is better regarded as a form of "deviance", for, as Malina & Neyrey suggest, a "deviance" model of conflict is appropriate given the more forensic (or at least the *potentially* forensic) nature of this sort of conflict ("Conflict", 99). In that case, a discussion of conflict in terms of roles, role expectations and role performance is quite appropriate.

II. WHAT CAUSES DIFFERENT CONFLICT RESPONSES?

The various factors shaping the network ties largely determine who the conflict will involve and why. They also help explain differences in conflict response, given that relationships are largely based on the need for another's action or approval. The culture of conflict theory also explains why a given trigger can produce different conflict responses in different societies.[57]

Therefore, a major step toward the development of a model of conflict is identifying what might provoke different conflict responses. According to Ross' theory, different conflict responses must be a product of a particular society's norms, values, beliefs, practices and institutions. Since the development of norms is dependent on socialization, variations in this process are clearly fundamental. Ross, himself, suggests that the propensity toward conflict is largely dependent on the warmth associated with socialization and the modelling of significant others.[58]

A high conflict culture is one where socialization is harsh and not particularly warm, where there are violent role models and a higher proportion of reinforcing ties. The overlapping of relational ties is important for, as Ross contends:

> When social organization reinforces a single dominant cleavage, conflicts escalate because few overlapping interests [between groups] reinforce mutual interests [within groups]; when lines of cleavage cross-cut each other and ties among the parties are well-established, the same precipitating incident often has far less severe consequences.[59]

On the other hand, a low conflict culture is one where socialization is warm and affectionate, there are fewer violent role models, and where there is a higher proportion of cross-cutting ties.[60] Indeed, in a society where there are many cross-cutting ties it is less likely that people will be mobilized to oppose each other, for both sides of a potential conflict will also be linked, and they will both have links to others.

---

[57] Ross, *Culture*, 35.
[58] Ibid., 188.
[59] Ibid., 11.
[60] Ibid., 188-90.

Consequently, it is in everyone's interest to avoid conflict or to see it resolved as quickly and smoothly as possible.[61]

Furthermore, a high conflict culture is one where resources are concentrated in the hands of a few.[62] Related to this is a society's organization of authority. That is, where power is concentrated in the hands of a small minority, and especially where this power is substantial and coupled with military capabilities, conflict will be more likely than when a society has a more egalitarian structure.[63] But in a society where resources are not widely distributed but there is a greater proportion of cross-cutting ties, particularly between the "haves" and "have-nots", conflict would probably be less than in an egalitarian society with mainly reinforcing ties.

Rodney Stark, drawing on C. S. Fisher's "Subcultural Theory of Urbanism", argues that the larger a population or society in numerical terms, the easier it is to "assemble a 'critical mass'" needed to form a deviant sub-culture.[64] By the same token, the larger the population size, the less likely it is that the plausibility structure will be co-extensive with the whole of the particular society. In such a case it is possible that there would be a greater tolerance towards divergent views, for it is likely that there will be more cross-cutting ties in a larger society.

Similarly, the ethnic composition of a society can influence the level and manifestation of conflict. This is especially related to the degree to which ethnic sub-cultures maintain their own norms, beliefs and customs, and/or seek relationships with people from the dominant culture. Based on these two variables there are four possible patterns: integration, segregation, assimilation, and deculturation.[65] The incidence of conflict will vary with each. It is likely that

---

[61] Ibid., 39-41, 171.

[62] Ibid., 11.

[63] Ibid., 11, 35.

[64] R. Stark, "Christianizing the Urban Environment: An Analysis Based on 22 Greco-Roman Cities" *Soc An* 52 (1991) 80.

[65] Landis & Boucher, "Themes", 24; cf. White, "Social Networks", 32. Integration involves cultural-retention and a commitment to positive relations with the wider society, while segregation retains the culture but rejects the relations (and is likely to lead to increased ethnic conflict). Assimilation involves a rejection of the culture and a commitment to relations (and is likely to cause internal conflict), while deculturation rejects both. See also J. M. G. Barclay, *Jews in the Mediterranean Diaspora from Alexander the Great to Trajan* (Edinburgh: T. & T. Clark, 1996) 92-101.

where the pattern is one of segregation conflict may be more marked, because there would be more reinforcing ties, than where there is a pattern of integration or assimilation.

In summary, then, conflict development is dependent on psychocultural and structural factors. Psychocultural factors determine the society's or group's disposition to conflict, and the strength of the conflict response, based on the pattern of norms, values and beliefs and the subjective commitment to them. As such they also determine what conflicts will be about. The structural factors, as representative of the patterns of relationships and relational networks, determine who the disputants will be and what might trigger the conflict.

Different conflict responses can be accounted for in terms of this model. Conflict will be more prevalent when socialization is harsh, ties are reinforcing, populations are smaller, ethnic heterogeneity manifests as segregation, and where resources and power are concentrated in the hands of a few (without cross-cutting ties). That is, there is a high incidence of conflict in a "high conflict culture". On the other hand, warmer and more affectionate socialization, more cross-cutting ties, a larger population size, overall ethnic homogeneity (or where the various ethnic groups are well integrated or assimilated), lower resource concentration and egalitarianism are associated with a lower incidence of conflict. In other words, there is a low incidence of conflict in a "low conflict culture".

According to Ross' theory, Mediterranean society would, in general terms, be a high conflict culture. Its pattern of socialization appears to be harsh, while it has already been suggested that socialization into a pattern of norms, values and beliefs is largely successful in Mediterranean society.[66] Furthermore, both its economic and political resources are generally concentrated in the hands of the few.[67] Indeed, Mediterranean society is recognized as an *agonistic* culture

---

[66] Indeed, Carney suggests that "in the traditional societies of antiquity, childhood, educational and job socialization generally inducted the recipient into authoritarian patterns of personal relationships" (*Shape*, 346-7, cf. 92-3, 118), while Malina recognizes that the agonistic nature of Mediterranean society is directly related to the harshness of primary socialization (*World*, 55-8).

[67] This is particularly evident in the anthropological model of "limited good", something that Malina has shown to be characteristic of Mediterranean society (*World*, 95-6).

because of the extent of conflict (both in terms of deviance and the challenge-response pattern of interaction).[68]

In summary, the preliminary model of conflict that will be tested against the first century data is based on an understanding of conflict as an escalating process between disputants. It begins with the recognition of differences, which become intolerable following some "trigger". The development of conflict depends on the psychocultural dispositions and structural factors of the society. Psychocultural dispositions determine the society's or group's disposition to conflict, and the strength of the conflict response, based on the pattern of norms, values and beliefs and the subjective commitment to them established via socialization. As such they also determine what conflicts will be about. Structural factors, as representative of the patterns of relationships and relational networks, determine who the disputants will be and what might trigger the conflict. In most cases, the disputants in a conflict will be the role set incumbents, and conflict will be based on role performance.

This model also explains why conflict responses can differ between different societies. High conflict cultures are ones where the socialization is harsh, ties are reinforcing, populations are smaller, there is ethnic heterogeneity and/or ethnic segregation, and hierarchical control of resources and power (in the absence of cross-cutting ties). Mediterranean society generally fits this category. Low conflict cultures occur where socialization is warmer and more affectionate, ties are more cross-cutting, there is a larger population size, overall ethnic homogeneity (or where different ethnic groups are present but well integrated), lower resource concentration and egalitarianism. While it is clear that Mediterranean society as a whole is a high conflict culture, at a lower level of abstraction, such as the level of individual Greek and Roman communities, it is possible that there might be variations, particularly in relation to city size, different norms and values, and the proportion of cross-cutting and reinforcing ties.[69] At this lower level of abstraction it is possible that individual communities may be classed as either high or low conflict cultures. This is yet to be seen.

---

[68] See Malina & Neyrey, "Conflict", 98; Malina, *World*, 37-8, 55.

[69] For example, ancient Greek society appears to have been unique among preindustrial societies in its democratic ideology and practices. See Sjoberg, *Preindustrial*, 235-6.

Chapter Two

PSYCHOCULTURAL DISPOSITIONS OF GRECO-ROMAN CITIES

The most appropriate first step in testing the model of conflict developed in the previous chapter must be a consideration of the psychocultural factors. That involves, in the first place, a consideration of socialization in the Greco-Roman world. In particular it is important to see how successful socialization was, which requires an investigation of the extent to which both Greek and Roman cities fit the *Gemeinschaft*-type.[1] At the same time, the manner in which it was carried out, and how harsh it was, will be important. Then, secondly, what is required is an exploration of the particular norms, values and beliefs into which people were socialized. To that end, this chapter will seek to present material drawn from significant primary sources and the work of classical and archaeological scholars that address these particular areas. As such, it will comprise something of an overview.

---

[1] The term "city" will be used here for the sake of convenience but it should not be confused with the modern understanding of the term. Cities in the Greco-Roman world comprised both an urban center (*astu* or *urbs*) and an area of farmed land belonging to it (*chora* or *territorium*). See D. W. Engels, *Roman Corinth: An Alternative Model for the Classical City* (Chicago: University of Chicago Press, 1990) 8, 24; S. E. Alcock, *Graecia Capta: The Landscapes of Roman Greece* (Cambridge: Cambridge University Press, 1993) 93, 117; R. Laurence, *Roman Pompeii: Space and Society* (London: Routledge, 1994) 138. That the Greek *polis* was unlike other pre-industrial cities in terms of its social and political structures does not negate this point. See R. Sallares, *The Ecology of the Ancient Greek World* (London: Duckworth, 1991) 3, 161-4, 192.

I. SOCIALIZATION IN THE GRECO-ROMAN WORLD

In the previous chapter it was argued that societies that resembled *Gemeinschaft*-type communities had successful socialization and an innate commitment to their norms, values and beliefs. Such a community is characterized by face-to-face relations involving mutual assistance, reciprocity and paternal authority such that the society is seen as an extended household. Concord and group loyalty are particularly valued. The relationships in such cities are usually marked by patronage and the formation of guilds and associations. Some of these features will be discussed later. At this stage, however, I would contend that both "Greek" and Roman societies were marked by a traditional religion, and that Roman society was centered on a well-defined patronage system, while peer assistance and reciprocal relationships were common to both.[2] The Romans also regarded their "state" as a "family", as can be seen in the public cult of *Vesta* and the frequent description of the Emperor as "Father of His Country" (*pater patriae* or *p.p.*).[3]

Greco-Roman cities were very much face-to-face societies. This is clearly evident in their spatial and social organization.[4] Despite some minor differences, Greek and

---

[2] The term "Greek" will be used to refer to communities and people who share norms, values and beliefs that may be broadly defined as Greek or Hellenistic, but may come from diverse geographical regions, such as Achaia, Macedonia, Asia Minor, the Greek Islands and so on.

[3] See, for example, *ILS* 112[b], 113, 140, 207-10, 214-18, 228, 231-2, 1986; Ovid *Fast.* 291-8; cf. W. K. Lacey, "*Patria Potestas*" in B. Rawson, ed., *The Family in Ancient Rome* (London: Routledge, 1992 [1986]) 125-30.

[4] See E. J. Owens, *The City in the Greek and Roman World* (London: Routledge, 1990) 153; D. Perring, "Spatial Organization and Social Change in Roman Towns", in J. Rich & A. Wallace-Hadrill, eds., *City and Country in the Ancient World* (London: Routledge, 1991) 273; cf. M. I. Finley, "The Ancient City: From Fustel de Coulanges to Max Weber and Beyond" *CSSH* 18 (1977) 306. As one historian actually to use Tönnies' typology, Dyson (*Community*, 12) suggests:

town planning and legal history have emphasized the qualities of *Gesellschaft* found in Roman communities, but the concept of *Gemeinschaft* has considerable potential for facilitating our understanding of Roman small-town...life.

The material that will be discussed in this chapter and the next suggests that the town planning of ancient cities does reflect a *Gemeinschaft* rather than a *Gesellschaft* type. Although Rome itself might come close to the latter, it still displays many features of *Gemeinschaft*.

Roman cities were normally laid out according to a regular grid-plan around one or more main roads, with smaller intersecting roads. Near the center of the grid, usually close to the main road(s), was a relatively large open space, the *agora* or *forum* — a square plaza or courtyard surrounded by colonnades, shops, temples and civic buildings.[5] By its location and structures, the *forum* or *agora* was the place where people gathered for a variety of reasons.[6] Dominic Perring contends that ancient town planning generally demonstrates that public life was focussed on a central core associated with an open public space.[7] While there may have been a number of foci, specifically in the center of the city and at its periphery, all of the public areas seem to have encouraged a gathering of people and demonstrate the very social nature of city life in the Greco-Roman world.

In prosperous and growing towns, specialized market buildings, *macella*, were developed and usually were situated in the vicinity of the *forum / agora*.[8] Many of these appear to

[5] Vitruvius *De Arch.* 1.1-4; cf. R. MacMullen, *Roman Social Relations 50 BC-AD 284* (New Haven, CT: Yale University Press, 1974) 57; J. B. Ward-Perkins, *Cities of Ancient Greece and Italy: Planning in Classical Antiquity* (New York: George Brazilier, 1974) 18-19, 28-9; J. E. Stambaugh & D. L. Balch, *The Social World of the First Christians* (London: SPCK, 1986) 108; J. E. Stambaugh, *The Ancient Roman City* (Baltimore: Johns Hopkins University Press, 1988) 147; Owens, *The City*, 74-5, 79-80, 124-5, 127-9; Perring, "Spatial Organisation", 278; Dyson, *Community*, 158; R. Tomlinson, *From Mycenae to Constantinople: The Evolution of the Ancient City* (London: Routledge, 1992) 22, 27. Many older Greek cities, such as Athens, developed haphazardly. But the regular "Hippodamian" plan, was followed in most purpose-built cities.

[6] Vitruvius *De Arch.* 3.1; Stambaugh, *Roman City*, 106; Owens, *The City*, 3, 153; A. Wallace-Hadrill, "Elites and Trade in the Roman Town", in J. Rich & A. Wallace-Hadrill, eds., *City and Country in the Ancient World* (London: Routledge, 1991) 258; Dyson, *Community*, 158, 168; J. M. Frayn, *Markets and Fairs in Roman Italy: Their Social and Economic Importance from the Second Century BC to the Third Century AD* (Oxford: Clarendon, 1993) 1-2, 104-5. Laurence has shown that there was a strong sense of neighborhood (*vicus*) identity. *Vici* had their own shrines and officials, and located at their boundaries were usually the public fountains that provided their water supplies (*Pompeii*, 39-46). Gathering to collect water would have been another social activity.

[7] Perring, "Spatial Organisation", 275-6.

[8] Ward-Perkins, *Cities*, 35; Dyson, *Community*, 165; Frayn, *Markets*, 2, 6. Successful market towns were normally situated on main roads, not closer than 30 km together, and with access to a port (Frayn, *Markets*, 41, 87). *Macella* normally sold a range of foodstuffs and were open daily. See Frayn, *Markets*, 3.

have been built by wealthy benefactors, and they probably would have controlled who could operate a stall.[9] This, in itself, fits the *Gemeinschaft*-type. Since the markets regularly drew many into the city from the surrounding areas, and were places that the lower classes in the city would visit frequently, they were clearly important social gathering points. Some of the control measures instituted at various times suggest that they were perceived by the authorities as places of gossip and potential unrest.[10] This fear, and the measures instituted, suggests there was a sense of paternal authority operating.

The social nature of city planning is also evident in the provision of public buildings for social purposes. In Greek cities there were *gymnasia*, which offered opportunities for exercise, recreation and social interaction.[11] Baths were virtually ubiquitous. Even relatively small towns could have more than one and these were generally located either near the *forum/agora* or at the periphery of the city along the main roads.[12] The latter is particularly seen when there was more than one bath house in the city or in Greek cities which had been Romanized.[13] At the baths there were games, exercises, massages, "take-away" food stalls and gardens. Bathing was enjoyed by all ages, sexes and classes — even merchants and artisans who otherwise worked long hours — not least because they were important places to make social/business contacts.[14] E. J. Owens is probably correct in

---

[9] Frayn, *Markets*, 38, 104.

[10] See R. MacMullen, "Market-days in the Roman Empire" *Phoenix* 24 (1970) 337; Stambaugh & Balch, *Social World*, 107; Dyson, *Community*, 156; Frayn, *Markets*, 27, 123.

[11] For example, A. H. M. Jones, *The Roman Economy* (Oxford: Blackwell, 1974) 23; Stambaugh & Balch, *Social World*, 107; Tomlinson, *From Mycenae*, 24. In earlier times they also had a civil function in the military training of young men, but in the Roman period only the social function would have been significant.

[12] Pliny boasts that the little village near his villa has three baths (*Ep.* 2.17); also see Owens, *The City*, 100, 135; Dyson, *Community*, 174.

[13] See the plans of various Roman cities in Owens, *The City*, 100-43.

[14] J. P. V. D. Balsdon, *Life and Leisure in Ancient Rome* (London: Bodley Head, 1969) 28-31; Stambaugh & Balch, *Social World*, 118; J. Shelton, ed., *As the Romans Did: A Sourcebook in Roman Social History* (New York: Oxford University Press, 1988) 311; Stambaugh, *Roman City*, 201; Dyson, *Community*, 174; Tomlinson, *From Mycenae*, 28. Except where they had their own separate baths, women probably used the baths early in the day, the more leisured classes used them about

describing them as "one of the most important social centres of the cities of the empire".[15]

In Roman cities, public latrines were frequently located near the *forum*. These usually consisted of rectangular rooms with large benches with regularly spaced holes along the three main sides, under which there lay sewers that were flushed. Along the main walls there were often numerous peep-holes. Both the complete lack of privacy, and the apparently social nature of even this most basic activity seems characteristic of ancient society. Given the design of these buildings it is quite likely that they also would have become social gathering places.[16]

Temples, shrines, and other sacred locations were normally situated in and around the *agora/forum* area, often at the most elevated point, to emphasize the protective nature of the gods.[17] Furthermore, statues of gods and shrines were common on street-corners. The Romans maintained cross-road cults (*compitalia*) for gods that were worshipped by the neighborhood (*vicus*) and to whom local people would offer prayers for the state's preservation.[18] Apart from their explicitly religious purpose, temples had a multitude of other uses. They were important as places where people gathered socially, so that many temples had gardens with seats, even aviaries and zoos, art galleries, or shops and stalls. Temples

---

the eighth hour, and the working classes used them in the evenings (Martial *Epigr.* 4.8, 10.48; Balsdon, *Life*, 25, 29, 54).

[15] Owens, *The City*, 155; cf. *CIL* 6.15258, 8.17938.

[16] MacMullen, *Social Relations*, 57; Stambaugh, *Roman City*, 133. Urinals were also provided in the front of fullers' shops, as urine was important for the tanning process (Stambaugh, *Roman City*, 133). It is likely that when men stopped at these to relieve themselves they would have engaged in conversation with others waiting to use them, as well as customers in the shop, and the shop-keeper.

[17] Stambaugh & Balch, *Social World*, 127; Owens, *The City*, 3-4, 153-4; Alcock, *Graecia Capta*, 181, 198. Tomlinson notes that while this was not always the case, as some temples could be situated outside city walls, it was normal to have at least one major temple located near the center of the city (*From Mycenae*, 18; cf. Dyson, *Community*, 157). Although the following material is largely drawn from Roman cities, because we have much more information on them in this period, many of the same principles can be assumed to apply to Greek cities.

[18] See, for example, Vitruvius *De Arch.* 4.5.2; MacMullen, *Social Relations*, 68; idem, *Paganism in the Roman Empire* (New Haven, CT: Yale University Press, 1981) 31; J. E. Stambaugh, "Social Relations in the City of the Early Principate: State of Research" *SBLSP* (1980) 88; Stambaugh & Balch, *Social World*, 130; Dyson, *Community*, 169.

also served as museums, meeting-places, repositories for valuables, and a place for beggars to wait for handouts.[19]

The social importance of public space is further highlighted by the cramped living conditions for most residents. James Packer states that, "the average Roman domicile must have served only as a place to sleep and store possessions".[20] For many, living in a small room or apartment, simply performing everyday functions would have meant relying on the public latrines, baths, cafés, shops, colonnades and streets. In effect, the street was an extension of one's house or shop.[21]

The planning of Greco-Roman cities shows that ordinary, everyday activities were highly sociable. It could therefore be said that, among other purposes, city planning sought to promote social cohesion.[22] One of the main contributing factors to this social cohesion was surely the lack of privacy resulting from the density of living.[23] A prominent feature of Greco-Roman cities is the narrowness of streets and the closeness of buildings. Although regulations at Rome dictated that *viae* be eight feet wide on the straight and sixteen on bends, few of them were, while in many provincial cities most roads were only a few metres wide.[24] Shops and

---

[19] See Stambaugh, "Functions", 556, 573, 588; MacMullen, *Paganism*, 35. Although these descriptions are of Roman temples, there is no reason why the same could not be said of Greek ones. This is apparent in the diagrammatic reconstruction of the Acropolis precinct at Athens in A. N. Oikonomides, *The Acropolis of Athens* (Athens: N. Gouvoussis, 1995).

[20] J. E. Packer, "Housing and Population in Imperial Ostia and Rome" *JRS* 57 (1967) 87; cf. Martial *Epigr.* 8.14. Few residences, other than houses, even had their own bathroom facilities. An *insula* apartment block might have a common latrine but it was seldom located higher than the second storey. See, for example, Stambaugh, *Roman City*, 175-6. If the plan of one such complex at Ostia is anything to go by, the individual apartments were very small, somewhere in the order of 9-$12m^2$ (ibid., 176).

[21] Packer, "Housing", 87; Balsdon, *Life*, 20; MacMullen, *Social Relations*, 62-4; J. M. Reynolds, "The Cities" in D. C. Braund, ed., *The Administration of the Roman Empire 241 BC-AD 193* (Exeter: University of Exeter Press, 1988) 20; Dyson, *Community*, 176.

[22] See Perring, "Spatial Organisation", 274; cf. Stambaugh, *Roman City*, 205.

[23] See Sallares, *Ecology*, 52.

[24] Martial *Epigr.* 1.86, 7.61; Varro *Ling.* 7.15; cf. MacMullen, *Social Relations*, 63-4; Ward-Perkins, *Cities*, 20; Stambaugh, *Roman City*, 188; Owens, *The City*, 11, 83, 157, 167.

cafés could also significantly protrude into and occlude streets.[25] Under such conditions, people would lean out of their windows to talk to neighbors across the street.[26] Consequently, there would have been very little privacy and almost no secrets.

This lack of privacy would be compounded if cities were small and densely populated. Scholars have sought to estimate the population size of a city by a variety of methods. None has been very successful.[27] The best attempt is that of Packer, who has estimated the urban population of Ostia from the numbers of apartment blocks and the number of tenements in these (assuming an average family of four) together with the number of houses and the numbers of bedrooms in these. His estimate is 27,000.[28] Given that the area within the city walls is sixty-nine hectares, this gives a density of 391 persons per hectare. This is lower than the estimates of Ramsay MacMullen (495 per hectare), Rodney Stark (507), and John Stambaugh (742), although these are based on Rome where the density can be assumed to have been higher.[29]

Yet Ostia was not a typical city. For it had many apartment blocks taller than two stories which were probably

----

[25] See, for example, Martial *Epigr.* 7.61; cf. Ward-Perkins, *Cities*, 35.

[26] Martial *Epigr.* 1.86; cf. MacMullen, *Social Relations*, 63-4; Stambaugh, *Roman City*, 184.

[27] See, for example, the attempts by T. Chandler & G. Fox, *3000 Years of Urban Growth* (New York: Academic Press, 1974) 2-9, 81. The difficulty is that census figures are notoriously unreliable, while other methods usually ignore that, in real terms, a city's population also included those living in its *territorium*. See K. Hopkins, "Economic Growth and Towns in Classical Antiquity", in P. Abrams & E. A. Wrigley, eds., *Towns in Societies* (Cambridge: Cambridge University Press, 1978) 69; P. R. Duncan-Jones, *The Economy of the Roman Empire: Quantitative Studies* (2nd ed.; Cambridge: Cambridge University Press, 1982), 259-65; T. G. Parkin, *Demography and Roman Society* (Baltimore: Johns Hopkins University Press, 1992) 4-5; Alcock, *Graecia Capta*, 96-7. Furthermore, cyclical fluctuations in population size are also largely ignored (Sallares, *Ecology*, 65, 70, 105-6).

[28] Packer, "Housing", 86.

[29] MacMullen, *Social Relations*, 62-3; Stambaugh, *Roman City*, 337 n. 4; R. Stark, "Antioch as the Social Situation for Matthew's Gospel", in D. L. Balch, ed., *Social History of the Matthean Community: Cross-Disciplinary Approaches* (Minneapolis: Fortress, 1991) 192. By comparison, modern Bombay has 450 per hectare and Calcutta has 300 per hectare (ibid.).

uncommon anywhere except Ostia itself and Rome.[30]
Consequently, the density of the urban centers of other
provincial cities would be considerably less than Ostia's 391
per hectare.[31] On the other hand, Packer's assumptions
regarding the numbers occupying tenements and rooms of
houses is too low. In any case, a figure in the vicinity of 200-
250 persons per hectare still indicates that we are dealing
with a very densely populated urban area within the city.[32]
Overall, the pattern is of a relatively sparsely populated
landscape with small, densely populated urban centers.[33]

Greek and Roman societies were both highly sociable.[34]
This is particularly apparent in the importance that was
placed on social eating. Dinner parties among the elite were
common. Apart from some Roman clients, the poor generally
relied on public banquets associated with festivals, held in
the *forum/agora*, and regular dinners associated with the

---

[30] Packer, "Housing", 81; cf. Juvenal *Sat.* 3.190-6; Duncan-Jones,
The Economy, 277; Reynolds, "Cities", 20; Dyson, *Community*, 176.
Nevertheless, Ephesus had at least two three-storey apartment blocks
in the first century. See A. G. McKay, *Houses, Villas, and Palaces in the
Roman World* (London: Thames & Hudson, 1975) 212-17. He also notes
that such complexes were also common at Babylon, Aradus and Tyre
(ibid., 217; cf. Strabo *Geog.* 16.1, 2.13, 2.23); cf. the three-storey complex
mentioned at Troas in Acts 20:8-9. However, McKay's interpretation of
the two complexes from Ephesus is not necessarily convincing. They
may have been more unique that he allows, especially given their
location on a hill-side. Nor is there any evidence to suggest, as he does,
that the Roman pattern was modelled on these.

[31] Engels, for example, suggests that for other cities which had only
one and two storey residences a figure closer to 160 persons per hectare
might be more accurate (*Roman Corinth*, 39, 82, 222-3 n. 68). Yet, he
does not explain why a figure that is considerably less than half that of
Ostia's is appropriate and his sources also potentially underestimate
populations by assuming only one person per bedroom in houses.

[32] Such a figure refers to the density of the population residing
within the city walls, i.e. the population density of the urban part of the
ancient city. The population density of the *territorium* would, by
comparison, be very much less. Hence, Sallares argues that the total
density of population in Attica was 35 per km[2] (*Ecology*, 73). In terms of
social interaction, however, the urban population density is still
meaningful.

[33] Compare the survey work of G. Barker, J. Lloyd & D. Webley in
"A Classical Landscape in Molise" *PBSR* 46 (1978) 43.

[34] Balsdon, *Life*, 20; MacMullen, *Social Relations*, 64; M. I. Finley,
Politics in the Ancient World (Cambridge: Cambridge University Press,
1983) 82; Reynolds, "Cities", 33; Stambaugh, *Roman City*, 187.

various clubs (*collegia*/θίασοι).[35] Poorer people also ate and
sought company at the numerous restaurants (*cauponae*)
and cafés (*popinae*), where they would gather to eat, drink,
talk and gamble. For example, Pompeii had 20 *cauponae* and
118 *popinae*.[36]

The sociability of life in Greco-Roman cities is also seen
in the frequent religious festivals. These were celebrated for a
particular god, to commemorate the founding of that god's
temple or, in the case of the older agricultural gods, related to
particular seasonal functions. On festival days, the temples
were decorated and opened, sacrifices were offered,
processions were held, and activities took on the
characteristics of a country fair. Markets were set up and food
and souvenirs were sold. There was singing, drinking,
musical and dramatic performances, mimes, dancers, and
chariot-races. The Greeks held athletic games, while the
Romans often held gladiatorial contests.[37]

Probably the high point of the festival was the feast,
normally laid on at public expense. The feast was usually
held in the temples and/or the *agora*/*forum*, and the statue
of the god was placed on a dining couch at the banquet to
indicate the god's communion with the people.[38] Participation
in the festivals was a personal religious duty and delight, a
major social activity, and a means of demonstrating
allegiance to the state.

Religious clubs (*collegia*, θίασοι) were an important
part of both the social and religious function of the cities.
Whether their primary purpose was religious/sacrificial,

---

[35] Seneca *Ep.* 56.1-2; MacMullen, *Social Relations*, 77; Stambaugh,
"Social Relations", 83; idem, *Roman City*, 205; Tomlinson, *From Mycenae*,
24-5; Alcock, *Graecia Capta*, 113. On the great frequency of festivals see:
Dio Cassius 60.17.1; Varro *Rust.* 3.2.16; cf. Balsdon, *Life*, 70-1.

[36] Balsdon, *Life*, 152-4; MacMullen, *Social Relations*, 86;
Stambaugh, *Roman City*, 208-9; Dyson, *Community*, 175. From the time
of Tiberius, however, restrictions were placed on their operation,
probably from fear of subversion. See Suetonius *Tib.* 34; cf. Balsdon,
Life, 153; Stambaugh, *Roman City*, 209. This, in itself, also reflects a
paternal authority and the importance of group loyalty and concord.

[37] Vitruvius *De Arch.* 5.3.1; *ILS* 5053; cf. Balsdon, *Life*, 70-1; J. E.
Stambaugh, "The Functions of Roman Temples" *ANRW* 2.16.1 (1978)
576-7; MacMullen, *Paganism*, 18-21; Stambaugh & Balch, *Social World*,
119-20; E. Ferguson, *Backgrounds of Early Christianity* (2nd ed.; Grand
Rapids: Eerdmans, 1993) 183.

[38] Dion. Hal. *Ant. Rom.* 2.23.2-5; Stambaugh, "Functions", 577-8;
MacMullen, *Paganism*, 36, 39; Dyson, *Community*, 210.

funerary, or as a trade guild, all adopted a patron deity and opened their meetings with prayer.[39] Most associations met in a building that comprised a shrine, a courtyard, dining-rooms for banquets, a kitchen and a meeting room.[40] Some associations performed special roles in various festivals and public rites, such as the guild of merchants at the festival of Mercury, or artisans at the feast of Minerva.[41] In this both Greek and Roman cities fit the *Gemeinschaft*-type.

Concord (ὁμόνοια) was one of the most important values of Greek society. It was regarded as "the avoidance of the evils of civil strife (*stasis*) and the preservation of national solidarity in the face of any external threat".[42] Devotion to the cause of one's native city was held to be one of the individual citizen's highest duties.[43] In the Roman period, this would have been expected to be manifest in the avoidance of disorder and hence Roman displeasure and intervention.

Furthermore, the Roman notion of *pax* (which will be discussed later in this chapter) seems to be quite close to the Greek idea. Indeed, citizens were expected to foster *concordia*, behave in an orderly manner when assembled and foster friendships for the sake of the state: to shun one's fellow-citizens and to try and live away from the public gaze

---

[39] Stambaugh, "Functions", 588; idem, "Social Relations", 83-4, 94; MacMullen, *Social Relations*, 82; A. Wardman, *Religion and Statecraft among the Romans* (London: Granada, 1982) 99; Reynolds, "Cities", 48. Religion was so integrated into ordinary civic life that there was no entirely secular social activity. Belonging to a trade guild or a funerary club, attending the market or the theatre, all involved some contact with, or participation in, "religion". See MacMullen, *Paganism*, 40; cf. Stambaugh & Balch, *Social World*, 127; Reynolds, "Cities", 32; Owens, *The City*, 155.

[40] Stambaugh, "Functions", 590-1; MacMullen, *Paganism*, 36-7.

[41] See Stambaugh, "Functions", 588.

[42] A. R. R. Sheppard, "*Homonoia* in the Greek Cities of the Roman Empire" *Anc Soc* 15-17 (1984-6) 229; cf. Thucydides 8.93.3; Philostratus *VA* 4.8; *SIG*³ 742.2; Finley, *Politics*, 105.

[43] See, for example, Plato *Resp.* 414E; Polybius 6.54; Josephus *Ap.* 2.30. Although Roman writers, such as Cicero (*Off.* 1.83, 86, 124; *Leg.* 1.20, 2.5) considered a citizen's first allegiance to be to Rome itself, devotion to one's native city was still an important duty. See also Reynolds, "Cities", 25; N. Wood, *Cicero's Social and Political Thought* (Berkeley: University of California Press, 1988) 139; P. Veyne, *Bread and Circuses: Historical Sociology and Political Pluralism* (London: Allen Lane, 1990) 39; Dyson, *Community*, 206; C. Nicolet, "The Citizen; Political Man" in A. Giardina, ed., *The Romans* (Chicago: University of Chicago Press, 1993) 24.

was regarded as treasonable.[44] In these matters both Greek and Roman cities fit the *Gemeinschaft*-type.

Religion was also deeply connected with the political life of cities, so much so that Ronald Mellor suggests that "belief and disbelief were political acts".[45] The role of religion in public life is also evident in the right of the state to punish offences against the gods. Cicero suggests that in the past the failure of public figures to comply with auguries was treasonable and had been punished as such.[46] Similarly, under the Principate, disloyalty to the Imperial cult was regarded as impiety, and cities could be charged for neglect of the cult or penalized for failure to fulfil promises of cult.[47]

Imperial cults were found in most cities, even villages, and were adopted enthusiastically in many parts of the East.[48] The basis of the cult lay in the recognition of the Emperor as the defender of the empire, the one who unites it, bringing peace and prosperity, through a pact with the gods.[49] In some sense, the Emperor himself was considered divine.[50] He was included in existing cults and festivals and

[44] Dio Chrys. *Or.* 48.2; Cicero *Off.* 1.124; cf. Balsdon, *Life*, 136-7; Woodhead, "Conflict", 8.

[45] R. Mellor, "The Goddess Roma" *ANRW* 2.17.2 (1981) 1026; cf. J. Helgeland, "Roman Army Religion" *ANRW* 2.16.2 (1978) 1471; J. R. Fears, "The Theology of Victory at Rome: Approaches and Problems" *ANRW* 2.17.2 (1981) 739; Wardman, *Religion*, 12; H. L. Hendrix, "Beyond 'Imperial Cult' and 'Cults of Magistrates'" *SBLSP* (1986) 301.

[46] Cicero cites the case of a certain Claudius who was tried for treason when his disregard for the auguries led to the defeat of his fleet. His colleague, Junius, committed suicide under similar circumstances (*Nat. D.* 2.7-8), presumable before the matter went to trial; cf. Finley, *Politics*, 94.

[47] See, for example, Tacitus *Ann.* 4.36; Price, *Rituals*, 66; A. Lintott, *Imperium Romanum: Politics and Administration* (London: Routledge, 1993) 184.

[48] Stambaugh, "Functions", 585; Wardman, *Religion*, 87; Price, *Rituals*, 83-4; cf. *CPJ* 153.29-48 (in J. L. White, ed., *Light from Ancient Letters* [Philadelphia: Fortress, 1986] 134-5).

[49] See, for example, Pliny *Pan.* 67.7, 68.1, 72.1-2, 94.1-2; Seneca *Clem.* 1.4.1; *ILS* 139-40; cf. R. M. Ogilvie, *The Romans and Their Gods in the Age of Augustus* (London: Chatto & Windus, 1969) 118; J. R. Fears, "The Cult of Jupiter and Roman Imperial Ideology" *ANRW* 2.17.1 (1981) 57-60, 64; Price, *Rituals*, 54.

[50] See, for example, *CIL* 10.6305; *SIG*³798; Tacitus *Ann.* 1.10; Suetonius *Aug.* 52; and the inscription found in R. K. Sherk, ed., *The Roman Empire: Augustus to Hadrian* (Cambridge: Cambridge University Press, 1988) 111; cf. A. N. Sherwin-White, *Roman Citizenship* (2nd ed.; Oxford: Clarendon, 1973) 415-16; Fears, "Jupiter", 97; S. R. F. Price,

specific imperial rites were established. In the provinces, worship frequently could be offered to the Emperor directly.[51]

Like other cults, the Imperial cult was important for the whole city, because its festivals attracted many visitors, and all residents were "expected" to participate in the processions and sacrifices.[52] There is also considerable evidence to suggest that it was personally significant for many individuals. Some *ex voto* inscriptions directed to the Emperor and the Imperial family have been found.[53] Likewise, some prayed to the Emperor.[54] In the provinces of Asia Minor and Bithynia there is also evidence for the existence of Imperial mystery rites.[55]

"Gods and Emperors: The Greek language of the Roman Imperial Cult" *JHS* 104 (1984) 85. Apparent references to the divinity of the living Emperor are ambiguous. Augustus, Tiberius, Claudius, and the young Nero all declined divine honors, but took the title of *divi filius* (See *ILS* 140; *SEG* 11.922-3; the inscription in Sherk, *Empire*, 103; Tacitus *Ann.* 4.38; Dio Cassius 51.20.8; Vell. Pat. 2.126.1; D. L. Jones, "Christianity and the Roman Imperial Cult" *ANRW* 2.23.2 [1980] 1024-5; F. G. B. Millar, "State and Subject: The Impact of Monarchy" in F. G. B. Millar & E. Segal, eds., *Caesar Augustus — Seven Aspects* [Oxford: Clarendon, 1984] 37). Even after his death, the Emperor was considered a *divus* not a *deus* (See Price, "Gods", 83-4, 88; Hendrix, "Imperial Cult", 305). Although the Emperor is sometimes equated with Zeus, Price argues, that may mean no more than he was seen as "Zeus-like" in the exercise of his power ("Gods", 86). Also, the *genius* of the Emperor appears to have been the focus of the cult for Romans in this period.
    [51] Dio Cassius 51.20.6-7; Suetonius *Aug.* 52; Pliny *Pan.* 72.1; Tacitus *Ann.* 4.37; *ILS* 112, 116, 5050; *P.Oxy* 2435; the inscriptions in Sherk, *Empire*, 13-14, 73-6; cf. H. W. Pleket, "An Aspect of the Emperor Cult: Imperial Mysteries" *HTR* 58 (1965) 334; Ogilvie, *Romans*, 123; D. Winslow, "Religion and the Early Roman Empire" in S. Benko & J. J. O'Rourke, eds., *The Catacombs and the Colosseum* (Valley Forge, PA: Judson, 1971) 247; Sherwin-White, *Citizenship*, 221; Fears, "Jupiter", 99; Mellor, "Roma", 977-83; Millar, "State", 37-8, 54; Price, *Rituals*, 3; Hendrix, "Imperial Cult", 305; Ferguson, *Backgrounds*, 194; Lintott, *Imperium*, 182.
    [52] Price, *Rituals*, 102-12. Price notes that householders in Asia were expected to sacrifice outside their homes as the procession passed.
    [53] For example, *ILS* 120; *SEG* 2.718; cf. Price, "Gods", 91-2.
    [54] For example, Horace *Carm.* 4.5; Ovid *Pont.* 4.9.105-16; cf. Price, "Gods", 92.
    [55] See Pleket, "Emperor Cult", 334, 337-9, 343-6, who cites a number of inscriptions in support. The evidence of *ex voto* inscriptions, prayers and mystery rites discredits the view of a number of scholars that it was not a religious phenomenon but simply a political ideology or a legitimation of power (so Winslow, "Religion", 247; K. Wengst, *Pax Romana and the Peace of Jesus Christ* [Philadelphia: Fortress, 1987] 48; Ferguson, *Backgrounds*, 185; and to some extent, J. G. Gager, *Kingdom and Community: The Social World of Early Christianity* [Engelwood

The nature of Greek and Roman religion will be discussed more fully in the treatment of norms, values and beliefs later in this chapter. Yet it should be apparent from the preceding discussion that Greek and Roman societies share many of the characteristics of *Gemeinschaft*-type societies. They had continual and close contact between residents (and a lack of privacy that fostered social cohesion), relationships were paternal but reciprocal, group loyalty and concord were highly valued.

As *Gemeinschaft*-type societies, we would expect that socialization in Greek and Roman cities would have been quite successful. Given the nature of the sources, this is difficult to verify or quantify, although the indirect evidence suggests that it was generally the case.[56] Family festivals and rituals that reinforced values associated with marriage, child-rearing, respect for ancestors and gender roles were very prominent.[57] Obedience, respect and devotion to parents, characterized by the Romans as *pietas*, was also strongly socialized. Apart from attestation to this in various writers it is also clear from the numerous funerary inscriptions set up

---

Cliffs, NJ: Prentice-Hall, 1975) 101). Furthermore, such views assume a distinction between religion and politics which cannot be supported in the light of the argument of this whole section. See also the criticisms of Price, *Rituals*, 52, 235, 248; idem, "Gods", 91. I am aware of the criticism of Hendrix against the use of the term "cult" in regards to this phenomenon ("Imperial Cult", 303-8). It is perhaps not the ideal term, since sacrifice was not a significant component of rites as he argues (ibid., 304, 308). He is also correct to highlight the possible variety of responses in different locations. Nevertheless, the phenomenon does involve a complex of prayers, festivals, *ex voto* inscriptions, processions and mystery rites, and offers of cult were often associated with requests for privileges. The last aspect is remarkably like the Roman cultic attitude of *do ut des* (this will be discussed later). Although not all of these elements may be found everywhere, I think there are sufficient grounds for regarding it as a genuine cult.

[56] Allowing for the biased view of elite authors, descriptions of values and beliefs such as those presented by Cicero in *De Officiis* give this impression. The strength of attachment to common values engendered by socialization is also manifest in accounts where such values are flouted. The examples of these in Cicero's work, alone, are many.

[57] See, for example, M. Golden, *Children and Childhood in Classical Athens* (Baltimore: Johns Hopkins University Press, 1990) 47-9; B. Rawson, "Adult-Child Relationships in Roman Society" in idem, ed., *Marriage, Divorce, and Children in Ancient Rome* (Oxford: Clarendon, 1991) 17.

by children for their parents.[58] Indeed, the Romans appear to have taken it for granted that such a value was universal.[59] Furthermore, Cicero suggests that a *pater* governs his children who obey him readily whereas he governs his slaves by coercion and sees it necessary to "break" them.[60]

As noted above, the sense of patriotism, duty and devotion to one's city seems to have been strongly held. That this sense of loyalty was strongly socialized is evident from the numerous conflicts that occurred between Greek cities during the Roman period.[61] Furthermore, according to Moses Finley the evidence suggests that the great majority of Greeks

> would have accepted as premises, one might say as axioms, that the good life was possible only in a *polis*, that the good man was more or less synonymous with the good citizen, that slaves, women and barbarians were inferior by nature...The main divergences were in practical judgments, not in the premises.[62]

Thus, while socialization in the Greco-Roman world was probably usually quite successful, it need not have been particularly warm and affectionate. The evidence for this is, in fact, very strong. In the first place, it does not seem that children had much contact with their parents, especially their fathers, during their early years. They were largely raised by slaves: wet-nurses and tutors/guardians. At the same time, family structures were not very stable or settled given the short life-expectancy, a high divorce rate (especially among the elite), and the frequent separation of slave families through sale. It is likely that this would have had a negative impact on children.[63]

---

[58] See, for example, R. P. Saller, *Patriarchy, Property and Death in the Roman Family* (Cambridge: Cambridge University Press, 1994) 105-14. See also C. S. de Vos, "'ΚΑΙ Ο ΟΙΚΟΣ...': The Nature and Religious Practices of Graeco-Roman Households as the Context for the Conversion and Baptism of Households in the Acts of the Apostles" (unpublished BTh[Hons] thesis, Flinders University, 1993) 15-16; cf. Seneca *Ben.* 3.38.2; Tacitus *Agr.* 4.2-4.

[59] See Saller, *Patriarchy*, 114.

[60] Cicero *Rep.* 3.37.

[61] See Sheppard, "*Homonoia*", 233-5.

[62] Finley, *Politics*, 125-6.

[63] See Golden, *Children*, 83, 100; Rawson, "Adult-Child", 7-8; cf. S. Dixon, *The Roman Family* (Baltimore: Johns Hopkins University Press, 1992), 116-18.

Among the Greeks, in particular, corporal punishment was used to ensure obedience was common. Its practice was held to be proper.[64] Aristotle, for example, argued that men should rule their wives like a magistrate does fellow-citizens, but his children like a king does his subjects.[65] Many Romans also considered severity in the raising of children as praiseworthy. A good example of this attitude is found in Seneca, who pictures God as a father who wishes, out of his love for men, that they be "harassed by toil, by suffering, by losses, in order that they may gather true strength" (*Prov.* 2.6).[66] The Romans were more reticent to use corporal punishment on their children, as distinct from their slaves. Nevertheless, they seem to have thought it appropriate to beat young children before they could be reasoned with.[67] Although Richard Saller claims that the child-rearing practices of the Romans were harsher than ours, they were probably no harsher than those of other preindustrial societies.[68] But, as was suggested in chapter one, these were also usually quite severe.

Furthermore, schooling in both Greek and Roman societies involved a very strict and brutal socialization into the values and norms of those societies. The severe beatings received from both teachers and *paidagogoi* are almost legendary.[69] Mark Golden even suggests that the "methods of instruction, like the emphasis on order, seemed tailor-made to stifle originality and self-expression, relying as they did on mimicry and memory".[70] While this is probably a little too modern and ethnocentric, it does suggest that schooling was a harsh, but effective, socialization into the dominant values of those societies.

---

[64] See, for example, Aristotle *Eth. Nic.* 1149B8; Plato *Prt.* 325D, *Resp.* 548B; Xenophon *An.* 5.8.18, *Cyr.* 2.2.14, *Oec.* 7.12; cf. Golden, *Children*, 103.

[65] Aristotle *Pol.* 1259A38-B18; cf. Golden, *Children*, 102.

[66] See also Seneca *Prov.* 1.5; cf. E. Eyben, "Fathers and Sons", in B. Rawson, ed., *Marriage, Divorce, and Children in Ancient Rome* (Oxford: Clarendon, 1991), 122-3.

[67] See Quintilian *Inst.* 1.3.14, 6.3.25; Seneca *Constant.* 12.3, *Clem.* 1.14.1; cf. Dixon, *Roman Family*, 117; Saller, *Patriarchy*, 145-7. With older children praise/criticism and rewards/penalties were thought to be more appropriate.

[68] Saller, *Patriarchy*, 130-2.

[69] See Golden, *Children*, 64-5; Dixon, *Roman Family*, 118-19; Saller, *Patriarchy*, 148; cf. Quintilian *Inst.* 1.3.13.

[70] Golden, *Children*, 65.

Finally, it was well-recognized that the father, as head of the household, served as an important role-model to his children. This is significant given the brutality that many Greeks and Romans showed towards the slaves in the household, and would have encouraged the children to see violence and domination as normal.[71] In fact, Juvenal suggests that "the son is brutalized, not by his own suffering, but by watching his father inflict pain on slaves".[72] Adding to this "education" would be the popular gladiatorial games and their own training as soldiers. Needless to say, in the case of slaves reared in households, who may have become citizens later, socialization was extremely harsh.

Overall, Greek and Roman societies share many features of *Gemeinschaft*-type societies. As such, they seem to have had generally successful socialization, and hence a strong commitment to their norms, values, beliefs and institutions. Nevertheless, socialization in the Greco-Roman world does not seem to have been warm and affectionate. According to the model, this would suggest that both Greek and Roman communities would have a high propensity to conflict. The evidence for that is overwhelming.[73] Since this is common to both societies, it does not help to explain possible differences in conflict response. Thus the different societies' patterns of norms, values and beliefs may be more important.

II. DIFFERENT NORMS, VALUES AND BELIEFS

Among the Greeks, a continuing commitment to the ideals of the city-state, and in many cases to democratic ideals, was important. These will be considered in more detail in the next chapter. However, the most significant differences, especially for the purpose of this study, are the religious attitudes of each society.[74] Given the broad geographical sweep and the

---

[71] See Golden, *Children*, 159-61; Saller, *Patriarchy*, 150.

[72] Juvenal *Sat.* 14.15-24, 63; cf. Saller, *Patriarchy*, 150.

[73] A similar point is made by Woodhead ("Conflict", 2). He notes that, for the ancients, recourse to violence was perceived to be the "complete answer in conflict resolution" (ibid., 19).

[74] I am not thereby suggesting that religious norms, values and beliefs operated in isolation, given the non-compartmentalization of life that is evident in the Greco-Roman world. But since the earliest Christians experienced conflict with their wider communities, at least overtly on the basis of these norms, values, and beliefs, they are the most relevant.

city-state origin of Greek cities, we would expect significant differences in the nature of religious practice and belief between them and Roman cities.[75] Furthermore, the attitude of each of these cultures to other cults and foreigners is also significant. Both of these will be examined in turn.

1. The Nature of Greek Religion

In the first century, "religion" in the Greek cities of the East involved traditional cults and practices, various philosophical schools, and numerous mystery cults.[76] A distinction ought to be made in Greek religion in respect to the beliefs and practices of the common people, and those of the educated and leisured classes.

Among the common people the traditional myths and gods were still important. In the Greek cities of the East there was a multiplicity of gods and cults and many cities had gods which were peculiarly their own, so that there was some location specificity. Besides these, Zeus and Tyche were among the most popular gods, given the number of dedications to them.[77] The traditional gods were largely understood anthropomorphically, such that they were invested with myth and personality, and thought to dwell among the people. When one approached a statue one, in fact, approached the god. Most found true delight in visiting the temple and participating in rites, festivals and sacrifices.

---

[75] Note the warning of Sallares against equating Greek and Roman cultures or societies (*Ecology*, 11); cf. MacMullen, *Paganism*, 65-7. Given the nature of the sources, C. R. Phillips argues that it is difficult to reconstruct religious mentality, for "at best, one can only examine the fundamental forms of religion: the psychology of religion is not available" ("The Sociology of Religious Knowledge in the Roman Empire to A.D. 284" *ANRW* 2.16.3 [1986] 2695); cf. W. Burkert, "Craft versus Sect: The Problems of Orphics and Pythagoreans" in B. F. Meyer & E. P. Sanders, eds., *Jewish and Christian Self-Definition* (vol. 3; London: SCM Press, 1982) 1. Although a full picture of religious perceptions and convictions cannot be known, the "forms of religion" do give some clue as to what the attitudes were.

[76] L. H. Martin, *Hellenistic Religions: An Introduction* (New York: Oxford University Press, 1987) 11.

[77] See J. Ferguson, *The Religions of the Roman Empire* (London: Thames & Hudson, 1970) 77; MacMullen, *Paganism*, 4; Ferguson, *Backgrounds*, 225-7; D. W. J. Gill, "Acts and Roman Religion: A. Religion in a Local Setting" in D. W. J. Gill & C. H. Gempf, eds., *The Book of Acts in its Graeco-Roman Setting* (BAFCS 2; Grand Rapids: Eerdmans, 1994) 81.

They believed that the gods were present, honored by the
rites, and accepted the worship. Many still believed that the
gods could visit in the guise of mortals.[78]

On the whole, Greek religion was non-exclusive, with
syncretism or assimilation common, since many local gods
were seen as equivalent.[79] The emphasis in traditional
worship was on piety, εὐσέβεια, which was understood as an
attitude of respect for the gods, as trying not to offend them,
and acquiring their support by the offer of the proper rites
and sacrifices.[80] Many of the common people also participated
in the mystery cults, which developed around and alongside
the traditional cults.[81]

Scholars often distinguish between the gods of the
mysteries and those that were traditional. The former are
portrayed as personal and immediate, dealing with the
spiritual concerns of individuals, while the latter are cold,
formal, transcendent, and community-oriented, not at all
concerned with an individual's spiritual well-being.[82] Such a
view does not explain the vitality of the traditional gods and
cults, something that is clearly demonstrated by inscriptions
and magical spells/amulets. It also involves a (Christian)
ethnocentric anachronism, namely, that genuine religion

---

[78] See, for example, Plutarch *Non posse* 1101D-1102A; Dion. Hal.
Ant. Rom. 2.20.2; Martin, *Hellenistic*, 52; B. W. Winter, "In Public and in
Private: Early Christian Interactions with Religious Pluralism" in A. D.
Clarke & B. W. Winter, eds., *One God, One Lord in a World of Religious
Pluralism* (Cambridge: Tyndale House, 1991) 116; Ferguson,
Backgrounds, 171. A good example of the continuing popular belief in the
visitation of the gods is found in Acts 14:11-8.

[79] Winslow, "Religion", 240-2; Martin, *Hellenistic*, 35; Ferguson,
Backgrounds, 161-5.

[80] For example, Diog. Laert. *Zeno* 119; cf. Stambaugh & Balch,
Social World, 134-5; Martin, *Hellenistic*, 11. Although Diogenes Laertius
adds that εὐσέβεια also means ἁγνούς θ' ὑπάρξειν, this may reflect
more of a philosophical, and particularly a Stoic, understanding than a
popular belief.

[81] Walter Burkert may be right in attributing the adoption of
mystery cults and rites, as well as the adoption of foreign gods such as
Isis and Osiris, to a development from votive religion (*Ancient Mystery
Cults* [Cambridge, MA: Harvard University Press, 1987] 14-15). Besides,
many of the Greek mystery cults, such as the Eleusinian rites, were
strongly linked to civic cults (see Ferguson, *Backgrounds*, 235).

[82] For example, Winslow, "Religion", 244; Mellor, "Roma", 1026;
Martin, *Hellenistic*, 9; Engels, *Roman Corinth*, 92-3.

must be individual and emotional.[83] Rather, both mystery and traditional cults are both expressions of piety and attempts to control nature and destiny.

The educated and the leisured classes largely treated the religious concerns and beliefs of the common people with considerable contempt. Popular religion was frequently derided as "superstition", δεισιδαιμονία. This term referred to the attitude and practice of taking ordinary events and ascribing divine causation to them, resulting in an irrational fear of phenomena like storms or darkness, attributing malicious intentions to the gods, and understanding the gods as the origin of pain, injury and suffering.[84]

Consequently, it was suggested that superstition resulted in irrational acts and rites in order to avert trouble, something that robbed festivals and religious rites of joy, and led to an attitude of disdain toward the gods.[85] Such a description is subjective and clearly reflects the pejorative attitudes of the educated and philosophically-inclined. Yet it must have had some basis in reality. In other words, the attitudes and practices which the educated and elite derided as superstition must reflect something of the nature of popular religion.

Philosophy was popular among the elite and educated of Greek cities. It had long been critical of the traditional Greek myths, and it tended to either totally debunk and thus reject them outright, or to reinterpret them allegorically.[86] Stoics understood the gods to be aspects or particular manifestations of the one transcendent God, and that this one God was called by many traditional names. Hence, they tended to use "god" and "gods" interchangeably. At the same time, their understanding of the nature of God was

---

[83] This will be discussed further below in the section on "The Nature of Roman Religion", and especially in relation to the importance of ancestral custom.

[84] For example, Plutarch *De superst.* 165B-E; idem, *Non posse* 1101D-E; cf. Ferguson, *Religion*, 80-1; MacMullen, *Paganism*, 70, 73.

[85] Dion. Hal. *Ant. Rom.* 2.20.2; Plutarch *De superst.* 166A, 169D-E; Ferguson, *Religion*, 80-1; MacMullen, *Paganism*, 73.

[86] See, for example, Dion. Hal. *Ant. Rom.* 2.20.1; H. W. Attridge, "The Philosophical Critique of Religion under the Early Empire" *ANRW* 2.16.1 (1979) 45-6; Stambaugh & Balch, *Social World*, 127-8; Martin, *Hellenistic*, 7-8, 40-2.

pantheistic and providential. Their approach to the myths was allegorical.[87]

Epicureans accepted the existence of the gods but rejected the idea that they cared about or intervened in the world, so that the traditional rites and sacrifices were futile and meaningless. As such, they were very close to "atheism" (ἀθεότης).[88] This was understood as a total disbelief in or disregard and disrespect for the gods. Plutarch, like most, considered this to be dangerous for it not only robbed ordinary religion of joy, but of meaning as well.[89]

Attitudes towards traditional religious practices were quite diverse among the various philosophical schools. Academics, such as Sextus Empiricus, allowed participation.[90] Epicureanism stressed piety, understood not as external worship but as a proper conception of the divine. Its adherents could continue to participate in the traditional rites, provided that they did so without believing they were thereby meriting the approval of the gods.[91] The Stoic Epictetus also links true piety with correct perception, but advocates moderation in sacrificial participation.[92] Neo-Pythagoreans, such as Apollonius of Tyana, regarded morality and spiritual worship as true piety, not external acts.[93] Plutarch also regards true piety as correct belief, and advocates an allegorical interpretation of traditional myths. He suggests that superstition should be avoided, but not in

---

[87] See, for example, Diog. Laert. *Zeno* 14, 119; Ogilvie, *The Romans*, 19-20; Price, "Gods", 80; Martin, *Hellenistic*, 8, 39; Winter, "In Public", 118-19. See also Cicero, *Nat. D.* 1.36-41, 2.66-71, 3.92-3.

[88] MacMullen, *Paganism*, 62; Martin, *Hellenistic*, 37; Winter, "In Public", 123; Plutarch describes the Epicurean position, quoting Menander, as ἔθυον οὐ προσέχουσιν οὐδέν μοι θεοῖς· (*Non posse* 1102B). See also Cicero *Nat. D.* 1.1-3, 18, 45, 56. As Attridge notes, however, Epicureanism was inherently conservative for the gods were still seen as fundamentally anthropomorphic in nature ("Critique", 52).

[89] Plutarch *De superst.* 165B, 169D-E; 170F, 171E-F; cf. Diog. Laert. *Zeno* 119; Winslow, "Religion", 246.

[90] Sextus Empiricus *Pyr.* 3.2-3; idem, *Phys.* 1.49; cf. Attridge, "Critique", 46-7.

[91] See, especially, *P.Oxy.* 215.1.4-23, 2.1-6; cf. Diog. Laert. *Epic.* 120; Attridge, "Critique", 52-3; Winter, "In Public", 125-6.

[92] Epictetus *Enchr.* 31.1. Attridge claims that "the classic Stoic position was one of accommodation to ordinary cult and belief", but he bases this entirely on Cicero *Nat. D.* 2.23-8, 59-72 ("Critique", 66).

[93] Philostratus *VA* 7.19; Attridge, "Critique", 70-1.

such a way as to destroy the faith of the common people in the gods.[94]

Thus, despite theological scepticism and criticism, most schools of philosophy tended to reach a position of accommodation with the traditional and popular rites. This meant avoidance of practices they found particularly unpalatable, or participation by reinterpretation, usually by allegorization.[95] Some, however, advocated maintaining traditional practices simply for the sake of the common people.[96] Indeed, among the Greeks, even an open expression of doubt about the gods could lead to punishment for atheism. For example, Anaxagoras was tried for impiety, ἀσέβεια, for saying the sun was a stone. Similarly, in the first century CE, Demonax of Athens was charged with atheism because he would not sacrifice to the gods and he had not been initiated into the Eleusinian mysteries.[97] In fact, Cicero even claims that Epicurus feigned piety to avoid popular hatred.[98]

Both the philosophical attitude to traditional practices and the actions against atheism show that the Greek religious mind considered religious belief to be important. This might also be described as a concern for congruity between belief and practice. For many, congruity meant reinterpreting the traditional practices, but the effect was that they tacitly appeared to maintain them, whereas for others, the need for congruity meant they rejected the traditional rites on principle.[99] The importance of congruity may be seen in the strong criticism levelled by some writers when they perceived it to be lacking.[100] This aspect of Greek

---

[94] Plutarch *Non posse* 1101B-C; idem, *De Is. et Os.* 355D, 381B-C; cf. Attridge, "Critique", 74-5.

[95] Attridge, "Critique", 45-6, 64.

[96] Plutarch *Non posse* 1102B; idem, *De Is. et Os.* 355C-D; cf. Winter, "In Public", 125-6.

[97] Plutarch *De superst.* 169F; Lucian *Demon.* 11; cf. Josephus *Ap.* 2.239; Attridge, "Critique", 59; MacMullen, *Paganism*, 62. Although Plutarch claims that superstition is actually a worse crime than atheism, he does not thereby deny that atheism itself is criminal (*De superst.* 169F, 170D).

[98] Cicero *Nat. D.* 1.63, 123, 3.3.

[99] This is particularly seen in the case of radical Cynics, such as Oenomaus and Demonax. See Attridge, "Critique", 56-60. Some Epicureans may also have advocated such a position.

[100] For example, Plutarch *De superst.* 170D. Epictetus uses the Jews as a model of congruity: καὶ ὅταν τινὰ ἐπαμφοτερίζοντα ἴδωμεν, εἰώθαμεν λέγειν, Οὐκ ἔστιν Ἰουδαῖος, ἀλλ' ὑποκρίνεται. ὅταν δ'

religious thought appears to be reflected in the observation of
W. H. C. Frend that, although the Roman concept of sacrilege
or impiety was concerned with specific offending acts, the
Greek idea of atheism also involved disbelief in the gods.[101]

2. The Nature of Roman Religion

Like the common people of the Greek world, many of the
Romans also maintained a firm belief in their traditional
gods. But in contrast, it would seem that this belief was not
simply confined to the common people.[102] The traditional civic
gods also remained the focus of private worship. People
stopped and prayed at the door of temples, had statues of
their favorite gods at home among their *lares* (household
gods) and hung garlands on statues in the streets.[103]

Jupiter seems to have remained the most popular god,
given the number of *ex voto* inscriptions in his honor, even
though he was officially understood as the chief protector of
the Roman state.[104] After him, the next most popular gods
were Fortuna, Mars, Victoria, Concordia and Salus.[105] The

ἀναλάβῃ τὸ πάθος τὸ τοῦ βεβαμμένου καὶ ᾑρημένου, τότε καὶ ἔστι τῷ
ὄντι καὶ καλεῖται Ἰουδαῖος (*Diss.* 2.9.19-20).

[101] Frend, *Martyrdom*, 95; cf. Cicero *Verr.* 4.111-12.

[102] For example, *IGRR* 4.1557; Cicero *Nat. D.* 1.61, 101; idem, *Pis.*
43; Dio Cassius 53.2.4; Martial *Epigr.* 10.92; Suetonius *Aug.* 31, 39; P. A.
Brunt suggests that the frequency with which Cicero appeals to religion
in public speeches shows this ("Laus Imperii" in P. D. A. Garnsey & C. R.
Whittaker, eds., *Imperialism in the Ancient World* [Cambridge:
Cambridge University Press, 1978] 167).

[103] Stambaugh & Balch, *Social World*, 129-30; de Vos, "ΟΙΚΟΣ",
31-4.

[104] For example, *ILS* 363, 2318, 2435, 2484, 2540, 2606, 2614,
2633, 2912, 3008, 3014-6, 3025, 3041-2, 3049-50, 3058, 3356, 3378,
3637-8, 4044, 4063; cf. Helgeland, "Army Religion", 1496; Fears,
"Jupiter", 47, 51; idem, "The Cult of Virtues and Roman Imperial
Ideology" *ANRW* 2.17.2 (1981) 926. As Fears points out, the role of
Jupiter as the protector of the state declined under the principate.

[105] For example, *ILS* 153, 2013, 2401, 2449, 2495, 2524, 2551,
2555, 2585, 2602, 3155-6, 3688, 3698, 3703, 3705, 3709, 3711, 3713,
3723, 3824, 9254, 9258; See Helgeland, "Army Religion", 1496; Fears,
"Virtues", 926, 935; idem, "Victory", 743. Numerous *ex voto*'s are found
to other Virtue-gods, such as Fata and Virtus (e.g. *ILS* 3756-60, 3762,
3765, 3795, 3800) as well as to other gods who could be described as
"abstract", namely, Vesta, Genii, Lares & Penates (e.g. *ILS* 2013, 2401,
2421, 3025, 3314, 3317, 3600, 3607-8, 3631, 3633, 3637-8, 3643ᵃ, 3647,
3655, 3661, 3667, 9252, 9262). Another way in which people
encountered the gods was via the coinage they used daily. Although the

fact that a number of the most popular gods were effectively "abstract" deities, suggests something very important about the Roman religious mentality.[106] Indeed, the Greek historian, Dionysius of Halicarnassus, recognized that the Romans saw their gods in a less anthropomorphic manner and early on had refused to adopt or copy the Greek myths.[107] This had changed, however, following two centuries of Hellenistic influence. But while the Romans still conceived of some divinities as numinous spirits and others as personalized and anthropomorphic, in regard to the latter they tended to avoid some of the excess of the Greeks.[108]

Nevertheless, the popularity of the cult of Virtues suggests that the Roman religious mentality considered the power of the gods to be of crucial importance. Indeed, this concern for power and benefits (*utilitates*) underlies Roman religion as a whole.[109] It meant the gods were understood as providential, benevolent, and in control of events and the elements.[110] This concentration on power and benefit explains why the Virtue-gods were normally not anthropomorphized, nor invested with myths or personality.[111]

A further indicator of the significance of this attitude is the fact that although the Greeks recognized Virtue-gods, theirs do not seem to have been adopted on a personal level,

---

particular gods displayed reflected imperial ideology more than popular devotion, Victoria, Mars and Fortuna were also the most commonly portrayed. See D. R. Sear, *Roman Coins and their Values* (4th ed.; London: Seaby, 1988).

[106] Further evidence of this is the number of inscriptions to the *genius* of the Emperor. See, for example, *ILS* 72, 116, 154, 192, 229-30, 1824, 2182, 3218, 6088-9, 7215, 9059, 9102a,b

[107] Dion. Hal. *Ant. Rom.* 2.18.2-3.

[108] Ovid *Fast.* 267-8; Juvenal *Sat.* 13.79-84; Seneca *Ep.* 41.3; Tibullus *Eleg.* 2.1.1-26; cf. Wardman, *Religion*, 1-2; Stambaugh & Balch, *Social World*, 128.

[109] Fears, "Virtues", 833, 837. It was also characteristic of the Greek attitude to religion, as evidenced by their adoption of the Imperial cult. The difference, as in some other aspects, is probably in the strength of the Roman attitude in this regard.

[110] See Cicero *Leg.* 1.21, 2.15-16; Horace *Carm.* 1.9.9-16; Juvenal *Sat.* 13.102-3; cf. Ogilvie, *Romans*, 10, 17; Fears, "Jupiter", 43.

[111] Cicero *Nat. D.* 2.60-1; Juvenal *Sat.* 1.115-16; Fears, "Victory", 740-1, 748. Despite appearing on a number of Imperial coins in human form, Pax, Victoria and Concordia were not truly anthropomorphized because they were not invested with myth and personality. They were perceived no more anthropomorphically than the various cults of *Genii*, despite their representation in *lares*.

as they were by the Romans.[112] The identification of gods by
their providential action on behalf of the Roman people gave
rise to another major religious attitude, namely, the
conviction that religious duty involved performance of the
correct gestures and rites. It was *this* that mattered, not
assent to "correct beliefs" or an ethical life. Since performance
of the traditional rituals in the past had always maintained
the goodwill of the gods, as evidenced by Rome's continued
success and prosperity, it was these rites that were crucial.[113]

The Romans' understanding that the gods were
benevolent, and that what mattered was their power and
benefit, was linked with the belief that their relationship with
the gods resembled a business contract. Whether this was like
a master-slave relationship, or a patron-client relationship,
does not ultimately matter.[114] What was important, however,
was the commercial understanding. In the manner of a
business contract, therefore, every aspect of the arrangement
was set down in black-and-white and debts were expected to
be paid in full, as promised, and at the agreed time.[115] This
"contract" involved striking a deal with a god, through prayer
and sacrifice. Votive offerings, with *ex voto* inscriptions, were
performed by way of payment for the god's fulfilment of the
deal. The attitude was one of *do ut des*.[116]

---

[112] Fears, "Virtues", 937. The Greeks worshipped personified
virtues: such as Eirene, Nike and Themis (ibid., 828). Fears suggests
that the Roman practice was derived from this ("Victory", 772-4), but he
does not explain, on this basis, why the Roman conception of these gods
remained abstract, rather than anthropomorphic. Whatever their
derivation, they remained distinctly Roman. On this distinctiveness, see
Sherwin-White, *Citizenship*, 406; P. D. A. Garnsey & R. P. Saller, *The
Roman Empire: Economy, Society and Culture* (Berkeley: University of
California Press, 1987) 39.

[113] See, for example, Cicero *Nat. D.* 3.87; J. North, "Conservatism
and Change in Roman Religion" *PBSR* 44 (1976) 8; Ogilvie, *Romans*, 17-
19; Wardman, *Religion*, 6; J. Scheid, "The Priest" in A. Giardina, ed., *The
Romans* (Chicago: University of Chicago Press, 1993) 75.

[114] Tomlinson, *From Mycenae*, 17; Wardman, *Religion*, 4; cf. Frend,
Martyrdom, 78. The differences between these two types of relationship
are somewhat relative, given the approach of the Romans to
manumission and the relationship of masters to their former slaves. See
de Vos, "ΟΙΚΟΣ", 11-12, 16-18.

[115] Ogilvie, *Romans*, 17; North, "Conservatism", 6; Frend,
Martyrdom, 78; Wardman, *Religion*, 7.

[116] Cicero *Nat. D.* 3.5; Ogilvie, *Romans*, 22-3; Ferguson, *Religion*,
156-7; North, "Conservatism", 6; Fears, "Virtues", 834; MacMullen,
Paganism, 52; Wardman, *Religion*, 7; Stambaugh & Balch, *Social World*,

Another way of describing this contract-type relationship with the gods, on a corporate level, was in terms of the concept of *pax deorum*. This concept was based on a belief that it was by the power, providence and decree of the gods that the Romans had conquered and continued to rule the world.[117] *Pax deorum* implied a treaty, whereby this state of affairs was maintained, provided the Romans fulfilled their obligations to the gods by the maintenance of cult.[118] Especially following Actium, the concept of *pax deorum* was linked to that of *pax Romana*. This link implied that the relationship between the gods and the Roman state was imperiled by civil strife. That is, besides properly attending to their religious duties, the continued goodwill of the gods (*pax deorum*) was also dependent on the Romans maintaining peace and order and showing mercy to those they had subjected (*pax Romana*).[119]

Given this contractual understanding, Roman rites were written down and recited word-perfect when performed. One tiny mistake in either word or gesture could offend the god and make the whole rite invalid. The rite would be repeated from the beginning until no mistakes were made.[120]

129; Ferguson, *Backgrounds*, 180. Votive offerings were also common among the Greeks (Burkert, *Mystery*, 12-13), but the sense of "contract" was not formalized as it was with the Romans.

[117] See, for example, Cicero *Har. Resp.* 19; idem, *Cat.* 3.21; Dion. Hal. *Ant. Rom.* 2.18.1; Horace *Carm.* 3.6.5-6; Pliny *NH* 3.39; Vergil *Aen.* 1.278-82; cf. Ogilvie, *Romans*, 112-13; Brunt, "Laus", 161; Fears, "Jupiter", 38-40; Wardman, *Religion*, 6; Wengst, *Pax Romana*, 47; T. Cornell, "The End of Roman Imperial Expansion" in J. Rich & G. Shipley, eds., *War and Society in the Roman World* (London: Routledge, 1993) 141.

[118] As Frend (*Martyrdom*, 78) and G. Woolf ("Roman Peace" in J. Rich & G. Shipley, eds., *War and Society in the Roman World* [London: Routledge, 1993] 176) note, *pax* is a term used in treaty arrangements; cf. Ogilvie, *Romans*, 23; North, "Conservatism", 8; Wardman, *Religion*, 9.

[119] Vergil *Aen.* 6.851-3; Cicero *Nat. D.* 2.8; cf. Lintott, *Imperium*, 176; Woolf, "Peace", 176-7. The concept of *pax Romana* does not necessarily imply that the period of the early Principate was free from all war — clearly something it was not. The great majority of residents, however, lived peacefully most of the time and enjoyed considerable financial benefits as a result. Things were certainly more peaceful that if such a state of affairs had not been instituted by Augustus. See Cornell, "The End", 150-3, 160, 167-8; Woolf, "Peace", 171, 186.

[120] For example, Pliny *NH* 28.10-11; Livy 6.41.8-9, 31.9.5-7; Cicero *Har. Resp.* 48; Dio Cassius 60.6.4; Tibullus *Eleg.* 2.1.1-36; *ILS* 5039, 5050; cf. North, "Conservatism", 1-2; Fears, "Virtues", 840; Wardman, *Religion*, 7; Stambaugh & Balch, *Social World*, 129.

Roman religion tried, as J. R. Fears puts it, "to fix in every detail the proper relationship between the community and the godhead and thus secure the continued beneficent operation of the divinity so recognized".[121] A major cause of offence to the gods was neglecting temples or rites.[122] When the gods had been offended, something that was usually indicated by portents and unfavorable omens and auguries, they had to be expiated by further rites and sacrifices.[123]

This Roman preoccupation with personal duty to the gods and ensuring that rites were scrupulously observed is normally referred to as *pietas*. This sense of duty was considered perhaps the most outstanding characteristic of the Romans.[124] Cicero, for example, claims that every aspect of life had its moral duties — one's duty was owed first to the gods, then to country, parents, children, *domus* and kin.[125] *Pietas* was as much admired and maintained by the elite as by the common people.[126]

The emphasis was on the correct performance of cult and ritual, not on belief or morality. Indeed, the gods only cared about the way people performed their duties.[127] This is apparent since even the priests, who were responsible for

---

[121] Fears, "Victory", 742; cf. L. de Blois, *The Roman Army and Politics in the First Century B.C.* (Amsterdam: J.C. Gieben, 1987) 25; Dyson, *Community*, 164.

[122] For example, Horace *Carm.* 3.6.1-4; cf. de Blois, *Roman Army*, 25; Dyson, *Community*, 164. Cicero suggests that the impiety of magistrates and generals could lead to the punishment of the Roman people (*Pis.* 85).

[123] Cicero *Nat. D.* 2.166; idem, *Div.* 1.29; idem, *Har. Resp.* 18-21; Livy, 22.1.14-20; 27.4.15; cf. North, "Conservatism", 8; Reynolds, "Cities", 32. In fact, Ogilvie claims that in the period immediately following Actium (31 BCE) many Romans attributed the turmoil they had just lived through to their failure to carry out their religious duties properly (*Romans*, 112).

[124] Cicero *Nat. D.* 1.116, 2.71; idem, *Har. Resp.* 19; Dion. Hal. *Ant. Rom.* 2.18.2-3; Polybius 6.56.6; See Frend, *Martyrdom*, 77; Winslow, "Religion", 239; North, "Conservatism", 2; Burkert claims that while the Greek was a "political-animal" *par excellence*, the Roman was *homo religiosus* ("Craft", 22). In *Nat. D.* 2.8, Cicero claims that compared to all other nations, *"religione id est cultu deorum multo superiores"*.

[125] Cicero *Off.* 1.4, 58, 160.

[126] For example, *IGRR* 4.1557; Dio Cassius 53.2.4; Suetonius *Aug.* 31, 39, 91; cf. Ogilvie, *Romans*, 114; Fears, "Jupiter", 60.

[127] See Cicero *Off.* 3.37; idem, *Leg.* 2.15-16; idem, *Pis.* 46; Juvenal *Sat.* 13.113-19; cf. A. M. Rabello, "The Legal Condition of the Jews in the Roman Empire" *ANRW* 2.13 (1980) 696; MacMullen, *Paganism*, 58.

performing the rites on behalf of the people, did not always believe in the gods. And they saw no problem with this.[128] Furthermore, MacMullen notes that at Pompeii "walls display dozens of blasphemous graffiti, insults to Venus (patron deity of the town)". Such a practice was probably common elsewhere as well.[129] This preoccupation with *pietas* and the correct performance of the traditional rites in order to maintain the favor of the gods constitutes the religious component of the Roman concept of ancestral customs or *mos maiorum*. These customs were considered to be the very essence of Roman society. Indeed, the strength of their conviction in this regard set them apart from the Greeks.[130]

Therefore, it is apparent that there were significant differences between the religious mentality of the Romans and the Greeks. In fact, the very characteristics which the Romans understood as *religio*, educated Greeks would have regarded as *superstitio*. This applies particularly to their contractual understanding of their relationship with the gods, namely, that their sacrifices and rites sought to win or maintain the favor of the gods.[131] Nevertheless, from the late Republic it did become fashionable for members of the Roman elite to adopt some philosophical stance, even if this had little impact on their society.[132]

Roman Stoics and Epicureans shared many of the characteristics of their Greek counterparts. Epicureans thought the gods were apathetic and not active in the world, and that traditional religion was both untrue and

---

[128] See, for example, Cicero *Nat. D.* 1.61.

[129] MacMullen, *Paganism*, 63.

[130] Frend, *Martyrdom*, 79; North, "Conservatism", 1; Stambaugh, "Social Relations", 78; Finley, *Politics*, 95; H. Conzelmann, *Gentiles/ Jews/Christians: Polemics and Apologetics in the Greco-Roman Era* (Minneapolis: Fortress, 1992), 128; Ferguson, *Backgrounds*, 160. As noted above, the Greek concept of εὐσέβεια has many similarities to the Roman *pietas*. There are, of course, nuances, but it was the extent and depth of Roman commitment to this concept that was probably distinct. See, for example, Polybius 6.56.6-8.

[131] See, for example, Polybius 6.56.7-11. Despite this, however, the concept of *superstitio* was also found among the Romans, understood as "excess", or, among some of the philosophical writers, as an irrational fear of natural events. See Cicero *Nat. D.* 1.117, 2.72, 3.16; Juvenal *Sat.* 13.223-34; Suetonius *Tib.* 69.

[132] J. P. V. D. Balsdon, *Romans and Aliens* (London: Duckworth, 1979), 49-50; MacMullen, *Paganism*, 77.

unnecessary.[133] Stoics allegorized the traditional gods and thought in terms of a single divine rationality.[134] Yet there were differences.

Many prominent Romans, such as Seneca and Cicero, were somewhat eclectic in their philosophy. In terms of a continuum from religion as true and necessary to untrue and unnecessary, many Roman philosophers, such as Varro and Cicero, adopted a middle position, such that religion was probable and necessary. Their attitude was modified by their convictions regarding *mos maiorum*.[135] Cicero maintains that "it is our duty to revere and worship these gods under the names which custom has bestowed upon them".[136] He adds that it was proper to uphold "the beliefs about the immortal gods which have come down to us from our ancestors, and the rites and ceremonies and duties of religion".[137] Such an attitude was expected even if one strongly doubted the existence of the gods.[138] In fact, Alan Wardman may be right in saying that the consensus among the educated was that traditional religion was defensible at least as custom.[139] Given

---

[133] Cicero *Nat. D.* 1.1-3, 18, 45; Wardman, *Religion*, 56.

[134] Cicero *Nat. D.* 2.66-70, 3.92-3; Ogilvie, *Romans*, 19.

[135] See Frend, *Martyrdom*, 78-9; Ogilvie, *Romans*, 19-20; MacMullen, *Paganism*, 64; Wardman, *Religion*, 53, 56; Winter, "In Public", 120; Varro, it is said, distinguished between mythical theology, as the untruths perpetuated by the poets, physical theology, as the musings of the philosophers which were not to be shared with the common people, and civil theology, which emphasized the gods as they have been found useful in practice (see Brunt, "Laus", 166; Wardman, *Religion*, 53-4; Conzelmann, *Gentiles*, 113). Although the elder Pliny was very critical, he still respects Roman practice, although somewhat reinterpreted (*NH* 2.5.18). Seneca was quite extreme, and was highly critical even of traditional Roman practices. He was, however, not typical. See Attridge, "Critique", 67.

[136] Cicero *Nat. D.* 2.71: *quoque eos nomine consuetudo nuncupaverit, hoc eos et venerari et colere debemus.*

[137] Cicero *Nat. D.* 3.5: *opiniones quas a maioribus accepimus de dis immortalibus, sacra caerimonias religionesque defenderem.* In the same passage this "belief" is understood as "belief as to the worship of the immortal gods" (*ex ea opinione quam a maioribus accepi de cultu deorum immortalium*); cf. Wardman, *Religion*, 61. While Winter may be right that the text of the previous note is representative of the general Stoic position ("In Public", 125), this one is distinctly Roman.

[138] Such as Cotta in Cicero *Nat. D.* 1.61 cf. 3.5.

[139] Wardman, *Religion*, 105-6. Yet, he adds that it served as a psychological crutch for the masses (ibid., 106-7). Such a statement fails to understand the nature of *mos maiorum*, and the depth of devotion to it among the educated as well.

the Roman conservatism and their dislike of "excess", he is probably correct.

Besides, as was noted earlier, the Roman understanding of "sacrilege" or "impiety" was quite different from the Greek notion of atheism. For despite scepticism about the gods and their interaction in the world, what counted for *pietas* was that the rites continued to be performed in the correct manner. Furthermore, there do not appear to have been any legal proceedings initiated against individual Romans on charges of atheism, as there were among the Greeks.[140] Now, it could be argued that the reason for this lay in the different political structure of Roman and Greek cities. Such proceedings were easier in the democratic structure of Greek cities, but difficult in the elite-controlled oligarchy of the Romans. Certainly, this may be a factor. But, there is enough evidence to suggest that the Romans were not really interested in beliefs, nor in a congruity between belief and practice.[141]

Thus, there are marked differences between Greek and Roman approaches to religion. The Romans generally

---

[140] See Frend, *Martyrdom*, 78; North, "Conservatism", 85. When charges were brought against Romans it was for impious acts (See Cicero *Verr.* 4.111-12; idem, *Nat. D.* 2.7-8; cf. Finley, *Politics*, 94).

[141] At one point, Cicero suggests that "the purest, holiest and most pious way of worshipping the gods is ever to venerate them with purity, sincerity and innocence both of thought and of speech" (*Cultus autem deorum est optimus idemque castissimus atque sanctissimus plenissimusque pietatis ut eos semper pura integra incorrupta et mente et voce veneremur — Nat. D.* 2.71). Yet the larger context here is concerned with *superstitio* and it is clear that this, like *religio*, is defined in terms of practice rather than belief (ibid., 2.72). The one real exception is Seneca, but as has been noted, his views were idiosyncratic (see *Ep.* 20.2). Phillips, however, is very critical of the notion that Roman religion was a matter of traditional practices and not of belief ("Sociology", 2697). Yet his criticism seems founded on the distinctions usually made in this regard between the elite and the common people such that "the Roman religion consisted of mindless actions on the part of the elite and base superstition on the part of all others" (ibid., 2705). He objects to the portrayal of Roman religion as a set of "empty cult acts" (ibid., 2710). My argument, however, is that the emphasis on acts over belief was as much a part of the common religious mentality as it was of that of the elite. Unlike Phillips, however, I would not argue that they were "empty" or "mindless". Phillips' argument seems to rest on the assumption that the Romans could not live with this sort of incongruity, when, as B. J. Malina argues, inconsistency and incongruity were much better tolerated in the ancient world (see "Normative Dissonance and Christian Origins" *Semeia* 35 [1986] 38).

conceived of their gods in a more abstract way. They saw the relationship as a business-contract, emphasized the maintenance of ancestral custom and *pietas*, but seem to have had little concern with the issue of congruity between belief and practice. While many of the elite were influenced by philosophy, this was normally modified by a commitment to the principles of *mos maiorum*. In contrast, the Greeks placed great importance on the continuity of belief and practice. While the common people generally believed in anthropomorphic gods and continued to serve them, the elite participated in the traditional rites probably out of expediency, or fear of popular hatred and charges of atheism.

3. Attitudes to Foreign Cults

John North argues that in the Roman period, religion changed from being a function of the *polis* to a choice between differentiated groups. In effect, it was analogous to a change from a monopoly to a market economy. He adds that this process would have reached a point where there was "no longer a dominant group...within the city's own religious traditions, but a plurality of groups in tension with one another".[142] In the case of Greek cities North may be incorrect. Their city-state origin still appears to have had a continuing influence, as evidenced by the esteem attached to the title of *civitas libera* and the numerous conflicts and rivalries between neighboring cities.[143] On the other hand, the right to use their own laws was a privilege granted by the Romans and theoretically could be revoked at any time.

It was well-known that the Greeks had both a great intellectual and cultural conceit. They divided the world into Greek and Barbarian, despising the latter on the grounds that no other peoples could match their achievements.[144]

---

[142] J. North, "The Development of Religious Pluralism" in J. Lieu *et al*, eds., *The Jews among Pagans and Christians in the Roman Empire* (rev ed.; London: Routledge, 1994), 178-9. He suggests that such changes are linked to "much wider social changes and movements of population in the history of the Mediterranean area" (ibid., 180).

[143] The significance of this title will be discussed in the next chapter. See also Dio Chrys. *Or.* 24.47, 38.22-31; Frend, *Martyrdom*, 95; Balsdon, *Romans*, 31; Sheppard, *"Homonoia"*, 233-5; P. A. Brunt, *Roman Imperial Themes* (Oxford: Clarendon, 1990) 165.

[144] See, for example, Gellius *NA* 19.9.7; Aelian *NA* 16.24; cf. A. Burford, *Craftsmen in Greek and Roman Society* (London: Thames & Hudson, 1972) 52; Balsdon, *Romans*, 30-3; Conzelmann, *Gentiles*, 78.

Even the Romans were regarded with disdain as brutal, dull, and unspiritual.[145] In general, Zvi Yavetz claims that the Greeks considered barbarians to be:

> obnoxious, ugly, rude, vulgar, superstitious, clumsy, stupid, uncivilized, illiterate, lawless, servile, cowardly, licentious, wild, cruel, mad, savage, violent, untrustworthy, greedy, passionate, gluttonous, treacherous, murderous.[146]

Such descriptions are largely caricatures and do not necessarily represent an attitude of abhorrence or loathing. But even an attitude of contempt could, under certain conditions, result in genuine and open hostility. Theoretically, there would have been no barriers to the adoption of foreign cults unless they promoted "atheism", but those adopted were Hellenized in the process.[147]

In many respects, the Romans held similar attitudes to foreigners as did the Greeks. For example, Sardinians were considered ugly and "congenital liars"; Narbonese Gauls were impetuous; Northern Gauls were gullible braggarts; Britons were uncivilized and inhospitable; Greeks were effeminate, dishonest, silly and vain; Balkans were uncouth; Egyptians, even Greek-Egyptians, were treacherous, base, foolish, boastful; Africans were fickle and dishonest.[148] Unlike the Greeks, however, there was not the same sort of cultural snobbery. For Cicero can admit that:

> if we care to compare our national characteristics with those of foreign peoples, we shall find that, while in all other respects we are only the equals or even the inferiors of others, yet...in reverence for the gods, we are superior.[149]

Admittedly, there is some respect for the wisdom of the ancient Egyptians, but this is limited (see Diod. Sic. 1.96-8; Plutarch *De Is. et Os.* 354D-F).

[145] Gellius *NA* 19.9.7; Dion. Hal. *Ant. Rom.* 1.89.4; cf. Balsdon, *Romans*, 30, 60; Stambaugh & Balch, *Social World*, 113.

[146] Z. Yavetz, "Judeophobia in Classical Antiquity: A Different Approach" *JJS* 44 (1993) 12; cf. Dion. Hal. *Ant. Rom.* 5.4.3; Gellius *NA* 19.9.7; Plutarch *De Alex. fort.* 329C-D; Polybius 1.65.7.

[147] The addition of mystery rites to the cult of Isis is typical of this response. See Burkert, *Mystery*, 2-3; Ferguson, *Backgrounds*, 235.

[148] See Balsdon, *Romans*, 25, 64-9, 301; cf. Burford, *Craftsmen*, 54-5; Stambaugh & Balch, *Social World*, 113; Cicero *Verr.* 4.112.

[149] Cicero *Nat. D.* 2.8: *Et si conferre volumus nostra cum externis, ceteris rebus aut pares aut etiam inferiores reperiemur, religione id est cultu deorum multo superiores.* See also Balsdon, *Romans*, 31.

Generally, the Romans showed considerable tolerance towards foreign religions. They permitted most groups to abide by their ancestral customs, and treated the religious customs and sanctuaries of their subjects with respect and restraint. Such toleration arose out of the Roman respect for ancestral practice, or for *longa consuetudo*, and the political expediency of maintaining the status quo.[150]

Furthermore, the Roman religious system was also highly syncretistic. Many local gods were adopted through association with Roman gods, although the new gods were seldom treated as the equals of their Roman counterparts.[151] Officially, however, it was expected that a Roman citizen would not practice foreign cults. To do so could be interpreted as an insult to the gods and the Roman people. In reality, however, there was no action taken provided that participants did not disturb the peace and order of society, or engage in any action that offended *mos maiorum*.[152]

Such an attitude appears to be prevalent, however, only in Republican times. It was probably related to the notion that a Roman could not be the citizen of two states.[153] This attitude changed under the Principate, and as the boundaries to citizenship opened up so did the boundaries to new cults. In fact, Wardman describes the Roman religious system as insatiable. Indeed, if the gods could be manifest in different forms in different times and places, and as the

---

[150] See, for example, Josephus *AJ* 16.36; idem, *BJ* 5.363; Suetonius *Aug.* 93; Dion. Hal. *Ant. Rom.* 2.19.3; F. F. Abbott & A. C. Johnson, *Municipal Administration in the Roman Empire* (New York: Russell & Russell, 1968) 74; MacMullen, *Paganism*, 43; Wardman, *Religion*, 5; *contra* Garnsey & Saller (*Empire*, 174) and J. North ("Religious Toleration in Republican Rome" *PCPS* 25 [1979] 85-6), who fail to consider the way the Romans themselves describe their attitude.

[151] Frend, *Martyrdom*, 79-80; Winslow, "Religion", 243; Fears, "Jupiter", 41; Garnsey & Saller, *Empire*, 168; Brunt, *Imperial*, 272. Wardman suggests that foreign gods were treated like conquered peoples: "sometimes despised, if they were the centre of rites unacceptable at Rome, or allowed to become half — or even full — citizens of Rome" (*Religions*, 59).

[152] A. N. Sherwin-White, *Roman Law and Roman Society in the New Testament* (Grand Rapids: Baker, 1992 [1963]) 79; Frend, *Martyrdom*, 79; Helgeland, "Army Religion", 1496.

[153] Cicero *Balb.* 11.28, 12.29; cf. Frend, *Martyrdom*, 79; North, "Conservatism", 11; Wardman, *Religion*, 3-4; G. Krodel, "Persecution and Toleration of Christianity until Hadrian" in S. Benko & J. J. O'Rourke, eds., *The Catacombs and the Colosseum* (Valley Forge, PA: Judson, 1971), 256.

Romans did not wish to ignore or offend any important god, they tended to assimilate the gods of those they conquered. Positively, this was seen as an accumulation of power.[154]

Consequently, when the Roman government did take action against the worshippers of foreign cults, this was not related to some general hatred but to some actual or threatened breech of law and order. Generally, such actions were sporadic and of short duration.[155] Sanctions were really only consistently maintained against practices that were considered savage and un-Roman, such as the human sacrifice practiced by the Druids.[156] For example, the Isis cult had existed in Italy since the mid second century BCE and was repressed several times between 59 and 48 BCE. A temple to Isis was approved by the triumvirs in 43 BCE but after Actium, "official propaganda came to treat Egypt as a subversive element" and the cult was repeatedly suppressed by Augustus.[157] Josephus claims that its suppression by Tiberius in 19 CE was linked to a scandal involving the deception and rape of a noblewoman.[158] But it was favored by

---

[154] Wardman, *Religion*, 3-4, 8, 172; cf. North, "Conservatism", 11. Yet, no new gods were adopted as *official* gods of the state in the early Principate (Garnsey & Saller, *Empire*, 170). Rather adoption was more unofficial and "personal". That foreign gods and rites (e.g. mystery cults) were adopted should not be understood as a response to some un-met religious need, nor that their traditional gods had become too formal and impersonal (*contra* Winslow, "Religion", 240). While the traditional rites were formal and corporate, the large number of *ex voto* inscriptions attests to the high level of personal devotion. Besides, the traditional Roman religion suited the Roman personality: it was legal, reflected a patronal-type relationship, and was moderate (cf. Wardman, *Religion*, 21, 58-9; Ferguson, *Backgrounds*, 160.

[155] Sherwin-White, *Roman Law*, 79; North, "Toleration", 86; Garnsey & Saller, *Empire*, 170-3; *contra* M. H. Moehring, "The Persecution of the Jews and the Adherents of the Isis Cult at Rome" *NovT* 3 (1959) 295, who claims that all Roman suppression of foreign rites was on moral grounds.

[156] See, for example, Balsdon, *Romans*, 65; Garnsey & Saller, *Empire*, 168-9.

[157] Stambaugh, "Functions", 595; cf. Dio Cassius 53.2.4; Moehring, "Persecution", 293-4; Frend, *Martyrdom*, 84; Garnsey & Saller, *Empire*, 172-3.

[158] Josephus *AJ* 18.65-80. S. Heyob argues that Josephus' account is largely propaganda and appears to resemble a Hellenistic romance, if not being an actual fabrication (*The Cult of Isis among Women in the Graeco-Roman World* [Leiden: E. J. Brill, 1975] 118-19). She claims this because the "foolishness of both husband and wife is scarcely credible" (ibid., 117), the punishment of the perpetrator lacks severity, especially

Gaius. Consequently, the temple of Isis at Rome was built during his reign and under subsequent emperors the cult became very popular and respectable.[159]

Fear of subversion appears to be the main reason for the suppression of the *collegia* at Rome by both Julius Caesar and Augustus. Nevertheless, those *collegia* which were of long standing remained unaffected by the ban.[160] Similarly, a fear of subversion also seems to have been the motivation behind the expulsions of the Chaldaean soothsayers, astrologers and magicians or the *Magi* from Rome on several occasions between 33 BCE and 52 CE.[161]

Livy's account of the actions against the Bacchanalia cult at Rome in 186 BCE is another example. The suppression of this cult appears to have arisen for political reasons, related to an incident of attempted fraud, and because the rites of the cult represented an innovation.[162] In other words,

given Tiberius' policies, and that Tacitus "who delighted to tell of the scandals at Rome" would not have passed over this in his account (ibid., 118). Her first argument is particularly weak, and represents something of an ethnocentric anachronism. The punishment given to Mundus, a member of the Roman elite, was appropriate for someone of his position while that handed to the Jews, despite Josephus' protestations, clearly reflects their social position (the matter of punishments will be discussed in the next chapter). Finally, there could be a number of reasons why Tacitus does not mention this incident. Given the esteemed position of the Isis cult in his time he may have chosen not to report it. Besides, even if Josephus' account is incorrect, it is likely that some sort of incident prompted Tiberius' action given other cases where religious suppression occurred.

[159] Moehring, "Persecutions", 294; Winslow, "Religion", 241; Stambaugh, "Functions", 595; Garnsey & Saller, *Empire*, 172-3; cf. *ILS* 4351-422.

[160] Suetonius *Iul.* 42.3; idem, *Aug.* 32.1; Josephus *AJ* 14.215-16; Philo *Leg.* 316; cf. R. A. Kraft, "Judaism on the World Scene" in S. Benko & J. J. O'Rourke, eds., *The Catacombs and the Colosseum* (Valley Forge, PA: Judson, 1971) 89; Rabello, "Legal Condition", 719.

[161] See Suetonius *Tib.* 63.1; Valerius Maximus 1.3.3 (in M. Stern, ed., *Greek and Latin Authors on Jews and Judaism* [vol. 1; Jerusalem: Israel Academy of Sciences and Humanities, 1974] #147a); Frend, *Martyrdom*, 67; Stambaugh, "Social Relations", 78; Garnsey & Saller, *Empire*, 179; R. MacMullen, *Enemies of the Roman Order: Treason, Unrest and Alienation in the Empire* (London: Routledge, 1992 [1966]) 128-33. MacMullen claims the repressions were based on a Sullan law of 81 BCE against those who destroyed another's crops by spells (*Enemies*, 124-5).

[162] Livy, 39.8-19. Several other factors are identified, such as the size of the group, the level of commitment required, the plebeian leadership (Frend, *Martyrdom*, 82; North, "Toleration", 87-8; idem,

it contravened the *mos maiorum*. But the suppression was not absolute, since private devotion was not banned, and groups of five could still perform the rites. Not only would it have been impossible to eliminate the cult but, given the Roman attitude to religion, to do so could offend the god.[163] By the time of the early principate, however, it was regarded as respectable.[164]

Finally, although Pythagoreanism gained a measure of popularity at Rome it was also included in the suppression of foreign rites under Tiberius in 19 CE.[165] Its suppression may have arisen because it was linked to magic and astronomy. More importantly, however, its radical lifestyle, its adoption of a system of communal property, and its sectarian nature probably generated fears of political conspiracy, as well as posing a threat to the established social order.[166]

Although these few examples cannot give a full picture of the Roman attitude to foreign cults, they do suggest that when action was taken it was a response to particular circumstances. It would also seem to have been usually of short duration. Otherwise, attitudes were more positive, especially if the rites had the force of ancient custom. Examples of Greek actions are scarce, but their general attitude to foreigners was one of disdain. They too had a great receptivity to foreign cults, but given a strong city-state mentality and a situation of foreign domination, the potential for conflict between Greeks and foreigners was high. The relations were potentially more volatile than those in Roman cities. This may be significant in terms of understanding the

"Development", 182).

[163] Livy, 39.18-19; cf. Frend, *Martyrdom*, 83-4.

[164] See Frend, *Martyrdom*, 84; North, "Toleration", 98; Stambaugh & Balch, *Social World*, 133-4.

[165] It was this suppression which prompted Seneca to renounce the Pythagorean lifestyle he had begun to adopt (*Ep.* 107.22); cf. MacMullen, *Enemies*, 95-6.

[166] Burkert, "Craft", 14-17; *contra* MacMullen, *Enemies*, 107-8. Of course, the two are not entirely synonymous, for most actions against magicians and astrologers were undertaken because of fear of conspiracy. At the same time, in the Greco-Roman world there was not a clear distinction between magic and religion (G. Luck, *Arcana Mundi: Magic and Occult in the Greek and Roman Worlds* [Baltimore: Johns Hopkins University Press, 1985] 4). While all levels of society seem to have believed in the validity of magic, and even practiced it, most actions taken against it were politically motivated (ibid., 5, 41). 'Sectarian' is used here in the sense of a voluntary religious group demanding strong commitment and emphasizing its radical separateness from society.

differing response to Christians in the first century CE. Of even more significance is their respective attitudes towards the Jews and their religion.

There has been a popular view that Judaism was universally disliked and treated with contempt, with only rare glimpses of sympathy.[167] But this relies on the opinion of a fairly small number of upper-class writers. It also fails to consider the dating of the different sources and the ethnic backgrounds of their respective authors.[168] Hence, the various writers will be examined here according to date and origin, followed by an analysis of the actual relationships between Greeks, Romans and Jews.

(i) Greek Attitudes to Judaism

The earliest recorded opinion of the Jews by Greek writers considered them to be philosophers. Such an unambiguously positive attitude is evident in Theophrastus (370-285 BCE), Megasthenes (c. 300 BCE), Clearchus (c. 300 BCE), and Hermippus (c. 200 BCE).[169] Hecataeus (c. 300 BCE) admires Moses and the Jewish manner of worshipping without images, and also regarded them as philosophers. He notes that, like the Greeks, they were descendants of foreigners expelled from Egypt due to plagues, and he attributes the anti-social lifestyle of the Jews to this experience.[170] Such an explanation gives the Jewish way of life some justification,

---

[167] See, for example, J. N. Sevenster, *The Roots of Pagan Anti-Semitism in the Ancient World* (NovTSup 39; Leiden: E. J. Brill, 1975) 16; Balsdon, *Romans*, 67; J. L. Daniel, "Anti-Semitism in the Hellenistic-Roman Period" *JBL* 98 (1979) 46-7.

[168] See J. G. Gager, *The Origins of Anti-Semitism: Attitudes toward Judaism in Pagan and Christian Antiquity* (New York: Oxford University Press, 1983) 36, 45. Although Sevenster acknowledges that the dating of the sources should be considered, he fails to do so, nor does he distinguish between Greek and Roman attitudes (see *Roots*, 7, 180-1).

[169] Stern, *Authors*, ##4, 14; Josephus *Ap.* 1.162-3, 175-85, 2.281. In fact, Josephus claims that nearly all the early philosophers recognized Judaism as a philosophy (*Ap.* 2.168). The latter may be an exaggeration, but his earlier claim is reasonable. It will be assumed that what Josephus presents as the opinions of authors is a fair representation. The same could not be said for some of his statements of historical fact, especially the legal-political privileges granted the Jews.

[170] Hecataeus served as the main source for Diodorus Siculus on the Jews (40.3.1-5). See Stern, *Authors*, 1.20. When referring to texts contained in Stern's work I will use #, but when I refer to his commentary on those texts I will cite page numbers, as here.

and it is used in a non-condemnatory way.[171] Overall, his attitude seems neutral or positive.

Euhemerus (c. 270 BCE) and Aristophanes (c. 200 BCE) attest to the antiquity of the Jews.[172] Manetho (third century BCE) inadvertently attests to it also.[173] Yet, it was he who introduced the idea that the Jews were expelled from Egypt as lepers, and adds that Moses was a renegade Egyptian priest.[174] Menahem Stern notes that Manetho himself was an Egyptian priest and intimately involved in the religious policy of the Ptolemies.[175] Thus, we would not expect him to be impartial. It is possible that the Jewish celebrations of the Passover were responsible for some of the animosity felt by Egyptians and prompted such accounts of the Exodus.[176]

Mnaseas (c. 200 BCE) also attests to the antiquity of the Jews, but he alleges that they worshipped the head of an ass, that is, at least Apion apparently contends that he did.[177] There is no direct evidence of this, however, so that his attitude cannot necessarily be assumed to have been hostile. Agatharcides (second century BCE) ridicules the superstition of the Jews, but he treats other nations similarly.[178] Besides, the mere attribution of the term "superstition" cannot be regarded as anything more than disdain, and certainly not as anti-Semitism.[179] It is just typical Greek xenophobia.

Thus, on the whole, in the period prior to the Maccabean revolt, really only the Egyptian Manetho shows any true animosity. Most are positive to neutral although the occasional writer, such as Agatharcides, shows some disdain.

[171] See Gager, *Origins*, 40; S. J. D. Cohen, "Respect for Judaism by Gentiles according to Josephus" *HTR* 80 (1987) 426; Conzelmann, *Gentiles*, 60; *contra* Sevenster, *Roots*, 189.

[172] Josephus *Ap.* 1.215-16.

[173] Ibid., 1.75-98.

[174] Ibid., 1.228-51.

[175] Stern, *Authors*, 1.62.

[176] See, for example, Frend, *Martyrdom*, 27; Stern, *Authors*, 1.64; cf. Josephus *Ap.* 1.223-6.

[177] Josephus *Ap.* 1.215-16, 2.112-14.

[178] Josephus *Ap.* 1.209-11, 220-22; idem, *AJ* 12.5-6.

[179] The term "anti-Semitism" will be used for the sake of convenience, although I am aware of the difficulties associated with it. In fact, from the copious amount written on suitable terminology, there would not appear to be any option that is without some difficulty. See, for example, Sevenster, *Roots*, 1-2; Daniel, "Anti-Semitism", 45-6. I will use the term to refer to a strong hatred towards Jews and/or Judaism rather than an attitude of disdain (which is similar to the Greek and Roman attitude towards other cultures).

But the criticisms of this period ought to be regarded as mild when compared to later ones.

Polybius (204-122 BCE) refers to the Jews in a neutral manner. He also regards Antiochus Epiphanes' looting of the Jerusalem temple as iniquitous, as does Apollodorus (second century BCE).[180] Theophilus (second century BCE) and Dius (second century BCE) attest to the antiquity of the Jews, while the latter also shows some appreciation of Solomon.[181] Melager (end of second century BCE) refers to the Sabbath without passing any judgment on it.[182]

On the other hand, Posidonius (135-51 BCE) is recognized by Josephus as one of Apion's sources for the accusation that the Jews despised the gods and worshipped the head of an ass.[183] Furthermore, Strabo claims that he regarded the Jews as sorcerers.[184] These tend to suggest a strongly negative opinion. Yet, it is commonly accepted that he was a major source for Diodorus Siculus' story of the refusal of Antiochus VII Sidetes to exterminate the Jews for impiety and misanthropy, contrary to the advice of his friends.[185] Therefore, Stern suggests that "we must pronounce a *non liquet* on the question of Posidonius' real views on the Jews". He adds that Posidonius' home-town had good relations with Jews later on.[186] But this is an argument from silence. For there is no reason to assume, even if this state of affairs existed in Posidonius' time, that he shared that view, while the evidence of Apion, Josephus and Strabo suggests he was hostile.

Apollonius Molon (first century BCE) claims that Noah was expelled from his homeland, that Moses was a fraud and con-man, and that the Jews were atheists, misanthropes and of no use to society. He also tries to undermine Jewish claims to antiquity.[187] However, Stern notes that he does not present the specifically Egyptian denigration related to the Exodus.[188] But this is inconsequential. For the Egyptian accusations may not have been known outside Egypt yet and, even if

---

[180] Josephus *AJ* 12.135-6; idem, *Ap.* 2.83-4.
[181] Josephus *Ap.* 1.112-15; 215-16; Stern, *Authors*, #37.
[182] Stern, *Authors*, #43.
[183] Josephus *Ap.* 2.79-80.
[184] Strabo *Geog.* 16.2.43.
[185] Diodorus Siculus 35.1.5; Stern, *Authors*, 1.143.
[186] Stern, *Authors*, 1.143.
[187] Josephus *Ap.* 2.16, 145-8; Stern, *Authors*, #46.
[188] Stern, *Authors*, 1.148-9.

they had, they would have had less impact on a Greek audience than the charges he actually makes.

Alexander Polyhistor and Hypsicrates (first century BCE) both relate aspects of Jewish history in a neutral manner.[189] Timagenes (first century BCE) speaks well of Aristobulus I, and is another who regards Antiochus Epiphanes' looting of the temple as unjust.[190] Diodorus Siculus (first century BCE) has a mildly positive attitude towards Aristobulus I and Moses, and is neutral towards Jewish customs.[191]

Therefore, it seems that during the period between the Maccabean revolt and the Roman conquest of Judaea, the majority of Greek writers still maintained a neutral attitude towards the Jews. Yet there were fewer holding a positive one. The two who reflect a hostile opinion, Posidonius and Apollonius Molon, make serious charges which amount to atheism and neither of them is associated with Egypt. This apparent spread and intensification of negative opinion may be related to the Maccabean revolt and the developing relations between the Jews and the Romans.

Nicolas of Damascus (64 BCE-c. 10 CE) displays the most favorable attitude towards the Jews, even acting as a champion of Jewish rights. No doubt this was a product of his friendship with Herod.[192] He records events of Jewish history from a neutral perspective, notes the piety of the Jews to their customs, and condemns Antiochus' looting of the temple.[193] Both Ptolemy the Historian and Ptolemy of Mendes (early first century CE) also record events involving Jews in a neutral manner.[194]

Strabo (64 BCE-24 CE) shows some admiration. He regards the Jews as civilized, speaks well of Aristobulus I, notes their piety to their customs, and condemns Antiochus'

---

[189] Stern, *Authors*, #51[a,b,c]; Josephus *AJ* 14.139.

[190] Josephus *AJ* 13.319; idem, *Ap.* 2.83-5. Josephus also includes Castor in the list of those critical of Antiochus.

[191] Diodorus Siculus 1.28.1-3, 1.55.5, 35.1.1-5; cf. Josephus *AJ* 13.319. Stern suggests that although Diodorus slavishly compiled the works of earlier historians, his own views reflect the same neutral attitudes as that of his sources (*Authors*, 167). This is an assumption, and Diodorus probably exercised more creative control than Stern allows, it is likely that his attitude was neutral.

[192] Josephus *AJ* 16.30, 42-5; cf. Gager, *Origins*, 69, 74-5.

[193] Josephus *AJ* 1.93-5, 159-60, 13.345-7, 14.66-8; idem, *Ap.* 2.83-5.

[194] Stern, *Authors*, ##146, 157[a,b].

looting.[195] He has a very high opinion of Moses. Indeed, he claims that Moses left Egypt because of his objection to the superstitious rites practiced there, and approves of his instituting a cult without images or anthropomorphic gods. But Strabo rebukes Moses' successors, whom he claims lapsed into superstition by instituting the Sabbath and pork-abstention.[196] While some scholars have suggested that this theme of deterioration in religion was common in popular philosophy, this does not lessen Strabo's criticism.[197] Although it is not anti-Semitism *per se*, as it involves no serious accusation or hostility, it does show disdain for contemporary Jewish custom. It also reflects the Greek concern for congruity between philosophical principles and practice.

The Egyptian attitudes seem to have reached their nadir in this period with the writings of Lysimarchus and Apion. Lysimarchus (late first century BCE or early first century CE), claims that the Jews were expelled from Egypt not as lepers, but for impurity and impiety, and that Moses taught them to be misanthropic and to desecrate the religious sanctuaries of those they conquered. He also regards Moses as a fraud and con-man.[198] Apion (early first century CE) undermines Jewish claims to antiquity. He repeats the accusations of Posidonius and Apollonius Molon, and adds that the Sabbath rite developed from a rest taken in the wilderness due to a groin disease. This is highly derogatory. He also claims that the Jews took an oath to be hostile to Greeks and that every seven years they fattened and sacrificed a Greek they had kidnapped. The Jews are also described as universal fomenters of sedition.[199] Two other Egyptians, Chaeremon and Nicarchus (both first century CE) also repeat the story of leper origins.[200]

---

[195] Strabo *Geog.* 16.2.35-8; Josephus *AJ* 13.319, 14.66-8; idem, *Ap.* 2.83-5; cf. A. N. Sherwin-White, *Racial Prejudice in Imperial Rome* (Cambridge: Cambridge University Press, 1967) 88; Gager, *Origins*, 74-5; Conzelmann, *Gentiles*, 72.

[196] Strabo *Geog.* 16.2.35-9; cf. Stern, *Authors*, 1.264; Gager, *Origins*, 74. Pseudo-Longinus (early first century CE), also admired Moses for his understanding of god. See Stern, *Authors*, #148.

[197] *Contra* Stern, *Authors*, 1.266; Gager, *Origins*, 74.

[198] Josephus *Ap.* 1.305-11, 2.145. The opinion of Stern (*Authors*, 1.382) and Conzelmann (*Gentiles*, 80) that he was the first to show true hostility cannot be supported.

[199] Josephus *Ap.* 2.17, 21, 68-9, 79-80, 91-111, 121.

[200] Josephus *Ap.* 1.288-93; Stern, *Authors*, #248.

This marked hostility, especially that of Apion, is most logically linked to the political conflict between Jews and Greeks in Alexandria. If the Jews were foreigners who had been expelled for sacrilege and atheism, they had no grounds to claim citizenship.[201] Furthermore, the very nature of these arguments shows that they are intended to foster support in the wider Greek world (appeals to atheism and hatred of Greeks) and with the Romans (Jews are seditious).[202] This is something of a shift compared to the earlier Egyptian criticisms, which were aimed at the domestic audience.

Thus, in the period prior to the first Jewish revolt, a number of writers show generally positive to neutral attitudes. Strabo's criticism of Judaism as superstition is not hostile, even if it involves some disdain, for it reflects a philosopher's critique of a failure of congruity between practice and principle. Actual hostility or anti-Semitism, however, is only evident among Egyptian authors. But it does show a marked intensification. The lack of evidence for a continuing spread of anti-Semitic ideas to the wider Greek world may simply reflect the gaps in the sources.

The philosopher Epictetus (50-130 CE) uses the Jews as a model for his fellow Stoics to imitate in regards to commitment and congruity of principles and practice. While this would appear to be reasonably positive, he also compares the food customs of Jews, Syrians, Egyptians and Romans in such a way that they cannot all be correct.[203] But this argument lacks any venom and cannot be considered anti-Semitic. His attitude would best be described as neutral.

Erotianus (late first century CE) displays a neutral attitude to Jewish customs.[204] Plutarch (45-125 CE), on the other hand, regards Jewish customs as superstition and he links them with Syrian customs.[205] Luke Johnson claims that this position should be seen as neutral, for his language is mild compared to that found in his criticism of rival

---

[201] See Gager, *Origins*, 47; Conzelmann, *Gentiles*, 90.

[202] The events in Alexandria during the Roman period will be discussed later in the chapter.

[203] Epictetus *Diss.* 2.9.19-20 cf. 1.11.12-13, 1.22.4. Gager claims that the comparison between these customs presents them all as viable options (*Origins*, 77). But this does not accord with the intent of Epictetus' discussion. The opposite is more to the point: if one of these is correct, the others must be wrong.

[204] Stern, *Authors*, #196.

[205] Plutarch *De superst.* 166A, 169C; idem, *De stoic. repug.* 1051E.

philosophical schools.[206] That Plutarch's criticism is so mild suggests that he does not acknowledge Judaism to be a true philosophical school. Dio Cassius (155-230 CE), however, not only regards Judaism as a foreign superstition, but charges the Jews with misanthropy and atheism.[207]

In general, writers in the period after the first Jewish revolt seem to consider Judaism to be a superstition, with an attitude of disdain rather than hatred or anti-Semitism. The fact that Dio Cassius does display hostility and charges the Jews with atheism may suggest that such views were to be found in some places at this time.

Overall, the bulk of the writers have a neutral or positive attitude. True hostility to the Jews seems to begin in Egypt early, but probably gained no foothold in the wider Greek world until after the Maccabean revolt. During the Roman period this attitude appears to worsen, especially in Egypt. The shift in Egyptian focus is significant, for early accusations appear to counter the anti-Egyptian flavor of the Jewish Exodus accounts but later the accusations appear to be directed so as to gain further support among the rest of the Greek world.

(ii) Roman Attitudes to Judaism

Cicero (106-43 BCE) is the first Roman to mention the Jews. He claims that it is praiseworthy to resist their *barbara superstitio*, that their customs are incompatible with *mos maiorum*, and that the gods clearly do not value them. He contends that Pompey's decision not to loot the Jerusalem temple was because of honor and expediency, not out of respect for the Jews.[208] Elsewhere he describes them as a people born to slavery.[209] A number of scholars have considered his attitude to be hostile.[210] Yet he makes similar disparaging remarks about Syrians, Phrygians, Mysians, Lydians, Greeks and Celts.[211] Besides, both cases in which he

---

[206] L. T. Johnson, "The New Testament's Anti-Jewish Slander and the Conventions of Ancient Polemic" *JBL* 103 (1989) 431; cf. Plutarch *Non posse* 1086c-1107c; idem, *De stoic. repug.* 1058E-1086B.

[207] Dio Cassius 37.17.1-4.

[208] Cicero *Flac.* 67-9.

[209] Cicero *Prov. Cons.* 5.10-12.

[210] See, for example, Frend, *Martyrdom*, 108; Balsdon, *Romans*, 67; Garnsey & Saller, *Empire*, 118.

[211] Cicero *Prov. Cons.* 5.10-12; idem, *Flac.* 65, 71; idem, *Font.* 30.

denigrates the Jews are made in a "courtroom" context, and Cicero himself admits that "it is the greatest possible mistake to suppose that the speeches we barristers have made in court contain our considered and certified opinions". Rather, the demands of the situation take precedence.[212] In the first occurrence the Jews are responsible for the prosecution case. His position reflects simply a typical Roman elitism, and may be linked to his understanding of citizenship.[213]

Varro (116-27 BCE) apparently equated Yahweh with Jupiter and approved of the Jewish manner of worshipping without images.[214] This is clearly positive. Asinius Pollio (first century BCE) presents a neutral record of events in Jewish history, although it is known that he too was a friend of Herod.[215] Tibullus (48-19 BCE) uses the Sabbath as an excuse not to leave his girlfriend.[216] This, in particular, shows a popular awareness of Jewish customs and perhaps almost a tacit acceptance.

Similarly, Horace mentions a friend who will not stop and discuss business concerns with him on the Sabbath out of respect for the Jews. Although Horace does not share his friend's opinion, he notes that many others do.[217] There is no hostility in this account and it attests to a widespread attitude of acceptance and support at Rome. Elsewhere, however, Horace alludes to the credulity of the Jews, something that seems to be proverbial. This is not anti-Semitic. It simply reflects a cultural disdain, and may actually relate to the class of the Jews with which he was familiar. On the other hand, Horace appears to claim that the Jews were active in proselytizing and that they were not averse to using intimidation in this manner.[218] However, as John Nolland contends, this text does not refer to proselytism, but to the way in which the Jewish mob at Rome intimidated opponents

---

[212] Cicero *Clu.* 139: *Sed errat vehementer, si quis in orationibus nostris, quas in iudiciis habuimus, auctoritates nostras consignatas se habere arbitratur.*

[213] Cicero's comments include nothing like the Greek accusations of atheism, misanthropy, nor even specific accusations of impiety. See, for example, Stern, *Authors*, 1.194; Gager, *Origins*, 41.

[214] Stern, *Authors*, #72[a,b,c].

[215] Josephus *AJ* 14.138; cf. Stern, *Authors*, 1.213.

[216] Tibullus *Eleg.* 1.3.15-18.

[217] Horace *Sat.* 1.9.68-72; cf. Stern, *Authors*, 1.325.

[218] Horace *Sat.* 1.4.142-3. This is the opinion of a number of scholars, such as Stern, *Authors*, 1.323.

to gain some measure of political leverage.[219] In any case, the
way in which Horace uses the analogy can only be described
as at least neutral. It may even contain a hint of admiration.

Livy (59 BCE-17 CE), it is said, notes the Jews
worshipped an unknown god and attests to the piety of the
Jewish priests to their rites.[220] This represents a neutral
attitude, as does the reference of Ovid (43 BCE-17 CE) to the
Sabbath,[221] and Lucan (39-65 CE) to the Jews' unknown
god.[222] Pompeius Trogus (early first century CE) claims that
the Jews originated from Damascus, a city he holds in high
regard, and that Joseph founded the science of dream-
interpretation. He shows some admiration for Moses, for the
justice of the Jews, and for their wisdom in quickly allying
themselves with Rome.[223] Furthermore, he claims that their
exclusiveness arose from their leper origin, such that they
tried to avoid contaminating their new neighbors. This is a
neutral, even positive, assessment and it clearly lacks the
hostility of the Alexandrian accounts.[224]

One version of Valerius Maximus (mid first century CE)
suggests that the Jewish expulsion from Rome in 139 BCE
was for proselytizing, linked to the expulsion of astrologers.
Another version claims it was for deception, fraud, and the
corruption of simple minds.[225] The former is considered to be
less accurate, while the latter may refer implicitly to a specific
incident and cannot be understood as representative.[226]

Seneca (4 BCE-65 CE) describes the Sabbath as
inexpedient and wasteful and he bemoans the fact that the
customs of this "accursed race" (*sceleratissimus gens*) are
spreading. However, his criticism appears directed more at
the Romans who are adopting these customs than at the
Jews themselves, for he claims that at least the Jews
understand the origin and meaning of their rites, unlike

---

[219] J. L. Nolland, "Proselytism or Politics in Horace *Satires* I,4,138-
143" *VC* 33 (1979) 347-53; cf. Cicero's allusion to the actions of the
Jewish mob in *Flac.* 66.

[220] Stern, *Authors*, ##133-4; Josephus *AJ* 14.68.

[221] Ovid *Ars Am.* 1.75-80.

[222] Lucan *Phars.* 2.592-3.

[223] Stern, *Authors*, #137.

[224] Stern, *Authors*, #137; cf. Gager, *Origins*, 71; Conzelmann,
Gentiles, 117-18.

[225] Compare Stern, *Authors*, ##147[a], 147[b].

[226] See Stern, *Authors*, 1.357.

others.[227] However, he also regards Jewish customs as superstition.[228] Given what is known of Seneca, his criticisms would derive from his philosophical critique and reflect his similar disdain of other foreign religions.[229] A similar attitude is found in Persius (34-62 CE).[230] Neither of their attitudes could be described as more than disdain.

Finally, Petronius (? mid first century CE) identifies circumcision as the distinguishing mark of the Jews — a neutral report.[231] He also criticizes a slave for having two faults: "he is circumcized and he snores" (*recutitus est et stertit*).[232] But this cannot be interpreted as some inherent criticism of Jews, especially since most Roman satire has sexual innuendos and this may well be the grounds of the complaint here.

Overall, then, the attitude of Roman writers prior to the Jewish revolt would best be described as neutral. When criticism is forthcoming it relates to Jewish customs, and there are none of the sort of accusations found in hostile Greek writers. A number of references indicate that some Jewish customs had been popularly adopted, but this is met with disdain or amusement rather than hostility.

Antonius Iulianus (late first century CE) claims that the crushing defeat the Jews received was what they deserved for their wickedness and obstinacy, and that their piety to their customs did not profit them at all.[233] The elder Pliny (23-79 CE) regards the Jews, and Moses in particular, as magicians and accuses them of despising the gods.[234] Quintilian (40-118 CE) describes Judaism as a superstition, Moses as a curse to other people, and the Jews themselves as full of vice.[235] Juvenal (end of the first century CE) associates the Jews with magicians. He also portrays Judaism as a silly

---

[227] Stern, *Authors*, #186: *Illi tamen causas ritus sui noverunt; maior pars populi facit, quod cur faciat ignorat.*

[228] Seneca *Ep.* 95.47, 108.22.

[229] See Stern, *Authors*, 1.429; Conzelmann, *Gentiles*, 118; cf. Seneca *Ep.* 95.47.

[230] Persius *Sat.* 5.179-82.

[231] Petronius *Sat.* 102.

[232] Ibid., 68.

[233] Stern, *Authors*, #201.

[234] Pliny *NH* 13.46; 30.11. He also has a number of references to Judaea which are neutral (ibid., 2.226, 5.66-73, 7.65). The accusation of being magicians is serious, given the Roman legislation and action against them, as mentioned above.

[235] Stern, *Authors*, #230.

superstition, and one that teaches people to hold Roman laws and customs in scant disregard.[236]

Tacitus (55-118 CE) comes closest to the attitude found among hostile Greeks, accusing the Jews of introducing practices contrary to all other nations, of worshipping the head of an ass, of misanthropy, hatred of the gods and disloyalty to country and family. He is the only Roman to refer to the leper story.[237] Suetonius (69-140 CE) claims Augustus praised Gaius for not visiting and sacrificing at the Jerusalem temple. Given that this would contravene normal protocol, and is inconsistent with what is known elsewhere of Augustus, it must reflect Suetonius' own prejudice.[238]

Martial (40-104 CE) thinks the Jews are lecherous beggars.[239] This, however, is not necessarily hostile, and may simply reflect the social status of the majority of Jews resident in Rome. As such it is disdain rather than anti-Semitism. Only Frontinus (30-104 CE) mentions the Jews with what appears to be a neutral attitude, although the very mention of Jerusalem being captured on the Sabbath would conjure images of the *barbara superstitio* of the Jews.[240]

Thus, in the period after the war there appears to be a marked degeneration in the attitude of Romans towards the Jews. Some of the comments of the satirists, however, must be treated cautiously since similar criticisms are made of other religious customs, and satire does not necessarily reflect real hatred.[241] At the same time, the criticism also appears to have shifted from a focus on Jewish customs to accusations like those of hostile Greek writers.[242] This change must be due to the war itself, for given the Roman concept of *pax deorum* and *pax Romana*, a charge of disrespect for the gods is tantamount to one of treason, and vice versa.[243]

---

[236] Juvenal *Sat.* 6.541-7, 14.96-106.

[237] Tacitus *Hist.* 4.1-2 & 5.1-5.

[238] On the protocol of prominent officials visiting temples see Thucydides 4.97-8; cf. Cohen, "Respect", 415.

[239] Martial *Epigr.* 7.30, 12.57.

[240] Frontinus *Str.* 2.1.17.

[241] See Gager, *Origins*, 57; Conzelmann, *Gentiles*, 104.

[242] See, for example, Daniel, "Anti-Semitism", 61; *contra* Gager, *Origins*, 56.

[243] Cohen, "Respect", 429; Conzelmann, *Gentiles*, 118-19; to some extent also M. D. Goodman, *The Ruling Class of Judaea: The Origins of the Jewish Revolt against Rome AD 66-70* (Cambridge: Cambridge University Press, 1987) 236-7. A number suggest the war is one of the causes, along with the status of the Jews and the success of Jewish

On the whole, and contrary to the assumption of many scholars, most of the Roman writers reflect at least a neutral or positive attitude. Genuine hostility toward or hatred of Jews arose in Egypt, but it does not appear to have been evident in the wider Greek world until after the Maccabean revolt. During the period of Roman domination the attitude towards the Jews seems to degenerate and spread to other parts of the Greek world. The Romans themselves, however, show a generally positive or neutral attitude prior to the war of 66-74 CE, although some disdain for Jewish customs is evident. Their attitude appears to change markedly in the aftermath of that war.

Nevertheless, it should not be assumed that the attitudes of the educated and elite (the *intelligentsia*) are necessarily representative of the whole of either Greek or Roman society. Already there have been several hints that popular attitudes included some sympathy towards and attraction to Jewish beliefs and customs, and this needs to be explored further. At the same time, there may also have been significant differences between the manner in which the Greeks and the Romans actually put their respective attitudes into practice.

(iii) Relations between Greeks, Romans and Jews

Under the Ptolemies, relations between Jews and Greeks, especially outside Palestine, seem to have been harmonious with little interference. Josephus claims that Ptolemy settled Jews in Alexandria with a variety of legal and political

---

proselytizing at Rome (see Sherwin-White, *Prejudice*, 98-9; Sevenster, *Roots*, 195; Daniel, "Anti-Semitism", 52-3). The criticisms of Martial clearly reflect some social snobbery, and may be a factor in other cases, although this is uncertain. Proselytism will be discussed further in the next section but, given that it did not begin in the post-war period, something must have changed if it did become a factor. The war showed to the Romans the treasonous and conspiratorial nature of the Jews and would make conversion a burning issue (see Cohen, "Respect", 429; Conzelmann, *Gentiles*, 118-19). Yavetz, however, argues "though the Jews were in many respects barbarians like all the others, they were in some respects a little more so" and adds that "even the most hated Graeculus in the days of Tacitus and Juvenal was better off than a tolerated Jew" ("Judeophobia", 13, 15). But he fails to appreciate the change in attitude following the war. The evidence presented is sufficient to show that while this may have been true in "the days of Tacitus and Juvenal" it was not earlier.

privileges.[244] Similarly, under most of the Seleucids the Jews
were apparently free to follow their own laws and customs.
This really changed only under Antiochus Epiphanes.[245] Both
his attitude and policy towards the Jews became intolerant as
Roman power and Jewish resistance increased. His
introduction of a ban on circumcision was not repeated until
the second century CE.[246]

Josephus claims that everywhere Jews attracted many
Greeks to their religious ceremonies and they had, in some
way, become associated with the Jewish community.[247] This
suggests that there was some degree of interaction. Jewish
names are also found in the *gymnasia* lists in a number of
cities. Furthermore, to pursue their livelihoods Jews must
have fostered relationships both within the Jewish
community and with the wider civic community.[248] Recently,
Paul Trebilco has shown that in the region of Asia Minor (in
cities such as Sardis, Lydia, Phrygia, Acmonia, Smyrna,

---

[244] Josephus *AJ* 12.7-8, 117-18; idem, *Ap.* 2.35; cf. Frend,
Martyrdom, 27; S. Appelbaum, "The Legal Status of the Jewish
Communities in the Diaspora" in S. Safrai & M. Stern, eds., *The Jewish
People in the First Century* (vol 1; Assen: van Gorcum, 1974) 428-32; E.
M. Smallwood, *The Jews under Roman Rule: From Pompey to Diocletian*
(SJLA 20; Leiden: E. J. Brill, 1976) 223; Conzelmann, *Gentiles*, 11, 21.
Diodorus Siculus claims Jewish customs were disturbed by both the
Persians and Macedonians (40.3.8), but there is little evidence of this.
Josephus' claims of Jewish privileges must be treated sceptically since
they are unsupported by other sources and his use of technical legal
terminology is inaccurate. This will be discussed later in this chapter.

[245] Frend, *Martyrdom*, 30; Appelbaum, "Legal Status", 454; Rabello,
"Legal Condition", 692; Gager, *Origins*, 39-40; T. Rajak, "Was There a
Roman Charter for the Jews?" *JRS* 74 (1984) 108; P. R. Trebilco, *Jewish
Communities in Asia Minor* (SNTSMS 69; Cambridge: Cambridge
University Press, 1991) 9. Although Epiphanes' attitude may not be
described as actual anti-Semitism, since he looted a number of temples
besides Jerusalem's, it did mark the beginning of specific official actions
against the Jews, as a number of these scholars point out.

[246] Josephus *AJ* 12.54; Frend, *Martyrdom*, 32-3; Rabello, "Legal
Condition", 699.

[247] Josephus *BJ* 7.45: ἀεί τε προσαγόμενοι ταῖς θρησκείαις πολὺ
πλῆθος Ἑλλήνων, κἀκείνους τρόπῳ τινὶ μοῖραν αὐτῶν πεποίηντο. See
also idem, *Ap.* 2.123, 282-3; cf. Kraft, "Judaism", 84.

[248] Appelbaum, "Legal Status", 447; Reynolds, "Cities", 45-6; A. F.
Segal, "The Costs of Proselytism and Conversion" *SBLSP* (1988) 350;
Trebilco, *Communities*, 173-7, 186; S. McKnight, *A Light among the
Gentiles: Jewish Missionary Activity in the Second Temple Period*
(Minneapolis: Fortress, 1991) 14; North, "Development", 176; cf. *SEG*
20.737.

Apamea and Pergamum), the Jewish communities were generally on friendly terms with their Greek neighbors and deeply involved in the life of their cities.[249]

At Cyrene, however, there were conflicts between the Greeks and Jews in the time of Augustus. For example, the city authorities prevented the Jewish residents from sending money to the temple in Jerusalem.[250] Latent hostility occasionally became outright conflict at Ephesus, Miletus, Laodicea, Tralles, Halicarnassus, Parium, Delos, and Antioch during this period. In these places the local authorities were generally responsible for actions taken against Jews.[251] Although these attacks were common during the civil wars of the late Republic, they were fairly rare during the first century CE.[252]

In the discussion of the attitude of writers towards the Jews it was noted that overt hostility began in Alexandria. Actions against the Jews seem to have originated there also, beginning during the Egyptian civil wars of the late second century BCE, and intensified by the assistance the Jews at Alexandria gave to the Romans when they invaded Egypt in

---

[249] See Trebilco, *Communities*, 10, 33-4, 38, 57, 83-4, 174-5; cf. Appelbaum, "Legal Status", 449; McKnight, *Light*, 14-15, 26-7; Conzelmann, *Gentiles*, 22 n. 63. Since the evidence from Sardis comes from the third century CE, however, it must be regarded with some tentativeness for the period in question. There is evidence of sporadic hostility at Lydia and Phrygia (see Trebilco, *Communities*, 33-4). At Acmonia the Jews had support among the elite of the city, such as Julia Severa who was a patron of the Jews and built their synagogue in the 60's CE, although she was a priestess of the Imperial cult (ibid., 83). Despite their integration and apparent assimilation, Trebilco notes that there is little evidence for syncretism or participation in pagan rites. Thus, in a number of cases concessions must have been made by individual cities to allow this (ibid., 180-7; cf. Appelbaum, "Legal Status", 443; Conzelmann, *Gentiles*, 46-7).

[250] See Josephus *AJ* 16.160, 169; cf. Appelbaum, "Legal Status" 445. These conflicts at Cyrene appear to have been part of a long standing dispute involving the Jews and the city.

[251] See Josephus *AJ* 14.8, 20-5, 213-14, 241-42, 245, 258, 264, 16.167-8; cf. Frend, *Martyrdom*, 101; Sherwin-White, *Prejudice*, 89-90; Rajak, "Roman Charter", 119; Trebilco, *Communities*, 34-5.

[252] Appelbaum, "Legal Status", 443; Sherwin-White, *Prejudice*, 91; Trebilco, *Communities*, 34-5, 183. In a number of places, but particularly in Syria, the start of the Jewish revolt in 66 CE provided an opportunity for cities to rise up against resident Jews. See Josephus *BJ* 2.457-63, 7.41-2.

55, 48 and 30 BCE.[253] At Alexandria, however, anti-Jewish
actions that included mob violence occurred particularly after
the Roman annexation of Egypt in 30 BCE.[254] Actions against
the Alexandrian Jews reached its apex in the governorship of
Flaccus. The Jews were herded into a ghetto, many were
bound and marched naked to the theatre where they were
whipped, women caught in the market were beaten and
forced to eat pork.[255] These actions were initiated by the
Greek leadership, who played on the precarious position of
the governor following Gaius' rise to power. Flaccus gave in
to the Greek leaders in order to maintain support.[256] The
situation remained volatile until Claudius' reign.[257]

It is suggested by some scholars that sporadic outbursts
might be reactions to active proselytizing by Jews.[258] Given
the demands placed on Jewish proselytes, this is possible.[259]
Martin Goodman, however, claims that there is no direct
evidence for resentment, let alone action, against Jews for
proselytism prior to 96 CE.[260] He is probably right. For recent
work has strongly questioned the idea that first century
Judaism was an actively proselytizing religion.[261] Rather, it

---

[253] Smallwood, *Jews*, 223-4; Gager, *Origins*, 237; Barclay, *Jews*, 48.
For example, during the the Egyptian civil war (145 BCE) Ptolemy
Physcon is claimed to have thrown some Jews into the theatre naked
and had them trampled by drunk elephants (Josephus *Ap.* 2.53).

[254] Smallwood, *Jews*, 234; Gager, *Origins*, 44, 49.

[255] Philo *In Flacc.* 73-5, 95-6. The conflict between Jews and Greeks
in Alexandria, probably may be classified as persecution rather than
simply conflict since, in many respects, the Jews were largely
scapegoats for anti-Roman sentiments.

[256] See Smallwood, *Jews*, 236-40; Gager, *Origins*, 47-8; Barclay,
Jews, 52.

[257] See Josephus *AJ* 19.278-9; Smallwood, *Jews*, 242-5.

[258] Cohen, "Respect", 417; Segal, "Costs", 350; M. D. Goodman,
"Jewish Proselytizing in the First Century" in J. Lieu *et al*, eds., *The Jews
among Pagans and Christians in the Roman Empire* (rev ed.; London:
Routledge, 1994) 59.

[259] Philo suggests this involves ἀπολελοιπότες πατρίδα καὶ φίλους
καὶ συγγενεῖς (*De spec.* 1.52). However, as with the case of the conflicts
between Christians and their wider civic communities, no explanation
has been given as to why such outbursts against the Jews were
sporadic.

[260] Goodman, "Proselytizing", 59.

[261] See, Cohen, "Respect", 423; McKnight, *Light* 116-17. Besides, if
proselytism was a major factor, then action would have been taken
against proselytes rather than Jews, but this did not seem to occur. See,
for example, Josephus *BJ* 2.461-3.

appears that whether or not conflict developed depended on the date at which the Jewish community was founded, the circumstances under which it developed, its size, and the attitude of the Greek majority.[262] There may have been an underlying resentment of Jews for their alleged misanthropy, social aloofness and atheism.[263] Their refusal to participate in the civic cults not only reeked of atheism but it potentially undermined the religious and political convictions of the Greek city-state mentality.[264]

In many places resentment of this refusal may have led to actions against Jews, even if not of the scale of the persecutions at Alexandria. For in a number of cases city councils appear to take it upon themselves to hinder Jews following their customs, such as the scheduling of court cases involving them on the Sabbath.[265] Specific causes are not mentioned. Such resentment and official hindrance may have been worse in a city where there was a large Jewish community that sought to be politically active and thus posed a potential threat to the Greek way of life.[266] In other words, the issue of citizenship might have contributed, for although Josephus seems to claim Jews were citizens in some cities, this is not supported by the evidence.[267]

The status of Jews living in Greek cities has often been linked to the concept of the πολίτευμα. Traditionally, this has

---

[262] See Trebilco, *Communities*, 188. These factors appear to correspond to those involved in the "culture of conflict" as the model suggests.

[263] Sherwin-White, *Prejudice*, 87; Sevenster, *Roots*, 5; Daniel, "Anti-Semitism", 53; Trebilco, *Communities*, 11; Conzelmann, *Gentiles*, 46-8.

[264] See Frend, *Martyrdom*, 95; Conzelmann, *Gentiles*, 46.

[265] For example Josephus *AJ* 14.245-6, 16.27-8.

[266] Frend, *Martyrdom*, 99; Sherwin-White, *Prejudice*, 100; to some extent also Appelbaum, "Legal Status", 452-3.

[267] Citizenship was clearly a major factor in the conflicts at Alexandria. Although the situation in Alexandria was unique, Josephus' emphasis on legal privileges and claims of citizenship in other cities suggest that the issue was widespread. See Josephus *AJ* 12.119, 16.160-1; idem, *BJ* 7.44; Appelbaum, "Legal Status", 435-6, 442; Smallwood, *Jews*, 234; Trebilco, *Communities*, 168; Barclay, *Jews*, 70. Although some Jews had Roman citizenship, they lacked citizenship in Greek cities. See Josephus *AJ* 14.228-35; Philo *Leg.* 155-7; Kraft, "Judaism", 89; Appelbaum, "Legal Status", 440-6. Josephus claims they had citizenship at Alexandria, but this is contradicted by Claudius' edict and is surely false (*AJ* 19.280-1; idem, *BJ* 2.487; *CPJ* 153.90-5 [in White, *Light*, 136]; Appelbaum, "Legal Status", 439-40; Smallwood, *Jews*, 231-2; Gager, *Origins*, 48; Barclay, *Jews*, 67).

been understood by most scholars as a "recognized, formally
constituted corporation of aliens enjoying the right of domicile
in a foreign city and forming a separate, semi-autonomous
civic body, a city within a city". In other words, it was
thought to have had its own constitution, administered its
own internal affairs, and appointed its own office-bearers.[268]
However, there is no real evidence to suggest that the
politeuma was a standard political or legal organization for
foreign communities in Greek cities. Rather, more recent work
suggests that the term *politeuma* may not have had such an
overtly political or legal sense. Indeed, in many cases the
term appears to have been synonymous with other terms
used to describe a *collegium*.[269] Nevertheless, it is likely that
some defined communal structure and degree of autonomy
may have been recognized, although probably only in the
larger cities and ones where the Jewish community had a
long history.[270]

Thus, for most Jews living in Greek cities there was
some ambiguity of status. This would have left them
vulnerable to a range of social, economic, and political
sanctions. Most often these would have been minor. Where
the Jews formed a large semi-autonomous community, the
commitment of Greeks to city-state principles may have
resulted in a strong resentment towards a foreign enclave

---

[268] Smallwood, *Jews*, 225; cf. Appelbaum, "Legal Status", 427;
MacMullen, *Social Relations*, 83; Rabello, "Legal Condition", 722;
Trebilco, *Communities*, 170.

[269] See C. Zuckerman, "Hellenistic *Politeumata* and the Jews. A
Reconsideration" *Scripta Classica Israelica* 8/9 (1988) 184-5; G. Lüderitz,
"What is the Politeuma?" in J. W. van Henten & P. W. van der Horst,
eds., *Studies in Early Jewish Epigraphy* (AGJU 21; Leiden: E. J. Brill,
1994) 202-21; *contra* Smallwood, *Jews*, 226; Rajak, "Charter", 109; A.
Kasher, *The Jews in Hellenistic and Roman Egypt: The Struggle for
Equal Rights* (Tübingen: J. C. B. Mohr, 1985), 181-2. Kasher's argument,
in particular, is sloppy and ignores a number of texts and misrepresents
others. For a thorough critique see especially Zuckerman, "Hellenistic
Politeumata". As both Zuckerman and Lüderitz point out, only at
Cyrenaica was the term *politeuma* actually used in relation to the
Jewish community. It may have had some sort of political sense there.

[270] See Trebilco, *Communities*, 171-2; Zuckerman, "Hellenistic
Politeumata", 184. At Cyrene, for example, the Jews were not even
accorded the status of "metics" (resident aliens). This would have placed
them in a precarious legal position. See Josephus *AJ* 14.114-18; cf.
Appelbaum, "Legal Status", 425.

outside their control.[271] Ill-feeling and the imposition of sanctions would have been exacerbated if the impetus for, and enforcement of, Jewish privileges came from Romans.[272]

Although the Romans continued earlier Greek tendencies to support traditional laws, these tendencies had never been formally defined as an explicit policy, let alone a universal one, prior to Roman control.[273] Realizing they would be better off under a more formal Roman policy of toleration, the Jews sought their favor. Given the inherent resentment of many Greeks in the *poleis*, this would have established a vicious circle: Jewish reliance on Roman support would lead to continued Roman intervention, increasing Greek resentment, and attempts to undermine Jewish privileges.[274]

Nevertheless, the Romans did not grant the Jews a specific political or legal status.[275] Support came in the form of specific grants from various Roman rulers. Julius Caesar granted Jews in Alexandria and Asia Minor the right to practice their ancestral customs and intervened when this right was undermined.[276] His policy was upheld by the Senate after his death, and by Agrippa in Ionia.[277] Augustus followed Caesar's example.[278] In fact, in the late Republican and early Imperial periods there was a series of edicts and

---

[271] Frend, *Martyrdom*, 97; Sherwin-White, *Prejudice*, 89, 94; Appelbaum, "Legal Status", 454; Kasher, *The Jews*, 356; Trebilco, *Communities*, 13.

[272] Greek resentment would have been even more intense if the Jews sought to maintain their privileges while claiming citizenship, especially given the belief that citizens ought to worship the gods of the city. Even Josephus acknowledges this connection (*Ap.* 2.65).

[273] Appelbaum, "Legal Status", 454; Rabello, "Legal Condition", 692; Trebilco, *Communities*, 9; cf. Josephus *BJ* 2.488. Conzelmann actually suggests that the Romans were the first to grant such a privilege (*Gentiles*, 14), but this is probably going too far.

[274] Sherwin-White, *Prejudice*, 93; Smallwood, *Jews*, 230-231; Gager, *Origins*, 43; Rajak, "Charter", 118. Many Greek cities sought to curtail Jewish rights while the Romans maintained them. See, for example, Josephus *AJ* 12.120-4; cf. Frend, *Martyrdom*, 102-3.

[275] See Rajak, "Charter", 107.

[276] Josephus *AJ* 14.211-16, 16.166; idem, *Ap.* 2.37; Philo *Leg.* 315-16; cf. Smallwood, *Jews*, 233; Garnsey & Saller, *Empire*, 169-70.

[277] Josephus *AJ* 12.125-6, 14.217-21, 16.167-8; cf. Rabello, "Legal Condition", 743.

[278] See Josephus *Ap.* 2.61-2; cf. Frend, *Martyrdom*, 89; Smallwood, *Jews*, 233; Garnsey & Saller, *Empire*, 169-70.

letters sent to various Greek cities to guarantee the right of
Jews to practice their ancestral customs.[279]

The effectiveness of these edicts, however, would have
depended on them being adopted and implemented by the
city councils and the local courts.[280] Of course, this could vary
considerably, as is seen from the need for them to be
repeated. The continual repetition of edicts also indicates that
they were not intended to be universal in nature or intent.[281]
Rather, the context and the spread of the edicts suggest that
they were *ad hoc* decisions that probably were made in
response to direct approaches from local Jewish groups, and
because of personal contacts that the Jews had in high
places.[282] Only the edict of Claudius comes close to being a
universal ruling.[283]

The basis of the Romans' intervention, and their
support of Jewish rights, would appear to be their concept of
ancestral custom. For according to Josephus the Romans
promised to uphold the rights of the Jews "while they abide
by their own customs".[284] A number of scholars, however,
have suggested that the intervention and support was given
simply because it was politically expedient and had nothing
to do with the antiquity of Jewish customs.[285] But it is

---

[279] Josephus *AJ* 14.207-8, 223, 226-7, 235, 241-2, 257-8, 16.48,
19.279, 283-90; Philo *Leg.* 311-13; *CPJ* 153; cf. Smallwood, *Jews*, 247-9;
Rabello, "Legal Condition", 694; Rajak, "Charter", 112; Cohen,
"Respect", 413; Garnsey & Saller, *Empire*, 170. Rajak notes that there
were about thirty in number ("Charter", 109). Although Josephus is the
main source we have for these edicts, apart from some inaccuracy on
the matter of citizenship, they should be considered as genuine. See
Rajak, "Charter", 107, 111; Trebilco, *Communities*, 7.

[280] See, for example, Sherwin-White, *Prejudice*, 90; Appelbaum,
"Legal Status", 457.

[281] Sherwin-White, *Prejudice*, 91; Rajak, "Charter", 113-15;
Trebilco, *Communities*, 10. Even Caesar's exemption of Jews from the
ban on *collegia* was probably only intended for Rome itself.

[282] Appelbaum, "Legal Status", 456; Rajak, "Charter", 112, 116-18;
Trebilco, *Communities*, 11, 16; cf. Josephus *AJ* 16.27.

[283] Claudius' edict was quickly implemented by provincial governors
(Sherwin-White, *Prejudice*, 91; Rajak, "Charter", 114-15), although
Trebilco suggests that it still formed only a general policy (*Communities*,
10).

[284] Josephus *AJ* 19.285: φυλάσσεσθαι δ' αὐτοῖς καὶ τὰ πρότερον
δικαιώματα ἐμμένουσι τοῖς ἰδίοις ἔθεσιν; cf. Smallwood, *Jews*, 246;
Rabello, "Legal Condition", 694; MacMullen, *Paganism*, 2.

[285] See Appelbaum, "Legal Status", 456; Gager, *Origins*, 55;
Garnsey & Saller, *Empire*, 169.

illogical, if political expediency is related to maintaining peace and order, to support the interests of a minority over those of the majority. Besides, in all the edicts emphasis is specifically placed on the very issue of ancestral customs and laws. Thus, Philip Esler argues that:

> in determining whether a Jew should be exempted from military service on account of religious scruples (δεισιδαιμονίας ἕνεκα), Roman provincial officials did not look just to the fact of circumcision to establish Jewishness; they ascertained whether the applicant for exemption actually lived the life of a Jew.[286]

Sympathy for, and adoption of, some Jewish practices by Romans on a popular level may testify to this concern for ancestral custom. It is likely that the motivation behind this would be a desire to maintain the *pax deorum*. For it was in the interest of the state that the Jews continued to worship their god in the traditional way. Furthermore, a number of Romans may have adopted Jewish customs so as to gain the favor of a potentially powerful god, who may, in any case, be a manifestation of Jupiter.

Some scholars claim that the Jews, and their customs, were tolerated by the Romans because they were conceived as an ethnic group and not as a religious one.[287] In one sense, this may be correct, given that the old notion of *religio licita* ("permitted religion") has been shown never to have been a Roman legal concept.[288] On the other hand, the concept of *collegium licitum* did exist, and the Jews at Rome were recognized as such a group.[289] This alone suggests that Judaism was not perceived as *merely* an ethnic group, and the focus of the edicts on Jewish religious scruples would tend to support this.

While the Romans officially supported the Jews, and intervened to protect their rights from Greek attempts to

---

[286] Esler, *Community*, 212-13. Encouraging ancestral customs may have been expedient in fostering political stability (ibid., 214-15).

[287] Appelbaum, "Legal Status", 455-6; Rabello, "Legal Condition", 695; Segal, "Costs", 348; North, "Development", 190-1; Barclay, *Jews*, 407; to some extent also see Frend, *Martyrdom*, 106.

[288] Appelbaum, "Legal Status", 460; Rajak, "Charter", 107; Esler, *Community*, 211; Trebilco, *Communities*, 9; *contra* Rabello, "Legal Condition", 695.

[289] See Appelbaum, "Legal Status", 460; Rabello, "Legal Condition", 719.

undermine them, there were instances of actions taken
against the Jews at Rome. The first of these, in 139 BCE, has
already been mentioned.[290] In that particular instance, the
most reliable version claims it was for deception, fraud and
the corruption of simple minds. Another version attributes it
to proselytism and association with astrology. If the
association with astrology were combined with the charge of
fraud and deception, this would make sense. But at this early
date, it may be due to some specific incident or it may simply
reflect the Republican dislike of foreign practices. In any case,
it is clear that the action was not due to proselytizing, as
may be seen in light of the incident of 19 CE.

Tiberius' expulsion of Jews in 19 CE has been recorded
by a number of writers and explained differently. Dio Cassius
claims it was for proselytizing, but in light of its context he
appears to link it with a similar ban on false prophecy.[291]
Tacitus connects it to a similar expulsion of Isis-followers and
attributes it to impiety and superstition.[292] Suetonius
associates it with the suppression of astrologers, but suggests
it was related to proselytism since apostasy from Judaism
could avert punishment.[293]

The most detailed account is found in Josephus. He
links it to a scandal involving the Isis cult and the fraudulent
rape of a Roman noble-woman. In Josephus' version the
repressive actions taken against the Jews were in response to
a scam involving a fugitive from Jerusalem who, with three
associates, defrauded money from a noble-woman
sympathizer.[294] Generally, scholars dismiss the account of
Josephus in favor of Suetonius or Tacitus. Proselytism is
therefore identified as a major factor in the sanctions
imposed. Some dismiss Josephus' version due to the apologetic
nature of his account and especially his habit in earlier works
of playing down any hints of proselytism.[295] It is argued that
under normal circumstances proselytism was tolerated as it
usually involved commoners, but when it reached the elite it
was perceived as a threat and sanctions were enforced.[296]

---

[290] See the discussion of Valerius Maximus above.
[291] Dio Cassius 57.18.5.
[292] Tacitus *Ann.* 2.85.
[293] Suetonius *Tib.* 36.
[294] Josephus *AJ* 18.65-84.
[295] See Smallwood, *Jews*, 190, 204; Gager, *Origins*, 87; Cohen,
"Respect", 424-8; Conzelmann, *Gentiles*, 26.
[296] See Smallwood, *Jews*, 205-9; cf. Goodman, *Ruling Class*, 237.

As has been suggested above, there is no clear evidence that proselytism was a genuine problem in the period prior to the Jewish war. There are no accusations of impiety or sacrilege, and the repression appears to have been only short-lived and selective. Furthermore, there are cases where members of the higher social classes were attracted to Judaism and no recorded action ensued.[297] Given the attitudes of Dio Cassius, Tacitus, and Suetonius to the Jews, it is quite likely that they were reading back their own prejudices and the issues of their own time to an earlier period.[298] Hence, Josephus' account should be accorded more credibility. It is likely that some specific action prompted the suppression, even if it was not as simple as Josephus portrays it, and a possible link of Judaism with magic and false prophecy is still a possibility.[299]

Philo's claim that Sejanus tried to exterminate the Jews finds no support elsewhere, and should be treated cautiously.[300] Meanwhile, Gaius' attempts to install his image in the Jerusalem temple is consistent with the rest of the inconsistencies of his regime, and is not representative of general Roman attitudes.[301] It is unclear what prompted Claudius' actions against the Jews at Rome in 41 CE. Proselytism, however, is not mentioned and is unlikely. Rather, possible disturbances and fears of subversion may have been involved, since the *collegia* were also suppressed at the same time.[302] Thus, Roman actions against the Jews

---

[297] See Sherwin-White, *Roman Law*, 81-2; idem, *Prejudice*, 100; Frend, *Martyrdom*, 108; Daniel, "Anti-Semitism", 64; McKnight, *Light*, 74; Goodman, "Proselytizing", 70; idem, *Ruling Class*, 237.

[298] To some extent this is suggested by McKnight, *Light*, 74.

[299] See Frend, *Martyrdom*, 107; cf. the implicit associations made by Dio Cassius (57.18.5) and Suetonius (*Tib.* 36).

[300] Philo *Leg.* 159f.; cf. Conzelmann, *Gentiles*, 27.

[301] Sherwin-White, *Prejudice*, 96; Rabello, "Legal Condition", 692; Cohen, "Respect", 415; cf. Josephus *BJ* 2.184-94.

[302] See Dio Cassius 60.6.6-7; cf. Smallwood, *Jews*, 215-16; Conzelmann, *Gentiles*, 28. That the sanctions did not involve expulsion may suggest that many were citizens, rather than that the Jews were too numerous. Yet, that they were allowed to continue to practice their customs *except* for meeting together strengthens the arguments associated with the ban on *collegia*. Claudius' reference to the Jews as a plague infecting the whole world (καθάπερ κοινήν τεινα τῆς οἰκουμένης νόσον ἐξεγείροντας) in his edict to Alexandria probably reflects his annoyance at having to deal with disturbances involving the Jews on two fronts. See *CPJ* 153.99-100 (in White, *Light*, 136); cf. Smallwood, *Jews*, 250. This incident is not the expulsion of the Jews related to "Chrestus",

ought to be seen as attempts to control order, prompted by specific offences.[303]

III. CONCLUSION

Greek and Roman societies share many of the features of *Gemeinschaft*-type societies. They seem to have had generally successful socialization into their particular patterns of norms, values and beliefs. At the same time, socialization in the Greek and Roman worlds (as represented by child-rearing and schooling practices) does not seem to have been particularly warm and affectionate. In other words, both Greek and Roman societies would have a high propensity to conflict. Since this is common to both cultures, it does not help to explain possible differences in conflict response. Thus the different societies' patterns of norms, values and beliefs may be more important.

In terms of religious norms, values and beliefs there are marked differences in Greek and Roman approaches. The Romans generally conceived of their gods in a more abstract way than the Greeks. They saw their relationship to them as a business-contract, emphasized the maintenance of ancestral custom, but seem little concerned with the issue of congruity between belief and practice. Even though many of the elite were influenced by philosophy, their beliefs were normally modified by a commitment to *mos maiorum*. On the other hand, the Greeks placed greater importance on the continuity of belief and practice. While the common people generally believed in and worshipped anthropomorphic gods, the educated and elite participated in the traditional rites probably only for the sake of expediency, or to avoid popular hatred and charges of atheism.

In the matter of attitudes toward foreigners and their religion, the general Greek attitude was one of disdain. While it had a great receptivity to foreign cults, a strong city-state mentality and a context of foreign domination made the potential for conflict between Greeks and foreigners high. The relations were potentially more volatile than those in Roman cities. For although Romans also showed some disdain, they were more tolerant if the rites had the force of

---

which Suetonius reports, and probably occurred around 49 CE. See Suetonius *Claud.* 25.4.

[303] See Frend, *Martyrdom*, 107; Goodman, *Ruling Class*, 237.

ancient custom. When action was taken it was a response to particular circumstances.

Correspondingly, the attitude of most ancient writers to the Jews is neutral or positive. Genuine hostility toward the Jews probably began in Egypt, but was not widespread in the Greek world until after the Maccabean revolt. During the period of Roman domination this attitude degenerated and spread. The Romans themselves show a generally positive or neutral attitude prior to the war of 66-74 CE, although some disdain is evident. This attitude changed markedly in the aftermath of the war. In terms of popular attitudes, that some were attracted to or sympathized with Judaism shows that Jews were active participants in the life of their cities. At the same time, it is likely that in most places, and at most times, Jews and their neighbors lived in a state of peaceful toleration.

In Greek cities, however, there would appear to be a current of resentment lying under the surface which could break out at any time into specific and official action against Jewish rights. The Jews suffered from an ambiguous legal and political status. A persistent city-state mentality also meant that the presence of a body of foreigners, in some respects outside their control, was a threat. This was exacerbated because the rights of the Jews were maintained by Roman intervention.

Roman policy, on the whole, sought to protect Jewish rights for a number of reasons. Support was largely based on respect for ancestral practices. The ruling elite was also tolerant because the Jews were not a political threat in Roman cities like they were in Greek ones. On a popular level, some Romans may have been sympathetic and adopted Jewish practices in an attempt to maintain the *pax deorum* and win the favor of a powerful god.

Overall, the pattern of socialization suggests that both Greek and Roman societies were high conflict cultures. And indeed, there was a high propensity towards conflict in both. Therefore the model appears to fit at this level. At the same time, however, there are considerable differences in their particular patterns of norms, values and beliefs so that it is likely that there would be considerable differences between Greek and Roman communities. Indeed, since Roman norms and attitudes towards other religions and ethnic groups are somewhat more tolerant, we would expect a slightly lower incidence of conflict in Roman communities than in Greek ones. Before we can suggest that some of these communities may be classed as low conflict cultures and others as high conflict cultures the social-structural factors (and the other factors that determine the "culture of conflict") must be explored and tested.

Chapter Three

SOCIAL-STRUCTURAL FACTORS OF GRECO-ROMAN CITIES

In the previous chapter it was suggested that the incidence of conflict may vary between individual Greek and Roman communities and that Roman communities may be lower conflict cultures than Greek ones. Before that can be asserted more positively, however, the social-structural factors that also determine whether a society is a high or low conflict culture need to be considered. Specifically, the extent of cross-cutting or reinforcing ties, the population size, the ethnic composition and pattern of interaction, the resource concentration, and the organization of authority must be examined. Thus, in this chapter the preliminary model will be tested against material drawn from significant primary sources and the work of previous scholars.

On the basis of the cities mentioned in the previous chapter, in relation to conflicts between Greeks and Jews, the contention of the preliminary model that conflict will be inversely proportional to city size cannot be supported. Generally good relations were maintained at Apamea (125,000 residents), Pergamum (120,000), Sardis (100,000) and Smyrna (75,000), while hostility was found in varying degrees at Alexandria (400,000), Ephesus (200,000) and Antioch (150,000).[1] By ancient standards all of these were large cities, and yet the incidence of conflict varied. Therefore, although corresponding data for smaller cities is lacking, it is likely that city size is not important, compared to other factors.

---

[1] Stark, "Christianizing", 78-9. These estimates of population size are meant as guides, given the difficulties involved in such estimates mentioned in the previous chapter.

I. PATTERNS OF SOCIAL RELATIONS

There appear to be significant differences in the planning of Greek and Roman cities in terms of the interaction of social groups. In the latter there is a particularly close association of public, commercial and residential buildings. All three types can be found in the proximity of the *forum*, and apart from certain streets or areas that were given over to particular commercial activities, most areas of the city show mixed use of space. Indeed, even the houses of the rich are not geographically separate from the residences of the poor (nor are residential and commercial buildings) in Roman cities.[2]

On the other hand, Plato argues that the working classes should be physically separate from the leisured classes.[3] Such a separation can be seen at Ostia, although this appears to have been a unique case given many other examples (including Pompeii). While there is some evidence for segregation at Rome, social and geographical mixing has even been identified there.[4] Although Plato's comments express an ideal rather than reality, it is nevertheless possible that there may have been some differences between Greek and Roman cities in the matter of social mixing, given the different household and patronal arrangements.[5] Furthermore, elsewhere in the Greek world there appears to

---

[2] Packer, "Housing", 81; MacMullen, *Social Relations*, 67; Reynolds, "Cities", 20; Wallace-Hadrill, "Elites and Trade", 252-3; Dyson, *Community*, 176; Laurence, *Pompeii*, 19, 67-8. Perring claims that in Roman cities this mixture of social strata and commerce may "suggest a society in which the clan-like ties of *familia* and *clientela* were more essential than any identification with class or economic interests" ("Spatial Organisation", 284). Laurence notes that brothels were frequently located at the rear of elite houses at Pompeii. Yet, "the elite structured their environment to distance themselves from those associated with *infamia* without creating zones" (*Pompeii*, 74-5).

[3] Plato *Resp.* 460c.

[4] See *CIL* 4.138, 1136; Wallace-Hadrill, "Elites and Trade", 261, 263-4; Perring, "Spatial Organisation", 284-5; *contra* Stambaugh, *Roman City*, 90. Although the elite of many Roman cities eventually exerted more planning control, distancing the commercial and (elite) residential, this is really only evident from the second century CE. See Perring, "Spatial Organisation", 274-5.

[5] S. S. Bartchy notes that among the Greeks, slaves often did not live in their master's house (*First Century Slavery and the Interpretation of 1 Corinthians 7:21* [SBLDS 11; Atlanta: Scholars Press, 1973] 42). See also N. R. E. Fisher, *Slavery in Classical Greece* (London: Bristol Classical Press, 1993) 69; cf. Heraclitus *Ep.* 9.

have been geographical separation of the leisured and working classes.[6]

Indeed, patronage was central to Roman society and to their social ideology.[7] A patronal relationship was seen as a bond of kindness, where the patron was to support, protect and care for his clients like a father for his children. Clients were expected to share the financial losses of their patron and to serve him.[8] Patronage was based on an exchange of goods or services, although uneven and different in kind, over a considerable period. Unlike the patron-freedperson bond, however, the relationship normally involved a moral, rather than a legal, obligation.[9] Effectively, the patronage system enabled the elite to control access to scarce resources, such as money, property and legal protection. In return, those supported formed the economic and political power bases of their patrons.[10] Since the number needing those resources was greater than those controlling them, this placed the elite in a position of great power.[11]

Among the Greeks, however, a patronage system did not operate and patronal relationships were generally avoided. In fact, the Greek ideology of democracy was inimical to patronage and strong measures were taken to

---

[6] There is some evidence for social segregation in the remains of Piraeus and Priene. See Tomlinson, *From Mycenae*, 71-2, 93. See also Burford, *Craftsmen*, 82.

[7] In fact, it was so central that Romulus was portrayed as its instigator. See Dion. Hal. *Ant. Rom.* 2.9.1-2; cf. Plautus *Men.* 571-84; Stambaugh, "Social Relations", 14; A. Wallace-Hadrill, "Patronage in Roman Society: From Republic to Empire", in idem, ed., *Patronage in Ancient Society* (London: Routledge, 1989) 63-5. The link to Romulus is as much polemical as it is mythical and idealistic.

[8] Dion. Hal. *Ant. Rom.* 2.9.3-10.2; cf. Martial *Epigr.* 3.46.

[9] Cicero *Off.* 1.56, 92-3; Dio Chrys. *Or.* 46.3-6; Dion. Hal. *Ant. Rom.* 2.10.4; Horace *Epod.* 7.55-9; idem, *Sat.* 2.2.99-105; Pliny *Ep.* 8.12; cf. P. Marshall, *Enmity in Corinth: Social Conventions in Paul's Relations with the Corinthians* (WUNT 2.33; Tübingen: J. C. B. Mohr, 1987) 143; R. P. Saller, "Patronage and Friendship in Early Imperial Rome: Drawing the Distinctions" in A. Wallace-Hadrill, ed., *Patronage in Ancient Society* (London: Routledge, 1989) 49-51; Wallace-Hadrill, "Patronage", 66; Veyne, *Bread*, 43-4.

[10] See, for example, J. H. D'Arms, *Commerce and Social Standing in Ancient Rome* (Cambridge, MA: Harvard University Press, 1981) 5-7; Wallace-Hadrill, "Patronage", 72-5; idem, "Elites and Trade", 268; cf. Cicero *Off.* 2.52; Seneca *Ep.* 19.4.

[11] See, for example, Cicero *Off.* 1.50, 2.54; Juvenal *Sat.* 3.152-3, 160-1; Plautus *Men.* 571-84.

avoid or hide it as something shameful. Although patronage was present in cities where democracy was less secure, and it became more common during the Principate, exchange between equals was generally much more preferred.[12] For example, there was a system of peer-loans (*eranoi*), such that a man in financial difficulty collected small contributions from each of his φίλοι and relatives until he had enough for his needs. It was expected that these loans would be repaid as soon as practical.[13]

Peer-support was found in both Greek and Roman societies. For example, neighboring farmers might form a co-operative while those of the same profession could form a trade *collegium*, and these may have acted as alternatives or supplements to the support they received from elite-patrons.[14] In this regard it was recognized that in order to do business or to obtain assistance, it was necessary to be popular, to have a good reputation, and to help others.[15] This co-operation and mutual assistance was, at least in part, the basis of the trade *collegia*.[16] Many such *collegia* also had a member of the elite as their patron and they supported him

---

[12] See P. Millett, "Patronage and its Avoidance in Classical Athens", in A. Wallace-Hadrill, ed., *Patronage in Ancient Society* (London: Routledge, 1989) 16-18, cf. Wallace-Hadrill's introduction to the volume; cf. Burford, *Craftsmen*, 37-8).

[13] See, for example, Theophrastus *Char.* 1.5, 15.7, 17.9, 22.9; Xenophon, *Oec.* 2.8; cf. Millett, "Patronage", 41-42; B. W. Winter, *Seek the Welfare of the City: Christians as Benefactors and Citizens* (Grand Rapids: Eerdmans, 1994) 55.

[14] P. D. A. Garnsey & G. Woolf, "Patronage and the Rural Poor in the Roman World", 155-7 and T. Johnson & C. Dandeker, "Patronage: Relation and System", 229, both in A. Wallace-Hadrill, ed., *Patronage in Ancient Society* (London: Routledge, 1989). Peer-support and assistance also would have been important following natural disasters, such as fires or earthquakes. See Garnsey & Woolf, "Patronage", 155; Veyne, *Bread*, 375. Although fires were perhaps less common in the provinces than at Rome (Juvenal *Sat.* 3.5-9; Martial *Epigr.* 3.52, 4.66), Pliny's request to Trajan for a local fire-brigade clearly shows they were still a problem (*Ep.* 10.33).

[15] So, for example Cato *Rust.* 4.2; Cicero *Off.* 2.39-40.

[16] See, for example, Martial *Epigr.* 1.2, 117, 9.59; Burford, *Craftsmen*, 159-60; MacMullen, *Social Relations*, 69, 72-3; Garnsey & Saller, *Empire*, 156; Stambaugh, *Roman City*, 150-1; Reynolds, "Cities", 20-1; Dyson, *Community*, 166; J.-P. Morel, "The Craftsman", in A. Giardina, ed., *The Romans* (Chicago: University of Chicago Press, 1993) 239-41.

in city elections.[17] In a few cases the trade *collegia* acted corporately to protect their interests.[18] This shows they had a significant role, although it is often noted that they were suppressed at various times. These suppressions, however, normally only involved recently formed *collegia* and usually occurred in periods of political unrest or when the groups were actually involved in disorder or strikes.[19]

Overall, it is likely that ties in Roman cities were more cross-cutting, given the strength of its patronage system that involved the association of people from different social strata. In contrast, ties in Greek cities were probably more reinforcing, given the weaker patronal structure, the ideology of democracy, and an emphasis on friendship and exchange between equals. A pattern of reinforcing ties is also likely in Greek cities since access to citizenship in their cities was quite restricted and their patriotism (which was restricted to their own particular city) was very parochial.[20] This contention that there was a significant difference in the pattern of relational ties between Greek and Roman societies and hence in the incidence of conflict development is also supported by the observation that *stasis* was regarded as a Greek rather than a Roman problem.[21]

It is likely, however, that there would be some variation in the pattern of relationships between Greek cities as well. Alexandria is a good example. It is probable that some of the

---

[17] For example, *CIL* 4.113, 206, 336, 373, 490, 497, 677, 710, 743, 826, 864, 960, 6672, 7164, 7273, 7473; cf. Jones, *Economy*, 41-3.

[18] MacMullen, *Social Relations*, 74-7; G. Alföldy, *The Social History of Rome* (Baltimore: Johns Hopkins University Press, 1985) 134; Morel, "Craftsman", 241. This is seen particularly in the case of the guild of salt merchants in Egypt (*P.Mich.* 5.245) and the strike of the bakers' guild in Ephesus (see Jones, *Economy*, 46).

[19] *Contra* Lintott, *Imperium*, 148. For example, Caesar suppressed the *collegia* following his defeat of Pompey (Suetonius *Iul.* 42.3) and Augustus suppressed newly formed ones soon after coming to power (Suetonius *Aug.* 32.1). Trajan's restrictions on *collegia* in Bithynia-Pontus appears related to disturbances there (Pliny *Ep.* 10.34; cf. Garnsey & Saller, *Empire*, 157). *Collegia* were suppressed in Pompeii in 59 CE following riots, while in Ephesus the bakers' guild was banned for striking (Tacitus *Ann.* 14.17; cf. Jones, *Economy*, 46).

[20] See, for example, Dio Chrys. *Or.* 34.21-3; Heraclitus *Ep.* 9; cf. Finley, *Politics*, 9; Sallares, *Ecology*, 189.

[21] Dio Chrysostom suggests that *stasis* was regarded by the Romans as a peculiarly Greek problem — Ἑλληνικὰ ἁμαρτήματα (*Or.* 38.38; cf. Winter, *Seek*, 90); cf. Finley, *Politics*, 105; cf. Sheppard, "*Homonoia*", 229; Woodhead, "Conflict", 2.

intensity of conflict in this city was linked to the segregation (physical, social and religious) and partial autonomy of the Jewish community.[22] The same could be said for Cyrene. Yet in at least two cities where the Jews and Greeks had positive relations, Sardis and Acmonia, there was a significant level of

---

[22] See Kasher, *The Jews*, 167, 312-21; L. H. Feldman, *Jew and Gentile in the Ancient World* (Princeton, NJ: Princeton University Press, 1993) 56-80. Although a small number of "progressive" Jews sought Greek citizenship, most did not (Smallwood, *Jews*, 225, 228, 234-5; Kasher, *The Jews*, 312-16; Feldman, *Jew*, 57-8; Barclay, *Jews*, 50-1); cf. Josephus *AJ* 18.159, 19.276, 20.100, 147. Kasher suggests that some Jews entered business partnerships with natives (*The Jews*, 70-1), but how common this was is unclear. Nevertheless, the Jews were largely organized into their own associations (ibid., 93). Although a large number of Jewish writings in Greek come from Alexandria this does not necessarily indicate that they were socially, religiously or politically integrated in the city as a whole. Such writings may represent a stretching of the boundaries but not their removal. In this regard, Barclay helpfully differentiates between assimilation (becoming like one's neighbors, i.e. social integration) and acculturation (adopting the language, and some of the ideology of one's neighbors) and notes that the two are not necessarily dependent on each other (*Jews*, 92). In particular, he notes that "Jews might acquire considerable expertise in Hellenistic *paideia* while exercising great caution in their social contacts with non-Jews" (ibid.). In any case, such writings may well represent the more "enlightened" view of the elite and intelligentsia (see Feldman, *Jew*, 56) and most probably comes from the more peaceful Ptolemaic period (Barclay, *Jews*, 126). Furthermore, the geographical separation of the Alexandrian Jews implies that a social, political and religious separation was also likely, given the strong integration of all these aspects in Greco-Roman city life (cf. Barclay, *Jews*, 117). This "segregation" is supported by Josephus, who claims that the Jews in Alexandria chose to be separate, and live together, so as to avoid contact with Gentiles (*BJ* 2.488; Feldman, *Jew*, 64). Feldman is also probably correct in suggesting that "the very size of the Jewish community in Egypt must have mitigated against assimilation", especially if they lived closely together (*Jew*, 65). Furthermore, the lack of concern writers, Philo in particular, show toward the issue of inter-marriage suggests that this social segregation was the norm (ibid., 77-9). Barclay, however, suggests a number of places where Philo condemns inter-marriage (*Jews*, 107-8). But his arguments are unconvincing and require much to be read into what are quite ambiguous statements. In any case, he earlier notes one case where a Jew who did have Alexandrian citizenship married a non-citizen Jewish woman (ibid., 67; cf. *CPJ* 144). If intermarriage was at all common, it would be expected in cases like this, where, presumably the man is more assimilated and marriage with another citizen would ensure his children were also.

integration.[23] In the case of Acmonia, the Jewish community was able to foster ties with members of the elite, gaining a prominent Roman as their patron (one who was also an Imperial Cult priestess), and the community itself was comprised of people drawn from across the social strata. Some of them held Roman citizenship, and at least one made public benefactions to the city.[24] In fact, one of the reasons given in chapter two for the Roman support of Jewish rights in general was that the Jews had "friends in high places".

In other words, the cases of Alexandria and Acmonia provide some support for the contention of the model regarding the importance of cross-cutting ties and the pattern of ethnic involvement. At the same time, the ability of a group to foster ties with a member of the elite seems to have been a major factor in avoiding conflict. Therefore, on the whole, while Roman cities may have more cross-cutting ties than Greek ones, wherever there was such a pattern, we would expect that conflict would be less prevalent.

II. RESOURCE CONCENTRATION

It is generally acknowledged that the first century CE was a time of great prosperity in the ancient world.[25] Yet, it remained largely a subsistence economy.[26] Keith Hopkins claims that there was a trickle down effect, such that the elite and wealthy fed slaves, erected buildings and spent money "which by its multiplier effects gave lots of people...enough or nearly enough money to buy food, shelter and clothing".[27]

---

[23] See Trebilco, *Communities*, 57, 83. Barclay, however, suggests that the Jews at Sardis sought to live close together and established a "close communal life" (*Jews*, 331) although he leaves open the possibility of assimilation.

[24] Trebilco, *Communities*, 82-3.

[25] Abbott & Johnson, *Municipal*, 143; Ward-Perkins, *Cities*, 35; Hopkins, "Economic Growth", 36; P. D. A. Garnsey & R. P. Saller, *The Early Principate: Augustus to Trajan* (Oxford: Clarendon, 1982) 28; M. Corbier, "City, Territory and Taxation", in J. Rich & A. Wallace-Hadrill, eds., *City and Country in the Ancient World* (London: Routledge, 1991), 211-12; Frayn, *Markets*, 163.

[26] I am using "subsistence economy" in terms of its most basic definition, namely, that "the unit of production, such as the peasant family, produces for its own immediate consumption" and "does not depend on the market for consumption". See *PDS* sv. "Subsistence Economy".

[27] Hopkins, "Economic Growth", 63.

Those at subsistence level, however, paid for everything whereas the wealthy sourced much of their food from their own estates and owned their own houses.[28] Therefore the effect of the "trickle down" may have been a widening socioeconomic gap. This is clear when the details are examined.

According to the elite, an annual income of 20,000 sesterces was the poverty line, but the great majority of the population would have been overjoyed to have had an annual income of 2,000 sesterces.[29] Day-laborers, for example, probably earned about 2-4 sesterces per day.[30] While this might be equivalent to 720-1,450 sesterces per annum, few would have worked all year.[31] Subsistence farmers, who would have made up the bulk of the population,[32] generally cultivated 2-10 *iugera* in an effort to produce enough for their own needs, and hopefully sell any surplus to purchase goods they could not produce themselves.[33] Cereal crops were usually sown at 4-8 *modii*

---

[28] Dio Chrys. *Or.* 7.105-6; *ILS* 5723, 6035; cf. Stambaugh, *Roman City*, 147.

[29] See, for example, Juvenal *Sat.* 9.140; cf. MacMullen, *Social Relations*, 120. Given the nature of the sources, costs and prices can only be estimated. After all, those mentioned may have been done so simply because they were extraordinary.

[30] Cicero *QRosc.* 28; cf. Stambaugh, *Roman City*, 154.

[31] B. W. Frier has estimated per capita income from annual subsistence annuities left in wills. Those recorded by the jurist Cervidius Scaevola generally have annuities of 376-600 sesterces, consisting of a monthly maintenance allowance and a yearly lump sum for clothing ("Subsistence Annuities and Per Capita Income in the Early Roman Empire" *CPhil* 88 [1988] 226-30). If this is taken as subsistence, then the amount needed to sustain a household of two adults and two children, given that allowances for children were 120-240 sesterces (ibid., 229), would be about 1,000-1,500 sesterces. However, these figures come from a later period and are probably over-inflated for the early first century.

[32] Since an ancient city comprised both an urban center and a rural area, farming can be considered an industry or occupation of the ancient city. Morel suggests that the proportion of the population engaged in agriculture was about 68% ("Craftsman", 229; cf. Hopkins, "Economic Growth", 37).

[33] *ILS* 7455; Varro *Rust.* 1.17.2; cf. J. M. Frayn, *Subsistence Farming in Roman Italy* (London: Centaur, 1979) 15-16. Engels claims that most ancient farmers were not at subsistence level and could retain something in the order of 30-50% of their surplus (*Roman Corinth*, 40-1). But his calculations are vague and are unsupported by any data. Compare, for example, Frayn, who notes that even in recent times most farms in small Italian villages are about 1.69 ha, i.e., 6.67 *iugera* (*Subsistence*, 29).

per *iugerum*, with a 4-8 fold yield in areas of reasonable fertility in good years. Assuming an average sowing rate of five *modii* per *iugerum*, and a five-fold yield, such a farmer might produce only 50-250 *modii* of grain, which would normally fetch about 150-750 sesterces.[34] Yet this does not allow for the prevalence of drought and disease in the Mediterranean area, nor for the need to retain some of the harvest for next season's seed, nor for the need to fallow land.[35] Most subsistence farms, however, were involved in mixed enterprises and consequently the returns may have been somewhat higher.[36]

The manufacture of goods, even in larger cities, appears to have been predominantly a cottage industry involving small workshop-residences. Although the largest workshop known may have had as many as seventy-five slaves, most would have had only a few.[37] This small scale meant that few

---

[34] Due to seasonal and other variations, grain could cost 1-48 sesterces per *modius* (Martial *Epigr.* 12.76; Hopkins, "Economic Growth", 45 n. 36; Duncan-Jones, *The Economy*, 50-1, 145-6; Garnsey & Saller, *Principate*, 11 n. 1). It was usually cheaper in rural areas, but 3 sesterces per *modius* is assumed to be the norm. On sowing rates and yields see Columella *Rust.* 2.9.1, 3.3.4; cf. Duncan-Jones, *The Economy*, 49; Garnsey & Saller, *Empire*, 80; L. Foxhall, "The Dependent Tenant: Land Leasing and Labour in Italy and Greece" *JRS* 80 (1990) 114 n.103. Sallares notes that Columella's figures for sowing rates are only a little higher than modern ones for farming in a similar semi-arid region (*Ecology*, 374-5). He estimates cereal yields as 400 kg/ha, which is comparable to the lower range of Columella's figures (ibid., 79), given than a *iugerum* is equivalent to 0.25 ha, and a *modius* is roughly 6.67 kg.

[35] See, for example, Garnsey & Saller, *Empire*, 6; Sallares, *Ecology*, 291-3, 379, 385-6, 393.

[36] These included cereals, vegetables, fruits, and grazing sheep for cheese and wool production. See Barker, Lloyd & Webley, "Landscape", 44-5; Frayn, *Subsistence*, 39-41, 44, 93; Duncan-Jones, *The Economy*, 34-6. Columella estimates the returns from grazing as, at best, 100 sesterces per *iugerum* (*Rust.* 3.3.3-4). Varro assumes that the returns on an average mixed farm were 150 sesterces per *iugerum*, but this is for a farm of 200 *iugera*, a size that allows more options in terms of productive enterprise (*Rust.* 3.2.16; cf. Frayn, *Subsistence*, 93). Both vineyards and olive groves produce huge yields, but are very capital expensive. See Cato *Rust.* 23.3-4; Varro *Rust.* 1.22.4; Columella, *Rust.* 3.3.5-13; cf. Duncan-Jones, *The Economy*, 40-8; Foxhall, "Dependent Tenant", 109.

[37] Packer, "Housing", 81, 85; Burford, *Craftsmen*, 62, 79; MacMullen, *Social Relations*, 98; Hopkins, "Economic Growth", 47; Garnsey & Saller, *Early Principate*, 29; Reynolds, "Cities", 48; Stambaugh, *Roman City*, 142, 151-2; Dyson, *Community*, 166, 176; Morel, "Craftsman", 232, 237; Laurence, *Pompeii*, 54-5.

artisans and merchants could have amassed great fortunes and, in fact, most seem to have lived near subsistence level. For example, Lucian claims that, by working hard and wearing themselves out from morning to evening with their toil, most artisans struggled to live of the wages they received.[38] However, while the vast majority of artisans, shopkeepers and merchants would have lived around subsistence level, some of the wealthy who owned and invested in commercial enterprises (instead of, or together with, their agricultural estates) profited substantially.[39]

---

[38] Lucian *Fug.* 17: πονοῦντας καὶ κάμνοντας ἔωθεν ἐς ἑσπέραν ἐπικεκυφότας τοῖς ἔργοις, μόγις ἀποζῶντας ἐκ τῆς τοιαύτης μισθαρνίας; also idem, *Somn.* 1; cf. Burford, *Craftsman*, 23, 27, 59, 143; MacMullen, *Social Relations*, 98-9; Morel, "Craftsman", 233; J. J. Meggitt, *Paul, Poverty and Survival* (SNTW; Edinburgh: T. & T. Clark, 1998), 44-6, 53-9.

[39] Lucian tells of a ship-owner who claims his vessel earned him over 250,000 sesterces annually (*Nav.* 13). Ship-owners who carried at least 324 tonnes of grain to Rome were also given taxation benefits (*Digest* 50.6.5.3-6 — in F. Meijer & O. van Nijf, *Trade, Transport and Society in the Ancient World: A Sourcebook* [London: Routledge, 1992] 76-7; cf. Jones, *Economy*, 58; Hopkins, "Economic Growth", 41; Duncan-Jones, *Structure*, 162). Meggitt underestimates the financial returns from ship-owning and ignores Lucian *Nav.* 13, although he elsewhere considers him sympathetically (*Poverty*, 44-9). Trade in marine or *murex* purple was also very profitable, but the raw materials were expensive and it was normally an Imperial monopoly involving Imperial slaves and *liberti* (see *New Docs.* 2.26-8; 3.54). This probably explains their social mobility (H. W. Pleket, "Urban Elites and Business in the Greek Part of the Roman Empire", in P. D. A. Garnsey, K. Hopkins & C. R. Whittaker, eds., *Trade in the Ancient Economy* [Berkeley: University of California Press, 1983] 142; Morel, "Craftsman", 221). It has often been argued that fortunes made from manufacture or trade were usually invested in land, since this was the only stable form of capital, and commercial enterprises, especially sea-trade, were precarious investments. See *ILS* 7519; Juvenal *Sat.* 14.265-304; Cato *Rust.* pref 1-4; Dio Chrys. *Or.* 46.5; Cicero *Off.* 1.151; the inscription in L. Casson, "The Role of the State in Rome's Grain Trade" in J. H. D'Arms & E. C. Kopff, eds., *The Seaborne Commerce of Ancient Rome* (Rome: American Academy in Rome, 1980) 33 and discussed in pp.26-7; cf. Jones, *Economy*, 30; MacMullen, *Social Relations*, 100; Hopkins, "Economic Growth", 60, 74; Stambaugh, "Social Relations", 77; D'Arms, *Commerce*, 15-16; Alföldy, *Social History*, 135; Veyne, *Bread*, 50-1; A. Giardina, "The Merchant", in idem, ed., *The Romans* (Chicago: University of Chicago Press, 1993) 246, 259-60. This was not always the case as the potential profits could outweigh the risks. Indeed, Plutarch (*Cat. Mai.* 5) claims that Cato considered investment in commercial enterprises to be much more reliable than agriculture, since the former were not at the mercy of the elements; cf. Plautus *Merc.* 73-9.

Juvenal, for example, mentions a man who owned five shops from which he claims he earned 400,000 sesterces annually.[40]

On the whole, therefore, the average income for the resident of a first century city, whether engaged in day-labor, farming, or small-scale manufacture or trade, was probably of the order of 750-1,200 sesterces annually. It has been suggested that this was the minimum required simply in order to survive. That this was indeed the case is clear when the figures for expenditure are also considered.

To purchase a modest house in Rome could cost 100,000-200,000 sesterces, while to purchase a small country villa could cost 40,000 sesterces.[41] Given annual incomes, renting a house was the only option for the vast majority of the population. In Italy, for example, the annual rent for an apartment was of the order of 400-500. This could represent something close to 40-50% of annual income, apart from the cost of food and clothing.[42]

The average working man consumed sixty *modii* of grain per year, as bread or gruel, and it is estimated that the average household living at subsistence level consumed about 150 *modii*.[43] If grain, on average, cost three sesterces

---

[40] Juvenal *Sat.* 1.103-6. However, Juvenal does not indicate what sort of shops they were. Such cases were probably exceptional, which is why attention was drawn to them. They cannot be taken as evidence of some sort of developing "middle class" for, as Burford notes, even those who owned and worked in their own workshops usually lived quite simply and did not earn very much (*Craftsman*, 59, 137).

[41] Martial *Epigr.* 3.52, 12.66; Varro *Rust.* 3.2.7; cf. Stambaugh, *Roman City*, 154. Unfortunately, most data on prices come from Rome where everything was more expensive than in the provinces (Martial *Epigr.* 4.66, 10.96, 11.54; Tacitus *Ann.* 3.55). Despite having no accurate figures for the cost of land, it is generally assumed to have been 500 sesterces per *iugerum*, depending on its location. A *iugerum* in Egypt, for example, only cost 141 sesterces in the first century CE. See Duncan-Jones, *The Economy*, 51; L. J. Keppie, *Colonisation and Veteran Settlement in Italy 47-14 BC* (London: British School at Rome, 1983) 76 n. 122.

[42] After his defeat of Pompey, Caesar gave a year's rent to those living in Italy, up to 500 sesterces (Suetonius *Iul.* 38.2; cf. Stambaugh, *Roman City*, 154). Figures for cities in other provinces are, naturally enough, difficult to attain, but it is possible that they were also of the order of those for Italy. They are most likely to be equivalent in the case of larger provincial cities.

[43] According to Seneca, working slaves were normally given about 5 *modii* of grain per month (*Ep.* 80.7); cf. Packer, "Housing", 88-9; Hopkins, "Economic Growth", 49 n. 36; Garnsey & Saller, *Principate*, 11

per *modius* (as mentioned above) this represents 450 sesterces per year. This would leave little, if any, from the average income when added to rental costs. In the case of subsistence farmers, it would represent something in excess of 60% of their total yield.

Consequently, more expensive foodstuffs, such as meat, poultry, or fish would have been quite uncommon.[44] An amphora of wine cost about five sesterces, but jugs of wine at cafés or inns were often 1-2 asses.[45] Furthermore, clothes had to be bought, even if infrequently, and tunics may have cost fifteen *denarii* (sixty sesterces).[46] Buying slaves was a considerable investment, since they began at 750 sesterces, with the average being 2,000. It could cost an extra 200 sesterces per year for food and clothing to support them. Consequently, it is unlikely that subsistence farmers or small-scale artisans would own any.[47] Social activities were quite cheap, but placed an additional strain on finances. For example, joining a *collegium* might cost 100 sesterces and an amphora of wine (a further five sesterces), and five asses monthly (fifteen sesterces annually). Office-bearers were expected to meet the expenses of banquets (four sesterces per head). Depending on the *collegium*, however, this assured them of a decent funeral costing somwhere between 300 and 2,000 sesterces.[48]

---

n. 1. Duncan-Jones notes that 5 *modii* per month is equivalent to an intake of 3,300 calories per day, which is quite satisfactory (*The Economy*, 147).

[44] Table birds: Varro *Rust.* 3.2.16, 3.6.3; cf. Frayn, *Markets*, 72-3. In the time of Tiberius, three mullets once sold for 30,000 sesterces, which prompted him to set a limit on salt-water fish of 24 *denarii* (96 sesterces) per pound (Suetonius *Tib.* 34; cf. Frayn, *Markets*, 69). The poverty of the common people, and the rarity of meat in their normal diet, is illustrated by Apuleius' description of a group salvaging the carcasses of bears which had died from some disease (*Met.* 4.14). Nevertheless, evidence that some meat was common in the average diet will be discussed in chapter 5 herein.

[45] Martial *Epigr.* 12.76; *CIL* 4.1679, 9.2689; cf. MacMullen, "Market-days", 339. An amphora was approximately 25.9 litres.

[46] Stambaugh, *Roman City*, 154. He does not, however, indicate what quality this garment might have been.

[47] See Duncan-Jones, *The Economy*, 42; Alföldy, *Social History*, 136-8; Stambaugh, *Roman City*, 154; Sallares, *Ecology*, 56.

[48] *CIL* 14.2112; cf. MacMullen, *Social Relations*, 79; Duncan-Jones, *The Economy*, 128; Frayn, *Markets*, 126-7. Another "social" activity, prostitutes, cost anywhere between 2-16 asses (*CIL* 9.2689; cf. MacMullen, "Market-days", 339; Dyson, *Community*, 176).

All of these extra costs, in addition to those for housing and the simplest food, show just how marginal the lives of many would have been.[49] The precariousness of their situation is even more apparent when the cost of taxation is also considered. Direct taxation in the Roman Empire was largely in two forms, a poll tax (*tributum capitis*) and a land tax (*tributum soli*). *Tributum capitis* was a flat annual rate on adults, with masters liable for slaves. It seems to have been low, perhaps eight sesterces.[50] *Tributum soli* was exacted either as a cash payment based on the value of the land and its improvements, or as a percentage of its produce, depending on the province. Where it was exacted in kind the rate varied from 10 to 20% of the harvest.[51] There were also a number of indirect taxes, such as custom duties (*portoria*), a tax on the sale or manumission of slaves, a tax on auctioned goods, and a tax on inheritance (for Romans).[52] Local city governments also collected their own tolls and imposed licence fees on market-stallholders, artisans, operators of bath houses and mines.[53]

---

[49] See also Meggitt, *Poverty*, 59-67, 99-100. While Meggitt and I largely concur on this, he has argued that the vast majority of the population (about 99%) lived *below* subsistence, and ignores some of the evidence which suggests that there was also a proportion who lived above, even comfortably above, that level (yet that need not mean there was a "middle class(, as Meggitt assumes). Unless it could be shown that there was a large-scale, progressive depopulation of the empire related to "poverty", it is probably better to assume that the bulk lived *around* subsistence.

[50] Josephus, *BJ* 7.218; Stambaugh & Balch, *Social World*, 78; Brunt, *Imperial*, 335-6; R. P. Duncan-Jones, *Structure & Scale in the Roman Economy* (Cambridge: Cambridge University Press, 1990) 187, 198; Corbier, "City", 217.

[51] Pleket, "Urban Elites", 132-3; Brunt, *Imperial*, 335-7; Duncan-Jones, *Structure*, 188-90. Judaea, Egypt, Asia, Sicily, Sardinia, Phrygia, Cyrene, Thrace and Pontus appear to have paid their taxes either largely or wholly in kind (see Duncan-Jones, *Structure*, 188-90; *contra* Brunt, *Imperial*, 335; Lintott, *Imperium*, 76).

[52] See, for example, Cicero *Att.* 2.16; Pliny *NH* 6.101; Tacitus *Ann.* 1.78, 11.35, 13.31; the inscription in Meijer & van Nijf, *Trade*, 80-1; *P.Lond.* inv.1562 verso (in Meijer & van Nijf, *Trade*, 78-9); *CISem* 2.3.3913 (in B. Levick, *The Government of the Roman Empire: A Sourcebook* [London: Croom Helm, 1988] 89-95); cf. Duncan-Jones, *Structure*, 193-6.

[53] Abbott & Johnson, *Municipal*, 138-40; Jones, *Economy*, 26-8; Reynolds, "Cities", 34-5; Duncan-Jones, *Structure*, 37; Dyson, *Community*, 163; Lintott, *Imperium*, 83-3; cf. *CISem* 2.3.3913 (in Levick, *Government*, 91).

Andrew Lintott claims that the normal level of taxation was not oppressive, unless harvests were low.[54] On the other hand, there are suggestions that some people were forced to sell their children into slavery to raise their tax dues, or to go into liquidation.[55] If Hopkins' estimate of the annual level of taxation as about fifteen sesterces per head is accurate, this clearly would have added to an already tenuous economic situation for many.[56]

Therefore many peasant farmers probably undertook seasonal work, especially given that the normal "manning ratios" were 1 to 25 *iugera* for cereals.[57] Those who lived in the town and commuted to their land could have supplemented their incomes through a trade such as pottery.[58] Co-operation and co-operatives between a number of small farmers also may have been able to offset some of the difficulties. In other words, arrangements may have been made for an exchange of labor during the harvest, mutual assistance in difficult times, and co-operative investment in larger items of equipment such as donkey-mills or teams of draft animals.[59]

Nevertheless, the average subsistence farmer would have needed the support of a wealthy land-owner. Tenancy relationships may have been the only way for many of them to produce enough in a good year, obtain injections of capital, or avoid starvation in a bad year by going into debt to a landlord. Such arrangements might also have been

---

[54] Lintott, *Imperium*, 95-6; cf. Veyne, who suggests that it was oppressive only during the reign of greedy emperors (*Bread*, 360).

[55] See Tacitus *Ann.* 4.72; cf. M. H. Crawford, "Rome and the Greek World: Economic Relationships" *EHR* 30 (1977) 49; Brunt, *Imperial*, 340. Crawford even suggests that the State may have actually encouraged the selling of children ("Rome", 49-50).

[56] K. Hopkins, "Taxes and Trade in the Roman Empire (200 BC-AD 400)" *JRS* 70 (1980) 104, 120; cf. Alcock, *Graecia*, 21.

[57] Varro *Rust.* 1.17.2; Columella *Rust.* 2.12.7-8; Dio Chrys. *Or.* 7.11; Pliny *Ep.* 9.37; cf. R. MacMullen, "Peasants during the Principate" *ANRW* 2.1 (1974) 254-7; Hopkins, "Taxes", 104 n.12; Duncan-Jones, *The Economy*, 39; Alföldy, *Social History*, 144-5; Garnsey & Saller, *Empire*, 72, 76, 111-12; Shelton, *As the Romans*, 7; Foxhall, "Dependant Tenant", 97, 105; Alcock, *Graecia*, 107, 113.

[58] Jones, *Economy*, 31; Frayn, *Subsistence*, 139; Duncan-Jones, *The Economy*, 260; Tomlinson, *From Mycenae*, 2.

[59] MacMullen, "Peasants", 257; Frayn, *Subsistence*, 21, 140-1; Garnsey & Woolf, "Patronage", 156. A pair of oxen could cost 10,000 *denarii* (Frayn, *Markets*, 156). It is possible that the *eranos*-system may have been called upon by Greek subsistence farmers.

advantageous where the market was "subject to political influences".[60] For the landlord it was an efficient system of management. As Lin Foxhall notes, "slaves, who would be fed, clothed and housed regardless of how hard they worked, might not have the same level of motivation as tenants". The latter had to work harder to produce enough for their own needs and to give the landlord his share.[61]

A similar set of circumstances would also hold for the majority of the traders, artisans, shopkeepers and merchants in towns. Those who became clients of a wealthy patron might receive a substantial daily allowance, while some provincial cities copied Rome in providing a grain-dole to citizens.[62] Especially in Roman towns, however, the vast majority of the artisans, merchants and shopkeepers were either slaves or freedpersons.[63] Such an arrangement occurred because masters generally trained their slaves to perform special skills or crafts in order to make them more valuable for re-sale or for leasing out.[64]

Most shops and businesses were probably rented, and the evidence from Pompeii shows that many of these were rooms in elite houses that had been divided off and rented to

---

[60] Hopkins, "Economic Growth", 76; Garnsey & Woolf, "Patronage", 160; Foxhall, "Dependent Tenant", 97-9, 101, 111-12. In the case of Greek farmers, in particular, seasonal or wage labor was also an important income supplement (Sallares, *Ecology*, 54-6).

[61] Foxhall, "Dependent Tenant", 101-2; cf. Columella *Rust.* 1.7.3-5; except where the tenants' debts became overwhelming and they kept the produce rather than pay rent (Pliny *Ep.* 10.37).

[62] Juvenal *Sat.* 1.120-1; Abbott & Johnson, *Municipal*, 146; Balsdon, *Life*, 22; Jones, *Economy*, 47. Significant cash allowances for clients may have been found only at Rome.

[63] For example *ILS* 1788, 7414, 7420a, 7428, 7486, 7491, 7496, 7503, 7539, 7558, 7600, 7626; the inscriptions in Casson, "Grain Trade", 33 and discussed in pp. 26-7; cf. S. R. Joshel, "The Occupations and Economic Roles of Freedmen in the Early Roman Empire: A Study in Roman Social and Economic Patterns" (unpublished PhD dissertation, Rutgers University, 1977), 201-2; D'Arms, *Commerce*, 16; Alföldy, *Social History*, 136; Stambaugh, *Roman City*, 97; Dyson, *Community*, 201-3; Morel, "Craftsman", 217; J. F. Gardner, *Being a Roman Citizen* (London: Routledge, 1993) 36.

[64] Balsdon, *Life*, 134-5; Alföldy, *Social History*, 141; Stambaugh, *Roman City*, 139; Dyson, *Community*, 166, 202; Gardner, *Roman Citizen*, 31; Morel, "Craftsman", 226.

clients for this purpose.[65] Therefore, members of the elite were involved in commerce by providing premises, investing capital and milking profits, while acting as silent partners or having their slaves or freedpersons act as their agents.[66] In fact, *operae*, an agreed number of days' work for their patron, was usually a contractual obligation imposed upon *liberti* at manumission. For those skilled in various crafts and trades, *operae* usually involved providing their skills for their patrons.[67] While patrons normally provided for their *liberti* when they performed *operae*, if the patron's expectations for *operae* were too demanding this could seriously hinder the viability of the artisan's business.[68]

Not all artisans and merchants had patrons, but those who did not might own their shop only because it had been bequeathed to them in their master's or patron's will.[69] Members of the elite also leased out ships which they owned, or they provided capital for their dependents to purchase them. For example, Cato loaned money or underwrote ships if a group of fifty ship-owners formed a company, in which he also purchased shares.[70]

The overall picture that emerges of the economic life of the first century city was that the majority of the population were engaged in small scale production around subsistence level. They relied heavily on the support of the wealthy who

---

[65] See, for example, *ILS* 5723, 6035; cf. Reynolds, "Cities", 20; Shelton, *As the Romans*, 60; Wallace-Hadrill, "Elites and Trade", 250, 266.

[66] For example, *ILS* 1949; Cicero *Att.* 5.21-6.1, *Font.* 5.11; *Historia Augusta Pertinax* 3.1-4 (in Meijer & van Nijf, *Trade*, 71); the inscriptions in Casson, "Grain Trade", 33; cf. Jones, *Economy*, 41; Burford, *Craftsmen*, 39-40; MacMullen, *Social Relations*, 99; D'Arms, *Commerce*, 16, 154, 169; Pleket, "Urban Elites", 133, 141; Stambaugh, *Roman City*, 97, 140; Wallace-Hadrill, "Elites and Trade", 250, 266; Dyson, *Community*, 203; Frayn, *Markets*, 117-18; Morel, "Craftsman", 222-3.

[67] Burford, *Craftsmen*, 38; Garnsey & Saller, *Early Principate*, 24; Gardner, *Roman Citizen*, 20, 31.

[68] Gardner, *Roman Citizen*, 27-8, 30-2. Burford suggests that the obligation could be "commuted to a cash payment, but even so the freedman [sic] suffered a limitation to his [sic] earning powers" (*Craftsmen*, 38).

[69] For example *ILS* 7029; Trimalchio in Petronius' *Satyricon*; cf. Stambaugh & Balch, *Social World*, 117; Wallace-Hadrill, "Elites and Trade", 266-7. Patronage was much less important for Greek artisans (Burford, *Craftsmen*, 19).

[70] Plutarch *Cat. Mai.* 6; cf. the inscriptions in Casson, "Grain Trade", 33; Pleket, "Urban Elites", 135-7.

could supply them with the property and capital investment that they needed. Indeed, it is likely that many subsistence farmers, artisans, or merchants could not have survived without support from wealthy investors and landlords.[71] There was one real exception to the dichotomy between the minority who possessed wealth, property and politico-legal resources and the majority engaged in various agricultural and commercial activities and were largely dependent on the former group for their economic survival. The exception was the soldier of the late Republic who became the veteran settler of the early Principate.

Julius Caesar raised the annual pay of ordinary legionaries to 225 *denarii* (900 sesterces).[72] While there were some deductions, it was still about subsistence level for the average family and it clearly was enough for a soldier's means, since many could afford to send presents home to their families.[73] Many of these soldiers also profited enormously from their campaigns.[74] Large donatives were the normal means of assuring the support of troops during the Civil Wars. Thus, a man who had served with Caesar in Gaul and was discharged after Philippi could have retired with

---

[71] See, for example, Stambaugh, "Social Relations", 82; Garnsey & Woolf, "Patronage", 153-4.

[72] For example, Polybius 6.39.12; Tacitus *Ann.* 1.17-35; cf. G. R. Watson, *The Roman Soldier* (London: Thames & Hudson, 1969) 89-91; Garnsey & Saller, *Early Principate*, 8; J.-M. Carrié, "The Soldier", in A. Giardina, ed., *The Romans* (Chicago: University of Chicago Press, 1993) 121; J. Patterson, "Military Organization and Social Change in the Later Roman Republic", in J. Rich & G. Shipley, eds., *War and Society in the Roman World* (London: Routledge, 1993) 99, 104.

[73] See, for example, Polybius 6.39.15; Tacitus *Ann.* 1.17; cf. Watson, *Roman Soldier*, 90; J. L. Jones, "The Roman Army" in S. Benko & J. J. O'Rourke, eds., *The Catacombs and the Colosseum* (Valley Forge, PA: Judson, 1971) 208; Stambaugh, "Social Relations", 91; Duncan-Jones, *Structure*, 44; Carrié, "Soldier", 121, 124. That Domitian limited the total sum in the savings scheme to 1,000 sesterces shows that prior to this deposits could have been much larger (Suetonius *Dom.* 7.3; cf. Patterson, "Military Organization", 97).

[74] Caesar occasionally gave them prisoners as slaves, as well as various donatives at the end of campaigns. In 51 BCE he gave each legionary 200 sesterces, and in 49 BCE he gave 2,000 sesterces. Following his defeat of Pompey, in 46 BCE, he gave a large sum, although the sources are unclear as to whether it was 20,000 or 24,000 sesterces. Appian *BCiv.* 2.47, 53, 102; Dio Cassius 43.21.3; Suetonius *Iul.* 26.3, 38.1; cf. Keppie, *Colonisation*, 41-2; de Blois, *Roman Army*, 48.

considerable cash reserves (50,000 sesterces or more).[75]
Indeed, soldiering was regarded as an extremely profitable
enterprise even in Imperial times when the rewards were
lower due to fewer chances to acquire booty.[76]

For the veteran of the Republic period, savings of this
magnitude, together with their settlement grants, placed
them in a comfortable position. They could enter civilian life
and engage in agriculture or commerce with few financial
worries, and be less dependent, if at all, on elite-patrons for
their economic survival. This was especially the case when,
prior to 13 BCE, they were also given land-grants upon
discharge.[77] Caesarean grants seem to have been about

---

[75] Brutus and Cassius gave 6,000 sesterces to each of their
legionaries and 30,000 to centurions on the eve of the battle of Philippi
(42 BCE). After the first battle Brutus gave a further 4,000 sesterces and
promised them the chance to plunder two Macedonian cities. When their
camp was plundered during fighting, Brutus gave them 20,000 sesterces
(and 100,000 to centurions) in compensation (Appian *BCiv.* 4.100, 118,
120; cf. Keppie, *Colonisation*, 43). Antony's troops nearly rioted in 44 BCE
when he offered them only 400 sesterces each. Many joined Octavian,
who gave his troops 10,000 sesterces each and offered another 20,000
sesterces before the battle of Philippi. Both he and Antony promised
their troops that if victorious they would go home wealthy. Indeed, after
their victory, they plundered their opponents' camp and took their
donatives as booty (Appian *BCiv.* 3.94, 4.126; Dio Cassius 45.13.2-4,
46.46.6; cf. Keppie, *Colonisation*, 41-2). During the proscriptions after
the war soldiers profited handsomely from the head-money offered.
Rewards of 100,000 sesterces were given for the capture of each
proscribed person, although Antony paid 1,000,000 sesterces to those
who killed Cicero (Appian *BCiv.* 4.11, 20; cf. Keppie, *Colonisation*, 41).
While awaiting settlement after Philippi, veterans living in Rome had
their rent remitted up to 2,000 sesterces or a rebate of 20% if they lived
in Italy. They were also given cash and houses that had been confiscated
from the proscribed (Appian *BCiv.* 5.13; Dio Cassius 48.9.5, 49.14.2-3).

[76] See Juvenal *Sat.* 16.1-3; cf. L. J. Keppie, *The Making of the
Roman Army: From Republic to Empire* (London: Batsford, 1984) 77;
Carrié, "Soldier", 120-4; Patterson, "Military Organization", 97-8.

[77] Juvenal maintains that following the Punic wars veterans were
given only two *iugera*, which he claims was enough to support the
veteran, his family and some slaves. But he complains that in his own
time such a plot was regarded as sufficient merely for a house-garden
(Juvenal *Sat.* 14.161-72). Given the details regarding subsistence
agriculture discussed above, this is clearly satirical exaggeration. It is
also not supported by other writers. Livy, for example, notes that
veterans were given two *iugera* for each year they had served (Livy,
31.49.5; cf. Keppie, *Colonisation*, 39; idem, *The Making*, 55). More
specifically, at the colonies of Mutina, Parma and Saturnia (183 BCE)
ordinary legionary veterans received grants of five, eight and ten *iugera*

twenty-five *iugera*, while grants made by the Triumvirs and Augustus were usually fifty *iugera*. But the size may have varied somewhat depending on the fertility of the land.[78]

Since most veterans of the Triumviral period had previously been discharged as veterans, and some had already been settled, it is likely that they would have received fresh allocations. These probably would have been larger.[79] Before the battle of Philippi, the Triumvirs promised their troops eighteen of the most fertile and prosperous cities in Italy for colonies. In light of this, and the natural desire for Italians to settle in Italy, any veteran who settled in the provinces must have been given a very generous grant.[80]

Some claim that most veterans, even with fifty *iugera*, would have lived on their property, or nearby and commuted each day, and worked it themselves with a couple of slaves.[81] Others suggest that most veterans had some education and expected a life of ease and an increase in status following service. Thus, they probably leased it to tenants and lived in town.[82] The latter is more likely when the economic details are considered. Two *iugera* probably would have been used for a farmhouse and buildings. If sixteen *iugera* were sown to

---

respectively, and this was probably combined with access to *saltus* (Livy, 39.55.6-9; cf. Keppie, *Colonisation*, 91; Patterson, "Military Organization", 100). At the colony of Vibo (192 BCE) they received fifteen *iugera* each (Livy 35.40.5-6).

[78] Although Caesar's grants in 63 and 59 BCE are said to have been only ten *iugera*, this assumes that there were 5,000 colonists (Cicero *Att.* 2.16; cf. Keppie, *Colonisation*, 92). But this would appear excessive. See Keppie, *Colonisation*, 13, 76 n. 122, 93-5; cf. Cicero *Phil.* 5.53; Patterson, "Military Organization", 103. Augustus claims in *Res Gestae* that he spent 860 million sesterces on land for 155,000 veterans. If land cost 500 sesterces per *iugerum* that would be 11 *iugera* each. But this does not allow for land that did not need to be purchased (see Duncan-Jones, *Structure*, 125). Keppie notes that 14 colonies founded in Italy after Philippi were centuriated into 50 *iugera* blocks (*Colonisation*, 99).

[79] Keppie, *Colonisation*, 62-4.

[80] Appian *BCiv.* 4.3; Keppie, *Colonisation*, 1, 61, 122; J. C. Mann, *Legionary Recruitment and Veteran Settlement during the Principate* (London: Institute of Archaeology, 1983) 5-7. Although there were Gallic veterans settled by the Triumvirs, it is unlikely that only they received land in the provinces. See Keppie, *Colonisation*, 55, 98; cf. Mann, *Legionary*, 3-4; P. A. Brunt, *Italian Man-Power 225 BC-AD 14* (2nd ed.; Oxford: Clarendon, 1987) 237, 240.

[81] Keppie, *Colonisation*, 124-6; J. E. Stambaugh, "Graeco-Roman Cities", *ABD* 1.1047.

[82] See, for example, Horace *Sat.* 1.1.28-32; Frayn, *Subsistence*, 96; Veyne, *Bread*, 38; Carrié, "Soldier", 129-32.

cereals, sixteen left fallow and sixteen grazed, the annual
returns would be in the order of 2,750 sesterces.[83]
Alternatively, it is possible that seven *iugera* could be used
for a vineyard. Capital investment for this would be quite
high, but so would the returns — such a vineyard could
return a nett profit of 2,125 sesterces.[84] If, then, seven *iugera*
were used for a vineyard, thirteen were grazed, fourteen
sown to cereals and fourteen left fallow, returns would be
about 4,430 sesterces.[85] In both of these scenarios, the
returns are sufficient for the veteran to have his land worked
by a tenant and two slaves, who would keep about 900
sesterces annually, and leave him with enough for a very
comfortable life in town. Besides, since many soldiers learned
particular crafts during their service, such as pottery, baking,
and construction, they may well have rented out their land
and worked at these crafts in the town. Some, of course,
would have invested in trade and commerce.[86]

---

[83] This figure assumes that sowing rates were probably higher (6
modii per *iugerum*) due to the colonist's large capital reserves, that there
was a five-fold yield producing 384 *modii*, (plus 96 *modii* for seed), grain
sold for 3 sesterces per *modius*, and the average returns for grazing were
100 sesterces per *iugerum* (as mentioned above)

[84] Columella suggests that a seven *iugera* vineyard required a total
capital investment of about 32,500 sesterces, including no returns for
two years, but in this case the cost of the land need not be figured in. He
estimates a nett return over six years of 55,320 sesterces, about 4,755
sesterces or 900 sesterces per *iugerum* based on a yield of 3 *cullei* or
wine (1,866 litres) per *iugerum* at a 300 sesterces per *culleus* plus 3,000
sesterces for sales of rooted cuttings (*Rust.* 3.3.5-13; cf. Duncan-Jones,
The Economy, 40-1). Duncan-Jones, however, claims that there are flaws
in Columella's sums. In particular, he suggests that a yield of 3 *cullei* per
iugerum is too high (more like 1.17 *cullei*), that the price of 300 sesterces
per *culleus* is too low (more like 540 sesterces), and there would not be
much income from the sale of rooted cuttings in the provinces. Therefore
he estimates the costs as 328 sesterces per *iugerum*, the gross returns
at 631.8 sesterces per *iugerum*, and hence a nett return of 303.8
sesterces per *iugerum*. For a 7 *iugerum* vineyard, the nett profit would be
2,125 sesterces (*The Economy*, 41-8, 53-6). Nevertheless, returns could
fluctuate wildly depending on the wine quality.

[85] As stated a 7 *iugera* vineyard would return a nett profit of about
2,125 sesterces, while 13 *iugera* grazed would return 1,300 sesterces. If
grain was planted at 6 *modii* per *iugerum* and yields were five-fold
(allowing for 84 *modii* to be kept for seed) the nett yield would be 336
modii. At 3 sesterces per *iugerum* that is a nett return of 1,008
sesterces.

[86] Horace *Sat.* 1.1.4; Jones, "Roman Army", 194-5, 206; Frayn,
Subsistence, 95.

In summary, therefore, the vast majority of the population was engaged in various small-scale agricultural and commercial enterprises, largely living at subsistence level and relying on the support of the wealthy for property, capital investment, and political and legal influence. Without this support many may not have survived, especially in bad years or following natural disasters. Co-operation between a number of small farmers or members of a trade *collegium* may have supplemented this. Only civil war veterans would be something of an exception, but they may well have joined the ranks of the local elite.

According to the preliminary model constructed in chapter one, we would expect a greater incidence of conflict, presumably in the form of "class conflict", in a society where resources are concentrated in the hands of a minority. While conflicts between "haves" and "have-nots" were prevalent in the first century, they were not related to notions of an egalitarian utopia, but to specific problems such as debt, land-shortage, and the failure of food supplies. The few labor disputes that have been recorded, such as strikes, relate to broken agreements between the State and the particular trade guild.[87] Similarly, when a riot erupted during a famine because the price of grain had risen very sharply, the accusation against the wealthy was that they were hoarding grain in an attempt to increase their profits.[88]

What these examples demonstrate is that conflicts related to resource concentration were, in real terms, nothing more than simple role conflicts. In fact, there is no clear evidence to suggest that there was any genuine questioning of the existing social system and its institutions, such as is normally presupposed by the sociological notion of "class conflict".[89] Given the strength of the Roman patronage

---

[87] See Burford, *Craftsmen*, 147, 241 n.392.

[88] See Dio Chrys. *Or.* 46; cf. Burford, *Craftsmen*, 155; MacMullen, *Social Relations*, 66; Finley, *Politics*, 109-10; Alföldy, *Social History*, 155; Philostratus *VS* 526.

[89] See Garnsey & Saller, *Roman Empire*, 109; Johnson & Dandeker, "Patronage", 223; Wallace-Hadrill, "Patronage", 69. Such an analysis is contrary to the arguments of C. L. Lee, "Social Unrest and Primitive Christianity" in S. Benko & J. J. O'Rourke, eds., *The Catacombs and the Colosseum* (Valley Forge, PA: Judson, 1971) 123-9; M. Reinhold, "Usurpation of Status and Status Symbols in the Roman Empire" *Historia* 20 (1971) 275-6; R. F. Newbold, "Social Tension at Rome in the Early Years of Tiberius' Reign" *Athenaeum* 52 (1974) 120-3, 134. These scholars argue that there was a serious, if latent or implicit,

system, and its ideology, it would be reasonable to assume that such conflicts between the classes may have been much less common among the Romans than among the Greeks.[90] While this may well be the case, because the pattern of resource concentration was probably fairly consistent for both Greek and Roman cities in the first century, this probably cannot be considered to have been a significant factor in determining the different incidence of conflict between different cities.

III. LEGAL & POLITICAL STRUCTURES OF CITIES

The preliminary model claims that conflict is less prevalent in societies with a more egalitarian organization of authority. Yet, it was suggested that an egalitarian pattern combined with reinforcing ties may result in a higher incidence of conflict than a hierarchical system where there were cross-cutting ties. There were considerable differences in the political and administrative structures of Greek cities (*civitates stipendiariae*, *civitates liberae*) and Roman cities

---

class-conflict due to a rising "middle-class" frustrated by the inequalities of the system which denied them social advancement, in a general climate of increased social mobility. Despite some social mobility in the early Imperial period, opportunities were still *extremely* limited and the bulk of the population, struggling at subsistence level, had no option but to accept their position. In any case, most of the social mobility of this period was downward (MacMullen, *Social Relations*, 101, 119; Stambaugh, "Social Relations", 83; Finley, *Politics*, 27-8; Alföldy, *Social History*, 151; Garnsey & Saller, *Roman Empire*, 123; Rohrbaugh, "Pre-Industrial", 128). Furthermore, according to classical Marxist theory, the questioning of the legitimacy of the social system only occurs with the development of "class consciousness", that is, where the disadvantaged become aware of their common conditions and interests as a social group. But such a development only occurs when the classes are polarized and the awareness of the injustice is raised by an intellectual group separate from the ruling class (Robertson, *Sociology*, 263; Waters & Crook, *Sociology*, 145-6; cf *PDS* sv. "Class Consciousness"). These conditions do not appear to have existed in the first century. See Carney, *Shape*, 94; D. G. Horrell, *The Social Ethos of the Corinthian Correspondence: Interests and Ideology from 1 Corinthians to 1 Clement* (Edinburgh: T. & T. Clark, 1996) 67.

[90] The Roman patronage system, and the relationships it entailed, specifically aimed to prevent social rebellion (Dion. Hal. *Ant. Rom.* 2.9.1; Finley, *Politics*, 45; Alföldy, *Social History*, 153; Garnsey & Saller, *Roman Empire*, 107; Wallace-Hadrill, "Patronage", 67). On the other hand, the conflict over grain prices that was discussed above took place in a Greek city (Dio Chrys. *Or.* 46).

(*municipia, coloniae, colonia iuris Italici*). Each will be examined in turn.

1. Greek Cities

The majority of the cities in the East were *civitates stipendiariae*. This designation meant that they were subject to the various forms of taxation, in particular the *tributum capitis* and *tributum soli*. It also meant that they were subject to the direct supervision, control, and interference of the provincial governors.[91] When a Hellenistic city was declared a *civitas libera*, it received a charter of privileges which normally included the clause *suis legibus uti*, meaning that it would maintain its traditional constitution and legal practices. It also meant that the state, in the guise of the provincial governor, generally would not interfere in the administration of the city.[92]

Such a designation was advantageous because, theoretically, such cities were not subject to the whims of governors and they were granted some economic privileges.[93] Under the Republic, most of these cities were classified as *libera et immunis*, meaning they were also free from *tributum soli*, but this became increasingly rare from the time of the Triumvirs.[94] Yet, these privileges were not always recognized by governors, many of whom did interfere in the affairs of these cities from the period of the late Republic.[95]

---

[91] Abbott & Johnson, *Municipal*, 48; Jones, *Economy*, 6; Reynolds, "Cities", 18.

[92] Abbott & Johnson, *Municipal*, 43; Jones, *Economy*, 6; Garnsey & Saller, *Empire*, 28; Reynolds, "Cities", 18; Lintott, *Imperium*, 19. Capital cases, however, were still to be referred to the governor (Jones, *Economy*, 20).

[93] See, for example Cicero *Att.* 6.2; Abbott & Johnson, *Municipal*, 44-5, 50-3; Lintott, *Imperium*, 38-9, 92. One such benefit was exemption from the requirement to billet troops. That this constituted a huge financial burden to cities can be seen from bribes, as high as 4.8 million sesterces, which were offered to governors to avoid it (Cicero *Att.* 5.21.7; Dio Cassius 47.14.3; cf. Lintott, *Imperium*, 93). Other benefits included the right to mint their own copper coins and impose customs duties.

[94] Abbott & Johnson, *Municipal*, 39-40; Sherwin-White, *Citizenship*, 245; Jones, *Economy*, 6; Garnsey & Saller, *Empire*, 28; Lintott, *Imperium*, 38.

[95] Abbott & Johnson, *Municipal*, 80; Veyne, *Bread*, 364; Lintott, *Imperium*, 57, 64.

Besides, it was possible that any of these privileges could be revoked at any time.[96]

Administratively, there was much variation between Hellenistic cities. Nevertheless, all had some pattern of elected magistrates, an elected council (*boulē*), and a popular assembly (*demos*) where the citizens met to hear reports and vote on proposals from the council.[97] The Romans imposed property qualifications on membership of the council, and encouraged some development towards oligarchy and away from strict democracy. But in most cases the ordinary citizens still retained a considerable degree of political and legal competence.[98] Nevertheless, under such a system an individual or a small minority group would effectively be quite powerless to initiate change.

2. Roman Cities

Most of the grants of the title *municipium* took place under Caesar and the Triumvirs.[99] Administratively, such cities were free to adopt a Roman constitution and legal code, but their citizens were still subject to *tributum soli*.[100] *Municipia* were politically autonomous. Nevertheless, their citizens had the right to trade with and to marry Romans and to pass on their estates according to Roman inheritance laws.[101] They

[96] See, for example, Suetonius *Aug.* 47; Abbott & Johnson, *Municipal*, 41; Jones, *Economy*, 7; Reynolds, "Cities", 18.

[97] See Abbott & Johnson, *Municipal*, 75; Jones, *Economy*, 11; Finley, *Politics*, 70, 76; Stambaugh, "Cities", 1044; Ferguson, *Backgrounds*, 41; Lintott, *Imperium*, 146-7.

[98] See, for example, Dio Chrys. *Or.* 34.16, 48.1f; Heraclitus, *Ep.* 7; cf. Abbott & Johnson, *Municipal*, 49, 70, 75; Jones, *Economy*, 12-3, 95; Finley, *Politics*, 70-1, 76; Reynolds, "Cities", 26; Brunt, *Imperial*, 270; Alcock, *Graecia*, 150-1. The continuing political importance of the *demos* is also presupposed by Plutarch's *Praecepta Reipublicae Gerendae* 798A-825E (cf. Lintott, *Imperium*, 147).

[99] Suetonius *Aug.* 47; Abbott & Johnson, *Municipium*, 8; Sherwin-White, *Citizenship*, 244; Brunt, *Man-Power*, 239.

[100] Cicero *QFr.* 1.1.11-12; Gellius *NA* 16.13.6-7; Tacitus *Hist.* 4.74; Abbott & Johnson, *Municipal*, 9; Jones, *Economy*, 27; F. G. B. Millar, *The Emperor in the Roman World* (London: Duckworth, 1977) 400; Levick, *Government*, 73; Garnsey & Saller, *Empire*, 27; Shelton, *As the Romans*, 271; Lintott, *Imperium*, 67.

[101] A. N. Sherwin-White, "The Roman Citizenship. A Survey of its Development into a World Franchise" *ANRW* 1.2 (1972) 25; Stambaugh, "Graeco-Roman", 1047; Lintott, *Imperium*, 161. In fact, Sherwin-White claims that Latin rights can be summed up by the ideas of *commercium*,

were rare outside Latin-speaking provinces, except for Stobi in Macedonia.[102]

A *colonia* differed from a Roman *municipium* in that it involved settlers sent out from Rome. Generally *coloniae* were planted in order to settle veteran soldiers, although Caesar also settled many *liberti* to reduce Rome's population.[103] Most were planted by Caesar, Augustus, and the Triumvirs when there were large numbers of veterans, but few were established after 13 BCE when the land grant was replaced with a cash gratuity.[104]

Coloniae were normally founded in established towns to which extra *territorium* was added. Native residents were seldom granted citizenship except, perhaps, the local elites.[105] *Coloniae* were strictly autonomous and governors were not to interfere. Their citizens had full Roman rights — they entered Roman marriages, were able to trade, and their estates were subject to Roman inheritance laws. Administratively, *coloniae* adopted a Roman constitution, legal code, and judicial structure. The main governing body was the council made up of ex-magistrates (*ordo decurionum*), which proposed legislation and nominated candidates for the magistracies, namely, *aediles, quaestores* and *duoviri*.[106]

Aediles controlled the markets and its prices, leased shops and stalls, tested weights and measures, and were responsible for maintaining public buildings and roads. *Quaestores* were the city treasurers. *Duoviri* were judges, and they organized and conducted the public meetings. In some colonies, the Emperor was elected sole *duumvir* and he

conubium and *ius mutandae civitatis* ("Survey", 25).

[102] Sherwin-White, *Citizenship*, 229; Jones, *Economy*, 8; Brunt, *Man-Power*, 250; Garnsey & Saller, *Empire*, 27. Although Claudius did grant citizenship to many Greeks, the grants were not to whole communities, as Sherwin-White notes (*Citizenship*, 246).

[103] Gellius *NA* 16.13.8; Abbott & Johnson, *Municipal*, 4; Sherwin-White, "Survey", 45; Jones, *Economy*, 3; Garnsey & Saller, *Early Principate*, 11; Hopkins, "Economic Growth", 67; Keppie, *Colonisation*, 1; Mann, *Legionary*, 2-3, 6; Reynolds, "Cities", 21-2; Owens, *The City*, 8;

[104] *Res Gestae* 5.28.1-2; Jones, *Economy*, 3; Mann, *Legionary*, 50; Brunt, *Man-Power*, 243; Nicolet, "Citizen", 31.

[105] Appian *BCiv.* 2.140; Strabo *Geog.* 12.3.11; Abbott & Johnson, *Municipal*, 138; Jones, *Economy*, 3; Sherwin-White, *Citizenship*, 248-9; Brunt, *Man-Power*, 247, 254; Reynolds, "Cities", 22.

[106] Gellius *NA* 16.13.8; Abbott & Johnson, *Municipal*, 72; Jones, *Economy*, 13; Garnsey & Saller, *Early Principate*, 2; Alföldy, *Social History*, 130-1; Dyson, *Community*, 159.

appointed a prominent local as his *praefectus iure dicundo*, and gave a lavish gift for the honor.[107] Those men elected to one of the magistracies normally had to be freeborn Roman citizens, at least thirty years old and of good character (no criminal record or engaged in a demeaning occupation). The property requirement for office varied with the size and wealth of the town. Usually it was 100,000 sesterces but in small towns it could be as low as 20,000.[108] Elected magistrates were expected to make civic benefactions or provide games, with payments usually being in the range of 4,500-35,000 sesterces.[109]

The voting rights of Roman citizens were mainly confined to electing magistrates and these votes were *en bloc* by *curia* (voting ward). Citizens were allocated to the *curiae* on the basis of their age and wealth, so that the whole system was strongly weighted in favor of the wealthier strata. The assembly of the people could still vote on motions brought by the council, but they could not make or debate proposals, and it only met when called by a *duumvir*.[110] Hence even their block vote was little more than a rubber stamp.

The designation of a *colonia* with the title *ius Italicum* first appears in the time of Caesar, and is found in the East where colonization was less prolific. In fact, such a grant was quite rare. It seems to have been given only for extreme loyalty, usually during the civil war period.[111] In light of this, Barbara Levick suggests that it was meant to help

---

[107] Cicero *Leg.* 3.6-8; Dio Chrys. *Or.* 46.14; *MW* 454.52-9 (in Levick, *Government*, 26-7); cf. Jones, *Economy*, 24, 46-7; Keppie, *Colonisation*, 113; Garnsey & Saller, *Empire*, 27; Reynolds, "Cities", 31-3; Stambaugh, *Roman City*, 125-6; idem, "Graeco-Roman", 1047; Veyne, *Bread*, 365; Owens, *The City*, 169; Dyson, *Community*, 163; Frayn, *Markets*, 123; Lintott, *Imperium*, 130, 145.

[108] See *MW* 454.54 (in Levick, *Government*, 26-7); Suetonius, *Aug.* 32.3; cf. MacMullen, *Social Relations*, 90; Stambaugh, "Social Relations", 79; Duncan-Jones, *The Economy*, 147; idem, *Structure*, 171; Finley, *Politics*, 87; Alföldy, *Social History*, 127-8; Garnsey & Saller, *Empire*, 114; Reynolds, "Cities", 26.

[109] See Abbott & Johnson, *Municipal*, 142; Duncan-Jones, *The Economy*, 148-9, 153.

[110] See *MW* 454.54 (in Levick, *Government*, 26); Jones, *Economy*, 13; Finley, *Politics*, 85-6; Duncan-Jones, *Structure*, 159; Dyson, *Community*, 161; Nicolet, "Citizen", 27, 34-5. Voting on legislation remained a privilege in provincial Roman cities even though it was abandoned at Rome in about 14 CE (cf. Tacitus *Ann.* 1.15; Millar, *Emperor*, 368; Dyson, *Community*, 2).

[111] Sherwin-White, *Citizenship*, 316-17; Levick, *Government*, 73-4.

expatriates settled in the provinces to maintain their distinctiveness from the natives around them.[112]

In a *colonia iuris Italici*, probably fewer natives were granted Roman citizenship, for the grant represents a legal fiction such that the city (*urbs* and *territorium*) was considered a part of Italy. Thus, its citizens were completely and automatically exempt from *tributum capitis et soli*.[113] Their land was also regarded as fully owned rather than merely possessed. A. N. Sherwin-White claims this was a distinction rather than an advantage for, apart from the tax benefit, the real benefit was greater status.[114]

It is possible that where a colony was formed in an existing Greek city, some of the local elite also may have remained in power in the newly founded colony.[115] Furthermore, it has been argued that when a colony was established in an existing town, the natives lost some land to the colonists but continued to exist independently as a *civitas* alongside the *colonia*.[116] As John Brunt notes, however, there is no solid evidence for this. Indeed, while a Roman community might exist within a native *civitas*, politically and economically speaking, the presence of the *colonia* would surely have extinguished (possibly legally, but certainly in real terms) the native city in which it was planted.[117] The political dominance of the city and control of its *territorium* by veterans would have ensured that. Thus, complete Romanization would have been especially likely in a *colonia iuris Italici*.

According to the model, an egalitarian system with reinforcing ties will have a higher incidence of conflict than an hierarchical one with cross-cutting ties. Greek cities generally fit the first category and Roman cities the second. There is also some evidence to support the link between the type of political system and the incidence of conflict, as the model suggests.

---

[112] Levick, *Government*, 316.

[113] See Abbott & Johnson, *Municipal*, 9; Jones, *Economy*, 8; Millar, *Emperor*, 407; Brunt, *Man-Power*, 253; Garnsey & Saller, *Early Principate*, 17; idem, *Roman Empire*, 27; Reynolds, "Cities", 23.

[114] See Sherwin-White, "Survey", 45; idem, *Citizenship*, 319.

[115] Stambaugh, "Social Relations", 79, 89; Keppie, *Colonisation*, 109; Garnsey & Saller, *Empire*, 191-2.

[116] See particularly MacMullen, *Social Relations*, 67.

[117] Brunt, *Man-Power*, 254; cf. Sherwin-White, *Citizenship*, 359.

For example, the apparent lack of conflict involving the Jews at Rome may well result from the oligarchic power structures and the presence of cross-cutting ties, since the Jews were able to gain support from the elite.[118] That conflicts with the Jews are not mentioned in provincial Roman cities may well be for the same reason.[119] A lack of conflict in the context of an oligarchy with cross-cutting ties is evident in elections in Roman cities. For example, in the Pompeiian elections of 79 CE, all the members of the Isis *collegium* supported Cn. Helvius Sabinus for *aedilis* except one of the priests, who supported his personal patron, C. Cuspius Pansa.[120] While this may have been a case of multiple role conflict, the text does not record any overt conflict between the priest and the *collegium*. Furthermore, there was considerable variability in support when the candidates were third-parties supported by patrons.[121]

At the same time, there is no apparent "class" basis to any particular political conflict at this stage, for where such conflicts arose, they were between the plebeian supporters of elite candidates. On the other hand, outright conflict, as a struggle between the "classes", was common in Greek cities.[122] This would seem to support the link between "egalitarian" political structures, reinforcing ties, and a higher incidence of conflict. Such a link may also be reflected in the language and ideology of *stasis*, which, as was mentioned earlier, was

---

[118] This is most clearly seen in the case of the Great Fire of 64 CE. It is widely believed that the Jews would have been made the scapegoats except for the fact that they had the sympathy of the Empress Poppaea Sabina. See, for example, Frend, *Martyrdom*, 126; Benko, *Pagan Rome*, 20; Feldman, *Jew*, 98; cf. Josephus *AJ* 20.195.

[119] Although this argument is one based on silence, it is logically feasible and coheres with the general attitude of the Romans towards the Jews.

[120] *CIL* 4.787, 1011; cf. White, "Finding", 16, 22 n. 26. Clients were expected to support their patron when he stood for local elections and to actively campaign on his behalf. See Dion. Hal. *Ant. Rom.* 2.10.3; Balsdon, *Life*, 22; Dyson, *Community*, 199; White, "Finding", 17. That *collegia* were prominent in supporting particular candidates is quite clear from the inscriptions. See, for example, *CIL* 4.576, 787; *ILS* 6411c, 6412a, 6419c; cf. MacMullen, *Social Relations*, 77; Wallace-Hadrill, "Elites", 249-50; White, "Finding", 16-17.

[121] See White, "Finding", 17.

[122] See, in particular, G. E. M. de Ste. Croix, *The Class Struggle in the Ancient Greek World* (London: Duckworth, 1981) 278-326; A. Lintott, *Violence, Civil Strife and Revolution in the Classical City* (London: Croom Helm, 1982) 254-5, 261-2.

primarily a "Greek problem". In other words, the claims of the model regarding the link between patterns of ties, organization of authority, and the incidence of conflict is generally supported.

IV. CONCLUSION

There are significant differences between Greek and Roman cities in the social-structural factors that determine conflict development. While the link between city size and incidence of conflict was not supported, the importance of relational patterns was quite apparent. The town-planning of Roman cities meant that there was considerable interaction of the various social classes, with no geographical separation between them. Indeed, in many cases shops were located within elite villas. On the other hand, in Greek cities there was a tendency towards social segregation.

At the same time there was a well-developed patronage system within Roman society. This seems to have reduced the incidence of conflict between the elite and the common people, and confirms the idea that a higher proportion of cross-cutting ties results in a lower incidence of conflict. While relationships in Greek cities would generally appear to have been more reinforcing, there were some differences. The cases of Alexandria and Acmonia support the contention of the model concerning the importance of cross-cutting ties and the pattern of ethnic involvement. Specifically, the ability of a group to foster ties with a member of the elite was a major factor in avoiding conflict.

The vast majority of the population was engaged in various small-scale agricultural and commercial enterprises, largely living at subsistence level and relying on the support of the wealthy for property, capital investment, and political and legal influence. In other words, there was a concentration of resources in both societies with a huge gap between rich and poor. Although civil war veterans may appear to have been an exception, it is most likely that they would have entered the ranks of the local elite.

Conflicts between the elite and the common people were prevalent in the first century, but they were largely restricted to specific problems. When they arose, it was usually over a (perceived) failure of role fulfilment. Since the pattern of resource concentration was probably fairly consistent for all first-century communities, this may not be a significant factor in explaining the different incidence of conflict development. On the other hand, there does not appear to have been conflict between the elite and common people in the political realm in Roman cities. The link of oligarchy and patronage (cross-cutting ties) seems to be largely responsible. Such conflicts were probably much more prevalent in Greek cities where there were more reinforcing ties and a strong democratic ideology.

Overall, then, examination of the evidence suggests that there were significant differences between Greek and Roman cultures in some of the factors that determine the culture of conflict. However the possibility that these differences were significant was suggested before testing began. In light of this testing it will be necessary to re-examine the preliminary model and refine it before it can be used to examine the different incidence of conflict in the specific Greek and Roman cities in question.

Conclusion

A MODEL OF CONFLICT FOR GRECO-ROMAN SOCIETIES

The preliminary model that was outlined in chapter one suggests that societies can be classified as high conflict cultures and low conflict cultures. A high conflict culture is one where the incidence of conflict is high, because socialization is harsh, relational ties are reinforcing, there is ethnic heterogeneity and/or ethnic segregation, and a hierarchical control of power and resources. It was noted that Mediterranean society, in general, is such a culture. However, at the end of chapter one it was hypothesized that, at a lower level of abstraction, specifically at the level of individual Greek and Roman communities, there would be considerable variation. The material discussed in the previous two chapters has supported this hypothesis. Consequently, the preliminary model requires some modification if it is to be useful at the level required to explain the differences in conflict response between Paul's churches and their wider civic communities. At the same time, in order more readily to facilitate its application to the three Christian and civic communities under consideration, the revised model will be expressed in the form of a series of propositional statements.

Comparison has suggested that the psychocultural dispositions which determine the predisposition to conflict and the strength of the conflict response were relatively uniform in the Greco-Roman world. Nevertheless, differences in the particular norms, values, and beliefs would produce some variation. At the same time, the structural factors, as representative of the patterns of relationships and relational networks, do appear to have determined who the disputants would be. Thus, the first proposition of the working model is that *conflicts between a Christian community and its wider civic community would center on the particular norms, values and beliefs of the civic community, especially those related to being a citizen or resident.*

It is clear from the previous two chapters that there were significant differences in the social structural factors between different Greek and Roman communities. Since some of these factors determine where a culture sits on a scale from low to high conflict, these factors tend to suggest that there would be differences in the conflict responses between different communities. According to the preliminary model, there is normally a link between population size and the incidence of conflict, such that the larger the population numerically the greater the tolerance of divergent world-views, and the less the incidence of conflict. But this has not been substantiated.

On the other hand, it is clear that the presence of cross-cutting ties is the most significant factor in determining the development of conflict. Thus, a second proposition is that *where there is a pattern of cross-cutting ties there will be a lower incidence of conflict, especially when those ties include members of the ruling elite, while a pattern of reinforcing ties will have a higher incidence of conflict*. Similarly, it is clear from the previous two chapters that the pattern of ethnic involvement is also important to the extent that it produces cross-cutting or reinforcing ties. Thus, a third proposition is that *where there is a pattern of ethnic integration or assimilation there will be a lower incidence of conflict*.

Somewhat similar is the link between conflict and the structure of authority. For Greek and Roman communities it is clear that this link is supported insofar as the authority structures are also associated with the pattern of relational ties. In particular, the incidence of conflict is reduced when the group includes members of the ruling elite and/or is able to foster positive ties with members of the ruling elite. Thus, a fourth proposition is that *where there is a hierarchical politico-legal system combined with strong cross cutting ties that include the elite there will be a lower incidence of conflict than where there is an egalitarian system with reinforcing ties*. Although the preliminary model also suggested that the pattern of resource concentration would have influenced the incidence of conflict, this pattern would have been similar for most communities. Consequently, it may be disregarded as significant for a model operating at the level of individual cities.

These propositions can now be used to explain the difference in conflict response between a Christian community and its wider civic community for different Greek and Roman cities. Having revised this model, the three specific churches and their cities will be examined in the next three chapters. Following that, the model will be used in an attempt to explain the different relationships (and hence different incidence of conflict in the relationships) of the Thessalonian, Corinthian and Philippian churches with their wider civic communities.

PART TWO

CHURCH & CIVIC COMMUNITY RELATIONS

Chapter Four

SOCIAL RELATIONS AT THESSALONICA

The reconstruction of a particular socio-historical context is a difficult enterprise. It involves accumulating evidence that is temporally, culturally and geographically specific. This is constrained by the extent of archaeological excavation, and the presence of other clues in historical texts. Therefore, some information needs to be "filled in" from evidence drawn from contexts that share two of these specificities in common. In the case of Thessalonica, such a reconstruction encounters a particular difficulty in that the city has never been fully $\leftarrow$ *!!!* excavated. Consequently, whatever primary evidence we have regarding the nature of the city and its way of life in the first century CE is patchy and potentially skewed. There is a real danger of overstating points, or of arguing from silence. Some details will also have to be assumed from what is known of other Macedonian and Greek cities.

This chapter will seek to reconstruct the nature of Roman Thessalonica, the Thessalonian church, and the relationship between this church and its civic community. The reconstruction of the social context of the city will draw on the work of ancient writers, epigraphic evidence and other historical data, as well as the work of previous scholars and, where relevant, chapters two and three herein. The reconstruction of the church, and the relationship between it and the wider civic community will rely primarily on Paul's

excluded
2 Thess.

first letter to the Thessalonians and from background material.[1] Overall, therefore, the methodology of this chapter will involve historical reconstruction via social description.

I. ROMAN THESSALONICA

The aim of this reconstruction of the nature of Roman Thessalonica is primarily to gather material that will be analysed by the model in chapter seven. According to the model outlined in part one of this study, the incidence of conflict is determined by the particular set of norms, values and beliefs, the pattern of relational ties, and the distribution of political power. Material related to these factors will be examined in this section, in terms of Thessalonica's history, its physical and demographic features, the nature of its social relations, its political features, and its religious profile.

1. History

Thessalonica was founded in 316/5 BCE by Cassander. One tradition suggests that he founded the city *de novo*, bringing together (physically and administratively) the populations of twenty-six towns on the Thermean Peninsular.[2] Strabo suggests that the inhabitants of at least two of these cities, Chalastra and Cissus, were Thracian. This is likely if, as he

---

[1] Along with the majority of scholars, I assume here that only canonical 1 Thessalonians is a genuine letter from Paul. Some suggest that 2 Thessalonians can be used to understand the context since the author bases his arguments either on personal knowledge of the Thessalonian situation or a reading of 1 Thessalonians. See, for example, J. L. Hill, "Establishing the Church in Thessalonica" (unpublished PhD dissertation, Duke University, 1990) 226 n. 653. But this assumes much, and ignores the possibility that there has been significant change or development in the intervening period. It is therefore safest to restrict consideration to 1 Thessalonians alone.

[2] Strabo *Geog.* 7 frag. 21; Dion. Hal. *Ant. Rom.* 1.49.4; See R. E. Davies, "The Macedonian Scene of Paul's Journeys" *BA* 26 (1963) 103; M. Vickers, "Hellenistic Thessaloniki" *JHS* 92 (1972) 159; idem, "Thessalonike" in R. Stilwell *et al*, eds., *Princeton Encyclopaedia of Classical Sites* (Princeton, NJ: Princeton University Press, 1976) 912; H. L. Hendrix, "Thessalonica" *ABD* 6.523; cf. T. Holtz, *Der erste Brief an die Thessalonicher* (EKKNT; Zürich: Benziger, 1986) 9; Hill, "Establishing", 20, 24; J. McRay, *Archaeology and the New Testament* (Grand Rapids: Baker, 1991) 293; R. F. Collins, *The Birth of the New Testament: The Origin and Development of the First Christian Generation* (New York: Crossroad, 1993) 5.

claims, most of Macedonia had at one stage been ruled by the Thracians.[3] Another tradition suggests that the city was founded on the site of the town of Therme.[4] Although this particular text is corrupt, it seems the more likely scenario since it was common for Macedonian rulers to found cities on existing sites. Furthermore, the remains of a fifth century BCE temple have been found to the west of the city.[5]

Together with the rest of Macedonia, Thessalonica became a part of the Roman empire following the defeat of Perseus in 168 BCE. The Macedonian Settlement, following this, declared the country free but divided it into four regions, and Thessalonica became the capital of the second.[6] Following the revolt of Andruscus in 149/8 BCE, the province was reorganized and the city became the provincial capital. At the same time, virtually all the Macedonian elite, and certainly all who had held some office, were transported to Rome along with their sons.[7] From then until the start of the civil wars, the province of Macedonia, and Thessalonica in particular, experienced frequent marauding raids from neighboring tribes. These may have continued into the first century CE, and were such a problem that the city required further fortification.[8] These may have created something of a siege

---

[3] See Strabo *Geog.* 7 frag. 11, 21, 24. That the original population included some Thracians will be important later in the discussion of demographic features.

[4] Strabo *Geog.* 7 frag. 24.

[5] See Hill, "Establishing", 22-3; Hendrix, "Thessalonica", 523; cf. Collins, *The Birth*, 5.

[6] Diodorus Siculus 31.8.6-8; Livy 45.17.1, 45.18.3-7, 45.19.4-9; Strabo *Geog.* 7 frag 47(8); See Papazoglou, "Macedonia", 192; McRay, *Archaeology*, 292; Hendrix "Thessalonica", 524; D. W. J. Gill, "Macedonia" in D. W. J. Gill & C. Gempf, eds., *The Book of Acts in its Graeco-Roman Setting* (BAFCS 2; Grand Rapids: Eerdmans, 1994) 400-1; cf. W. A. Meeks, *The First Urban Christians: The Social World of the Apostle Paul* (New Haven: Yale University Press, 1983) 47; Collins, *The Birth*, 6.

[7] See Livy 45.32.3-6; cf. Vickers, "Thessalonike", 912; Meeks, *First Urban*, 47; K. P. Donfried, "The Cults of Thessalonica and the Thessalonian Correspondence" *NTS* 31 (1985) 344; McRay, *Archaeology*, 292; Hendrix, "Thessalonica", 524; Gill, "Macedonia", 402. Although Gill implies this was largely a popular revolt, the deportation of the elite suggests that it was more complex.

[8] See Cicero *Prov. Cons.* 4; idem, *Pis.* 38-40, 61, 84; Florus 1.39; *SIG*[3] 700; *SEG* 3.378; cf. J. O. Larsen, "Greece and Macedonia from Augustus to Gallenius" in T. Frank, ed., *An Economic Survey of Ancient Rome* (vol. IV; Baltimore: Johns Hopkins University Press, 1938) 423, 427; Papazoglou, "Macedonia", 193; Gill, "Macedonia", 402.

mentality, and may well have increased the sense of community within the city.

Thessalonica became Pompey's base in 49-8 BCE, when he was joined by two consuls, and two hundred senators and *equites* from Rome. However, they stayed less than a year.[9] During the civil wars, the Thessalonians developed a habit of backing the losers. In particular, they supported Brutus and Cassius (but switched to the Triumvirs between the first and second battles at Philippi) and M. Antony (until his defeat at the battle of Actium). Yet, they quickly heaped lavish honors on Octavian, and received benefits from him, following his victory and ascendancy to the title of *Princeps*.[10] In light of this history, the city seems to have developed an attitude of strong dependence on Roman, and especially Imperial, benefaction.[11]

2. Physical Features

Thessalonica is located on a bay, which forms a naturally sheltered harbor.[12] The city lay on/near the *Via Egnatia*, the main highway traversing mainland Greece.[13] This would have made it an important stop for travellers and merchants, especially since it was the provincial capital. Its plan is odd, in that it comprises two sections: a southern part, whose streets follow the coast, and a northern part, whose streets are more regularly aligned. That there are two quite distinct plans is apparent in that the streets in the two sections do not align.[14]

---

[9] See Papazoglou, "Macedonia", 194; Collins, *The Birth*, 7; Hendrix, "Thessalonica", 524; Gill, "Macedonia", 402.

[10] See Papazoglou, "Macedonia", 195; Hendrix, "Thessalonica", 524; Collins, *The Birth*, 7.

[11] This will be discussed further in regard to the Imperial Cult.

[12] Davies, "Macedonian Scene", 103; McRay, *Archaeology*, 293; Hill, "Establishing", 24; Hendrix, "Thessalonica", 523; cf. Meeks, *First Urban*, 46; Holtz, *erste Brief*, 9; A. J. Malherbe, *Paul and the Thessalonians: The Philosophic Tradition of Pastoral Care* (Philadelphia: Fortress, 1987) 6; Collins, *The First*, 5.

[13] Although both Polybius (34.12.7) and Strabo (*Geog.* 7.7.4, 7 frag. 10) imply that the city lay on the *Via* (ἐκεῖθεν...μέχρι Θεσσαλονικείας cf. 7 frag. 10 — ὁδῷ...ἕως Θεσσαλονικείας), modern historians of the city assert that it did not pass through the city itself. See, for example, Vickers, "Hellenistic", 157 n.4.

[14] M. Vickers, "Towards Reconstruction of the Town Planning of Roman Thessaloniki" in B. Laourdas & C. Makaronas, eds., *Ancient Macedonia* (Thessaloniki: Institute for Balkan Studies, 1970) 240, 244;

The most likely explanation for this is that the two sections were laid out at different times.[15]

Dividing the plan are paired parallel main roads, running east-west, each about ten metres wide. Most of the other roads in the city were typically narrow, about 1.5-2.0 metres wide.[16] The section between these main roads appears to have been a regular Hippodamian plan, with standard *insula* blocks of about one hundred by fifty metres.[17] By comparison, the *insula* blocks in the south-eastern part appear to have been smaller, while those to the north are larger (although this may reflect its later development).

Since the western part of the southern section has fewer streets and larger blocks, there may have been a number of public buildings located there. It is generally agreed that there would have been an *agora* in this area, given the activity around the harbor and the fact that most Greek cities had two *agorae*. One formed the administrative center and the other the main market area. An *agora* has been found in the northern section, dating from at least 60 BCE, and since this was later transformed into a Roman *forum*, it was more likely the administrative center. The

---

Hill, "Establishing", 28-9, 35. It was normal for a city, especially one which was purposely built, to have only one plan.

[15] Michael Vickers originally claimed that the southern part was probably laid out at the city's founding, since a plan following the coast is consistent with other cities founded in the fourth century BCE, so that the northern part was probably later. *IG* 10.2.1.4 attests to a gymnasium in the northern section and is dated to 95 BCE. An earlier dating for that section is likely given the existence of the Sarapeum, on the same alignment, which is referred to in an inscription dated 187 BCE (*IG* 10.2.1.3). See Vickers, "Hellenistic", 164-5; Hill, "Establishing" 35-7; Hendrix, "Thessalonica", 523. C. F. Edson dates the Sarapeum to the third century BCE ("Cults of Thessalonica [Macedonica III]" *HTR* 41 [1948] 181). Later Vickers appears to have changed his mind, claiming the whole plan was laid out at its founding (Vickers, "Thessalonike", 912) since the section between the main roads is a regular Hellenistic plan (Vickers, "Hellenistic", 169; idem, "Thessalonike", 912; cf. Gill, "Macedonia", 414). Thus, the most likely scenario is that the southern section may correspond to the remains of old Therme, and the central and northern sections to its Hellenistic founding. This is a possibility Vickers raised in his earliest article, but promptly dismissed. See Vickers, "Reconstruction", 245.

[16] D. Pandermalis, "Monuments and Art in the Roman Period" in M. B. Sakellariou, ed., *Macedonia: 4000 Years of Greek History and Civilization* (Athens: Ektodike Athenon, 1983) 211.

[17] Vickers, "Hellenistic", 169; idem, "Thessalonike", 912; cf. Gill, "Macedonia", 414.

presence of a commercial *agora* in the southern part of the
city, near the harbor, would also be logical.[18]

One important feature of the city is its harbor. Most
scholars assume this was a busy commercial port, given the
city's location and status, and the harbor's natural
protection.[19] But the head of the gulf suffers seriously from
silting. In the fifth century BCE the city of Pella was near the
coast but in the first century CE it was twenty kilometres
inland. Even the bay on which Thessalonica was built had to
be dredged before construction began and the city's coastline
was also continually moving inland.[20]

Furthermore, little is known of the harbor in ancient
times. Both Livy and Diodorus Siculus mention that, during
the wars with the Romans, Perseus had ordered the
dockyards (*navalia* or τὰ νεώρια) at Thessalonica to be
burned, but this was not carried out.[21] Vickers, however,
points out that Zosimus, writing at the end of the fifth
century CE, claims there "was no harbour as such until
Constantine built one in 322", a reference he accepts since
Zosimus "was no friend of Constantine and would hardly
have given him the credit for something he had not done".[22]
Thus, it may be safest not to assume too much concerning the
prominence of the port and its impact on the life of the city
during the first century CE.

Consequently, while Thessalonica may have been a
busy and bustling city, its planning suggests that it operated
as a *Gemeinschaft*-type community. The planning also
suggests that the commercial activity of the city may have

---

[18] Vickers, "Hellenistic", 163, 169; Hill "Establishing", 38; Hendrix,
"Thessalonica", 523; Gill, "Macedonia", 415. Near the northern *agora*
there was also a *gymnasium*, possibly a stadium, and another sacred
area/temple. See, for example, Vickers, "Reconstruction", 249; Hill
"Establishing", 38, 41; Hendrix, "Thessalonica", 524. This difference in
the function of the two *agorae*, which I have suggested, I also found in the
commentary to the map of the ancient city in the Archaeological
Museum of Thessaloniki, when I visited in February 1996.

[19] This appears to be the assumption of most of those cited in note
12 above.

[20] See M. Cary, *The Geographic Background of Greek and Roman
History* (Oxford: Clarendon, 1949) 294; cf. Hill, who states that "ancient
descriptions of the city confirm that the coastline of the unprotected
harbor area has moved about fifty meters further out into the Thermaic
Gulf". ("Establishing", 26).

[21] See Livy 44.10.1-2; Diodorus Siculus 30.11.1.

[22] See Vickers, "Hellenistic", 169.

been somewhat separated from the administrative and political activity.

3. Demographic Features

Thessalonica was the capital of the province of Macedonia, and also the largest city. Cicero complains that travel in and out of the city was difficult due to the large volume of traffic.[23] Based on the density rate proposed in chapter two (200-250 per hectare), its population would have been somewhere in the range of 40,000-50,000. Indeed, when allowances are made for the additions to the walls in the early fourth and fifth centuries CE, and for the later development of the northern section, the effective area of the city would have been about 203 hectares.[24]

Given that it was the provincial capital, near the main highway of the province, and with a harbor, most scholars assume that Thessalonica was a cosmopolitan city.[25] Yet, as some note, and as would be expected, native Macedonians probably made up the bulk of its population.[26] However,

---

[23] Cicero *Att.* 3.14; cf. Strabo (*Geog.* 7.7.4) describes it as νῦν μάλιστα τῶν ἄλλων εὐανδρεῖ. Livy describes it as *celeberrima*, which might mean either the most flourishing or the most famous (45.30.4), but the latter is clearly the intent. Although Cicero complains that during his exile there he was unable to occupy his mind (*Att.* 3.15), this reflects his attitude to his situation more than the nature of the city. See J. W. Loomis, "Cicero and Thessaloniki, Politics and Provinces" in *Ancient Macedonia II* (Thessaloniki: Institute for Balkan Studies, 1977) 170.

[24] Hill estimates the total area as 363 hectares but excludes the northern section to give an effective living area of 203 hectares. Since the acropolis only housed a garrison of Roman soldiers (perhaps 2,000), this can be largely neglected. But her estimate of 75,000-100,000 is too high since she assumes a density of 495 per hectare ("Establishing", 46-8). For the inadequacy of this figure, see section I of chapter two herein.

[25] For example, Meeks, *First Urban*, 46; Malherbe, *Paul*, 6; Hill, "Establishing", 49; G. H. R. Horsley, "The Politarchs" in D. W. J. Gill & C. Gempf, eds., *The Book of Acts in its Graeco-Roman Setting* (BAFCS 2; Grand Rapids: Eerdmans, 1994) 420.

[26] Hill, "Establishing" 50; Gill, "Macedonia", 404-6; cf. R. Jewett, *The Thessalonian Correspondence: Pauline Rhetoric and Millenarian Piety* (Philadelphia: Fortress, 1986) 119. Hill claims that the names found in *IG* 10.2.1 are "peculiar to Macedonia or surrounding areas or are of general Greek or Latin background", and most with Latin names are of Macedonian extraction ("Establishing", 51, 199). Although analysis of names alone is not a sound basis for argument, she is probably correct.

apart from the governor, his entourage, and the garrison, there was clearly also a group of quite wealthy Roman businessmen.[27] The inscriptions suggest that there were also some residents who had come from Achaia, Asia Minor, Egypt, Syria and Thrace.[28]

More uncertain is the attempt to locate the origin of people based on what appears to be an ethnic name. It is likely that T. Claudius Aegyptus is from Egypt. Similarly, it is possible that Asiaticus, son of Phila, and Xanthion, son of Asiaticus, are of Asian descent, and that L. Minatius Byblos is from Phoenicia.[29] That a number have Thracian names, however, need not mean they were from Thrace since the populations of at least two Thracian cities were involved in the original settlement of the city. Consequently, although there is some ethnic diversity, the extent and range is difficult to tell. Yet it should not necessarily be assumed that the city was cosmopolitan.

Many scholars assume there was a Jewish presence in Thessalonica at the time Paul visited and wrote, based on Luke's account of Paul preaching in the synagogue there (Acts 17:1-9).[30] But the earliest certain evidence of Jews is

---

[27] See *IG* 10.2.1.32, 33; cf. Papazoglou, "Macedonia", 196, 201. See also Jewett, *Correspondence*, 119; Malherbe, *Paul*, 6; Hill, "Establishing", 51. The Roman presence at Thessalonica was small given the few Latin inscriptions found. Of the approximately 150 inscriptions that may be dated before the end of the first century CE, only one is bi-lingual (*IG* 10.2.1.878) and seven are in Latin, and most of these come from Romanized-Macedonians (*IG* 10.2.1.29, 74, 339, 378, 688, 690, 927).

[28] See *IG* 10.2.1.48, 69, 119, 254, 255, 291, 301, 309. *IG* 10.2.1.49 refers to the city of Phylakia in northern Pieria, another region of Macedonia. The claim that the adoption of foreign gods from Egypt and Asia Minor in some way reflects the ethnic composition is weak (*contra* Horsley, "Politarchs", 420; cf. Meeks, *First Urban*, 46; Malherbe, *Paul*, 6). Jewett's claim that there were some Celts (*Correspondence*, 119) is unsupported by the inscriptions or any material remains. The references to a person from Lydia and a group of Asians (*IG* 10.2.1.291, 309) come from at least the second century CE, so that it cannot necessarily be assumed that they reflect the situation in Paul's time (*contra* Malherbe, *Paul*, 6; C. J. Hemer, *The Book of Acts in the Setting of Hellenistic History* [Winona Lake, IN: Eisenbrauns, 1990] 231).

[29] All of these individuals are named in *IG* 10.2.1.68-9 and will be discussed further below.

[30] V. C. Pfitzner, *Paul and the Agon Motif: Traditional Athletic Imagery in the Pauline Literature* (NovTSup 16; Leiden: E. J. Brill, 1967) 113; I. H. Marshall, *Acts* (TNTC; Leicester: IVP, 1980) 275-6; Papazoglou, "Macedonia", 207; Donfried, "The Cults", 356 n. 93;

probably from the third century CE, while a Samaritan synagogue most likely dates from the fourth century CE.[31] To attempt to use material from such a late date to reconstruct the situation of the first century CE is totally unjustified.[32]

Judith Hill, however, argues that while archaeological evidence is lacking, it would be logical to expect Jews at Thessalonica. Jews were widespread in the Empire and it would be reasonable to suppose they would be found in the largest city in the province. This is even more likely, given that there was a Jewish community at Stobi dating from the late first or early second century CE. She argues that since Stobi is only 140 kilometres from Thessalonica, that it is an inland rather than a coastal city, and that Thessalonica lay at the start of the road to Stobi, it is reasonable to assume that there was an earlier community at Thessalonica.[33]

Nevertheless, the archaeological evidence for Jewish communities in Macedonia as a whole is comparatively rare. Philo's attempt to show how widespread Judaism was in his time mentions Macedonia only in general and not Thessalonica specifically, compared to, for example, Corinth.[34] Elsewhere, however, Philo shows a lack of knowledge of Macedonia and he makes sweeping geographical references, seldom mentioning main cities.[35] In any case, the fact that his statement about how widespread the Jews were is found in *De Legatione ad Gaium* — a completely apologetic document

---

Malherbe, *Paul*, 6-7; McRay, *Archaeology*, 293. E. Haenchen bases his claim on much later data (*The Acts of the Apostles* [London: Blackwell, 1971] 506). For a discussion of the unreliability of Luke's account of Paul in Thessalonica see section II below.

[31] *IG* 10.2.1.633, 772, 789; cf. I. Levinskaya, *The Book of Acts in its Diaspora Setting* (BAFCS 5; Grand Rapids: Eerdmans, 1996), 154-7. This inscription probably comes from the fourth century CE. See, Marshall, *Acts*, 276; Malherbe, *Paul*, 6-7; Hill, "Establishing", 55; Collins, *The Birth*, 8; *contra* Hemer, *Book*, 115. Donfried ("The Cults", 356 n. 93) mistakenly dates it to the fourth century CE. Jewett's dating of it to the third century BCE (*Correspondence*, 119-20) is completely inexplicable.

[32] H. Koester, "From Paul's Eschatology to the Apocalyptic Schemata of 2 Thessalonians" in R. F. Collins, ed., *The Thessalonian Correspondence* (BETL 87; Leuven: Leuven University Press, 1990), 442-3.

[33] Hill, "Establishing", 53, 55-6; cf. Meeks, *First Urban*, 46; Jewett, *Correspondence*, 119-20.

[34] Philo *Leg.* 281; cf. D. Lührmann, "The Beginnings of the Church at Thessalonica" in D. L. Balch, E. Ferguson & W. A. Meeks, eds., *Greeks, Romans and Christians* (Minneapolis: Fortress, 1990) 239.

[35] See, for example, *De gig.* 7; *Plant.* 12; *Deus Imm.* 174.

— suggests that his comments should be seen as an over-generalization and treated cautiously.

Furthermore, Hill's arguments regarding Stobi are also weak. It is just as likely that some Jews had travelled east to the city from Rome via Dyrrachium, as it is that they came west via Thessalonica. Besides, as was mentioned in chapter three, Stobi was unique among Macedonian cities in that it was a *municipium*. Given the more favorable attitude of Romans to Jews, it is quite possible this city was chosen ahead of the very Greek Thessalonica. Thus, there is no clear evidence to suggest that there was a Jewish community in Thessalonica apart from Acts 17:1-9 (and perhaps implied by the use of the aorist ἐκδιωξάντων in 1 Thess 2:15).

Another demographic feature is the extent of ethnic integration in Thessalonian society. Most of the Roman residents probably remained somewhat separate. With the garrison stationed in the citadel, it is likely that the governor and his entourage, along with the other Roman residents, nearby. The most likely location would have been the newer, and larger, areas in the northern section.[36] Hill contends that there may have been ethnic enclaves at Thessalonica like there was at Alexandria.[37] While the latter was unique, as has been noted, the historical links between Alexandria and Macedonia should not be ignored. Her claim that people were located according to occupation rather than ethnic group is not strong since it is based on Rome and, as suggested in chapter three, there was probably more physical separation in Greek cities.

The inscriptions suggest that the Roman businessmen formed a community and were considered somewhat separate from the rest of the city.[38] In one inscription, Macedon

---

[36] See Hill, "Establishing", 57-8. "Roman", here, refers to ethnic Romans, and not to those Macedonians with Roman citizenship.

[37] Hill, "Establishing", 56-7.

[38] See *IG* 10.2.1.32-3; cf. C. F. Edson, "Macedonica" *HSCP* 51 (1940) 130. This seems clear from the dedication, which is from ἡ πόλις καὶ οἱ συμπραγματευόμενοι Ῥωμαῖοι. This title seems to draw a clear distinction between the *city* and the Roman *conventus*. Holland Hendrix claims that the latter was somehow associated with the city's government ("Archaeology and Eschatology at Thessalonica" in B. A. Pearson, ed., *The Future of Early Christianity* [Minneapolis: Fortress, 1991] 114). But there is no mention of the more normal *politarchs, boule* or *demos*, which would probably be expected if Hendrix was right. Rather, the use of πόλις tends to suggest there was *no* political association.

(probably a native-Thessalonian) was honored by the θίασος of Asiani as their fellow-μύστης.[39] Yet this inscription is dated to the second or third century CE.[40] Similarly, a Thyatiran was honored by the guild of purple-dyers, but no other clues are given regarding its composition and the inscription comes from the second century CE.[41] Given their late dating, neither of these can be assumed to reflect the situation of the first century, especially as the date at which the *collegia* began is unknown. Nevertheless, the presence of such groups may well reflect an attitude to ethnic origin and non-integration that was prevalent at Thessalonica.

Leaving aside lists of civic officials, there are eight lists of names in the inscriptions that appear to represent some sort of socio-religious grouping. Two inscriptions (*I G* 10.2.1.68, 69) list the members of a θίασος dedicated to *Theos Hypsistos*, and are dated towards the end of the first century CE. The second list, however, is probably later than the first.[42]

---

[39] *IG* 10.2.1.309; cf. Edson, "Cults", 154. Edson notes that the other known associations of Asiani are only found in the Balkans (ibid., 157).

[40] Since integration and assimilation normally occur slowly, if this *thiasos* existed in the first century it may well have been ethnically homogeneous. See Edson ("Cults", 158), who makes a similar point.

[41] See *IG* 10.2.1.291. Jewett's claim that the marauding barbarians of the first century BCE were by now well integrated is without foundation, for there is no suggestion they settled in the city. They were simply raiding parties. See Cicero *Prov. Cons.* 4-5; idem, *Pis.* 38-40, 84; *contra* Jewett, *Correspondence*, 119.

[42] Lists of magistrates can be largely ignored. Those found for this period have names which are common Macedonian or generic Greek. There appear to be two exceptions: (1) a Zopa, son of _, is listed as a *politarch* in an inscription from 27 BCE-14 CE (*IG* 10.2.1.31). This name is probably derived from the Thracian Zopas. But given the incorporation of Thracian towns in the origin settlement of Thessalonica, it is most likely that he was a native Thessalonian; (2) an Athenogenes, son of Plousia, is listed as a *politarch* (*IG* 10.2.1.133). This inscription is unclear and badly damaged in places. Thus, Edson dates it to the second century CE in the commentary in *IG* 10.2.1, but others reconstruct the text differently and date it to 18-19 CE (see H. L. Hendrix, "Benefactor/Patron Networks in the Urban Environment: Evidence from Thessalonica" *Semeia* 56 [1992] 46). While this name may appear to originate in Athens, a man of foreign origin could not have been *politarch*. To assume the highest political office in a Greek city he had to be a citizen, and to be a citizen of the city he had to be freeborn of freeborn parents, and born in the city of native parents (see Heraclitus *Ep.* 9; Aristotle *Pol* 1275A-B). Thus, it must be assumed that both these men were native Thessalonians. Besides, other Athen- names are known from Macedonia, such as an Athenagoras, son of Apollodorus (96/5 BCE). See D.

In the first list, forty members are named, although two of those names are now indistinguishable and one is inexplicably repeated. Of the remaining, one is specifically labelled as a Thessalonian, six are clearly Macedonian, seven are probably Macedonian, eleven may be Macedonian, six may be of servile origin, two have names that cannot be identified, and one may come from Asia, one from Egypt, and one from Phoenicia.[43] Overall, there may be no more than

Kanatsoulis, *Prosopographia Macedonica from 148 B.C. to the Time of Constantine the Great* (ed. A. N. Oikonomides; Chicago: Ares, 1979) #10.

[43] The group's leader is clearly Macedonian (T. Flavius Amunta f. Euctimeni), four have characteristically Macedonian names (Eubulides, son of Hyacynthus; Philip, son of Epigonos; Paramonos, son of Certimmas; Cassander, son of Axioma). Another, Theodes Prota, has a Greek name but is specifically labelled Θεσσ(αλονικεύς). Seven have generic Greek names (_, son of Dioscurides; _, son of Nicopolis; Theodas, son of Dioscurides; Theodorus, son of Epimenus; Moschus, son of _; Dionysius, son of Cleopater; Antiphanes, son of Epicrates). Although they are given no ethnic appellation, it is probably fair to assume that they too were native Macedonians. Four have Roman names with generic Greek cognomina (Ti. Claudius Agathopus x2, Cn. Octavius Euhemerus, Q. Pomponius Sosibius, M. Mutilius Thyrsus). Another eleven have common Roman names (L. Fesius Halimus, M. Vivius Onesimus, L. Atellius Secundus, Q. Minucius Rufus, L. Trebius Primgenus, L. Petronius Vales, M. Antonius Potitus, P. Popillius Balbus, M. Servilius Crescus, T. Claudius Cerdon, A. Avius Laetus). Of these, Agathopus, Cerdo, Thyrsus, and Onesimus are most likely of servile origin given their cognomina. This is not conclusive, for Papazoglou notes that the use of servile labor was not widespread in Macedonia until the second century CE ("Macedonia", 200). A number also bear the nomina of rulers and former governors (M. Antonius, Ti. Claudius, Q. Minucius, Q. Pomponius, M. Servilius) so that it is also possible that these are enfranchised Macedonians. Indeed Hill admits that many of the Roman citizens at Thessalonica were of Macedonian origin ("Establishing", 51). Two have uncommon names which cannot be identified: M. Hermerotus and C. Iulius Rheglus. By the way they are listed, two appear to be slaves of other members (Geminus, Hermes). That leaves (1) Asiaticus, son of Phila — while "Asiaticus" would appear to indicate an origin in Asia Minor, it actually originated as the name given to the conqueror of that province, but "Phila" is similar to a common Macedonian name; (2) T. Claudius Aegyptus probably comes from Egypt, (3) L. Minatius Byblus may come from the city of that name in Phoenicia. The final two are M. Herennius Zosimus and M. Herennius Romanus — Herennius was the nomen of a prominent Macedonia family (see *IG* 10.2.1.239-41), but the cognomen "Romanus" does not necessarily indicate he was a native Italian since the name had by this time lost all geographical correlation (see I. Kajanto, *The Latin Cognomina* [Helsinki: Societas Scientarium Fennica, 1965] 50-1). "Zosimus" appears Thracian, but it was one of the commonest names found in Macedonia (see *IG* 10.2.1,

eleven out of forty (28%) from different ethnic backgrounds. That no two of those with ethnic names come from the same background does not suggest a major integration of ethnic groups.[44] A later list for this same θίασος shows even less diversity. Some of those with clearly ethnic names are no longer listed, and the only new members who may come from different ethnic groups are a Xanthion, son of Asiaticus, and a Thallus, son of Eutyches. The latter is specifically identified as Κορίνθιος — the only one given an ethnic appellation.[45] This tends to suggest significant homogeneity.

In another group (*IG* 10.2.1.124, dated 42-32 BCE) all the names are either Macedonian or generic Greek, and none has an ethnic appellation. This is largely the case with another list of seven names, although one patronym, Dionysophanes, is uncommon except at Athens and Euboea. But given the prominence of other Dionys- names in Macedonia, there is no reason to doubt that the man was a native-Thessalonian.[46] Another list of six names has two which are distinctly Macedonian, possibly one which is Thracian, one which is generic Greek and two which are uncertain. There are no ethnic appellations.[47]

Another inscription (*IG* 10.2.1.243, dated either first or second century CE) lists three columns of names, with sixteen in each of the first two columns and three in the third. One of the thirty-five names is indistinguishable. Of the others, four are characteristically Macedonian, two are possibly Thracian and the rest are generic Greek names or Roman/Greek. There

---

SIGLM, and Kanatsoulis, *Prosopographia*), and he was probably a native. On the ethnicity of names, see Kajanto, *Cognomina*; the indices of *ILS*, *SIGLM* and *IG* 10.2.1 (and notes); P. M. Fraser & E. Matthews, *A Lexicon of Greek Personal Names* (vol 1; Oxford: Clarendon, 1987); M. J. Osborne & S. G. Byrne, *A Lexicon of Greek Personal Names* (vol 2; Oxford: Clarendon, 1994). See also *New Docs* 4.179-81.

[44] Although it could be argued that it would take time to achieve the necessary status to be accepted into such a group, the fact that only one of each ethnic group is found may imply that only a few wished to achieve such a level of integration; cf. the case of the *thiasos* of Asiani.

[45] See *IG* 10.2.1.69. That an ethnic appellation is significant is also seen in the inscriptions found in other places that list certain people as *Thessalonian* (*IG* 10.2.1.1024, 1029, 1031, 1033). This implies that such a title was retained with a sense of pride.

[46] *IG* 10.2.1.129. This is dated to the first century BCE or CE. Dionysophanes is the man's patronym, his personal name is Stilbon.

[47] *IG* 10.2.1.242. That one name is Thracian is uncertain: Alexander, son of Dorzinthus — while his personal name is the most popular name in Macedonian his patronym is Thracian.

are no ethnic appellations. Again, this tends to suggest a considerable degree of ethnic homogeneity.[48]

A *thiasos*, dedicated to a number of deities (*I G* 10.2.1.259, dated first century CE), lists eighteen names (one indistinct). Five are clearly Macedonian, the rest are either Roman or Roman/Greek. The priest, L. Fulvius Felix, is most likely of servile origin.[49] But there are no ethnic appellations. The final list of six people (*IG* 10.2.1.263, dated sometime before the mid first century CE) has only Macedonian or generic Greek names, no Romanized names, and no ethnic appellations. It is possible that it was entirely native in origin.

The analysis of the ethnic composition of these groups on the basis of names must remain extremely tentative. Nevertheless, the impression is that there was not a great ethnic diversity nor much interaction, given the lack of geographical names and ethnic appellations.[50] That there was probably limited ethnic integration is also implied by the example of the Roman *conventus*. In fact, both this group and the *thiasos* of Asiani suggest that most people of foreign origin may have retained a strong commitment to their heritage and sought to maintain a sense of ethnic identity. This was common in Greek cities and may also reflect typical Greek xenophobia (as discussed in chapter two above).[51]

4. Social Relations

Another factor of city life is the pattern of relations between people from different socio-economic strata. Holland Hendrix has suggested that patronal networks were becoming increasingly important in Thessalonian society, even if the

---

[48] That only a small proportion have Romanized names suggest it may be earlier rather than later. See Edson, "Macedonica", 129; idem, "Cults", 184. Two other lists, most likely dated to the second century CE show an increased proportion of Roman or Roman/Greek names, and without apparent ethnic diversity (see *IG* 10.2.1.245, 252).

[49] Kajanto claims that of the 3542 occurrences of the cognomen Felix, 529 were of servile origin (15%) (*Cognomina*, 273), although he admits that it was one of the commonest slave names (ibid., 73, 134).

[50] The latter were frequently included as an indicator of origin (and presumably a sense of pride), as can be seen from the inscriptions of Thessalonians found away from Thessalonica (e.g. *IG* 10.2.1.1024, 1028-9, 1031-3, 1040), as well as in many inscriptions at Corinth (e.g. Merritt ##2, 14-16, 71) and at the Sarapea at Delos (see F. Mora, *Prosopografia Isiaca* [Leiden: E. J. Brill, 1990]).

[51] See Lüderitz, "Politeuma", 193-201.

highly developed Roman system was not transplanted intact.[52] Yet his first two examples concern benefaction of groups, such as the gymnasium, not personal patronage bonds.[53] A third inscription refers to a Damon who dedicated a statue to Q. Caecilius Metellus for his benefaction to the Macedonians, the Greeks in general, and to himself personally.[54] His final example is the Thessalonian poet, Antipater, whom Hendrix claims accompanied his "patron", L. Calpurnius Piso, on a journey to Asia Minor.[55] But there is nothing in the text Hendrix cites to suggest that there was actually a patronal bond between Antipater and Piso.

In fact, Hendrix does acknowledge that there is little evidence for patronal relationships prior to the second century.[56] Of the examples he cites, only the third and fourth are relevant. But in both cases, the patron is a senior Roman official in the province and the client is a prominent local. All of the other cases of patronal relations in the first century CE (or earlier) involve a patron who was Roman or strongly Romanized, and clients who were *liberti/libertae*.[57] Since there are fewer than ten cases recorded in more than a thousand inscriptions from Thessalonica, it cannot be said that patronal relationships were an important element in social networks there during the first century.[58] It is more likely that people relied on their peers for support, as has been suggested in chapter three.

---

[52] Hendrix, "Networks", 40-1.

[53] *IG* 10.2.1.4, 133; cf. Hendrix, "Networks", 44-6, 49.

[54] *IG* 10.2.1.1031; cf. Hendrix, "Networks", 47-8.

[55] See Hendrix, "Networks", 48.

[56] Ibid., 56 n. 1; cf. *IG* 10.2.1.297, 811, and possibly 658, which come from a later period.

[57] See *IG* 10.2.1.310, 339, 354, 399, 405, 688, 878. In the case of #405, the dedication is from Ferusa to Hilarus her "husband and patron". Both are Roman names, and probably reflect a servile origin. Hilarus was certainly a common servile name (see Kajanto, *Cognomina*, 68-9). She was most likely his *liberta* since "marriages" between a slave and a slave girl that he owned and freed to marry were common (see de Vos, "ΟΙΚΟΣ", 22-4). To this could be added the two slaves mentioned in the *thiasos* to *theos hypsistos* (*IG* 10.2.1.68-9).

[58] Papazoglou suggests that the use of servile labor was not common in Macedonia until the second century CE ("Macedonia", 200). Note the important distinction made by Johnson and Dandeker between patronage relationships and a patronage system ("Patronage", 220-1). Not only is there no evidence for a patronal *system* at Thessalonica, we would not expect it given the more democratic form of government.

The discussion of ethnic integration and social contact between the different socio-economic status groups suggests that in the time of Paul, it is possible that most of the boundaries between groups at Thessalonica were quite strong. While there may have been some interaction between members of different ethnic and socio-economic status groups, these may have been only casual and incidental, not regular and organized as they would be under a patronal system.

5. Political Features

According to Livy, the Macedonian settlement of 167 BCE involved a grant of freedom such that the people were able to keep their own laws and to elect annual magistrates. Most scholars suggest that it was only following the Triumviral victory of 42 BCE that Thessalonica was officially designated a *civitas libera*. It is quite possible, however, that such a status needed reconfirmation, especially given the city's support for Brutus and Cassius. In any case, Thessalonica clearly had this designation in Paul's time.[59]

Despite this grant of freedom to the province, some scholars contend that the Romans encouraged the adoption of a form of republican government, on the premise that Macedonian cities had not been autonomous under their

___

[59] Livy 45.19.4; Pliny *NH* 4.36. See Larsen, "Greece", 449; Edson, "Macedonica", 133; Papazoglou, "Macedonia", 192, 198; cf. Meeks, *First Urban*, 47; Jewett, *Correspondence*, 123; Gill, "Macedonia", 414. Holland Hendrix argues that after the victory of 42 BCE, the Triumvirs granted Thessalonica the status of *libera et immunis*. Before then, he suggests, it is possible that for some cities, including Thessalonica, there were unofficial arrangements involving concessions ("Thessalonicans Honor Romans" [Unpublished ThD dissertation, Harvard University, 1984] 350-64). The initial settlement of the province did not involve a grant of immunity (Larsen, "Greece", 457; Papazoglou, "Macedonia", 198; Collins, *The Birth*, 6). Thessalonica could not have had immunity at the time that Cicero prosecuted Piso or else Cicero would have used this to strengthen his case (Hendrix, "Honor", 358-9). Hendrix argues that the declaration of *homonoia* between Thessalonica and Rome, based on the example of Byzantium, makes it likely that there was an official ratification of its status of *libera et immunis* (Hendrix, "Honor", 360, 363-4; cf. Donfried, "The Cults", 345; Collins, *The Birth*, 7). But this is just speculation. Although fragmentary, the inscription dealing with the grant of *libera* gives no hint of *immunis* (*IG* 10.2.1.6), and as mentioned in chapter 3, grants of *immunis* were uncommon in the Triumviral period. The declaration of *homonoia* is explicable as a reaffirmation of its earlier status given the city's support for Brutus and Cassius.

kings.[60] Most, however, assert that the Macedonian cities had been largely autonomous and had functioned as democracies, even if not to the extent of the Athenian model. Certainly in the first century BCE, Thessalonica had a classical Greek structure of a popular assembly (*demos*), a council (*boule*) and a group of magistrates (*politarchs*).[61]

Some scholars claim that the Romans replaced democracy in Macedonian cities with oligarchy, effectively depriving the common man of political power.[62] But this is unlikely. Indeed, in most Macedonian cities Roman rule produced little novelty and most probably retained their

---

[60] J. H. Oliver, "Civic Constitutions for Macedonian Communities" *CPhil* 58 (1963) 164; Jewett, *Correspondence*, 123. However, it is clear that Alexander himself established democracies in a number of cities. See *SIG* 1.283; Arrian *Anab.* 1.17.10, 1.18.2; cf. Lüderitz, "Politeuma", 187.

[61] *IG* 10.2.1.5-9, 11. See Larsen, "Greece", 308; Papazoglou, "Macedonia", 197-8; Gill, "Macedonia", 411; cf. Marshall, *Acts*, 276; Meeks, *First Urban*, 47; Holtz, *erste Brief*, 9; Collins, *The Birth*, 7. There has been much discussion of Luke's term for the magistrates of Thessalonica, πολιτάρχης, in Acts 17:6. It is now known that this office was widespread in Macedonia, and that the *politarchs* formed a collegial body whose numbers varied in different cities and from time to time. At Thessalonica the range is 3-7. See *IG* 10.2.1.26-8, 30-1, 86, 109, 128, 133, 252; cf. C. Shuler, "The Macedonian Politarchs" *CPhil* 55 (1960) 90; Oliver, "Constitutions", 164; C. Koukouli-Chrysanthaki, "Politarchs in a New Inscription from Amphipolis" in H. J. Dell, ed., *Ancient Macedonian Studies in Honor of Charles F. Edson* (Thessaloniki: Institute for Balkan Studies, 1981) 240; Horsley, "Politarchs", 425-6. The *politarchs* appear to have been the chief magistrates who convened the assembly and council, introduced motions, and confirmed and carried out decrees. The office was annual but repeatable (Shuler, "Politarchs", 90-1; Horsley, "Politarchs", 425-6). It has been suggested that they became the chief magistrates of Macedonian cities only under the Romans (see Shuler, "Politarchs", 93-4; Oliver, "Constitutions", 164). But newer inscriptions show that they probably dated from at least the time of Perseus (Koukouli-Chrysanthaki, "Politarchs", 235-8, 240; Papazoglou, "Macedonia", 195-6; McRay, *Archaeology*, 294; cf. Collins, *The Birth*, 7). Although Horsley still expresses some reservations about this ("Politarchs", 424-5), he is perhaps overly cautious.

[62] Larsen, "Greece", 308, 440, 443-4; Jewett, *Correspondence*, 123. Oliver claims that while the classical Greek democracy had a large council (Plato suggested 360 in *Leg.* 756B-E), the council in another city at the time of Antoninus Pius was only 80 — a common size of Roman councils — so that Macedonian cities had Roman rather than Greek constitutional forms ("Constitutions", 165). But his argument is based on one isolated case from the mid second century CE. It suggests no more than that an increasing Romanization of Macedonian cities occurred.

judicial authorities and a form of democratic government, even if it was moderated. There is no reason to assume the average citizen of Thessalonica lost political power as this certainly did not happen in many other places.[63]

6. Religious Profile

Much of the religion of Macedonia, and presumably Thessalonica, was traditionally Greek. Important gods included Zeus, Apollo, and Heracles, to which were added the healing gods (Asclepius, Hygeia), Harpocrates, the Dioscuri, the Egyptian gods, Roma and Roman benefactors and the Imperial Cult. There was also an element drawn from the original "ethnic substratum" of Macedonia. Elements of this included the mystery cults of Dionysus and Kabirus.[64]

Some scholars have attempted to link the cult of Kabirus at Thessalonica with the cult of the Kabeiroi at Samothrace. But this is highly questionable, given that the cult at Thessalonica was quite distinct in that its focus was a single god, Kabirus, and not twin gods. It was more likely an indigenous Macedonian cult. Nevertheless, there is evidence that the Macedonian elite were interested in the Samothracian cult as well.[65]

---

[63] See, in particular, *IG* 10.2.1.5-9, 11; cf. Heraclitus *Ep.* 7; Dio Chrys. *Or.* 34, 48; the inscription in R. K. Sherk, *Rome and the Greek East to the Death of Augustus* (Cambridge: Cambridge University Press, 1984) #59a. See also section III.1 of chapter 3 herein; cf. Sherwin-White, *Law*, 96; Papazoglou, "Macedonia", 199. In Acts 17:5, Luke implies that the *demos* still retained considerable power. Although some aspects of Luke's account are historically questionable, in matters of politics and law he is generally very accurate. See, for example, Sherwin-White, *Law*, 96; R. J. Cassidy, *Jesus, Politics and Society: A Study of Luke's Gospel* (Maryknoll, NY: Orbis, 1978) 13-15; Donfried, "The Cults", 342-3.

[64] Edson, "Macedonica" 136; idem, "Cults", 160, 190-2; R. E. Witt, "The Kabeiroi in Macedonia" in *Ancient Macedonia II* (Thessaloniki: Institute for Balkan Studies, 1977) 73; Papazoglou, "Macedonia", 204-5; Hendrix, "Honor", 259; idem, "Thessalonica", 525; Hill, "Establishing", 61-6; Gill, "Macedonia", 408; cf. Donfried, "The Cults", 338. Of these, Dionysus, Kabirus, Zeus, and the Dioscuri were also commonly represented on Thessalonian coins. See B. V. Head, *A Catalogue of Greek Coins in the British Museum. Macedonia Etc.* (London: British Museum, 1879).

[65] Papazoglou, "Macedonia", 205; and to some extent Donfried, "The Cults", 339; *contra* Edson ("Cults", 188-9) and Witt ("Kabeiroi", 71-2, 78) who assume that it was imported from Samothrace. Concerning the interest of the Macedonian elite in the Samothracian cult see Edson,

A number of scholars have singled out the cult of Kabirus as being particularly important at Thessalonica. Indeed, by the middle of the first century CE Kabirus was the most common deity represented on Thessalonian coins, while one inscription refers to him as πάτριος θεός. The latter has led some scholars to suggest that there was almost a Kabiric monotheism.[66] But such a claim is an overstatement, for it is based on relatively late data (the inscription comes from the third century CE) and ignores the fact that other gods, such as the Dioscuri, were also found on a series of coins and in inscriptions during the same period.[67] Besides, representation on coins does not necessarily mean that a particular god had *popular* appeal.[68]

Robert Jewett argues that the cult of Kabirus began as the worship of a "laborer's hero" but was usurped by the elite and incorporated into the civic cult creating a religious vacuum that prepared the way for Christianity.[69] But he misunderstands the relationship between public and private worship.[70] Jewett also overstates what is known about the cult and, in so doing, he relies on work which uncritically extrapolates from the cult of the Kabeiroi from other regions

---

"Cults", 189-90; Witt, "Kabeiroi", 73-4; Koester, "Eschatology", 443.

[66] *IG* 10.2.1.199; Edson, "Cults", 190-3; Witt, "Kabeiroi", 78; Papazoglou, "Macedonia", 205; cf. Jewett, *Correspondence*, 127-8; Hill, "Establishing", 66-7; K. P. Donfried, "The Theology of 1 Thessalonians" in K. P. Donfried & I. H. Marshall, *The Theology of the Shorter Pauline Letters* (Cambridge: Cambridge University Press, 1993) 15. See Head, *Catalogue*.

[67] See the evidence presented by J. S. Kloppenborg, "Φιλαδελφία, Θεοδίδακτος and the Dioscuri: Rhetorical Engagement in 1 Thessalonians 4.9-12" *NTS* 39 (1993) 283-6; cf. *IG* 10.2.1.56; Hendrix, "Honor", 148-51.

[68] This is something that even Hill acknowledges ("Establishing", 65). Surprisingly, in the latest volume of the British Museum collection of coins the only god who appears more than once in coins minted at Thessalonica is Nike, and no coin has either Kabirus or the Dioscuri. See A. Burnett et al, *Roman Provincial Coins* (vol 1; London: British Museum Press, 1992) ##1551, 1556, 1582-4, 1593, 1595, 1597, 1604. Even in the early catalog by Head, the most common god represented on coins in the last century BCE was Ianus. Yet no one has suggested that either Nike or Ianus were prominent, let alone popular, at Thessalonica.

[69] See Jewett, *Correspondence*, 124-32.

[70] This has been discussed in chapter three. See also Koester, "Eschatology", 443-4; J. M. G. Barclay, "Conflict in Thessalonica" *CBQ* 55 (1993) 519 n. 24.

and from Clement of Alexandria's polemics. In fact, little is known of the practices of the Thessalonian cult of Kabirus.[71]

Another prominent indigenous cult was that of Dionysus, a state cult that is known at Thessalonica from at least the late Hellenistic period.[72] The Egyptian cults were prominent in the city, although their actual importance is difficult to assess. That Philip V (187 BCE) wrote to the city regarding the use of the Sarapeum's funds suggests that the cult was important.[73] While the importance of the Egyptian cults might reflect the historic links between Macedonia and Alexandria, such an explanation is entirely conjectural.[74] Although at Thessalonica they may have been salvation-cults, the details of the rites of the cults are unknown.[75]

In Paul's time the Imperial cult was particularly important. Soon after Augustus became Princeps, the city erected a temple to *Divus Caesar*, as an expression of their loyalty to Augustus. Along with the lavish honors they bestowed on him, this honor probably reflects the political insecurity that the city felt, given their history, and an awareness that their continued position depended on maintaining Imperial benefaction.[76] This was probably an extension of an earlier cult in Thessalonica to Roma and Roman benefactors, begun soon after the revolt of 148 BCE was crushed.[77]

Overall, not very much is actually known of Thessalonian religious practices. It is reasonable to suppose, however, that the Thessalonians shared many of the religious values and norms that were characteristic of other

---

[71] Jewett relies on Witt, "Kabeiroi", 73 (Jewett, *Correspondence*, 129-30). This is strongly rebutted by Koester, "Eschatology", 443-4. Donfried ("The Cults", 338) also overstates the details of the cult.

[72] Edson, "Cults", 160-1. Donfried ("The Cults", 337) claims the cult began in 187 BCE, and wrongly cites Edson in support.

[73] *IG* 10.2.1.3; Papazoglou, "Macedonia", 207; Hill, "Establishing", 63; Hendrix, "Thessalonica", 523. Jewett claims that the Isis cult was "less well supported by the civic establishment" at Thessalonica (*Correspondence*, 126-7). This is clearly contrary to the inscriptions found, not least *IG* 10.2.1.3. See also *IG* 10.2.1.76, 86, 97, 108-9, 115.

[74] Gill, "Macedonia", 408-9.

[75] Donfried, "The Cults", 337.

[76] Hendrix, "Honor", 303-7, 337. He is probably correct in asserting that at Thessalonica the honors were given to the recipients as human rather than divine. See also Hendrix, "Imperial Cult".

[77] Edson, "Macedonica", 134; Hendrix, "Honor", 318; Donfried, "The Cults", 345.

Greek cities.[78] That is, they probably valued a continuity between religious belief and practice and expected their citizens to participate in their religious practices and festivals.

In summary, then, Thessalonica in the first century CE was a large and busy city. Nevertheless, it has many characteristics of a community: close and very public living and a strong integration of the various aspects of city life. Its planning suggests there may have been some geographic separation of different groups. It is unclear whether the city was ethnically cosmopolitan or homogeneous. The available inscriptions suggest possibly the latter, but at least that there probably was not a high degree of ethnic integration. In fact, given Greek xenophobia, ethnic boundaries may have been strongly enforced. There is little to suggest whether there was or was not a Jewish community in Thessalonica. The nature of the social interactions suggests that there would not have been much interaction between members of different socio-economic status groups and possibly only limited interaction of different ethnic groups. Administratively, the city was the provincial capital with the status of *civitas libera* (but probably not *immunis*). Its administrative/political structures were typically Greek and democratic, and there is no reason to assume that the average citizen of the city had lost his political power.

Not much is actually known of Thessalonian religious practices. They worshiped a number of typically Greek gods, as well as the Egyptian gods, while mystery cults centered on Dionysus and Kabirus were probably indigenous. It is reasonable to suppose that their religious outlook was typically Greek. The strong emphasis on the Imperial cult at Thessalonica, along with the earlier cult of Roma and Roman benefactors, probably reflects their sense of dependence on Roman benefaction, and their political insecurity.

---

[78] The fact that the goddess Nike was found on several Thessalonian coins need not negate this. For although such "abstract" gods were not generally among the popular gods in Hellenistic cities (apart from Tyche), it is likely that she would have been identified with the Roman Victoria and hence associated with the Imperial Cult — something that was important at Thessalonica, especially among those who would have decided the images on coins. Although it may be suggested that I am drawing inferences here from other regions and thus doing what I have been so critical of with Jewett, there is a considerable difference in our approaches. My argument is concerned with the *general* religious mentality of the city, while his argument is about *specific* details of a particular cult.

II. THE CHRISTIAN COMMUNITY AT THESSALONICA

The Christian community at Thessalonica that Paul founded, and to which he wrote, could be described in a number of ways. There are three main features, however, that will be important for understanding the nature of the relationship between the Christian and civic communities and the development of conflict. These are the ethnic composition, the social profile and the size of the Christian community.

1. Ethnic Composition

Normally, when Paul wrote to one of his churches he used a locative expression that emphasized the *geographical location* of the church. In 1 Thess 1:1, however, Paul addresses the letter τῇ ἐκκλησίᾳ Θεσσαλονικέων ἐν θεῷ. This unusual expression seems to specifically emphasize its *ethnic* composition, implying that the Christian community consists of native-Thessalonians.[79] Although Hill admits that

---

[79] Romans is addressed πᾶσιν τοῖς οὖσιν ἐν Ῥώμῃ (1:7); 1 & 2 Corinthians are addressed τῇ ἐκκλησίᾳ τοῦ θεοῦ τῇ οὔσῃ ἐν Κορίνθῳ (1 Cor 1:2; 2 Cor 2:1); Philippians is addressed πᾶσιν τοῖς ἁγίοις...οὖσιν ἐν Φιλίπποις (1:1). Although it does not have the ἐν-construction, Gal 1:2 (ταῖς ἐκκλησίαις τῆς Γαλατίας) has the same geographical sense. See also Hill, "Establishing", 196-7; A. J. Malherbe, "God's New Family in Thessalonica" in L. M. White & O. L. Yarbrough, eds., *The Social World of the First Christians* (Minneapolis: Fortress, 1995) 117-19; cf. Holtz, *erste Brief*, 38; *contra* E. Best, *A Commentary on the First and Second Epistles to the Thessalonians* (BNTC; London: A. & C. Black, 1977) 62. As E. J. Richard notes, the genitive in 1 Thess 1:1 is probably a "partitive genitive", so the sense is "the community made up of Thessalonians" (*First and Second Thessalonians* [SP; Collegeville, MN: Michael Glazier, 1995] 38). This particular expression is found only in 1 & 2 Thessalonians. The ἐν θεῷ clearly qualifies ἐκκλησία and thereby draws a contrast between the Christian ἐκκλησία and the civic ἐκκλησία (*contra* Richard who claims that ἐκκλησία here refers to the Hellenistic synagogue [*Thessalonians*, 38]). Since the latter referred to the meeting of the *demos* (*TDNT* 3.513) this strengthens the ethnic sense of the phrase (*nomen gentilicum*), as such a contrast would be most meaningful to those who were members of the civic ἐκκλησία. Although there is a reference to ἡ Λαοδικέων ἐκκλησία in Col 4:16 this church also may have been ethnically homogeneous — but there are no other indicators of its composition. In 1 Thess 2:14 Paul speaks of the αἱ ἐκκλησίαι τοῦ θεοῦ αἱ οὖσαι ἐν τῇ Ἰουδαίᾳ ἐν Χριστῷ Ἰησοῦ. The sense of the comparison in 2:14-15 implies that he was using this expression in an ethnic, rather than geographical sense. This does not, however, negate

this particular designation is unique, she contends that it has a local rather than a racial meaning, referring to those who had been resident in the city for a long time.[80] Similarly, other scholars dilute the sense, suggesting that it means the church is *primarily* Thessalonian.[81] However, they fail to explain why Paul would have chosen this designation rather than his more usual and inclusive locative expression.

It is unlikely, however, that Paul would have used the term in any other sense. Indeed, even if the majority of the church were native Thessalonians, to use a term which seems to impute such a status to some who were not would have caused great offence to the majority who were.[82] Therefore, it

---

the ethnic sense and the uniqueness of the expression in 1 Thess 1:1. While the ἐν expression is, strictly speaking, semantically ambiguous, and depends on the context for its meaning, the use of the *nomen gentilicum is ethnically specific* and does not include the geographic.

[80] Hill, "Establishing", 197. She also suggests that such a designation was only used in civic affairs or when referring to "the background of a person living or visiting elsewhere" (ibid., 199). But this is not supported by the use of the term Θεσσαλονικεύς in *IG* 10.2.1.68.

[81] See Jewett, *Correspondence*, 118; B. C. Johanson, *To All the Brethren: A Text-Linguistic and Rhetorical Approach to 1 Thessalonians* (ConBNT 16; Stockholm: Almqvist & Wiksell, 1987) 49; cf. Hill, "Establishing", 250-1.

[82] For example, the Jews in one city are clearly described as "the Jews in...". See *CIG* 3.5361; cf. Lüderitz, "Politeuma", 211-12. Also, Claudius' letter to the Alexandrians is addressed Ἀλεξανδρέων τῇ πόλει and clearly distinguishes between Alexandrians and Jews (*CPJ* 153.15-16, 82-3 [White, *Light*, 133-6]). That Jews claimed the title of natives most likely contributed to the conflict between Jews and Greeks. See Smallwood, *The Jews*, 228-9; Trebilco, *Communities*, 172. D. Delia has shown that the term Ἀλεξανδρεύς was always used in legal documents from the Roman period to refer to those with Alexandrian citizenship but that in informal correspondence it could refer to both citizens and resident non-citizens (*Alexandrian Citizenship during the Roman Principate* [Atlanta: Scholars, 1991] 26-7). It is difficult to know whether Paul's letter was an official document or informal correspondence. In any case, there is also a huge difference between informal correspondence between two individuals and a letter, like this, addressed to a group. To use the same term to address a group that included both citizens and resident non-citizens would, given the strong sense of civic-pride and patriotism evident in inscriptions and conflicts between cities, surely have been an insult. Paul does use ethnic terms for addressees in 2 Cor 6:11 (Κορίνθιοι), Phil 4:15 (Φιλιππήσιοι) and Gal 3:1 (Γαλάται), but in each case he is moved by emotion, and it is unlikely that he was as careful in his use of language than when he was making the more formal address to the letter (cf. Winter, *Seek*, 129). Besides, it is doubtful that the provincial term, "Galatians", carried the same weight as a civic one.

could refer only to people who were natives and therefore citizens of the city.[83] This would seem to fit with the earlier tentative suggestion that there was a tendency towards ethnic segregation at Thessalonica. The reference to conflict with their συμφυλέται also suggests strongly that the Christians were citizens of the city.

The main reason that scholars try to dilute the clear ethnic sense of 1:1 is to include Jews in the church. Acts 17:2 states that on arriving in Thessalonica Paul preached first in the synagogue. However, κατὰ δὲ τὸ εἰωθός suggests that Luke is applying a formula and his account of Paul in Thessalonica is heavily shaped by his theological agenda. Luke's account must be considered somewhat suspect for, apart from this contradiction regarding the composition of the church, there are a number of other significant discrepancies.[84] Furthermore, the fact that Paul never cites or

---

[83] The citizen of a Greek democracy was traditionally defined as an adult male who was born in the city of citizen parents. See, for example, Aristotle *Pol.* 1275A-B; Heraclitus *Ep.* 9; cf. E. S. Staveley, *Greek and Roman Voting and Elections* (London: Thames & Hudson, 1972) 78; Delia, *Citizenship*, 28. It could be argued that the Thessalonian Christians could not have had a political role even in the *demos*, since citizenship was not open to all who even fitted these characteristics because a certain level of wealth was required. For example, J. C. Lentz claims that "full citizenship in a Greek city was reserved, even in the city of Tarsus…, for those of landed wealth and was a mark of status that many longed for but few achieved" (*Luke's Portrait of Paul* [SNTSMS 77; Cambridge: Cambridge University Press, 1993] 33). But Tarsus may have had a timocratic form of government — one that was certainly not universal in Greek cities. For example, Staveley notes that there was no such requirement at Athens. In fact, the bulk of those who did attend *demos* meetings in that city were artisans. The very "poor" did not attend because they could not afford to forgo their wages, not because they were not entitled (*Voting*, 78). But Dio Chrysostom seems to imply that even at Tarsus artisans such as dyers, cobblers and carpenters were citizens (*Or.* 34.23). See also Meggitt, *Poverty*, 83.

[84] See Haenchen, *Acts*, 506-7, 510-11; Jewett, *Correspondence*, 117; Malherbe, *Paul*, 8; F. W. Hughes, "The Rhetoric of 1 Thessalonians" in R. F. Collins, ed., *The Thessalonian Correspondence* (BETL 87; Leuven: Leuven University Press, 1990) 96-7; Lührmann, "Beginnings", 237-40; C. A. Wanamaker, *A Commentary on 1 & 2 Thessalonians* (NIGTC; Grand Rapids: Eerdmans, 1990) 85; Collins, *The Birth*, 31-3, 36; *contra* Marshall, *Acts*, 275; Donfried, "Theology", 54. The discrepancies include Luke claiming Timothy stayed in Beroea whereas Paul suggests he accompanied him to Athens; Luke claims that Paul only stayed in

appeals to the OT, refers to any OT figure, or uses any OT cultic language, seems to exclude the possibility that there were Jews in the Thessalonian church.[85] Paul's contention that they turned ἀπὸ τῶν εἰδώλων δουλεύειν θεῷ (1:9) would also rule this out.[86]

Consequently, it is most likely that the Christian community at Thessalonica was comprised entirely of native Thessalonians who had been converted from their traditional Hellenistic religions. Contrary to Luke's account, there does not appear to have been any Jews within the church. It is also likely that the Thessalonian Christians were citizens of the city. Such a profile would be consistent with the earlier (tentative) suggestion that social groupings at Thessalonica tended to be ethnically homogeneous.

2. Social Profile

It is generally assumed that the social profile of the Thessalonian church was similar to that of the Corinthian church, being based in a large villa provided by a wealthy patron within the community, and comprising a cross-section of society.[87] The assumption that the church had a broad

Thessalonica for three weeks, but Paul's reference to receiving two gifts from the Philippians while there (Phil 4:16) means it must have been considerably longer; Luke deliberately seems to ignore the fact that Paul worked while in Thessalonica; Luke claims that the opposition to Paul's ministry at Thessalonica comes from Jews but in 1 Thess it clearly comes from Thessalonians. This will be discussed further below.

[85] See Lührmann, "Beginnings", 239. Holtz accepts that it was a Gentile church, but suggests that its members had had some contact with Judaism prior to their conversion (*erste Brief*, 10). But there is no evidence in 1 Thess to support this claim. Nor does anything suggest they were "God-fearers" (*contra* R. Russell, "The Idle in 2 Thess 3.6-12: An Eschatological or a Social Problem?" *NTS* 34 [1988] 111).

[86] Hughes, "Rhetoric", 96-7; Lührmann, "Beginnings", 239; E. J. Richard, "Early Pauline Thought: An Analysis of 1 Thessalonians" in J. M. Bassler, ed., *Pauline Theology, Volume I* (Minneapolis: Fortress, 1991) 40-1. I. H. Marshall contends that Jews could be included as theirs was a conversion from "a false attitude to God to a true one" (*1 & 2 Thessalonians* [NCB; Grand Rapids: Eerdmans, 1983] 57), but this involves a psychological and doctrinal anachronism that misconstrues the nature of first century Judaism(s).

[87] See, for example, Meeks, *First Urban*, 73; Jewett, *Correspondence*, 103, 120-1; Johanson, *Brethren*, 51; Hill, "Establishing", 218-19; Winter, *Seek*, 47. Winter presupposes that Paul's call for the Thessalonian Christians to work and to be "dependent on nobody" (4:11-12) is encouraging them not to become clients. He adds that since the

social profile also relies on Luke's account in Acts 17, and a later reference to Aristarchus from Thessalonica in Acts 19:29 and 20:4.[88] Scholars often acknowledge that Luke has a particular bias towards showing that Christianity attracted converts from the upper classes. But there is no reason to assume that this particular Aristarchus was a member of the Thessalonian elite. Indeed, it is likely that Luke would have drawn attention to that fact if that were the case.[89]

Some scholars claim that the Jason mentioned in Acts 17:5-9 was a wealthy patron who provided hospitality to Paul during his stay, and that the Thessalonian church met in his home.[90] But even assuming the authenticity of Luke's account at this point, it is still a presumption. Rather, Jason may have owned the workshop where Paul worked, like the arrangement with Aquila and Prisca at Corinth. And since Paul engaged in manual labor at Thessalonica it is likely that he stayed in an *insula*-workshop, and not in a luxury *villa*.[91]

---

elite only sought clients from those with some status or way of repaying, the Thessalonian Christians therefore could not have been the "urban poor" (*Seek*, 42-3, 45-6). But he assumes a Roman system of patronage which did not exist (see section II of chapter 3 herein), and that artisans ranked among the urban poor. Furthermore, it will be suggested in the next chapter that the Corinthian church itself may not have met in the villa of a wealthy member.

[88] See, for example, Winter, *Seek*, 46.

[89] The assumption is usually based on the mention of Aristarchus son of Aristarchus, a politarch in *IG* 10.2.1.30, 50. But, as a number of commentators point out, it was a common Macedonian name. See Hemer, *Book*, 236; Lührmann, "Beginnings", 241; Horsley, "Politarchs", 429. On Luke's bias towards the elite see Malherbe, *Paul*, 16; L. T. Johnson, *The Acts of the Apostles* (SP; Collegeville, MN: Michael Glazier, 1992) 306-10; Collins, *The Birth*, 33.

[90] For example, Meeks, *First Urban*, 62-63; Hill, "Establishing", 253; F. Morgan-Gillman, "Jason of Thessalonica (Acts 17,1-9)" in R. F. Collins, ed., *The Thessalonian Correspondence* (BETL 87; Leuven: Leuven University Press, 1990) 41, 49; Kloppenborg, "Φιλαδελφία", 276; Collins, *The First*, 15. Although the name "Jason" was frequently used by Diaspora Jews as a substitute for "Joshua", it was also a very common Greek name. Consequently, there is no real reason to identify this particular Jason with the one described as a Jewish Christian in Rom 16:21 (Haenchen, *Acts*, 507; Lührmann, "Beginnings", 240-1; Johnson, *Acts*, 307; *contra* Morgan-Gillman, "Jason", 40. Indeed, Malherbe suggests that the portrait of Jason in Acts 17:5-9 presents him as a Gentile (*Paul*, 14).

[91] Malherbe, *Paul*, 15-17; cf. R. F. Hock, *The Social Context of Paul's Ministry: Tentmaking and Apostleship* (Philadelphia: Fortress, 1980) 35-7. Since the elite strongly disdained manual labor it is most unlikely that Paul would have stayed with a member of this group, let alone have been

Others contend that since Aquila and Prisca were Christians before Paul met them, Lydia at Philippi (Acts 16:14-15), who was converted and then offered hospitality, may be a better parallel.[92] But they ignore the possible uniqueness of Paul's relationship with the Philippian Christians.[93] Nor does Paul seem to have worked at Philippi.

Furthermore, the assumption that all of Paul's churches met in villas presumes that they all followed the Corinthian pattern. This is unlikely.[94] Indeed, Jewett has recently pointed out that there were probably Christian communities at Rome that were comprised entirely of people of low social status. He suggests that such churches could easily have met in an *insula*-shop, as occurred later. This, he contends, also occurred at Thessalonica.[95] His argument is supported by the

---

introduced to his/her peers. The fact that some of the elite and well-to-do were converted while Paul worked and ministered at Corinth (although it is only implied in the text that Paul himself was responsible for their conversion) need not negate this argument. Given that there was a significant Jewish presence in the Corinthian church, unlike at Thessalonica, some of the well-to-do may have been converted via relationships with prominent Jews or "God-fearers" (such as Stephanas or Crispus). It is also possible that their conversion comes during the time when Paul no longer worked to support himself, after the arrival of the Philippians' gift and of Timothy and Silas (if the account in Acts is to be relied upon).

[92] Morgan-Gillman, "Jason", 41, 49; Collins, *The First*, 15.

[93] This will be discussed in chapter six.

[94] See n. 87 above. Sallares has recently argued that scholars should not assume that there was a uniformity of population structures across the Greco-Roman world (*Ecology*, 44). Barclay makes a similar point in relation to different Diaspora Jewish communities, especially in terms of varying patterns of assimilation and acculturation (*Jews*, 92-3).

[95] See R. Jewett, "Tenement Churches and Communal Meals in the Early Church: The Implications of a Form-Critical Analysis of 2 Thessalonians 3:10" *BR* 38 (1993) 24-32. He notes that οἶκος refers to a variety of residence types, including the *insula* flat, and that there is evidence for *insula*-workshop churches after Paul's time (ibid., 24-7, esp. n. 19). An analysis of the names in Rom 16:14-15 suggests that these represent two "house" churches comprised of people from servile origins without patronage, who would have been based in such a setting (ibid., 28-31). Despite the title of his article, Jewett's contention that the Thessalonian church was a tenement church is largely based on the pattern of communal living suggested by 1 Thess 2:9, 4:9-12. 2 Thess 3:10 gives additional support for this (ibid., 39-42). Furthermore, Kloppenborg has recently demonstrated that the main context in which the Thessalonian Christians would have heard the term φιλαδελφία (4:9) would have been the cult of the Dioscuri ("Φιλαδελφία", 282-3). That the only known ritual associated with this cult was a feast provided

example of the church at Troas that met in an upstairs *insula*-apartment (Acts 20:7-9). Since such apartments were very small, it is unlikely that they would have met in one if there had been wealthier members in the community.[96]

The Thessalonian church probably did not include slaves. Some scholars suggest such a scenario since there are no references to slaves or slavery compared to Paul's other letters (1 Cor 7:21-22; Gal 3:28; Phlm 15-16).[97] Furthermore, if there were no wealthy patrons there would have been few slaves, given the incidence of household conversions.[98] That there were no slaves, however, is most likely given Paul's expectation that the Christians should be self-sufficient (1 Thess 4:12).

This same injunction would also seem to rule out freedpersons. In the case of slaves freed by Roman masters, they would have been required to perform *operae* and remained financially liable to their former masters and their families. In the case of slaves owned by Greek masters (which, if there were slaves in the Thessalonian church, would have been the more likely scenario) the incidence of manumission would have been much less and its arrangements much harsher. Indeed, Greek "freedpersons" were never really free.[99] Consequently, the Thessalonian

---

for the poor by the rich (ibid., 286; cf. Jewett, "Tenement", 39-40) may be further evidence of the social position of the Thessalonian Christians. However, Kloppenborg's contention that Paul *intended* the term θεοδίδακτος to refer to the Dioscuri also (ibid., 287-9) is untenable.

[96] McKay, however, notes that two three-story *insula* apartment-blocks found at Ephesus had shops on the ground floor and "luxury apartments" on the other two floors (*Houses*, 213-17). But nothing suggests that these blocks were representative for the Greek world, given that they were built on the slopes of a hill and that substantial remodelling occurred over time. These apartments and McKay's analysis was discussed more fully in section I of chapter 2 herein.

[97] Hill, "Establishing", 228; cf. Jewett, *Correspondence*, 120.

[98] See Jewett, *Correspondence*, 120; cf. chapter 3 of de Vos, "ΟΙΚΟΣ".

[99] Fisher notes that unlike Roman *liberti* who became citizens, Greek freedpersons were regarded as metics and treated as such in respect to legal status and in harsher taxation (*Slavery*, 68). Manumission contracts after 200 BCE normally involved an agreement that such freedpersons would work for the former masters, and they could be quite restrictive (ibid., 68-70; cf. W. L. Westermann, *The Slave Systems of Greek and Roman Antiquity* [Philadelphia: American Philosophical Society, 1955] 35, 38). The rate of manumission was also much less (Fisher, *Slavery*, 70). See also Bartchy, *Slavery*, 41-4.

church was probably comprised of free people from the artisan class.

Some scholars have suggested this reconstruction, based on Paul's reference to the poverty of the Macedonian Christians in 2 Cor 8:2 (ἡ κατὰ βάθους πτωχεία αὐτῶν).[100] But others contend that this passage is heavily rhetorical, to the point of being hyperbolic.[101] Those who insist that the Thessalonian Christians were poor use this to argue that they experienced a sense of relative deprivation (in a situation of increasing socio-economic prosperity their aspirations were unjustly thwarted) or status inconsistency (their status in one area, such as level of wealth, did not match their status in another, such as legal rights).[102] Both of these ideas involve ethnocentric anachronisms. As was argued in chapter three, artisans, like the vast majority of the population in the ancient world, lived near subsistence level. This is no reason to assume they experienced feelings of frustration or disillusionment. Those who reject the idea that the Thessalonian Christians were artisans usually do so as a means of negating such arguments.[103]

In pre-industrial societies that operate on the basis of honor-shame, poverty normally refers to a *loss* of one's inherited social status.[104] Under normal circumstances, therefore, the Thessalonian Christians may not have been "poor", but this does not negate the likelihood that they were artisans living at subsistence level. Ultimately this text gives no clues to the socio-economic status of the church, except that it had declined. Besides, it is possible that in 2 Cor 8:2 Paul implies that the poverty of the Macedonian Christians, including the Thessalonians, is linked to their experience of θλῖψις, as something they have experienced as a result of their faith.

---

[100] See, for example, Jewett, *Correspondence*, 120; Johanson, *Brethren*, 50. Both, however, suggest that this applied to *most* of the church.

[101] Meeks, *First Urban*, 66; Barclay, "Contrasts", 56 n. 8; idem, "Conflict", 519 n. 23; cf. Hill, "Establishing" 245 n. 703.

[102] See, for example, Meeks, *First Urban*, 73; Jewett, *Correspondence*, 121-3.

[103] This would appear to be the intention of Barclay ("Contrasts", 56; "Conflict", 519-20).

[104] Malina, *World*, 105-6.

Paul's instruction that they work with their hands (1
Thess 4:11) also suggests that they were artisans.[105] Barclay
argues that this is not a good basis for determining their
social level since Paul might have *assumed* that such work
was appropriate.[106] Dio Chrysostom discusses a range of
occupations, listing them as acceptable or unacceptable
depending on whether they are harmful to the health or
immoral.[107] But even those which are acceptable are
considered so *only* for commoners. Since Paul expects the
Thessalonian Christians to be respected by outsiders for
engaging in manual labor, as the ἵνα of 4:12 seems to
indicate, this could only mean that they were already
members of the "working class".

For that reason, also, the recent argument of Abraham
Smith must be rejected. He contends that Paul's instruction in
4:11, and his reference to his own labor in 2:9, draws on an
ancient tradition associating work with a life of virtue and
simplicity.[108] This would make 4:11 no more than a call to a
virtuous life. But it is not at all apparent that Paul is drawing
on such imagery in 4:11. Smith's argument is also negated by
the expectation in 4:12 that working will earn the Christians
respect from outsiders, something which must be related to
the "appropriateness" of such behavior.

The main reason for thinking that the Thessalonian
Christians were artisans is the context in which Paul
preached in the city. Given that his base would not have
been a synagogue, since the church seems to have included
no Jews, and that he admits to having worked to support
himself, the most likely scenario is that Paul preached while
he worked.[109] The workshop was also a common place where

---

[105] See, for example, Best, *Commentary*, 176; Meeks, *First Urban*,
64-5; Jewett, *Correspondence*, 120; to some extent also Russell, "The
Idle", 112-13; Kloppenborg, "Φιλαδελφία", 274.

[106] Barclay, "Contrasts", 56 n. 8; idem, "Conflict", 519 n. 23.

[107] Dio Chrys. *Or.* 7.109-23; cf. also Richard, *Thessalonians*, 212.

[108] A. Smith, *Comfort One Another: Reconstructing the Rhetoric and
Audience of 1 Thessalonians* (Louisville: WJK Press, 1995) 38-9; cf.
Marshall, *Enmity*, 171; Richard, *Thessalonians*, 220. Although Smith
mainly relies on Seneca's *Helv.* 10.7-8 (*Comfort*, 119 n. 66), other
examples could be given, including Horace's fable of the "Country Mouse
and City Mouse" (*Sat.* 2.6.79-117).

[109] See Hock, *Social Context*, 31-41; Malherbe, *Paul*, 18-19;
Marshall, *Enmity*, 166-7; Hill, "Establishing", 249; Wanamaker,
Commentary, 106; Collins, *The Birth*, 12-17; Kloppenborg, "Φιλαδελφία",
274; cf. Meeks, *First Urban*, 51. It is normally assumed that Paul worked

Cynic philosophers taught. And if Paul preached while he worked in a workshop, those who heard would also have been other artisans.[110]

Furthermore, it is unlikely that Paul simply preached in the *agora* or on street-corners. That was the practice of the Sophists, and Paul clearly sought to distance himself from them — something that is very evident in 2:3-6.[111] In addition, since his aim was to establish a community, rather than simply call individuals to follow a moral life, a more private setting and a form of teacher-student relationship was required. This is supported by Paul's reference to individual instruction in 2:11.[112]

as a tent-maker or leather-worker, largely based on Luke's description of him in Acts 18:3 as a σκηνοποιός (e.g. Hock, *Social Context*, 20-5; F. F. Bruce, *1 & 2 Thessalonians* [WBC; Waco, TX: Word, 1982] 34; Hill, "Establishing", 248; Wanamaker, *Commentary*, 104; Collins, *The First*, 12, 14-15). But Paul himself does not identify his trade, and it may be unwise to extrapolate from Luke's description. See Smith, *Comfort*, 38. That Paul regularly engaged in some form of craft is also apparent from 1 Cor 4:12. Contrary to Smith (ibid.), however, even if this was Paul's trade, that does not necessarily mean that *all* the Thessalonian Christians shared it, although it is possible (see Kloppenborg, "Φιλαδελφία", 274-5).

[110] Although Socrates is said to have taught in a shop, he seems to have taught more frequently in the *stoai* and *gymnasia*. Only the Cynics seem to have regularly taught in workshops. See Hock, *Social Context*, 37-9, 41. And most of them appear to have come from the artisan class (ibid., 38; cf. Lucian *Fug.* 12-13, 17, 28, 33; idem, *Pisc.* 12-13, 34, 40). Although Hock assumes that there would be members of the elite among the customers in Paul's workshop, this is based on the presumption that his trade was a tent-maker (ibid., 33-4). It is also doubtful that many members of the elite would visit such shops, but would instead send slaves. The idea that Paul's converts were from among his own artisan class is supported by the observation that conversion normally occurs along social networks. See R. Stark, "Jewish Conversion", 318-19, 321-5; N. H. Taylor, "The Social Nature of Conversion in the Early Christian World" in P. F. Esler, ed., *Modelling Early Christianity: Social-scientific Studies of the New Testament in its Context* (London: Routledge, 1995) 128, 132; cf. de Vos, "ΟΙΚΟΣ", especially p.59. Kloppenborg assumes that the same crafts tended to be concentrated together and thus the convert may have shared the same, or similar trades ("Φιλαδελφία", 274-5). The evidence for such clustering at Thessalonica is non-existent. Whether or not it did occur, it is likely that people of the same craft socialized together so that the Thessalonian church may have been a converted trade *thiasos* as Kloppenborg also suggests (ibid.).

[111] See, for example, Wanamaker, *Commentary*, 95-8.

[112] Hock, *Social Context*, 42; Malherbe, *Paul*, 9-11; Wanamaker, *Commentary*, 104-6. Luke represents Paul as preaching ἐν τῇ ἀγορᾷ

Taken together, Paul's instruction to pursue manual labor and the fact that a workshop was the most probable base for his missionary activity make it highly likely that the Thessalonian Church was of a relatively uniform socio-economic level. In light of this is also quite unlikely that there were any members of the elite, and any slaves or freedpersons in the community. Consequently, the church was most probably comprised of freeborn artisans and manual-workers.

3. Size

Hill suggests that the Thessalonian church could not have been so small that the death of some members (4:13) did not severely devastate the community numerically. At the same time, she claims that it could not have been too large or it would have attracted the attention of the Roman authorities. Consequently, she suggests that the church at Thessalonica may have numbered up to seventy-five.[113]

This argument, however, clearly assumes a potential situation of "persecution" by the Roman authorities. But such an assumption is clearly anachronistic. As will be apparent in the next section, the Christian community was already causing a stir, and that *per se* would have been sufficient to attract Roman attention. Under such conditions size is quite irrelevant. Ultimately, her estimate is based on the further assumption that the church met in a villa. But if it met in an *insula*-workshop, as is more likely, it would have been much smaller, perhaps comprising no more than twenty to twenty-five members.[114]

In summary, then, the most likely picture of the Thessalonian Christian community is of a very small group of native Thessalonians, who were both citizens and artisans. Given such a profile, it is likely that the church met in an *insula*-workshop.

(Acts 17:17), but it is more likely that he preached in a workshop, most of which were located around the *agora*. See Hock, *Social Context*, 42. Luke also has Paul preaching in the stoas, but this reflect his apologetic agenda of portraying Paul as a respectable philosopher.

[113] Hill, "Establishing", 247-8.
[114] See Jewett, "Tenement", 24-5.

III. CHURCH AND CIVIC COMMUNITY RELATIONS

If the language of 1 Thessalonians is any guide, it is clear that the relations between the Christian and civic communities involved considerable conflict. Indeed, especially in the first three chapters there are numerous references to suffering and struggling: ὑπομονή (1:3), θλῖψις (1:6; 3:3, 7), θλίβω (3:4), πάσχω (2:2, 14), ἀγών (2:2), ἐκδιώκω (2:15), ἀνάγκη (3:7). Although ἐν πολλῷ ἀγῶνι in 2:2 has been interpreted as Paul's mental effort in proclaiming the gospel, the context makes this unlikely, as does the use of παρρησιάζεσθαι, which suggests a sense of courage. There seems to be no question that there was some external conflict.[115] Indeed, that the community was still experiencing this suffering and conflict is suggested by Paul's act of sending Timothy to support them. It is also implied that all the Thessalonian Christians experienced this conflict.[116]

1. Conflict/Repression

1 Thess 1:6 clearly suggests that the conflict Paul's readers experienced was directly related to their conversion. Presumably this arose because they had "turned to God from idols" (1:9), abandoning their traditional religious practices *and*, perhaps more significantly, all of the associated social interaction. In this regard, language like that listed in the introduction to section III, was used by converts to philosophy and Judaism to describe their experiences of social alienation.[117] As was noted, however, the language of suffering in 1 Thessalonians does assume an actual external threat not just mental anguish or a sense of alienation. It is

---

[115] See Pfitzner, *Agon Motif*, 112-13; cf. Best, *Commentary*, 91-2; Bruce, *Thessalonians*, 25; Marshall, *Thessalonians*, 64; Wanamaker, *Commentary*, 81.

[116] Marshall, *Thessalonians*, 92; Jewett, *Correspondence*, 178; Johanson, *Brethren*, 50; Hill, "Establishing", 235; Lührmann, "Beginnings", 242-3; Barclay, "Contrasts", 53; idem, "Conflict", 513.

[117] See, for example, Heraclitus *Ep.* 7; Epictetus *Diss.* 3.13.1-3; *Joseph & Aseneth* 12.12(11)-13; cf. A. J. Malherbe, "Self-Definition among Epicureans and Cynics" in B. F. Meyer & E. P. Sanders, eds., *Jewish and Christian Self-Definition* (vol. 3; London: SCM Press, 1982) 54-5; idem, *Paul*, 37-8, 44; idem, "'Pastoral Care' in the Thessalonian Church" *NTS* 36 (1990) 387-8. But Epictetus also suggests that Cynic converts ought to expect *actual* "persecution" (*Diss.* 3.22.53-5).

more likely that given the Christians' rejection of their traditional religious practices they would have been branded as ἄθεοι. Their abandonment of such practices may have been perceived by many as a threat to the civic community from the wrath of the gods.[118]

Given the integration of religion and politics that was noted in the third chapter herein, it is likely that such "atheism" would have been understood as politically subversive. This is even more likely if the Christians also claimed to follow another king. Such an idea could easily be construed from Paul's use of political language in 2:12 (βασιλεία τοῦ θεοῦ), 4:15 (παρουσία τοῦ κυρίου) and 5:3 (εἰρήνη καὶ ἀσφάλεια), or even the way in which he uses ἐκκλησία (1:1).

Most scholars associate the conflict at Thessalonica with the charge against Christians in Acts 17:7 of contravening the "decrees of Caesar".[119] These may refer to bans, imposed by Augustus and reinforced by Tiberius, against predicting the change of Emperors.[120] It is more likely, however, that they refer to oaths of loyalty that were sworn by the residents of provincial cities to the Imperial house, and which included promises to hunt down and report any who contravened them. Usually the magistrates were responsible for administering and regulating these oaths.[121] Even if this is not the explanation of Acts 17:7, and if this aspect of the narrative is unreliable, it is likely that such oaths would have been taken at Thessalonica. Indeed, in a city that was acutely aware of its dependence on Imperial benefaction it would be

---

[118] This has been well noted by Barclay, "Conflict", 514-15.

[119] E. A. Judge, "The Decrees of Caesar at Thessalonica" *RTR* 30 (1971) 2-3; Donfried, "The Cults", 344; idem, "Theology", 16; Jewett, *Correspondence*, 125; Hemer, *Book*, 167; Koester, "Eschatology", 450; Wanamaker, *Commentary*, 113; Hendrix, "Archaeology", 110-12, 118; and to some extent D. Georgi, *Theocracy in Paul's Praxis and Theology* (Minneapolis: Fortress, 1991) 28-30. In this regard, it must be noted that, as mentioned earlier, Luke is generally accurate when dealing with legal and political matters.

[120] See Dio Cassius 56.25.5-6, 57.15.8; cf. Judge, "Decrees", 3-4; Hemer, *Book*, 167; Wanamaker, *Commentary*, 113.

[121] See, for example, *ILS* 8781; *IGRR* 4.251; *SEG* 18.578; cf. Judge, "Decrees", 5-7; Jewett, *Correspondence*, 125; Donfried, "The Cults", 343-4.

quite surprising if such expressions of loyalty were not performed enthusiastically.[122]

Therefore, the conflict between the Christian and civic communities may have operated at several levels. The rejection of traditional religious practices may have led to unofficial, or even official, charges of "atheism". Linked to this may well have been charges of breaking the oath of loyalty to the Emperor and fears of political subversion. There was also very likely a degree of social dislocation and strained relationships. Overall, the response of the civic community was one of isolation and repression, presumably aimed at reversing the beliefs and practices of the Christian converts.

In Acts 17:5-6, Luke appears to suggest that the *demos* was the competent body to hear charges of political subversion against Paul and the other missionaries. However actions against residents, who may have been citizens of the city, were referred to the *politarchs*.[123] Such a distinction is likely, given that Luke is generally accurate when dealing with legal/political matters.

Luke, however, also portrays the Jews as responsible for initiating these repressive actions. But it fits his apologetic agenda to claim they were the troublemakers. He also suggests that the actions involved the Jews stirring up the dregs of society (τῶν ἀγοραίων ἄνδρας τινάς πονηρούς — Acts 17:5) against the elite Christians.[124] Given the nature of the opposition mentioned above, and the nature of the church, this scenario is unlikely. It is more likely that such conflict would have been initiated by other Thessalonians. They would have been most threatened by, and had the most to lose from, such "atheism" and political subversion. This is also supported by Paul's claim that the conflict involved their συμφυλέται (1 Thess 2:14), which clearly implicates their fellow-Thessalonians.[125]

Nevertheless, some scholars have tried to suggest that the term συμφυλέται should be understood in a local rather than a racial sense. The only justification for this, however, is

---

[122] See Hendrix, "Archaeology", 115-17; cf. Donfried, "Theology", 17; Barclay, "Conflict", 514.

[123] Sherwin-White, *Law*, 96; cf. Marshall, *Acts*, 278-9; Hemer, *Book*, 115; Collins, *The Birth*, 34.

[124] See Malherbe, *Paul*, 17; Lührmann, "Beginnings", 243.

[125] See Jewett, *Correspondence*, 117-18; C. J. Schlueter, *Filling up the Measure: Polemical Hyperbole in 1 Thessalonians 2.14-16* (JSNTSup 98; Sheffield: JSOT Press, 1994) 65.

the desire to reconcile Luke's claim of Jewish initiative in the conflict with what amounts to a contradiction by Paul.[126] But this term cannot have been applied to Jews since, in the perception of both Greeks and Romans, they constituted a distinct *ethnos*.

A number of scholars have questioned the authenticity of 1 Thess 2:14-16, claiming that it is a later interpolation.[127] Yet, as others have shown, the arguments against an interpolation are strong, especially when the letter is understood from the perspective of ancient rhetoric.[128] Indeed, many of the problems that are cited to justify an interpolation argument are also overcome when the passage is regarded as polemical hyperbole.[129]

---

[126] See, for example, Marshall, *Thessalonians*, 78; Best, *Commentary*, 114; Holtz, *erste Brief*, 102; K. P. Donfried, "The Theology of 1 Thessalonians as a Reflection of its Purpose" in M. P. Horgan & P. J. Kobelski, eds., *To Touch the Text* (New York: Crossroad, 1989) 250; Morgan-Gillman, "Jason", 44; Collins, *The Birth*, 111. Wayne Meeks notes that the term in fact applies to people belonging to the same *tribe* (φυλή). However, he immediately dilutes this without explanation ("The Social Functions of Apocalyptic Language in Pauline Christianity" in D. Hellholm, ed., *Apocalypticism in the Mediterranean World and the Near East* [Tübingen: J. C. B. Mohr, 1983] 691). Richard assumes 2:14-16 refers to Jewish opposition at Thessalonica, which he admits is inconsistent with the letter as a whole, and hence concludes that 2:14-16 must be an interpolation (*Thessalonians*, 18). But the term συμφυλέται was quite specific, and cannot be used in such senses. See Still, "Θλῖψις", 214-22.

[127] The main exponents of this view are B. A. Pearson, "1 Thessalonians 2:13-16: A Deutero-Pauline Interpolation" *HTR* 64 (1971) 79-94; D. Schmidt, "1 Thess 2:13-16: Linguistic Evidence for an Interpolation" *JBL* 102 (1983) 269-79; cf. Morgan-Gillman, "Jason", 43; D. Georgi, *Remembering the Poor: The History of Paul's Collection for Jerusalem* (Nashville: Abingdon, 1992) x; Richard, *Thessalonians*, 17-19. Bruce leans this way, but ultimately does not commit himself to one position (*Thessalonians*, 49). Richard offers an alternative reconstruction, claiming that 2:13-4:2 represents a short earlier letter inserted into a latter one comprising 1:2-2:12+4:3-5:28 ("Early", 41-42; *Thessalonians*, 11-19). But his argument is unconvincing, not least because the contents of the two letters he identifies are not as incompatible as he claims.

[128] See, especially, Johnson, "Slander", 421 n. 4, 429-35, 441; Hughes, "Rhetoric", 102; Donfried, "Reflection", 250; Wanamaker, *Commentary*, 29-37; 115-16.

[129] This has recently been argued by Schlueter, *Filling*, 41-2, 47-8, 51, 65-73, 105-6.

Paul's reference to Satan in 2:18, and the satanic allusion of 3:5, may imply that the city authorities were responsible for the actions against the Christians. It is possible that Paul was demonizing the authorities because they were acting as Satan's agents in tempting the Thessalonian Christians to reject their faith.[130] It could be argued, however, that these references to Satan may simply reflect a standard apocalyptic eschatology. However, this does not necessarily rule out an association between earthly actors and cosmic ones.[131]

Most scholars claim that there is nothing in 1 Thessalonians to suggest that the conflict and repression that the Christians experienced were very severe. In fact, they argue that the measures taken against them probably involved no more than discrimination, ostracism, insults and other verbal abuse. Certainly, these scholars argue that there is no evidence that the lives of the Thessalonian Christians were thought to be in any danger.[132] Karl Donfried, however, claims that some Thessalonican Christians were martyred for their faith. His argument depends on linking the deaths discussed in 4:13-18 with the conflict, drawing a parallel between the use of κοιμάω in 4:13 and Luke's account of the martyrdom of Stephen (Acts 7:60), and from the language of 1 Thess 2:14-16.[133] Nowhere, however, does Paul specifically link these deaths with the conflict.[134] Both Luke and Paul use κοιμάω elsewhere to refer to death without any sense of

---

[130] See Donfried, "Reflection", 253; idem, "Theology", 19-20; Wanamaker, *Commentary*, 132. Elaine Pagels argues that although "Satan" is not used in the Gospels for the Roman authorities, it does refer to the Jewish authorities opposing Christianity; however she notes that it can refer to the Roman authorities in John ("The Social History of Satan, Part II: Satan in the New Testament Gospels" *JAAR* 62 [1994] 19). Admittedly, none of Paul's other uses of the term have this sense (e.g. Rom 16:20; 1 Cor 5:5, 7:5; 2 Cor 2:11, 11:14, 12:7), but that need not rule it out here.

[131] *Contra* J. S. Pobee, *Persecution and Martyrdom in the Theology of Paul* (JSNTSup 6; Sheffield: JSOT Press, 1985) 110.

[132] See, for example, Best, *Commentary*, 113; Meeks, *First Urban*, 174; Holtz, *erste Brief*, 47, 102; J. Reumann, "The Theologies of 1 Thessalonians and Philippians: Contents, Comparison, and Composition" *SBLSP* (1987) 522; Barclay, "Contrasts", 53; Schlueter, *Filling*, 52. Furthermore, as suggested earlier, 2 Cor 8:2 may imply that the repression included some sort of economic measures as well.

[133] Donfried, "The Cults", 349.

[134] Barclay rightly points this out ("Contrasts", 53; "Conflict", 514).

martyrdom (Acts 13:36; 1 Cor 7:39, 11:30, 15:51).
Furthermore, as mentioned above, the language of 1 Thess
2:14-16 is probably hyperbolic, and it probably arises from
Paul's current situation, not the one at Thessalonica.[135]

John Pobee suggests on the basis of 4:14 that there
may have been some martyrs. He argues that διὰ τοῦ Ἰησοῦ
should be taken with κοιμηθέντες rather than with ἄξει,
"since οἱ κοιμηθέντες διὰ τοῦ Ἰησοῦ" is "an obvious parallel
with νεκροὶ ἐν Χριστῷ" (4:16), and means "those who have
died because of Christ".[136] While this may be the correct
structure, it is not necessary to assume that διὰ is causative.
Even Donfried, whose own argument would be strengthened
by Pobee's translation, suggests that it more simply means
"those who were 'in relationship with' Christ at the time of
their death".[137]

Thus there is no textual basis for the idea that some
were executed. But if the repressive measures were in
response to charges of "atheism" or breaches of the oath of
loyalty, physical violence and even death, cannot be ruled
out. Besides, Paul does hold up the church as an example in a
way that suggests the sufferings and repressive measures
were severe and that such conflict was not the experience of
other churches in Achaia and Macedonia at that time.[138]

2. The Response of the Thessalonian Christians

Paul's instruction in 1 Thess 5:15, ὁρᾶτε μή τις κακὸν ἀντὶ
κακοῦ τινι ἀποδῷ, ἀλλὰ πάντοτε τὸ ἀγαθὸν διώκετε [καὶ] εἰς
ἀλλήλους καὶ εἰς πάντας, suggests that the Christians were
retaliating against the repression they experienced. Indeed,
the καὶ εἰς πάντας clearly seems to be aimed at their relations

---

[135] *Contra* Richard, *Thessalonians*, 18, 214.

[136] Pobee, *Persecution*, 113.

[137] Donfried, "Theology", 33, 51. This is interesting given his support
for Pobee's interpretation in an earlier work ("Reflection", 256); cf.
Wanamaker, *Commentary*, 169; *contra* Best, *Commentary*, 188-9; Bruce,
Thessalonians, 97, 99; Koester, "Eschatology", 447 n. 34.

[138] See Wanamaker, *Commentary*, 82-3; cf. Donfried, "Theology",
22; *contra* Barclay, "Conflict", 514. In this regard it may be significant
that only the Thessalonian Christians are said to *have become imitators*
of Jesus and Paul (1:6), whereas the Corinthian (1 Cor 4:16; 11:1) and
Philippian Christians (Phil 3:17) are urged to *become imitators*. See
Donfried, "Reflection", 252-3.

with non-Christians.[139] Barclay claims that this retaliation was linked to aggressive evangelism, that is, that the Christians denigrated the gods of non-believers, predicted their forthcoming doom, and perhaps even vandalized temples or shrines.[140] But this finds no real support in the text. Although ἀφ' ὑμῶν...ἐξήχηται ὁ λόγος τοῦ κυρίου (1:8a) appears to suggest that they were engaged in proclaiming the gospel,[141] Paul claims that this had occurred ἐν τῇ Μακεδονίᾳ καὶ ἐν τῇ Ἀχαΐᾳ. It is highly improbable that the Thessalonians had become itinerant missionaries throughout these two provinces.[142]

Furthermore, in 1 Thess 1:8b Paul clearly assumes that what has gone out is the report of their faith. This surely qualifies the sense of 1:8a.[143] Hence, in this instance, it is likely that Paul equates the report of their conversion and their faithfulness to the gospel in the face of conflict with the proclamation of the gospel itself. At the same time, the recipients of the "news" of 1 Thess 1:8 are clearly believers, not non-believers (1:9). Finally, nowhere is their suffering specifically linked to any proclamation.

Rather, the nature of the church's retaliation is probably indicated by the instructions of 4:11-12. These seem to address the Thessalonians' situation most specifically, that is, Paul charges them φιλοτιμεῖσθαι ἡσυχάζειν καὶ πράσσειν τὰ ἴδια καὶ ἐργάζεσθαι ταῖς [ἰδίαις] χερσὶν ὑμῶν. Yet Abraham Malherbe argues that "quietness" (ἡσυχία) was a goal of most philosophical schools, understood as avoiding the distractions of the world. That it could be taken too far, and lead to withdrawal from society and a neglect of civic duties, was a common complaint. For this reason, Cynics were

---

[139] Barclay, "Conflict", 520; implied by Best, *Commentary*, 177; to some extent also Marshall, *Thessalonians*, 152-3.

[140] Barclay, "Contrasts", 53; idem, "Conflict", 520-1, 524 n. 44. In the latter he also links this with 4:11-12.

[141] So, for example, J. Ware, "The Thessalonians as a Missionary Congregation: 1 Thessalonians 1,5-8" *ZNW* 83 (1992) 127-31.

[142] See Wanamaker, *Commentary*, 83. Richard claims that the only grounds for dismissing this possibility is the assumption that Paul's stay in Thessalonica was very brief and the letter was written very soon afterwards (*Thessalonians*, 71-2). Richard's argument presupposes his partition of the letter (with this section falling into the so-called "later missive"). Nevertheless, the length of time is largely irrelevant. Such an undertaking would not have been logistically possible for a relatively poor, harassed community such as this.

[143] *Contra* Richard, *Thessalonians*, 51, 71-2.

regarded as "atheistic, misanthropic, socially irresponsible, and sexually immoral".[144]

Since Paul expects that their quietness will earn them the respect of outsiders (something that is implied by the ἵνα clause of 4:12), a "philosophical" interpretation cannot be sufficient in this case. Consequently, Malherbe takes the three injunctions together to argue that the Thessalonian Christians were being interfering nuisances, perhaps akin to Cynic converts who were criticized for leaving their trades to become itinerant preachers.[145] But it is not at all clear from the text of 1 Thessalonians that preaching was in any way directly linked to their experience of conflict.

"Quietness" was also a political term, and a political sense would seem to be intended here given the combination of φιλοτιμεῖσθαι and ἡσυχάζειν. As a number of scholars have noted, this is an oxymoron that means something like "make your ambition to be non-ambitious".[146] Strengthening the political sense is the next instruction, "mind your own business" (πράσσειν τὰ ἴδια) that, together with ἡσυχάζειν, forms a common expression meaning "to retire from public life".[147] It is generally argued, however, that a political sense

---

144 See Malherbe, "Self-Definition", 49-50, 54-5; idem, *Paul*, 105-6; cf. Hill, "Establishing", 165-6; Barclay, "Conflict", 523.

145 Malherbe, *Paul*, 19, 99-101; cf. Frend, *Martyrdom*, 74; Barclay, "Conflict", 522; While Kloppenborg agrees with the context ("Φιλαδελφία", 270) he contends that the three expressions cannot be taken together since they are connected by καί. But he ignores the sense of ἵνα in 4:12; cf. Richard, *Thessalonians*, 221.

146 E. von Dobschütz, *Die Thessalonicher-Briefe* (7th ed.; Göttingen: Vandenhoeck & Ruprecht, 1909) 179; Best, *Commentary*, 174; Hock, *Social Context*, 46; Malherbe, *Paul*, 105-6; Hill, "Establishing", 166 n. 468. Calvin Roetzel dismisses the idea that ἡσυχάζειν has a political connotation since Philo uses it to refer to the "eschatological rest" ("*Theodidaktoi* and Handwork in Philo and 1 Thessalonians" in A. Vanhoye, ed., *L'Apôtre Paul: Personnalité, style et conception du ministère* [BETL 73; Leuven: Leuven University Press, 1986] 324-31; cf. Philo *De migr.* 29-30; idem, *De praem.* 157). Not only is it doubtful that a Philonic tradition would have been widespread in the diaspora, but the suggestion ignores the way in which the intended readers would have heard it. Indeed, not only is there no evidence for a Jewish influence among the Thessalonian Christians, the idea of a Philonic influence is completely untenable. Kloppenborg is also correct that Roetzel's suggestion "would be rhetorically ineffectual" ("Φιλαδελφία", 280).

147 Dio Cassius tells of a Vinicius who ἡσυχίαν ἄγων καὶ τὰ ἑαυτοῦ πράττων ἐσῴζετο in Claudius' time (60.27.4). Plutarch links ἡσυχία with ὁμονοία as a major goal of the politician (*Praec. rei. ger.*

cannot have been intended, since the Thessalonian Christians were common people and thus not involved in public affairs.[148] But such an argument ignores the democratic political structure of the city. Since the Thessalonian Christians were most likely citizens of the city, they would have been members of the city's *demos*, and consequently they did have a public/political role via that body. Not only should a political connotation not be excluded, but the force of the combined expression makes such a sense most likely.

Furthermore, the combination of a strong political expression with an injunction to engage in manual labor suggests that the latter may also have some political connotation. Indeed, Paul links the three injunctions together under the same aim. What is unusual is that Paul expects their retirement and manual labor to earn the respect of outsiders, and presumably prevent escalation of the conflict. This can only be a logical outcome if the Thessalonian

---

824E). Philo argues that a woman "should not be a busybody, meddling with matters outside her household concerns, but should seek a life of seclusion" (μηδὲν οὖν ἔξω τῶν κατὰ τὴν οἰκονομίαν πολυπραγμονείτω γυνὴ ζητοῦσα μοναυλίαν μηδ' οἷα νομὰς κατά). This is in direct contrast to a man, whose life should revolve around "market-places and council-halls and law-courts and gatherings and meetings" (*De spec.* 3.169-71). Although Philo does not use ἡσυχία or ὁμονοία there are the same ideas of interfering, busybodiness and minding one's own business in relation to the political/legal sphere of public life. The same link between quietness and retiring from public/political life can also be seen in Pliny Ep. 2.11. On the political meaning of "to mind one's own business" see also Plato Resp. 433A, 496D; cf. Hock, Social Context, 4. Even Malherbe admits that "the expression 'to remain quiet and mind one's own business' came to describe the person who withdrew from the political arena, particularly in the late Roman Republic and early Empire, when renunciation of public life was a particularly attractive choice for thoughtful people" (*Paul*, 97).

[148] For example, Best, *Commentary*, 175; Marshall, *Thessalonians*, 116; Malherbe, *Paul*, 98; Barclay, "Conflict", 522. On the other hand, see Hock, *Social Context*, 46-7. The chief exponent of a political interpretation was von Dobschütz (*Briefe*, 180-3), but his views have largely been ignored. Although he suggested that the giving up of work and political agitation was linked to eschatological expectation, he also assumed that it was linked to a sense of social deprivation. While the latter is unlikely, the strong political sense of the terms in 4:11-12 must be taken seriously.

Christians were thereby doing something that was appropriate for them.[149]

It is likely that their retaliation involved some form of civic disturbance or political agitation that included stopping work. One way a group of artisans could be active in public affairs, but inappropriately, was by going on strike. Although infrequent, such actions did occur.[150] While the Christians were few in number, so were those guilds which engaged in such activity relative to the size of the cities. Indeed, even small groups can have a significant impact. Another form of action could have involved disrupting meetings of the *demos*. The purpose of such actions by the Thessalonian Christians would most likely have been a protest against the treatment they were receiving. It is also possible that they used the gathering of the *demos* as an occasion for preaching the gospel. In support of this interpretation is the common perception that members of *collegia* and *thiasoi* were political agitators and potentially subversive.[151] To the average Thessalonian, the Christian community probably would have resembled a *thiasos*.

Such an interpretation may be further supported by Paul's description of some in the church as ἄτακτοι (5:14). Originally, this was a military term used for those who were undisciplined, insubordinate, or not battle-ready.[152] Many scholars, however, associate the term with the injunction to work in 4:11 and interpret it as "idle". They argue that some of the Thessalonian Christians have stopped working on account of their fervent and imminent expectation of the

---

[149] Dionysius of Halicarnassus contends that if the plebs quit their jobs the result is sedition and the demise of the state (*Ant. Rom.* 6.86.5).

[150] The strike of the bakers' guild at Ephesus has been mentioned (cf. Jones, *Economy*, 46). That the linen-workers' guild at Tarsus was accused of causing θόρυβος, ἀταξία and στάσις suggests that something similar was occurring there also (Dio Chrys. *Or.* 34.21).

[151] Later Christian groups were also considered to be political agitators. See Jewett, "Tenement", 42. On *collegia* as agitators see chapter 3 herein. Although small in number, they could still have had a big impact, as vocal minority groups often do, even if their actions and protests were ultimately doomed to failure because of their numbers.

[152] See Marshall, *Thessalonians*, 150; Jewett, *Correspondence*, 104; Hill, "Establishing", 224; cf. BAGD sv "ἄτακτος"; e.g. Isocrates *Paneg.* 150 — although this reference also draws an association between the term and the ideal of the good citizen.

parousia, something that is largely based on their perception of the meaning of ἀτάκτως in 2 Thess 3:6-13.[153]

In neither 4:11-12 nor 5:14 does Paul specifically use eschatological arguments. But especially given that 4:13-5:11 is heavily eschatological and that there is an enormous emphasis on eschatology and the parousia in 1 Thessalonians, an expectation of an imminent eschatological intervention may be involved. On the other hand, the force of Paul's argument in 4:11-12, especially its strong political implications, means that an explanation in terms of eschatological fervor alone is inadequate.[154] Besides even the problem in 2 Thess 3:6-13 seems to have a major social component.[155] Consequently, it is likely that their eschatological fervor may be linked to their political activism and retaliation.

What is usually ignored, is the fact that ἄτακτος and its cognates were commonly used in the sense of civil disobedience or disturbance.[156] Dionysius of Halicarnassus even links this sense of civil disturbance with a failure to maintain ancestral customs.[157] Therefore, it is probably better to understand the ἄτακτοι as some who were "disobedient", rather than "idle", in that they did not perform their expected civic duties or roles. This probably refers back to the injunctions of 4:11-12, for immediately following the

---

[153] For example, Best, *Commentary*, 175, 230; Bruce, *Thessalonians*, 91, 122; Marshall, *Thessalonians*, 117; Hill, "Establishing", 225-6. Jewett argues this mainly on the basis that such actions are common among "millenarian movements" (*Correspondence*, 173).

[154] A number of scholars have rejected the eschatological explanation in favor of a social one. See, for example, Hock, *Social Context*, 43; Malherbe, *Paul*, 106 n. 27; idem, "Pastoral Care", 389; Marshall, *Enmity*, 170-1; Winter, *Seek*, 43, 53-4; cf. Russell, "The Idle", 110. Walter Schmithals (*Paul and the Gnostics* [Nashville: Abingdon, 1972] 158-9) claims that the idleness is somehow related to problems from Gnostics (ibid., 159-60), but this is weak and without textual support. What most have ignored is that the two interpretations need not be exclusive or contradictory.

[155] Russell, in particular, advocates a social problem rather than an eschatological one ("The Idle", 107-9; cf. Marshall, *Enmity*, 170-1). Here, too, they are not necessarily exclusive.

[156] See, for example, Aristotle *Pol.* 1302B, 1319B; Dio Chrys. *Or.* 34.21; Dion. Hal. *Ant. Rom.* 3.10.6; Plato *Leg.* 780D; Plutarch *Aem.* 32.2.

[157] Dion. Hal. *Ant. Rom.* 3.10.6.

injunction to admonish the ἄτακτοι (5:14) is the expectation
that they should not retaliate (5:15).[158]

While some of the Thessalonian Christians retaliated,
others struggled to maintain their faith. This is suggested by
Paul sending Timothy to support them (3:1-10). Paul's fear
that the repression was so severe that some of them might
have apostatized is indicated by his use of σαίνεσθαι (3:3).
Although he considered this a possibility, Timothy's report
shows his fears to be ungrounded.[159] However, some were
afraid or losing heart, as is suggested by Paul's instruction to
encourage the ὀλιγόψυχοι in 5:14. It is also implied by his
emphasis on their recalling the circumstances of their
conversion, and by what appears to be a lengthy apology for
his ministry in 2:1-12.[160]

Paul's defence of his ministry may have been prompted
because some of the Thessalonian Christians blamed Paul for
their situation and for abandoning them, like a Sophist, to

---

[158] Richard suggests that this disobedience was exhibited within the
community (*Thessalonians*, 276). Yet if so, then this particular "label"
has a different sense from the other two in 5:14 that refer to an attitude
that is characteristic of their Christian lives generally. He also ignores
the sense of nonretaliation in 5:15. Besides, as will be argued later in this
section, all three probably need to be seen in terms of the context of
conflict. Jewett suggests that the "disobedience" is shown towards the
leaders of the Christian community on account of spiritual enthusiasm,
class conflict, and sexual libertinism (*Correspondence*, 102-5). Barclay
rightly rejects this. Yet he claims that if there was any disobedience it
was probably directed at Paul and not the local leaders ("Conflict", 525 n.
46). However the injunction of 5:13, immediately preceding this,
encourages them "to be at peace among yourselves". It is much more
likely that this relates to some disagreement or dispute within the
community (see, for example, Richard, *Thessalonians*, 269) and may well
concern the Church's response to the conflict. Nevertheless, the sense of
civil disobedience cannot be excluded. To some extent this is also
suggested by Russell, "The Idle", 108-11.

[159] Best, *Commentary*, 135; E. Bammel, "Preparation for the Perils
of the Last Days: 1 Thessalonians 3:3" in W. Horbury & B. McNeil, eds.,
Suffering and Martyrdom in the New Testament (Cambridge: Cambridge
University Press, 1981) 94-6, 99; Marshall, *Thessalonians*, 93; Bruce,
Thessalonians, 62-4; Donfried, "The Cults", 347; Jewett, *Correspondence*,
93; Wanamaker, *Commentary*, 129. Donfried notes that "apostasy" was
a common theme in Jewish literature dealing with persecution
("Reflection", 253).

[160] See Hill, "Establishing", 156-7, 231; Lührmann, "Beginnings",
241; Wanamaker, *Commentary*, 197; Collins, *The Birth*, 9-10.

face it alone.[161] Yet, nothing in the text suggests any problem between Paul and the community. On the contrary, 1 Thess 3:6 makes it clear that their relationship was strong.[162] It is rather more likely that since a few Christians had died so soon after their conversion, some outsiders had derided their beliefs in salvation. In fact, some may have even suggested that since the deaths occurred so soon after their conversion it clearly proved that they were being punished by the gods for their atheism.[163]

Malherbe, however, claims that the language of 2:1-12 merely follows the "convention of a philosopher offering himself as a paradigm for his followers" of the "ideal moral philosopher".[164] But he does not explain why Paul would have used this image unless something in the context of the Thessalonian Christians had prompted it.[165] Since there is no evidence in the letter of opponents of Paul, nor of tension between Paul and the community, it may well be a response to slander and accusations from outsiders.

In 1 Thess 5:14, Paul also instructs the Christian community to help the ἀσθενεῖς among them. Usually this term referred to people who found the moral life difficult to follow because they were tempted by pleasures. Here it probably refers to some who found it difficult to maintain the Christian way of life.[166] However, given the context of the letter, and the thrust of the rest of this verse, it may refer to some in the church who were tempted to compromise in response to the conflict. In fact, retaliation, apostasy and

---

[161] For example, Best, *Commentary*, 91; Bruce, *Thessalonians*, 27; Marshall, *Thessalonians*, 62, 65; Donfried, "The Cults", 352; idem, "Theology", 25; Holtz, *erste Brief*, 94; cf. Dio Chrys. *Or.* 32.11.

[162] Hughes ("Rhetoric", 101) claims that:
> since no such charges are taken up in the three-part *probatio*, and since Paul in the *narratio* consistently praises himself and then praises the Thessalonians' positive response to him, it does not appear that Paul was defending himself against charges.

cf. Johanson, *Brethren*, 52-3.

[163] See, for example, Barclay, "Contrasts", 53; idem, "Conflict", 513, 516; cf. Marshall, *Thessalonians*, 73; Holtz, *erste Brief*, 92-5; Johanson, *Brethren*, 54.

[164] Malherbe, *Paul*, 52-5; cf. Wanamaker, *Commentary*, 91.

[165] Marshall, *Thessalonians*, 61; Jewett, *Correspondence*, 102; Richard, "Early", 48; cf. Donfried, "Reflection", 258.

[166] Malherbe, "Pastoral Care", 379-80; Richard, *Thessalonians*, 277; cf. Best, *Commentary*, 231; Marshall, *Thessalonians*, 151.

compromise are probably the most likely reactions to such a situation of extreme conflict and repression.

Nevertheless, 1 Thess 4:1-10 makes it quite clear that none of them has actually lapsed, for Paul glowingly praises their moral conduct.[167] Despite this, some have suggested that there may have been a case of sexual misconduct within the church given the instructions of 4:3-7.[168] But this is unnecessary. In fact, this particular text reads more like a reinforcement of the conviction that their new life demanded a complete break from the old.[169]

Therefore, the response of the Thessalonian Christians would seem to have been mixed. Some retaliated. Some had begun to lose heart. But as yet none appear to have apostatized or sought some form of social/religious/moral compromise.[170] Overall, their response appears to have been towards an increasing separation from their society. This is also seen in their strongly eschatological perspective. The Thessalonian Christians appear to have adopted the apocalyptic theology in which Paul had instructed them (1:9-10; cf. 5:1-5). This theology, with its dualisms, helped to explain their experience of conflict and to strengthen the boundaries of the group relative to the wider society. In fact, Barclay suggests that there was a vicious circle at work:

> The more they are ridiculed or ostracized, the more clearly defined is the distinction between believers and nonbelievers...and thus the more obviously correct is the

---

[167] Bammel, "Preparation", 91; Marshall, *Thessalonians*, 103-5; Johanson, *Brethren*, 55; Lührmann, "Beginnings", 248; Wanamaker, *Commentary*, 146; Barclay, "Contrasts", 51; *contra* Schmithals, *Paul*, 156; Donfried, "The Cults", 341-42.

[168] Best, *Commentary*, 166; Marshall, *Thessalonians*, 111; Wanamaker, *Commentary*, 191.

[169] See Bruce, *Thessalonians*, 82.

[170] Malherbe argues that 5:14 does not refer to specific groups within the church, but to certain tendencies or attitudes ("Pastoral Care", 375). He is largely correct. Other clues suggest that these attitudes or tendencies were not acted on. But in regard to disobedience/retaliation it seems that some had, given that (1) the injunction not to retaliate follows 5:14, (2) there is a dispute between the leaders and some in the church as suggested by 5:12-13 and (3) the leaders are the ones who admonish (5:12) while the ἄτακτοι require admonishing. As Donfried contends the ἄτακτοι "constitute the only truly distinct group of Thessalonians identified by Paul" (*The Birth*, 95; cf. Holtz, *erste Brief*, 250-1).

apocalyptic division between those destined for salvation and...for wrath.[171]

Some scholars contend that because the Thessalonian Christians readily adopted an apocalyptic world-view their pre-conversion experience must have been one of dissatisfaction.[172] This is usually linked with the theories of relative deprivation or status inconsistency.[173] But, as noted above, these theories are ethnocentric anachronisms, and the way they are used implicitly assumes some sort of determinism.[174] Rather, as recent social-scientific studies of conversion have shown, a religion's beliefs are seldom the primary attraction for prospective converts. Such beliefs really only become important following conversion, during the processes of resocialization and legitimation.[175]

Thus, in support of Barclay's interpretation, it is more likely that apocalyptic theology was adopted after conversion because it helped to explain the suffering they experienced in converting.[176] The church's apocalyptic theology, with its dualism and future eschatological hope, helped explain their experience of conflict while strengthening the group boundaries. Together with a tendency to retaliate, this

---

[171] Barclay, "Conflict", 518-19; idem, "Contrasts", 50, 54-5.

[172] So Meeks, *First Urban*, 172; Jewett, *Correspondence*, 161; Wanamaker, *Commentary*, 114.

[173] Meeks, "Social Function", 688; Jewett, *Correspondence*, 161-3; L. M. White, "Shifting Sectarian Boundaries in Early Christianity" *BJRL* 70 (1988) 16; Wanamaker, *Commentary*, 114.

[174] Holmberg, *Sociology*, 137-41; Barclay, "Contrasts", 55; idem, "Conflict", 520 n. 26.

[175] Stark points out that "people typically must be taught to attribute their conversion to features of the doctrine, for seldom does conversion culminate a spiritual search" ("Conversion", 318-19); cf. de Vos, "OIKOΣ", 59; Taylor, "Social Nature", 136.

[176] Of course, other factors may have helped this process: a growing anti-Roman sentiment in the provinces (Newbold, "Social Tension", 121-2), a series of famines and earthquakes in c. 40-50 CE which were seen as divine portents (Wanamaker, *Commentary*, 53-4), and a strong tradition of post-mortem judgment ideas among Greek writers and a looking to the gods for vengeance/recompense (D. W. Kuck, *Judgment and Community Conflict: Paul's Use of Apocalyptic Judgment Language in 1 Corinthians 3:5-4:5* [NovTSup 66; Leiden: E. J. Brill, 1992] 99-101) and the promise of a better life after death to initiates of some mystery cults (ibid., 104-9).

suggests the Christian community at Thessalonica had a separatist outlook.[177]

On the whole, then, the relationship of the Thessalonian Christian community to its wider civic community involved a severe conflict. This was a direct result of the conversion of the Christians. It is most likely that the conflict centered on the rejection of the traditional religious practices of the city and a withdrawal from many social/religious activities. This was probably met with discrimination, ostracism and insults. Yet their conversion may also have led to charges of atheism and of breaking the oath of loyalty to the Emperor. Although there is no evidence for physical violence and executions, these cannot be ruled out on this basis. It is also possible that the Christians were fined. Overall, the response of the civic community was one of repression aimed at a restoration of the former relations.

The response of the Thessalonian Christians was strong and even provocative. Some of Paul's injunctions suggest that they were retaliating against the repression they were experiencing, possibly by engaging in some form of civil disturbance. This may have involved disrupting *demos* meetings by preaching or by protesting at the treatment they were receiving. At the same time, however, the Christian community displayed a strong separatist attitude.[178] Some of them had begun to lose heart, and although some were tempted to seek a compromise, none seem to have apostatized.

IV. PAUL'S RESPONSE TO THIS RELATIONSHIP

Paul's response to the situation is indicated by the type of letter he wrote, since this reflects his overall intent. The genre

---

[177] However, given the problems associated with the term "sectarian", to describe them as such may not be helpful. See, in particular, Holmberg, *Sociology*, 77-114. Added to these difficulties are the recent sociological distinctions between "sects" and "cults". See White, "Sectarian", 17-23.

[178] Although this separatist tendency appears to be incompatible with their retaliation, it is only apparently so. It is possible that they used whatever (limited) power they had to achieve their aim of being left in peace — even if it was a futile effort (cf. the response of the authorities to the other strikes mentioned in n. 150 above). It is also possible that there is a contradiction, in which case we need to be careful not to judge it by our own standards. After all, the societies of the first century probably allowed for a greater dissonance in their beliefs and experiences/ actions than we would like. See Malina, "Normative Dissonance", 38.

of this letter has been described as a "praising letter", while its rhetorical genre has been classed as epideictic. That is, its primary concern was praising the readers and persuading them to hold on to, and to maintain, the writer's point of view.[179] Such a rhetorical classification, however, is not really appropriate for a letter such as this one.[180]

Recently, it has been observed that 1 Thessalonians has many characteristics of the "letter of consolation" (παραμυθητικὸς λόγος) genre. Such letters were common, particularly among relatives and friends.[181] As the name suggests, they were addressed to people experiencing some form of suffering, whether due to bereavement, poverty or social scorn.[182] They exhorted the recipients to "accept bravely the misfortune which is connatural to the human condition, not to be overcome excessively by grief and, in consequence, to neglect one's duties". Hence, they combined both consolation and exhortation.[183] A letter of consolation is appropriate, given the Thessalonian Christians' context and Paul's inability to visit them.[184] Furthermore, Paul's use of παραμυθέομαι, which is found only in 1 Thessalonians among Paul's letters (2:12, 5:14), shows that comfort was an important purpose of the letter.[185] Therefore, it would be pertinent to examine what Paul says by way of consolation and exhortation.

---

[179] Jewett, *Correspondence*, 71-2; Wanamaker, *Commentary*, 47; Hughes, "Rhetoric", 97.

[180] T. H. Olbricht, claims that Aristotle's classification of rhetorical genres was not intended to be rigid and that praise/blame could be found in all three types: epideictic, forensic and deliberative. Furthermore, each of these genres were historically linked to a particular setting— the *agora*, the law court, the *demos* — none of which fits the probable context of 1 Thessalonians ("An Aristotelian Rhetorical Analysis of 1 Thessalonians" in D. L. Balch, E. Ferguson & W. A. Meeks, eds., *Greeks, Romans and Christians* [Minneapolis: Fortress, 1990] 224-7).

[181] Malherbe, "Pastoral Care", 387; Donfried, "Reflection", 259-60; J. Chapa, "Is First Thessalonians a Letter of Consolation?" *NTS* 40 (1994) 150-1; Smith, *Comfort*, 49-59.

[182] See Malherbe, "Pastoral Care", 387.

[183] Chapa, "Consolation", 151 (especially n. 8), 152-3, 155.

[184] Chapa, "Consolation", 156-7. Although Chapa finds many elements of such letters in 1 Thessalonians, ultimately he does not accept that it is, strictly speaking, a "letter of consolation" (ibid., 158-9). For a contrary view, see Smith, *Comfort*, 52-8. In either case, the intent, and presumably the effect, would be the same.

[185] Malherbe, "Pastoral Care", 388; Donfried, "Reflection", 259.

1. Comfort and Reassurance

Theologically, Paul seeks to reassure them and strengthen
their resolve by reminding them that they are loved and
chosen by God (1:4, 2:12). The idea that God creates and
sustains the church may also be intended if ἐν τῷ θεῷ in 1:1
also has an instrumental sense.[186] This is given a strong
eschatological and apocalyptic flavor by reference to their
membership in the βασιλεία τοῦ Θεοῦ (2:12), and by a
reminder that their salvation is assured (4:13-18, 5:23-4) and
they are υἱοὶ φωτός (5:5). The apocalyptic perspective is also
seen in Paul's assurance that they will ultimately be
vindicated and those responsible for their suffering will be
punished (1:10, 5:3-9).[187]

In fact, Paul's chief consolation involves an emphasis on
a future eschatological hope. This is seen in his reference to
Christ's *parousia*. Indeed, Paul may have been the first to
use this particular term in a peculiarly Christian way, and
his use of it in this letter may also be the first such
instance.[188] Nevertheless, Paul's consolation is not entirely
future-oriented.[189] For in 5:23-4, Paul assures them that God
will sanctify them and will protect them from apostasy.
Therefore, although Paul does not expect an end to their

---

[186] Such an instrumental sense to ἐν τῷ θεῷ is possible given that
Paul uses it in 2:12 and the idea of the nurture of god was a *topos* in Stoic
thought. See Malherbe, "New Family", 119-20.

[187] Best, *Commentary*, 221; Pobee, *Persecution*, 111; Wanamaker,
Commentary, 88; Georgi, *Theocracy*, 27.

[188] Indeed, the idea/term is not found in traditional apocalyptic
material and is drawn from the realm of Greco-Roman politics: Jesus'
coming is portrayed as the arrival of the Emperor. See Koester,
"Eschatology", 446; cf. R. H. Gundry, "The Hellenization of Dominical
Tradition and the Christianization of the Jewish Tradition in the
Eschatology of 1-2 Thessalonians" *NTS* 33 (1987) 162.

[189] Donfried, "The Cults", 347; Reumann, "Theologies", 525-6; cf.
Best, *Commentary*, 221; Bruce, *Thessalonians*, 19. There are no grounds
for the view that 1 Thess presents a realized eschatology (*contra*
Schmithals, *Paul*, 167; Jewett, *Correspondence*, 96-100). J. W. Elias
argues that it relates to present deliverance more than future ("'Jesus
Who Delivers Us from the Wrath to Come' [1 Thess 1:10]: Apocalyptic
and Peace in the Thessalonian Correspondence" *SBLSP* [1992] 123-4),
but he eschews the amount of evidence in the letter for a future
eschatology.

suffering, he assures them that God will sustain them in the midst of it (3:3-5).[190]

2. Exhortation

The aim of Paul's exhortation seems to have been the strengthening of boundaries. This is apparent from the various injunctions and the large body of paraenetic material found in the letter. Firstly, Paul draws on a classical apocalyptic dualism between the Thessalonian Christians, who are destined for salvation as the children of light, and outsiders, who are destined for wrath. In fact, most of Paul's statements concerning non-Christians are negative: they are idolaters, lustful and without hope (1:10, 4:5, 4:13, 5:6).[191] This in itself creates, or at least encourages, a dichotomy between those inside and outside the Christian community. It would further reinforce the separatist tendency of the church.

Secondly, Paul uses a number of familial terms in 1 Thessalonians. When he addresses the Thessalonian Christians, which he does fourteen times, he calls them ἀδελφοί (1:4, 2:1, 2:9, 2:14, 2:17, 3:7, 4:1, 4:10, 4:13, 5:1, 5:4, 5:12, 5:14, 5:25) and he refers to them as ἀδελφοί on other occasions (4:6, 5:26).[192] Furthermore, Paul also compares his relationship to them with a wet-nurse caring for her children (2:7) or with a father encouraging his children (2:11). He also describes them as υἱοί (5:5). The heavy concentration of this language in 1 Thessalonians strongly suggests that Paul is trying to "nurture a new, fictive kinship" among the Christians there.[193]

---

[190] Elias, "Jesus", 131. In fact, Paul seems to equate their suffering with the eschatological woes preceding the *parousia*. See Best, *Commentary*, 79, 135-6; Pobee, *Persecution*, 115; Johanson, *Brethren*, 57; Wanamaker, *Commentary*, 109, 131.

[191] See, for example, Malherbe, *Paul*, 95; idem, "New Family", 124; P. Perkins, "1 Thessalonians and Hellenistic Religious Practices" in M. P. Horgan & P. J. Kobelski, eds., *To Touch the Text* (New York: Crossroad, 1989) 332-3; Wanamaker, *Commentary*, 181; Barclay, "Contrasts", 54.

[192] This has also been noted recently by Malherbe, who suggests that it is "the highest incidence of the term in all of Paul's letters" ("New Family", 122). While the incidence may be numerically higher in Romans and 1 Corinthians, the concentration of use (i.e. the ratio of "use" to "size of letter") is the highest in 1 Thessalonians.

[193] See, for example, Malherbe, "Pastoral Care", 388; idem, "New Family", 121-2; cf. Wanamaker, *Commentary*, 146, 149. It is also supported by Paul's allusion to the philosophical ideal of φιλαδελφία

Furthermore, Paul tries to foster bonds between the Christians at Thessalonica and Christians in other places. Indeed, he highlights their love for the ἀδελφοὶ ἐν ὅλῃ τῇ Μακεδονίᾳ (4:10) and he refers to the appreciation of the latter, and those of Achaia, for them. Paul also associates their sufferings with those of the Judaean Christians while he points out that the perpetrators were their συμφυλέται (2:14). This may well have been intended to loosen their ties to their fellow-Thessalonians outside the church.[194]

Thirdly, Paul's exhortation is aimed at strengthening the community's boundaries by encouraging internal unity. He encourages them to be at peace with each other and to respect their leaders (5:13). His injunctions to admonish, encourage, help, be patient and encourage each other (4:18, 5:11, 5:14) would have a similar function.

Fourthly, Paul's paraenetic material would help reinforce the boundaries. For the content of this paraenetic material is largely that of Hellenistic-Jewish ethics that Paul is applying to Gentile converts.[195] At the same time, some suggest that Paul is deliberately countering the practices of certain Thessalonian mystery cults in 4:4-5 and 5:5-7.[196] Although care must be taken not to overstate this, given the paucity of information available on these cults, it is a reasonable assumption.[197]

(4:9). See Hill, "Establishing", 164-5.

[194] See Barclay, "Contrasts", 54; cf. Wanamaker, *Commentary*, 86; Schlueter, *Filling*, 164. It might be suggested that this "love" for Christians in the rest of Macedonia may indicate that the Thessalonian Christians did travel widely or were in the practice of giving material support to other churches. However, as Wanamaker notes, the support Paul encouraged was "not primarily of a material character, but of a psychological nature" (*Commentary*, 161). The frequency with which he passed on greetings between churches and groups would tend to support this (e.g. Rom 16:21-3; 1 Cor 16:19-20; Phil 4:22). Yet even if they had made some financial contribution to other churches in their province, the amounts may not have been very substantial and need not imply that the economic level of the Thessalonian church was higher that I have suggested earlier in this chapter. As the saying goes, "it's the thought that counts".

[195] G. P. Carras, "Jewish Ethics and Gentile Converts: Remarks on 1 Thess 4, 3-8" in R. F. Collins, ed., *The Thessalonian Correspondence* (BETL 87; Leuven: Leuven University Press, 1990) 314; cf. Wanamaker, *Commentary*, 150-1.

[196] For example, Bruce, *Thessalonians*, 82; Donfried, "The Cults", 342.

[197] On the need for care see Koester, "Eschatology", 445.

Finally, Paul's injunctions in 4:11-12 may have sought to have a similar effect in relation to the boundaries between the Christian and civic communities.[198] As mentioned above, Paul encourages them to withdraw from public/political life and this would ultimately entail forgoing their right to participate in meetings of the *demos*. As such, Paul calls on them to renounce their citizenship and become like metics. By contrast, when the guild of linen-workers at Tarsus were treated as metics for civil disobedience and rioting, Dio Chrysostom advised the city to regard them as citizens.[199] In both cases, civil disturbances seem to have been a response to the disdain and hostility of the rest of the *demos*.

Paul's encouragement to the Thessalonian Christians to retire from public life may have been prompted by the common belief that to be a citizen one had to worship the gods of that city. Since the rest of the civic community would have shared this belief, withdrawal may have helped reduce the conflict, although it would have further encouraged the separatist tendency of the church. Thus, Paul's injunctions to admonish the ἄτακτοι (5:14) and not to retaliate (5:15), appear aimed at reducing the escalation of the conflict.[200]

V. CONCLUSION

In the first century CE Thessalonica was a large and busy city. Yet it probably retained many characteristics of a community (such as very public living), although there may have been some geographic separation of different groups. It is unclear whether the city was ethnically cosmopolitan or homogeneous, although the available inscriptions tend to suggest the latter. The nature of social interactions in the city imply that there may have been limited interaction between members of different ethnic and socio-economic status groups.

---

[198] Winter argues that the second aim of the injunctions of 4:11-12 is to discourage the Thessalonian Christians from entering patron-client relations (*Seek*, 56-7). But he ignores the strong political overtones of the injunction. Thus, it is better to understand it according to the Stoic idea of self-sufficiency. See Best, *Commentary*, 178.

[199] Dio Chrys. *Or.* 34.21-3. Paul may even be drawing on the tradition that expected metics to mind their own business and not meddle in the political affairs of a city to which they did not legally belong. See Dio Chrys. *Or.* 48.2; Cicero *Off.* 1.124.

[200] Similarly, Barclay argues that Paul resembles a man in damage-control ("Conflict", 530); cf. Malherbe, *Paul*, 95, 105; Perkins, "Practices", 333-4.

The city was the provincial capital with the status of *civitas libera* (but probably not *immunis*). Its structures were typically Greek, and at least moderately democratic, and there is no reason to assume that the average citizen of the city had lost his political power.

Little is actually known of Thessalonian religious practices. They worshipped a number of typical Greek gods and the Egyptian gods, while mystery cults of Dionysus and Kabirus were probably indigenous. It is reasonable to suppose that their religious outlook was typically Hellenistic. The strong emphasis on the Imperial cult, along with the earlier cult of Roma and Roman benefactors, probably reflects their sense of dependence on Roman benefaction, given a history of support for the losing sides in the civil wars.

The Thessalonian Christian community most likely comprised a small group of free-born, native Thessalonians who were citizens of the city. They were artisans and manual-laborers, so that as a church they probably met in an *insula*-workshop. Their relations with the wider civic community involved severe conflict, which arose directly from their conversion. Most likely, the conflict centered on the rejection of traditional religious practices and a withdrawal from social/religious activities.

The response of other Thessalonians was probably discrimination, ostracism and insults. Yet it may also have led to charges of "atheism" and of breaking the oath of loyalty to the Emperor. Although there is no evidence for physical violence and executions, these cannot be ruled out. It is also possible that the Christians were fined. Overall, the repression by the civic community aimed to restore the former relations. The reaction of the Thessalonian Christians to this was generally strong, even provocative. Some of Paul's injunctions suggest that they retaliated to the repression, possibly via some political protest or civic disturbance. At the same time, the Christian community displayed a strong separatist attitude. Nevertheless, some had begun to lose heart. Thus, Paul's response was to write a "letter of consolation", both to comfort and encourage them.

His consolation centered on Christian eschatology. He reminded them that they were loved and chosen by God and members of God's kingdom and he reassured them of their salvation. Paul also affirmed that they would ultimately be vindicated and those responsible for their suffering would be punished. Yet he also assured them that God would sustain them in the midst of their suffering.

Paul's exhortation focused on strengthening group boundaries. He did this via apocalyptic dualism, and a concentration on familial language to nurture a sense of (fictive) kinship with other Christians at the expense of their compatriots. Paul sought to encourage unity and respect for leaders. His moral exhortations were derived from diaspora Jewish ethics and may have deliberately countered those of certain mystery cults. He also called on them to renounce their citizenship and assume the position of metics within their own city. While all of these encouraged the church's separatist tendencies, Paul sought to prevent some escalation of the conflict by calling on them not to retaliate.

Chapter Five

SOCIAL RELATIONS AT CORINTH

The aim and approach of this chapter will be similar to that of the previous one. In other words, this chapter will seek to reconstruct the nature of Roman Corinth, the Corinthian church, and the relationship between the church and the civic community at Corinth. My reconstruction of the social context of the city in the first century CE will draw on the work of ancient writers, epigraphic evidence, and other historical data, as well as the work of previous scholars and, where relevant, chapters two and three of this study. The reconstruction of the Corinthian church, and the relationship between the church and civic community, will primarily rely on canonical 1 Corinthians and background material.[1]

While reconstruction of the socio-historical context of Thessalonica is difficult due to the lack of thorough excavation, this is not a problem with Corinth. The difficulty for Corinth is the poor quality of the material remains. Most of the inscriptions are only fragmentary (many of them are also late), and little is known of the city apart from the central *forum* area.[2] Consequently, some of the data needed for reconstruction must be extrapolated from other sources.

---

[1] For the purposes of this reconstruction I have chosen to focus on 1 Corinthians since it appears to deal with issues arising from contact with the wider society (and hence is useful for the purposes of this chapter) but the issue in 2 Corinthians is largely "false teachers" and the strained relations between Paul and the church. In other words, the latter deals mainly with different issues than those found in 1 Corinthians. Where 2 Corinthians does add to this discussion (e.g. the matter of Paul's weakness as a rhetor and preacher — section III.2 below) it will be considered.

[2] See H. A. Stansbury III, "Corinthian Honor, Corinthian Conflict: A Social History of Early Roman Corinth and its Pauline Community" (unpublished PhD dissertation, University of California at Irvine, 1990) 21-4.

I. ROMAN CORINTH

As with the case of Roman Thessalonica, the aim of the reconstruction of the nature of Roman Corinth is primarily to gather material that will be interpreted by the model in chapter seven. According to the model outlined in part one of this study, the incidence of conflict is determined by the particular set of norms, values and beliefs, the pattern of relational ties, and the distribution of political power. Material relevant to these factors will be explored in this section, in terms of the city's history, its physical and demographic features, the nature of its social relations, its political structures, and its religious profile.

1. History

Probably the most significant event in Corinth's history, at least in the Roman period, was its destruction in 146 BCE by L. Mummius. This action was taken in response to the revolt of the Achaean League.[3] Most of the ancient reports suggest that the city was (almost) completely destroyed and left deserted, with the men killed and the women and children taken into slavery.[4] The archaeological evidence, however,

---

[3] Cicero *Leg. Agr.* 1.5; Florus 1.32.1; Pausanias *Descr.* 2.1.2; Strabo *Geog.* 8.4.8, 8.6.23; cf. O. Broneer, "Corinth: Center of Saint Paul's Missionary Work in Greece" *BA* 14 (1951) 82; H. S. Robinson, "Corinth" in R. Stilwell *et al*, eds., *Princeton Encyclopaedia of Classical Sites* (Princeton, NJ: Princeton University Press, 1976) 242; J. R. Wiseman, "Corinth and Rome I: 228 BC-AD 267" *ANRW* 2.7.1 (1981) 461-2; D. G. Romano, "Post 146 BC Land Use in Corinth, and Planning of the Roman Colony of 44 BC" in T. E. Gregory, ed., *The Corinthia in the Roman Period* (JRASup 8; Ann Arbor: University of Michigan Press, 1994) 12. In light of its destruction, and the way in which it was rebuilt and reinstituted 102 years later, the history prior to 146 BCE is largely irrelevant for a reconstruction of Corinth in the first century CE.

[4] See Ser. Sulpicius Rufus in Cicero *Fam.* 4.5.4; Cicero *Leg. Agr.* 2.87; Florus 1.32.5-7; Pausanias *Descr.* 2.1.2; Strabo *Geog.* 8.6.23, 10.5.4; Vel. Pat. 1.13.1; Polystratus (*Greek Anthology* 7.297); Antipater of Thessalonica (*Greek Anthology* 7.493); Antipater of Sidon (*Greek Anthology* 9.151); cf. Broneer, "Corinth", 82; Robinson, "Corinth", 242; Wiseman, "Corinth", 462; C. K. Williams II, "The Refounding of Corinth: Some Roman Religious Attitudes" in S. MacReady & F. Thompson, eds., *Roman Architecture in the Greek World* (London: Society of Antiquities of London, 1987) 26; cf. D. W. J. Gill, "Achaia" in D. W. J. Gill & C. Gempf, eds., *The Book of Acts in its Graeco-Roman Setting* (BAFCS 2; Grand Rapids: Eerdmans, 1994) 434.

shows it was far from completely destroyed. Indeed, many buildings were left relatively intact and the remains suggest that there was some level of continued occupation.

Furthermore, Cicero notes that when he visited in 63 BCE there were farms in the region and some inhabitants who were probably descendants of survivors.[5] Yet these inhabitants were probably no more than squatters or tenants and there is nothing to suggest there was any semblance of a normal city — it had effectively ceased to function. The squatters showed little interest in the ruins themselves (unlike Cicero), and none in rebuilding.[6] After the destruction, some of the city's territory was handed over to the Sicyonians, and some of it was declared *ager publicus* and leased out.[7] It is probable that the squatters Cicero encountered were tenants on this *ager publicus*.

---

[5] Cicero *Tusc.* 3.53-4. On evidence for some occupation and a less than complete destruction see Wiseman, "Corinth", 493-6; Engels, *Roman Corinth*, 16; McRay, *Archaeology*, 312; W. L. Willis, "Corinthusne deletus est?" *BZ* 35 (1991) 237-9; R. S. Stroud, "The Sanctuary of Demeter on Acrocorinth in the Roman Period" in T. E. Gregory, ed., *The Corinthia in the Roman Period* (JRASup 8; Ann Arbor: University of Michigan Press, 1994) 65.

[6] Cicero *Tusc.* 3.53-54. See also Wiseman, "Corinth", 496; Stansbury, "Corinthian Honor", 103-4, 109-10; Tomlinson, *From Mycenae*, 8; D. W. J. Gill, "Corinth: A Roman Colony in Achaea" *BZ* 37 (1993) 262; Romano, "Land Use", 13; C. K. Williams II, "Roman Corinth as a Commercial Center" in T. E. Gregory, ed., *The Corinthia in the Roman Period* (JRASup,8; Ann Arbor: University of Michigan Press, 1994) 31; cf. A. D. Clarke, *Secular and Christian Leadership in Corinth: A Socio-Historical and Exegetical Study of 1 Corinthians 1-6* (Leiden: E. J. Brill, 1993) 9. This lack of interest and any traces of civic life mean that Willis' claim that there was considerable continuity ("Corinthusne", 241) cannot be supported. The lack of continuity will be even more apparent in later sections, especially "Physical Features" and "Religious Profile". Willis' contention that continuity is also indicated by the consistency of Corinthian bronze from the Roman city compared to the Greek city, given its unusual composition (ibid., 239), is not strong. Indeed, it is now apparent that the so-called "Corinthian Bronze" was actually manufactured at several places besides Corinth. See Gill, "Corinth", 261-2.

[7] Cicero *Leg. Agr.* 1.5; Strabo *Geog.* 8.6.23; cf. Larsen, "Greece", 308, 312; Robinson, "Corinth", 242; Wiseman, "Corinth", 26; Engels, *Roman Corinth*, 15-16. Although there is evidence that an attempt at centuriation was made in 111 BCE to prepare the *ager publicus* for sale, the process was apparently never completed and the sale did not go ahead. See Romano, "Land Use", 12; cf. *CIL* 1²585; Stansbury, "Corinthian Honor", 110.

The city was refounded as a *colonia* in 44 BCE, and was given the name *Colonia Laus Iulia Corinthiensis*.[8] Although this title strongly suggests that it was a Caesarean colony, the actual role that Julius Caesar played in the process is not clear. The most likely scenario, however, is that some settlement had begun prior to his assassination, but that it was only completed by his successors.[9] Upon colonization the city was extensively rebuilt. Although a number of surviving buildings were repaired and restored it was essentially a new city, one that bore little resemblance to the former Greek city. It was also thoroughly Roman in its character and ethos. This is quite apparent from its town-planning, architecture, political structures, entertainments, and social and religious institutions. Even the name (*Corinthiensis*) seems to reflect a deliberate attempt to distinguish it from the former Greek city.[10] Indeed, Corinth remained a thoroughly Roman city

---

[8] See, for example, Kent #130; Robinson, "Corinth", 242; Wiseman, "Corinth", 26; McRay, *Archaeology*, 320; cf. V. P. Furnish, "Corinth in Paul's Time: What Can Archaeology Tell Us?" *BARev* 15.3 (1988) 16.

[9] See Appian *Pun.* 136; Pausanias *Descr.* 2.1.2; Strabo *Geog.* 8.4.8, 21, 23; cf. Larsen, "Greece", 446; Robinson, "Corinth", 242; Wiseman, "Corinth", 497; Stansbury, "Roman Honor", 118-19; Tomlinson, *From Mycenae*, 81; Gill, "Achaia", 438; Romano, "Land Use", 12; *contra* Broneer, "Corinth", 82; Williams, "Commercial Center", 31.

[10] Broneer, "Corinth", 78, 93-5; Robinson, "Corinth", 242-3; Wiseman, "Corinth", 512-13; Williams, "The Refounding", 26-9, 32; Engels, *Roman Corinth*, 62, 69; Stansbury, "Corinthian Honor", 112, 124-5; McRay, *Archaeology*, 324, 335; Alcock, *Graecia*, 168; cf. Clarke, *Leadership*, 9-10; Gill, "Corinth", 262-3. Williams argues that with the exception of the Asclepion:

> the Romans knew about and tried to revive the Greek sanctuaries of the city, if possible even on their original sites, but were not concerned to restore them to their original form or recreate their original Greek ritual with any great precision or accuracy. Roman "modernization" seems to have been much preferred to ancient Greek authenticity. ("The Refounding", 32).

Although some of the minor (and "unusual") Greek cults were found in the Roman city this may indicate a deliberate "antiquarian revival", even a need "to propitiate the gods who controlled the city" without implying any significant continuity. Besides, even these cults were not immune to significant change at the hands of the Roman colonists. See Engels, *Roman Corinth*, 94; cf. Stansbury, "Roman Honor", 112; *contra* Willis, "Corinthusne", 238.

until at least the end of the first century, if not until Hadrian's time.[11]

2. Physical Features

Corinth lies near the narrow isthmus separating the Peloponnesus from the mainland. To its west is the port of Lechaeum on the Gulf of Corinth, about 3 kilometres away, and to its east is the port of Cenchreae on the Saronic Gulf, about 9-10 kilometres away.[12] It is located in a small plain at the base of Acrocorinth, which rises sharply to about 570m.[13] The annual rainfall of the area is quite low and the soil is generally not very productive, having a heavy clay component and many rocks.[14]

Corinth was laid out according to a Roman grid-plan comprising two major east-west roads and a major north-south road. The latter, the Lechaeum Road, was about 15m wide (including footpath), while the east-west roads were, on average, about 5m wide and other north-south roads were about 3.5m wide.[15] This grid gave *insulae* ranging between

---

[11] Williams, "The Refounding", 35; Engels, *Roman Corinth*, 62, 71-3; Stansbury, "Corinthian Honor", 152; Gill, "Corinth", 263-4; idem, "In Search of the Social Élite in the Corinthian Church" *TynBul* 44 (1993) 327 n. 35. Some NT scholars assume, apparently based on Favorinus (Dio Chrys. *Or.* 37), that the city was already strongly Hellenized in Paul's time (e.g. Meeks, *First Urban*, 47; V. P. Furnish, *II Corinthians* [AB; Garden City, NY: Doubleday, 1984], 12; Willis, "Corinthusne", 241; D. Litfin, *St. Paul's Theology of Proclamation: 1 Corinthians 1-4 and Greco-Roman Rhetoric* [SNTSMS 79; Cambridge: Cambridge University Press, 1994] 141). But they fail to consider the significant changes under Hadrian. See Gill, "Social Élite", 327 n. 35.

[12] Cicero *Leg. Agr.* 2.87; Pausanias *Descr.* 2.1.5; Pliny *NH* 4.9-11; Polystratus (*Greek Anthology* 7.297); cf. Cary, *Geographic*, 80; Robinson, "Corinth", 240; Wiseman, "Corinth", 441; Stansbury, "Corinthian Honor", 55-60; Tomlinson, *From Mycenae*, 75. At its narrowest point the isthmus is only about 6 km wide (Stansbury, "Corinthian Honor", 59-60).

[13] Pausanias *Descr.* 2.4.6-7, 2.5.1; Pliny *NH* 4.11; Strabo *Geog.* 8.6.21; cf. Wiseman, "Corinth", 439; Engels, *Roman Corinth*, 9; Stansbury, "Corinthian Honor", 55.

[14] Cicero *Leg. Agr.* 1.5, 2.51; Strabo *Geog.* 8.6.23; Cary, *Geographic*, 81; Wiseman, "Corinth", 444-5; Engels, *Roman Corinth*, 10-12, 27; Stansbury, "Corinthian Honor", 52, 54, 61-3; cf. Furnish, "Corinth", 17.

[15] Romano, "Land Use", 15-19; cf. Stansbury, "Corinthian Honor", 124; McRay, *Archaeology*, 335.

0.5 and 2 *iugera*.[16] The actual area of the *urbs* is unclear. Donald Engels suggests it was 2,100 *iugera* (about 525 hectares) but David Romano claims that it was 812 (about 203 hectares).[17] Engels gives no solid reason for his figure, whereas Romano's is well supported and should be preferred.

In the Greek city, houses were located close to the *agora*. Remains of Roman houses, however, have been found throughout the *urbs* and not concentrated in any particular area.[18] While Engels claims that only elite houses were found in the central area of the city so that there would have been a geographical separation of social groups, he admits that commercial property was central.[19] In fact the arrangement of space in the city shows a close connection between the commercial, religious, political, social and residential aspects of life.[20] Bronze-foundries were very close to the *forum*: one was almost adjacent to the *macellum* and another lay between at least two temples.[21] Many trade guilds met in temples: merchants in the temple of Mercury/Hermes (western end of the *forum*) and sea-traders in the *peribolos* of Apollo.[22] This close association of commercial, administrative, religious and social facilities also suggests there may have been a considerable interaction of the various social groups.

Given the nature of its planning, with the mix of commercial and residential (elite and common), it is

---

[16] Romano, "Land Use", 19. Many of the colony's roads were laid over former Greek ones, but the city's plan does not align with that of the old Greek city. For example, the old *agora* lies to the north-east of the *forum*. See Wiseman, "Corinth", 512-13; Stansbury, "Corinthian Honor", 124; McRay, *Archaeology*, 324; Tomlinson, *From Mycenae*, 78; Romano, "Land Use", 19.

[17] Engels, *Roman Corinth*, 81-2; cf. Romano, "Land Use", 19.

[18] Robinson, "Corinth", 242-3; cf. Furnish, *II Corinthians*, 12.

[19] Engels, *Roman Corinth*, 183-4.

[20] Many of the thirty-three shops in the South Stoa that were originally *tabernae* and *popinae* were converted into offices, possibly for Games officials, some time in the first century CE. See Broneer, "Corinth", 92-3; Robinson, "Corinth", 241; Wiseman, "Corinth", 513; cf. Stansbury, "Corinthian Honor", 174. While this might suggest that there was a tendency to move the commercial activities away from the *forum*, it is likely that these conversions would have been a gradual change, as "governmental services proliferated and became more complex" (Williams, "Commercial Center", 37). They do not necessarily reflect specific planning intentions.

[21] See Wiseman, "Corinth", 512; cf. Furnish, *II Corinthians*, 9.

[22] See Robinson, "Corinth", 243; Stansbury, "Corinthian Honor", 176-7.

reasonable to assume Corinth followed the pattern of other Roman cities. The narrowness of the roads and small size of the *insulae*, together with the large open spaces,[23] suggest life would have been very communal and that the city functioned as a *Gemeinschaft*-type community. Therefore, it is also reasonable to assume that much of what has been discussed in relation to city life, especially in the case of Roman cities, would also apply to Corinth.

3. Demographic Features

Roman Corinth was a very large city. Recent estimates suggest its population was about 80,000-87,000 for the *urbs* and 20,000 for the *territorium*. But the figure for the *urbs* is based on a population density rate of 160 person per hectare.[24] Based on the density rate proposed in chapter two (and used in the previous chapter) and an area of 812 *iugera*, Corinth's population (*urbs*) would be in the order of 100,000-130,000.

It is generally assumed that Corinth was a very cosmopolitan city. This is possibly indicated by the range of places represented by pottery sherds and coin finds.[25] A considerable ethnic diversity is very likely, given that the city was the provincial capital, and was a very large and extremely wealthy city, it was an important trade center, and hosted the Isthmian Games.[26] Indeed, the fact that it was

---

[23] Corinth's *forum* comprised 6 *iugera*, not including the building and structures in the *forum* (Broneer, "Corinth", 90; Engels, *Roman Corinth*, 60; Williams, "Commercial Center", 33), although Romano suggests it was 12 *iugera* including the buildings ("Land Use", 19). Stansbury notes that it was one of the largest known ("Corinthian Honor", 172-4).

[24] Engels, *Roman Corinth*, 33, 82; Alcock, *Graecia*, 160; Gill, "Social Élite", 333. Furnish suggests 130,000 for *urbs et territorium* (*II Corinthians*, 10). Other estimates cite it as 100,000 (Chandler & Fox, *3000 Years*, 81; Stark, "Christianizing", 79).

[25] See K. M. Edwards, *Corinth: Results of Excavations. Volume VI: Coins 1896-1929* (Cambridge, MA: Harvard University Press, 1933). J. M. Harris, "Coins Found at Corinth" *Hesp* 10 (1941) 148-52; K. S. Wright, "A Tiberian Pottery Deposit from Corinth" *Hesp* 49 (1980) 174-5; cf. Furnish, *II Corinthians*, 8.

[26] See, for example, Merritt #14; cf. Broneer, "Corinth", 78, 83; Engels, *Roman Corinth*, 12, 42-50. Given that the voyage around the Peloponnesus was extremely hazardous, Corinth's location near the isthmus meant it could control virtually all the sea-trade between the east and the west. See Cicero *Leg. Agr.* 2.87; Pliny *NH* 4.10; Strabo *Geog.* 8.6.20; Cary, *Geographic*, 82; Broneer, "Corinth", 78-80; Wiseman,

extremely wealthy and an important trade and "tourism" center, means that we would expect there to have been a large migrant population of merchants and artisans.[27]

Besides, the majority of the original colonists sent out from Rome were *liberti*, although there was a small number of veterans among them.[28] Most scholars, however, have simply assumed that the *liberti*-colonists were of Greek

---

"Corinth", 446; Engels, *Roman Corinth*, 9, 50; Stansbury, "Corinthian Honor", 59-60, 65; McRay, *Archaeology*, 313; Tomlinson, *From Mycenae*, 75; Williams, "Commercial Center", 38. On the importance of the Isthmian Games see Dio Chrys. *Or.* 8.6; Strabo *Geog.* 8.6.20; Broneer, "Corinth", 95; Engels, *Roman Corinth*, 50-1; Stansbury, "Corinthian Honor", 68; McRay, *Archaeology*, 313. It is likely that in the period between 40 BCE and the late 50's CE the games were staged in Corinth itself, not at the village of Isthmia. See E. R. Gebhard, "The Isthmian Games and the Sanctuary of Poseidon in the Early Empire" in T. E. Gregory, ed., *The Corinthia in the Roman Period* (JRASup 8; Ann Arbor: University of Michigan Press, 1994) 79-85.

[27] In fact, a substantial part of Corinth's wealth appears to derive from its extensive manufacturing industries, e.g. Corinthian bronze, dyeing, marble-carving, pottery, and it may have been the main center for the slave-trade in the region. See Florus 1.32.6-7; Josephus *BJ* 5.201; Robinson, "Corinth", 241-2; Bartchy, *Slavery*, 58 n. 185; Wiseman, "Corinth", 512, 520; Engels, *Roman Corinth*, 10, 35-8, 42; Stansbury, "Corinthian Honor", 30, 55, 81, 233, 238; McRay, *Archaeology*, 326; Williams, "Commercial Center", 38; cf. Marshall, *Enmity*, 294. This may also be suggested by the very large number of shops found in the city. Engels estimates that shops occupied some 23,200m² (*Roman Corinth*, 60). In any case, some of the names in the inscriptions do suggest an ethnic origin, e.g. C. Curtius Lesbius (Kent #198) — possibly from Lesbos; C. Iulius Spartiaticus (Merritt #70) — from Sparta, along with other members of the Euryclids who were prominent at Corinth e.g. C. Iulius Eurycles, C. Iulius Deximachus, C. Iulius Laco (West #67); M. Antonius Milesius (Kent #311) — possibly from Miletus; even C. Iulius Syrus (Kent #57) — possibly from Syria. See also Stansbury, "Corinthian Honor", 183.

[28] Polystratus (*Greek Anthology* 7.297); Strabo *Geog.* 8.6.23; Wiseman, "Corinth", 497; Brunt, *Man-Power*, 256; Engels, *Roman Corinth*, 16, 67; Stansbury, "Corinthian Honor", 120; Alcock, *Graecia*, 168; Romano, "Land Use", 12. Keppie suggests that in Caesarean colonies only 20-25% of colonists were veterans (*Colonisation*, 58). Thus, K.-K. Yeo's designation of Corinth as a military colony (*Rhetorical Interaction in 1 Corinthians 8 and 10* [Leiden: E. J. Brill, 1995] 85) is quite mistaken. A. C. Wire contends that the colonists would have "had to compete for dignity and with prime Greek families who returned to Corinth" as well as with "foreign merchants and traders" (*The Corinthian Women Prophets: A Reconstruction through Paul's Rhetoric* [Minneapolis: Fortress, 1990] 62). But she misunderstands the nature of a *colonia* and seems to assume Corinth was a Greek rather than a Roman city.

origin.[29] Although there may have been some descendants of the original inhabitants, and some may indeed have been of Greek origin, the bulk of available *liberti* in 44 BCE would have been Jews, Syrians, Egyptians, Gauls, and people from Asia Minor.[30]

Upon colonization, the squatters would have generally become *incolae*, while many other residents would have been drawn in from the surrounding areas. Immigrants also came from throughout Greece and the East.[31] Given that the city was founded as a *colonia*, it is also probable that a number of Italians migrated to the city, especially businessmen (*negotiatores*) who had been living in Achaia and Greece.[32] It is also likely that a number of Jews would have settled in Corinth following Tiberius' expulsion in 19 CE and Claudius' expulsion in 49 CE.[33]

It is likely that there were Jews among the colonists since Pompey had taken a large number back to Rome as slaves in 61 BCE, many of whom would have been *liberti* at the time the colonists were chosen. Furthermore, during the civil war between Caesar and Pompey the Jews probably supported Caesar. Thus it is quite conceivable that in reward

---

[29] Larsen, "Greece", 446; Wiseman, "Corinth", 497; Meeks, *First Urban*, 48; P. Richardson, "On the Absence of 'Anti-Judaism' in 1 Corinthians" in P. Richardson & D. Granskou, eds., *Anti-Judaism in Early Christianity, Vol. I* (Waterloo, Ont.: Wilfred Laurier University Press, 1986) 61; Engels, *Roman Corinth*, 70; Alcock, *Graecia*, 168; Romano, "Land Use", 12; B. Witherington III, *Conflict and Community in Corinth: A Socio-Rhetorical Commentary on 1 and 2 Corinthians* (Grand Rapids: Eerdmans, 1995) 6; Yeo, *Interaction*, 85; Timothy Savage cites Strabo *Geog.* 17.3.15 in support of this (*Power Through Weakness: Paul's Understanding of Christian Ministry in 2 Corinthians* [SNTSMS 86; Cambridge: Cambridge University Press, 1996] 37), but the text simply calls them ἐποίκους.

[30] Rightly identified by Furnish, *II Corinthians*, 7; idem, "Corinth", 16.

[31] Wiseman, "Corinth", 497; Engels, *Roman Corinth*, 70; Alcock, *Graecia*, 160.

[32] For example, L. Aeficius Certus, *duumvir* in 43/2 BCE, and M. Insteius Tectus, *duumvir* in 43/2 BCE, 37/6 BCE and 34/3 BCE, were both clearly freeborn immigrants (Kent ##149, 345; cf. Engels, *Roman Corinth*, 68); cf. Brunt, *Man-Power*, 244; Engels, *Roman Corinth*, 8; Gill, "Achaia", 439.

[33] See, for example, Wiseman, "Corinth", 503; Stansbury, "Corinthian Honor", 378-80; McRay, *Archaeology*, 319; Witherington, *Conflict*, 26.

for this loyalty Caesar designated some as colonists.[34] Apart from the likelihood of Jews being among the colonists, Philo explicitly mentions Corinth as having a Jewish community. Given that he mentions Corinth as well as Attica and Peloponnesus it is possible that there was a large community at Corinth.[35] Unfortunately, the only known Jewish inscriptions date from the third or fourth century CE.[36] Conclusive proof, therefore, is unavailable but it is most likely that there was a strong Jewish community at Corinth in the first century CE. The Jewish community may have been well integrated and on good terms with the wider community since there is no record of any conflict.[37]

There is limited evidence with which to assess the extent of ethnic integration at Corinth. Based on the large transient and migrant populations it would be reasonable to assume there was a degree of tolerance, and perhaps integration. Unfortunately the only inscription of a *collegium* is one for imperial *liberti*, whose descendants could be of any ethnic origin, but who would have been quite well Romanized.[38] Nevertheless, men who were not native Corinthians were elected as magistrates and this would have necessitated considerable interaction with the Corinthian elite and probably with the ordinary Corinthian population

---

[34] Furnish, *II Corinthians*, 20; Stansbury, "Corinthian Honor", 377-8. Although there is no direct evidence of the Jews taking Caesar's side it is likely given their deep grief at his murder (Suetonius *Iul.* 84), and his history of support for their privileges (Josephus *AJ* 14.213-22).

[35] Philo *Leg.* 281; cf. Wiseman, "Corinth", 503 n. 255; Furnish, *II Corinthians*, 20; Meeks, *First Urban*, 48; Richardson, "Absence", 61; Stansbury, "Corinthian Honor", 378-9; McRay, *Archaeology*, 319; Gill, "Achaia", 450; Witherington, *Conflict*, 25-6. Stansbury suggests that the reference to a Jewish community at Sicyon in 1 Macc 15:22-3 is to some Jews who escaped the destruction of Corinth and settled in Sicyon. He claims that some of their descendants moved back after colonization ("Corinthian Honor", 378). But this is speculative and unsupported.

[36] See, for example, Meeks, *First Urban*, 48; McRay, *Archaeology*, 319. The most well known inscription is Merritt #111; Marshall (*Acts*, 292) mistakenly dates this to the first century CE.

[37] That Prisca and Aquila settled there (Acts 18:2) may imply that Corinth was known to be tolerant towards Jews. Furnish's claim that the Jews lived in a separate area due to anti-semitism (*II Corinthians*, 21-2) is unsupported, and unlikely given the general absence of such sentiments among the Romans. See section II.3 of chapter 2 herein.

[38] See, for example, Merritt #14; Kent #62; cf. Chow, *Patronage*, 65.

as well.[39] Therefore, the impression is that there was reasonable ethnic diversity and integration.

4. Social Relations

Despite the manner of its colonization, Corinth was not an egalitarian community. The colonists would have differed in wealth, education and social connections, and the commissioners deliberately sought to recreate a stable oligarchy and a society that was "hierarchic and elitist, and therefore safe".[40] Indeed, the colonization process itself ensured that land, wealth and magistracies were confined to those whom the commissioners designated as the colony's elite.[41] Consequently, although there were probably more opportunities for social advancement in Corinth than in most other cities, it was still very difficult. Indeed, from the inscriptional evidence it is clear that the ruling elite at Corinth remained quite stable over a long period of time.[42] The elite seem to have used a number of social control mechanisms to restrict access to their group, including wealth, marriage and social ties.[43]

Since Corinth was a Roman *colonia*, it should be expected that patronage ties were very important.[44] For example, since the main market appears to have been built by Q. Cornelius Secundus and his family, it is likely that they

---

[39] For example, Ti. Claudius Dinippus, *duumvir* (West ##86-92), C. Curtius Lesbius, *aedilis, duumvir, agonothetes* (Kent #198), L. Papius Lupercus, *aedilis, duumvir, agonothetes* (West #105), did not belong to Corinthian tribes.

[40] Stansbury, "Corinthian Honor", 120-1; *contra* G. Theissen, *The Social Setting of Pauline Christianity* (Philadelphia: Fortress, 1982) 99-100.

[41] Stansbury, "Corinthian Honor", 126.

[42] Stansbury, "Corinthian Honor", 86-8; *contra* Theissen, *Social Setting*, 99-100; Witherington, *Conflict*, 20; Savage, *Power*, 39. The elite's stability is seen in that certain families continued to act as civic benefactors and to fill magistracies (e.g. Cornelii, Heii, Rutilii) and that many of the elite belonged to the tribe Aemilia (e.g. West ##12, 80, 82, 106, 124; Kent, ##152, 156, 164, 175, 208-9, 212, 224, 237, 321, 327).

[43] Stansbury, "Corinthian Honor", 86-7, 268, 283; Clarke, *Leadership*, 11; cf. West #124; Kent #321. The elite also showed marked snobbery (Dio Chrys. *Or.* 9.10; cf. Stansbury, "Corinthian Honor", 32-3).

[44] See, for example, Chow, *Patronage*, 38-42; Clarke, *Leadership*, 35; cf. West ##16, 68.

would have controlled who could operate stalls there.[45] Since many of the colonists were *liberti*, they would have remained as clients of their former masters, and it is likely that many acted as business-agents for these prominent Romans in the new colony.[46] Furthermore, when *liberti* did break into the elite it was largely because they were well connected.[47] This strongly suggests both that there was some degree of interaction of people from different social groups and that patronage ties were important.

5. Political Features

Corinth was the capital of the province of Achaia, at least following Claudius' designation of Achaia as a senatorial province in 44 CE. Prior to 27 BCE it fell under the jurisdiction of the governor of Macedonia, and again from 15-44 CE when it was designated an imperial province.[48] As a *colonia*, however, it was largely self-governing. Nevertheless, it was an ordinary *colonia* and was not granted *ius Italicum*.[49]

As a colony, Corinth had a Roman form of government. The chief officials of the city were the *duoviri*, designated *duoviri quinquennales* every fifth year when they took the census and appointed new members to the *ordo decurionum* from among the former office-holders, and the *aediles*.[50] But

---

[45] See West ##124-5; Kent #321; cf. D. W. J. Gill, "The Meat-Market at Corinth (1 Corinthians 10:25)" *TynBul* 43 (1992) 390; Williams, "Commercial Center", 39-46.

[46] See Williams, "Commercial Center", 33. Many of the Corinthian elite also had substantial business interests in other provinces. See Stansbury, "Corinthian Honor", 131, 194, 261-2; Alcock, *Graecia*, 156; Gill, "Social Élite", 329.

[47] It was only via wealth and good connections that a former *libertus* could become a magistrate (see West ##98-101; Kent #50; Chow, *Patronage*, 53-9; Clarke, *Leadership*, 10). However, in one unusual case, the daughter of a Corinthian nobleman (Cornelia Secunda) married her grandfather's *libertus* (Q. Maecius Cleogenis). See Kent #321.

[48] Pliny *NH* 4.12; Stansbury, "Corinthian Honor", 168-9, 195; Wiseman, "Corinth", 501-3; cf. Larsen, "Greece", 437-8; Broneer, "Corinth", 82; Robinson, "Corinth", 242; Engels, *Roman Corinth*, 8; Tomlinson, *From Mycenae*, 82; Gill, "Achaia", 434-6.

[49] Sherwin-White, *Citizenship*, 316; Stansbury, "Corinthian Honor", 170.

[50] See Wiseman, "Corinth", 398-99; D. W. J. Gill, "Erastus the Aedile" *TynBul* 40 (1989) 294; Engels, *Roman Corinth*, 18: Stansbury, "Corinthian Honor", 157; cf. Clarke, *Leadership*, 14-16. See also section III.2 of chapter 3 herein.

there is no evidence to suggest that there were actually *quaestores* at Corinth and it is likely that the *aediles* fulfilled their role.[51] The Corinthian *aediles* were unusual in that they did not manage the Games. This was undertaken by the *agonothetes*, whose office was accorded the highest honor in the city.[52] A *curator annonae* appears to have been elected irregularly to deal with famines, ensuring there was sufficient grain for the city's need at a reasonable price.[53]

While it was possible for *liberti* to be elected to public office at Corinth this was uncommon elsewhere.[54] Yet, even at Corinth, *liberti* may have been barred from holding the highest offices, particularly those of *duumvir quinquennalis* and *agonothetes*.[55] The average resident of Corinth had limited political power in a hierarchic and oligarchic system.[56]

---

[51] Wiseman, "Corinth", 499; Stansbury, "Corinthian Honor", 156; cf. Clarke, *Leadership*, 52-3. *Quaestor* is not listed among the cursus of a Corinthian from any known inscription. Furthermore, another Caesarean colony from 44 BCE, Urso, did not elect *quaestores* according to its *Lex Colonia*. See Stansbury, "Corinthian Honor", 159.

[52] Wiseman, "Corinth", 499-500; Gill, "Erastus", 294; Engels, *Roman Corinth*, 18; cf. Clarke, *Leadership*, 15-17; Witherington, *Conflict*, 12. There was also the position of *praefectus fabrum* (chief engineer) — an equestrian appointed by the governor to oversee public works (Wiseman, "Corinth", 499; Stansbury, "Corinthian Honor", 156).

[53] Those appointed include: M. Antonius Achaicus, in the time of Trajan (Kent ##164, 224), Ti. Claudius Dinippus (West ##86-90), who probably assumed the position in 51 CE, and an un-named man (West #83) some time between 47 and 51 CE. The fact that Dinippus was appointed to the post of *curator annonae* on three separate occasions (West #88), and that at least one other individual held it in the same period, strongly suggests that there was a series of famines from the mid-40's to mid-50's CE. See also Wiseman, "Corinth", 505; Stansbury, "Corinthian Honor", 300; Clarke, *Leadership*, 18-19.

[54] For example, Cn. Babbius Philinus (West ##2, 98-101) and C. Heius Pamphilus (Kent #150). See Wiseman, "Corinth", 498; Gill, "Erastus", 295; idem, "Social Élite", 328; Engels, *Roman Corinth*, 68; Stansbury, "Corinthian Honor", 157; cf. Chow, *Patronage*, 59; Clarke, *Leadership*, 14. Engels claims that the right of *liberti* to hold office in *coloniae* was revoked by Augustus (*Roman Corinth*, 18), but this is clearly not the case. See, for example, Stansbury, "Corinthian Honor", 255.

[55] This is suggested by the absence of these from the cursus of Cn. Babbius Philinus (Stansbury, "Corinthian Honor", 256; cf. West ##98-101).

[56] Engels argues that the *incolae* at Corinth were permitted to vote in elections, but were not permitted to hold office (*Roman Corinth*, 17). But this would be unusual in a Roman *colonia*.

Real power resided with the magistrates (especially the *duoviri / duoviri quinquennales*) and the decurions. As with any Roman city, it is likely that patronage ties were very important in this regard, for clients provided the power base for potential office-holders, while such patrons were the only means of access to the machinery of government. Patronage therefore entailed security.

6. Religious Profile

The gods and cults adopted or revived by the Corinthians included Apollo, Aphrodite/Venus, Asclepius, Athena, Athena Chalinitis, Demeter and Kore, Dionysus, Ephesian Artemis, Hera Acraea, Hermes/Mercury, Jupiter Capitolinus, Poseidon /Neptune, Tyche/Fortuna and Zeus. Also important were the Egyptian cults, the Imperial cult and the *Genius* of the Colony.[57] According to the number of temples, shrines and statues, and the number of images on coins, the two most important and popular gods were Poseidon/Neptune and Aphrodite/Venus.[58]

The popularity of Poseidon/Neptune was associated with his role as the god of the sea (and hence relevant to Corinth's economy) and of earthquakes (which were prevalent). Furthermore, the Isthmian Games were also at least nominally in his honor.[59] It is sometimes assumed that the popularity of Aphrodite/Venus was because Corinth was a particularly "immoral" city. While it is likely that the Corinthians valued sensual pleasure, they were probably no more immoral than residents of other wealthy cities.[60] Besides, Strabo's account of 1,000 sacral prostitutes at the

---

[57] See Pausanias *Descr.* 2.1.6-7, 2.2.6-8, 2.3.1-3, 2.4.1-5; Apuleius *Met.* 10.35-11.24; Dio Chrys. *Or.* 37.42; Broneer, "Corinth", 83-6; Engels, *Roman Corinth*, 101-2; Stansbury, "Corinthian Honor", 178-9; McRay, *Archaeology*, 322; cf. Furnish, *II Corinthians*, 15, 18-19; Richardson, "Absence", 61 n. 5; Yeo, *Interaction*, 104-5; Savage, *Power*, 50.

[58] See Engels, *Roman Corinth*, 93-4, 97; Yeo, *Interaction*, 104-5; cf. Dio Chrys. *Or.* 37.42; Burnett et al, *Coins*.

[59] Dio Chrys. *Or.* 37.42; Broneer, "Corinth", 84. Every four years the Isthmian Games were held in combination with the Caesarean Games (i.e. the "Greater Isthmian Games") and thus a link with the Imperial Cult became strong.

[60] See Engels, *Roman Corinth*, 89; Stansbury, "Corinthian Honor", 70; cf. Litfin, *Proclamation*, 142; Yeo, *Interaction*, 108; *contra* Haenchen, *Acts*, 533.

temple of Aphrodite was no more than a legend, and one that related to the Greek city in any case.[61]

Apart from these two gods, most of the extant inscriptions and dedications were offered to the Imperial cult, as well as to Victoria, Concordia, the *Genius* of the Colony, Jupiter Optimus Maximus, Isis and Sarapis, and Apollo.[62] While there is some overlap between the gods commonly found in inscriptions and those on Corinthian coins (Nike/ Victoria and Apollo are also common there), the most common ones depicted on coins after Poseidon/Neptune and Aphrodite/ Venus are Bellerophon and Pegasus, and Melicertes.[63]

Despite the assumption of some scholars, the cult of Demeter and Kore appears to have been much less important in Roman times than earlier, in Greek times. The temple on Acrocorinth was substantially remodelled after colonization, making it much smaller and omitting the dining rooms altogether, and there is no clear evidence for any sacrifices in the Roman period.[64] Thus, it is likely that the rites also were modified substantially.

Although a few of the gods were specific to Corinth (Bellerophon, Melicertes), and many Greek gods were worshipped, most of the popular or important gods were Roman. This suggests a more Roman religious mind-set.[65]

---

[61] See H. Conzelmann, *1 Corinthians* (Hermeneia; Philadelphia: Fortress, 1975) 12; Furnish, *II Corinthians*, 16; Stansbury, "Corinthian Honor", 69; Witherington, *Conflict*, 13. The suggestion that these sacral-prostitutes may have been located in the city rather than the temple on Acrocorinth (McRay, *Archaeology*, 315; Yeo, *Interaction*, 108) cannot be supported. While there were probably many prostitutes in Corinth itself (cf. Pompeii), Furnish may be right in asserting that "sacred prostitution was not common in Greece" ("Corinth", 25).

[62] Engels, *Roman Corinth*, 101-2.

[63] See the catalogs by Edwards and Burnett *et al*; cf. Engels, *Roman Corinth*, 99; Yeo, *Interaction*, 104-5.

[64] See Stroud, "The Sanctuary", 67-72; McRay, *Archaeology*, 316; *contra* P. D. Gooch, *Dangerous Food: 1 Corinthians 8-10 in Its Context* (ESCJ 5; Waterloo, Ont.: Wilfred Laurier University Press, 1993) 5-12; Savage, *Power*, 50. It is possible that meals were held in the open air (Stroud, "The Sanctuary", 71; cf. Gooch, *Dangerous Food*, 4). Gooch's argument that meals still occurred in the sanctuary relies on the practices of the Eleusinian cult (Gooch, *Dangerous Food*, 5-12; cf. Yeo, *Interaction*, 110) but this is a huge, and unfounded, assumption.

[65] This is evident in the importance of the non-anthropomorphized gods. See section II.2 of chapter 2 herein; cf. Stansbury, "Corinthian Honor", 237; Alcock, *Graecia*, 168. That the known priesthoods at Corinth were of the Imperial Cult, Jupiter Capitolinus, Ianus, Victoria,

Some, however, contend that the Imperial cult was only supported by the elite, since they are responsible for most of the inscriptions related to it.[66] In fact, K.-K. Yeo claims that:

> Demeter and Kore, Isis and Sarapis, and Cybele appeared less on coinage in the first century for one reason: they were the cults of the poor, slaves, freedmen, women, and not the Italian colonists or aristocrats.[67]

The idea that the prevalence of inscriptions to the Imperial cult implies that it was the domain of the elite is an argument from silence. The elite are, in any case, the ones most likely to set up inscriptions. Besides, the fact that Isis and Sarapis are also commonly mentioned in inscriptions seems to rule out Yeo's contention — a contention that is without any supporting evidence. Similarly, Yeo would have to argue that because Tyche/Fortuna was often found on coins she too was a goddess of the elite.[68] But this clearly is not the case.

Overall, the religious profile of Corinth is mixed. This would be consistent with the varied nature of its population: some Greek and some Roman cults. Although it would be unwise to allocate these on either a "class" or ethnic basis, it is possible that the Roman cults would have been especially prominent among the city's citizens. Given the mixed population it would be reasonable to assume a variety of religious mentalities, Greek and Roman, as well as the more philosophical approach of the educated elite and the "superstition" of the common people.

In summary, then, first century Corinth was an extremely large and busy city. Nevertheless, it probably retained many of the characteristics of a community, with close and very public living and a strong interaction of the various aspects of city life. The city's planning, and the manner of its colonization, suggest that there may have been a reasonable association and interaction of different social

---

Saturn and the *genius* of the Colony (Engels, *Roman Corinth*, 101) would support this. Furthermore, that there was no cult of Roma at Corinth until Hadrian's time suggests that the Corinthians very much thought of themselves as Romans (see Williams, "The Refounding", 30-1).

[66] See, for example, Engels, *Roman Corinth*, 101; Alcock, *Graecia*, 169; cf. Yeo, *Interaction*, 113.

[67] Yeo, *Interaction*, 110; cf. Engels, *Roman Corinth*, 106.

[68] Yeo's argument seems to reflect that of Robert Jewett in respect to the cults at Thessalonica. For a critique of the latter see section I.7 of the previous chapter.

groups. This is even more likely given the strong patronal ties and patronal networks operating in the city.

Despite a lack of clear evidence, it seems likely that the city was very heterogeneous in its ethnic composition. The numerous to the city, in conjunction with shipping and the Isthmian Games, and presumably a large migrant population of merchants and artisans would have added to that. It is also likely that there was a strong Jewish community at Corinth. Although there is limited evidence regarding the overall level of interaction between members of different ethnic groups, given its cosmopolitan nature and the reliance of the city on foreign visitors, a fairly high degree of integration is likely. The city was the provincial capital with the status of a *colonia*. Its political structure was elitist and oligarchic, following a Roman pattern. However, there were ties between officials and the common people via the patronage system. The religious pattern of Corinth shows a mixture of Greek and Roman gods, and presumably of religious beliefs also.

II. THE CHRISTIAN COMMUNITY AT CORINTH

The nature of the Corinthian church will be reconstructed in a similar manner to that of the Thessalonian church in the previous chapter. In other words, its ethnic composition, its social profile and its size will be considered. Indeed, these are the most relevant aspects for understanding the nature of the relationship between the Christian and civic communities and the development of conflict.

1. Ethnic Composition

Paul's opening address in 1 Corinthians 1:2 (τῇ ἐκκλησίᾳ τοῦ θεοῦ τῇ οὔσῃ ἐν Κορίνθῳ) follows his more usual pattern of a locative expression, and gives no clue about the ethnic composition of the church. However, it is quite apparent from the letter that the majority of the Corinthian Christians had come from a background in Greek and Roman religion.[69] This is certainly evident in 6:9, 8:7-10, 12:2.

---

[69] See Richardson, "Absence", 63; G. D. Fee, *The First Epistle to the Corinthians* (NICNT; Grand Rapids: Eerdmans, 1987) 3-4; Furnish, "Corinth", 26; W. Baird, "'One Against the Other': Intra-Church Conflict in 1 Corinthians" in R. T. Fortna & B. R. Gaventa, eds., *The Conversation Continues* (Nashville: Abingdon, 1990) 120; Witherington, *Conflict*, 24.

On the other hand, it is clear that there was a number of Jews and/or God-fearers in the community. Their presence in the church is very likely given Paul's assumption that some were circumcised (7:18), his attention to Jewish concerns and sensibilities (1:22-4; 9:20-2), and his direct appeals to the Torah as an authority (9:8-10; 14:34). Although it is not conclusive, the quotes from and references to the OT (6:16; 9:9-10; 10:7, 26; 15:27, 32, 45, 54-5) also suggest this.[70] Furthermore, Luke identifies some of the members as Jews, namely Prisca, Aquila (18:2) and Crispus the former ἀρχισυνάγωγος (18:8). He also claims that Titius Iustus was a God-fearer (18:7). There is no compelling reason to doubt this.[71]

The majority of Corinthian Christians who are named in Acts 18, in 1 Corinthians, or in Romans 16:23, have Latin names (Achaicus, Crispus, Fortunatus, Gaius, Quartus, Titius Iustus), while a few have Greek names (Chloe, Erastus, Phoebe, Stephanas).[72] Nevertheless, some of the latter were probably also Romanized (especially Erastus).

---

[70] See Witherington, *Conflict*, 24-5; cf. Richardson, "Absence", 63-4; Baird, "Intra-Church", 121; Wire, *Women Prophets*, 64; Horrell, *Social Ethos*, 91. While Jewish-Christians would have been concerned with the issue of idol-meat and involvement in Greco-Roman cultic meals, 1 Cor 8 and 10 are clearly aimed at Greco-Roman members of the church. See section III.1 below.

[71] E. A. Judge, "The Early Christians as a Scholastic Community" *JRH* 1 (1961) 129; C. K. Barrett, *A Commentary on the First Epistle to the Corinthians* (BNTC; London: A. & C. Black, 1971) 47; Haenchen, *Acts*, 535; Marshall, *Acts*, 294; Fee, *First Epistle*, 62; Johnson, *Acts*, 323; Gill, "Social Élite", 327; Witherington, *Conflict*, 102; Yeo, *Interaction*, 86. NT Scholars are generally agreed that Luke's account of Paul at Corinth in Acts 18 is mostly reliable. See Haenchen, *Acts*, 537-40; Marshall, *Acts*, 292; Furnish, "Corinth", 14; Johnson, *Acts*, 324; Chow, *Patronage*, 86 n. 2; Yeo, *Interaction*, 86. Haenchen is sceptical of the vision to Paul and of the appearance before Gallio (*Acts*, 540-1). Yet the latter is reasonable when the notion of *religio licita* is rightly rejected as non-existent (*contra* Haenchen, *Acts*, 536; Johnson, *Acts*, 329, 334) along with some idea of rampant anti-semitism. It is feasible in terms of Gallio's "personal indignation at this awkward public situation" i.e. at being approached spontaneously in public after giving a public address (Stansbury, "Corinthian Honor", 395) or that he considered it an internal Jewish matter related to their own customs cf. Pilate (Witherington, *Conflict*, 73). The identity of the πάντες who beat Sosthenes is decidedly ambiguous.

[72] Compare, for example, Meeks, *First Urban*, 48, 212 n. 264; Yeo, *Interaction*, 89.

Consequently, it is likely that the Corinthian church was comprised of an ethnic mix, with some Romans, some "Greeks", and some Jews (who probably had assumed some Roman and/or some Greek customs).[73]

2. Social Profile

In 1 Cor 1:26 Paul reminds his readers that there were οὐ πολλοὶ σοφοὶ κατὰ σάρκα, οὐ πολλοὶ δυνατοί, οὐ πολλοὶ εὐγενεῖς among them. These terms (σοφοί, δυνατοί, εὐγενεῖς) are traditional ones for the elite.[74] Although there were "not many" of them, there is a growing consensus that Paul's statement infers that a *few* of the Christians were members of the elite.[75] Some suggest that those who fit this description are: Crispus, Phoebe, Titius Iustus, Stephanas, Chloe, Erastus and Gaius.[76]

As a former ἀρχισυνάγωγος, Crispus (Acts 18:8; 1 Cor 1:14) would have been reasonably wealthy and acted as a

---

[73] Yeo argues that those with Latin names are elite and should be identified with the "strong" in 1 Cor 8-10, while Greeks are the "weak" (*Interaction*, 114). This is too simplistic. See section III.2 below.

[74] See, for example, Aristotle *Ars* 2.12.2; Dio Chrys. *Or.* 31.74; Plutarch *De lib. ed.* 5C-D; cf. Theissen, *Social Setting*, 70-3; L. L. Welborn, "On the Discord in Corinth: 1 Corinthians 1-4 and Ancient Politics" *JBL* 106 (1987) 96-7; idem, "The Pursuit of Concord: A Political Ideal in Early Christianity" (unpublished PhD dissertation, Vanderbilt University, 1993) 47-8; Clarke, *Leadership*, 26, 44-5. Meggitt, however, contends that the three terms are "substantially more equivocal than has been assumed" (*Poverty*, 103-5). While εὐγενής may be used by those who were not, strictly speaking, nobles (he does not consider Dio Chrysostom's claim in *Or.* 15.29-30 [discussed below] that such a term was applied by the common people to those who were rich), he fails to consider the weight of the three terms together. Paul is not just referring to those who were σοφός or δυνατός or εὐγενής, but to those who were σοφός *and* δυνατός *and* εὐγενής.

[75] See Theissen, *Social Setting*, 55, 70-2; Furnish, *II Corinthians*, 25; Fee, *First Epistle*, 80; Baird, "Intra-Church", Chow, *Patronage*, 26; Clarke, *Leadership*, 42; Gill, "Social Élite", 324; D. B. Martin, *The Corinthian Body* (New Haven, CT: Yale University Press, 1995) 61; Witherington, *Conflict*, 22; with some modification also Horrell, *Social Ethos*, 95-8.

[76] See Judge, "Scholastic Community", 128-30; Baird, "Intra-Church", 122; Stansbury, "Corinthian Honor", 460-61; Engels, *Roman Corinth*, 108; Chow, *Patronage*, 89-91; Clarke, *Leadership*, 46; Witherington, *Conflict*, 34-5; Yeo, *Interaction*, 86-8.

patron to the Jewish community and been responsible for the
upkeep of the synagogue.[77] While he may have been well-
respected by the wider community, he probably had high
status only within the Christian community and formerly in
the Jewish community. There is no reason to consider him a
member of the city's ruling elite.[78] Both Phoebe (Rom 16:1)
and Titius Iustus (Acts 18:7) were of at least moderate means
since they owned houses and hosted Paul.[79] Stephanas (1 Cor
1:16, 16:15-17) would also be similarly placed as he could
visit Paul in Ephesus with his dependants.[80] It is likely that

---

[77] Bernadette Brooten claims that the position had both liturgical
and financial responsibilities (*Women as Leaders in the Ancient
Synagogue: Inscriptional Evidence and Background Issues* [BJS 36;
Chico, CA: Scholars, 1982] 28-9). However, the fact that both women
and children received such titles makes this unlikely. See T. Rajak & D.
Noy, "*Archisynagogoi*: Office, Title and Social Status in the Greco-Jewish
Synagogue" *JRS* 83 (1993) 83-7. Rather, the primary role of the
ἀρχισυνάγωγος was as a benefactor/patron (ibid., 87-8); cf. Stansbury,
"Corinthian Honor", 461; Chow, *Patronage*, 89; Clarke, *Leadership*, 46.

[78] See Chow, *Patronage*, 89; Rajak & Noy, "*Archisynagogoi*", 88;
contra Haenchen, *Acts*, 535; Theissen, *Social Setting*, 74-5; Yeo,
Interaction, 88.

[79] See Theissen, *Social Setting*, 90-1; Meeks, *First Urban*, 60;
Stansbury, "Corinthian Honor", 460-1; Chow, *Patronage*, 88-9, 102;
Witherington, *Conflict*, 34-5; Yeo, *Interaction*, 86. That Phoebe was a
patron is clearly intended by προστάτις (Rom 16:1). See BAGD sv
"προστάτις". Meggitt is probably correct to reject the idea that Phoebe
was a member of the elite, but he tries to downplay even her moderate
level of wealth. Although the term προστάτις need not indicate she was
wealthy, it is a reasonable assumption and Meggitt's arguments as to
how she could be cited as such and not be at least moderately wealthy
are weak (*Poverty*, 143-9). While it was unusual for a client to
recommend a patron, as Paul seems to do in her case, the situation is
more nuanced than Meggitt allows, since Paul had very high status
within the church, but not necessarily high social status. It is on the
basis of the former that he could recommend her to the church in Rome
while in regard to the latter she could support him. The attempt to
identify Titius Iustus with Gaius (i.e. as C. Titius Iustus) is without
foundation (Haenchen, *Acts*, 535; *contra* Marshall, *Acts*, 295;
Witherington, *Conflict*, 102). The use of the praenomen in the case of
Gaius may be because his cognomen was of servile origin, and being of
high social status (see below) he would not have wanted to emphasize
that. Since Paul did not use his nomen this may suggest that it was a
particularly common one. Thus, it is possible that his name may have
been C. Iulius _____.

[80] See Fee, *First Epistle*, 82, 829; Stansbury, "Corinthian Honor",
460; Chow, *Patronage*, 88-9, 102; Clarke, *Leadership*, 46; Yeo,
Interaction, 88; cf. Meeks, *First Urban*, 57-8. Theissen contends that

he was a merchant, rather than a member of the elite, given this method of travelling. In fact, none of these three qualify. Nor does Chloe (1:11). She has some means, since she owns slaves (or has *liberti*) who travel as her business agents, but that does not necessarily mean she was a noblewoman.[81]

In Rom 16:23 Paul identifies Erastus as ὁ οἰκονόμος τῆς πόλεως. Given this description, it is most likely that he is the same Erastus who laid a pavement to the east of the theatre at Corinth in return for having been elected an *aedilis*.[82] For

Fortunatus and Achaicus could not have been slaves since Paul requests the church to submit to their leadership (*Social Setting*, 92). But Fortunatus was a very common servile name (see Kajanto, *Cognomina*, 13, 273; cf. Fee, *First Epistle*, 831). Fee claims that Achaicus was also a common servile name (Fee, *First Epistle*, 831). Although the name is recorded for a member of the Corinthian elite in Trajan's time (Kent ##164, 224), it is actually quite rare in inscriptions. Besides Kajanto notes that such ethnically derived cognomina are overwhelmingly associated with freeborn, and many of these were probably children of *liberti*. (*Cognomina*, 48). However, the mention of these two with Stephanas just after the mention of his οἰκία strongly suggests they were his dependants (16:15-17). In any case, submission to the leadership of slaves or *liberti* would be a problem for *Paul* only if one accepts Theissen's model of love-patriarchalism. See section IV.2 below. Given that Stephanas himself has a Greek name it is entirely likely that he too was a *libertus*, especially since it was a common servile name (see *ILS*).

[81] See Stansbury, "Corinthian Honor", 461; Chow, *Patronage*, 91. It is most likely that "Chloe's people" (οἱ Χλόης — 1:11) are slaves "since members of a family would have used their father's name, even if he were deceased" (Theissen, *Social Setting*, 57, 93; cf. Barrett, *Commentary*, 42; Meeks, *First Urban*, 63; Welborn, "Discord", 98; Baird, "Intra-Church", 122; Witherington, *Conflict*, 99). Some claim they cannot be her slaves or *liberti* but are her followers since the construction is the same used in the slogans in 1:12 (e.g. E. Schüssler Fiorenza, "Rhetorical Situation and Historical Reconstruction in I Corinthians" *NTS* 33 [1987] 394-5; Yeo, *Interaction*, 88 n. 17). But Paul *does* construe those slogans in terms of servile dependence. See M. M. Mitchell, *Paul and the Rhetoric of Reconciliation: An Exegetical Investigation of the Language and Composition of 1 Corinthians* (Louisville: W/JK Press, 1991) 83-6. See section III.2 below.

[82] *Erastus pro aedilit[at]e s. p. stravit* (Kent #232). Most scholars consider them to be the same person. See Broneer, "Corinth", 94; Wiseman, "Corinth", 499 n. 226; Furnish, "Corinth", 20; Engels, *Roman Corinth*, 108; Stansbury, "Corinthian Honor", 321; McRay, *Archaeology*, 331; A. D. Clarke, "Another Erastus Inscription" *TynBul* 42 (1991) 151; idem, *Leadership*, 54-6; Welborn, "Concord", 80; Gill, "Achaia", 451; Witherington, *Conflict*, 33; Yeo, *Interaction*, 87; Savage, *Power*, 40 n. 153; Horrell, *Social Ethos*, 97; *contra* Hemer, *Book*, 235. Meggitt's difficulty with this text leads him to suggest an emendation from Erastus to

his was an uncommon cognomen, and it is highly unlikely that two prominent Corinthians would have had such a name when no other officials at Corinth are known to have had it.[83] Indeed, Paul's description of him as ὁ οἰκονόμος τῆς πόλεως would seem to be the equivalent of *aedilis*. Although ἀγορανόμος is the more usual Greek equivalent, οἰκονόμος could refer to either an *aedilis* or *quaestor*.[84] Furthermore,

Eperastus (*Poverty*, 135-41). But his argument is weak and speculative.

[83] See Furnish, "Corinth", 20; Clarke, "Erastus", 151; idem, *Leadership*, 54; McRay, *Archaeology*, 332; cf. Stansbury, "Corinthian Honor", 321. While another inscription mentioning an Erastus has been found at Corinth, it is dated to the second century CE, and there is no indication that this individual was a prominent person. He seems to be a *libertus* of the other dedicators. See Clarke, "Erastus", 147-8. "Erastus" was a cognomen found among prominent citizens of Ephesus (Gill, "Erastus", 299-300; Hemer, *Book*, 235; Clarke, "Erastus", 150). Some scholars suggest that the term οἰκονόμος referred to a public slave, and hence that the two cannot be the same individual, (see, for example, Meggitt, *Poverty*, 135, 139). As D. B. Martin notes, the term normally referred to either a public slave, who was quite high in the official bureaucracy, or an elected office-holder (*Slavery as Salvation: The Metaphor of Slavery in Pauline Christianity* [New Haven: Yale University Press, 1990] 15-16, 174-6). Paul's mention of his position, something that was unusual for him to do, suggests that this Erastus had a high standing in society. Meggitt claims that Paul's use of the title could not mean Erastus was elite, since 1 Cor 1:27-8 and 6:1 are evidence that Paul "shows antipathy to the notion of secular prestige in his epistles" ("Economic", 135). Apart from the fact that this requires an unusual reading of 6:1, his argument ignores the fact that Paul's use of the title occurs in the letter to the Romans, possibly intended to introduce Erastus to them, and it is not addressed to Erastus personally. His suggestion that the title referred to a church-office is weak, for even though *collegia* borrowed civic titles for their offices, there is no reason why it would include τῆς πόλεως and not simply be ὁ οἰκονόμος or ὁ οἰκονόμος τῆς ἐκκλησίας. In either case, he would have had reasonable status, something that is generally ignored by NT scholars. See Theissen, *Social Setting*, 76; Gill, "Erastus", 300; idem, "Social Élite", 323; Clarke, *Leadership*, 56; Witherington, *Conflict*, 30; but see Meeks, *First Urban*, 58. An identification with the paver/*aedilis* is still most likely since the name was so uncommon *at Corinth*. While the cognomen was found irregularly in the inscriptions, it is its rarity *at Corinth* that is important. *Contra* Meggitt, *Poverty*, 139-41.

[84] See Gill, "Erastus", 297; Stansbury, "Corinthian Honor", 322; Clarke, *Leadership*, 15 n. 30, 50; Witherington, *Conflict*, 33-4. Theissen claims that Paul describes him in the earlier post of *quaestor* (*Social Setting*, 80-3; cf. Meeks, *First Urban*, 59), but ignores the fact that there does not seem to have been such a post at Corinth. But H. J. Mason lists three inscriptions where οἰκονόμος does mean *aedilis*: *IGRR* 4.813, 1435, 1630 (*Greek Terms for Roman Institutions: A Lexicon and Analysis* [ASP

given that the Corinthian *aedilis* did not manage the Games, the term οἰκονόμος fits the job-description of the *aedilis* well.[85] Despite having attained this position in society, the paving inscription implies that Erastus was probably a *libertus* since there is no space for his father's name or tribe.[86]

Gaius (Rom 16:23; 1 Cor 1:14) was obviously wealthy since he acted as a patron/host to Paul (who wrote the letter to the Romans from his house) and the whole church.[87] Furthermore, the way that Erastus' greetings are linked with Gaius' suggest the two are of a similar social standing. Indeed, Gerd Theissen suggests that Rom 16:23 reads as if Erastus had visited Gaius' house just as the letter was being written.[88] While this cannot be proved, it is quite plausible. If that was the case, it could imply that Gaius was somewhat

---

13; Toronto: Hakkert, 1974] sv "οἰκονόμος"); cf. Clarke, "Erastus", 151. Meggitt ignores the fact that such a term is used for high ranking local officials, disregards the evidence presented by Mason, and assumes that such a term *must* refer to a poor and lowly slave (*Poverty*, 135-9).

[85] See Gill, "Erastus", 298; idem, "Social Élite", 325; McRay, *Archaeology*, 332; Clarke, *Leadership*, 15 n. 30.

[86] See Gill, "Erastus", 294-5; idem, "Social Élite", 325; Stansbury, "Corinthian Honor", 321; Clarke, *Leadership*, 47-8; Witherington, *Conflict*, 33; Yeo, *Interaction*, 87. As a *libertus*, and given the Neronian dating, to have acquired such a position suggests that he was particularly well connected. See Stansbury, "Corinthian Honor", 324-5. *Contra* Meggitt (*Poverty*, 138) who claims that this dating of the inscription is disputed.

[87] See Theissen, *Social Setting*, 55, 89; Meeks, *First Urban*, 57; Fee, *First Epistle*, 62, 82; Stansbury, "Corinthian Honor", 460-2; Chow, *Patronage*, 90; Clarke, *Leadership*, 46; Yeo, *Interaction*, 88; *contra* Meggitt, *Poverty*, 132-5. Yeo, however, contends that the idea that "Gaius was hosting Paul and the whole church of Corinth...which Priscilla, Aquila and Titius Justus attended is textually and archaeologically unfounded" (*Interaction*, 88 n. 18). But he assumes that Prisca was a "Latin noblewoman" (his further contention that Aquila was a "Jewish handworker of slave background" is totally without foundation and most improbable). Despite the attempt of some to portray them as elite, there were most likely modest artisans (Baird, "Intra-Church", 122; Stansbury, "Corinthian Honor", 461-2; *contra* Judge, "Scholastic Community", 129-30; Haenchen, *Acts*, 538; Meeks, *First Urban*, 59). Indeed, according to Acts, Paul moved from their home to that of Titius Iustus, something that suggests he was of a higher social standing (Theissen, *Social Setting*, 91). Yeo also assumes that the reference to Gaius in Rom 16 refers to him as "hosting" the whole church (i.e. in his home). But this is not necessary if he had provided the church with its own meeting-place, as will be discussed in the next section.

[88] Theissen, *Social Setting*, 89.

socially superior: Erastus' visit may have been as an *amicus* *(cliens)* to his "patron" who was promoting his career.

Overall, although Paul names a few who seem to have been modestly wealthy (and presumably acted as benefactors and patrons to the church), only Gaius and Erastus could genuinely be considered to fit the category of the "elite".[89] But even Erastus would not seem to fit the designation of εὐγενεῖς in 1:26.[90] However, Dio Chrysostom complains that those called "noble and well-born" (τοὺς γενναίους καὶ τοὺς εὐγενεῖς) were often labelled as such simply because they had wealth and status.[91] Besides, as we have seen, some Corinthian *liberti* were members of the elite even if they were not strictly εὐγενεῖς.

In any case, of those named, only these two seem to fit. The issues discussed in the letter, however, suggest there were others who would fit the category but whom Paul does not name because they were opposed to him.[92] Hans Dieter Betz may well be correct that at Corinth "the Pauline mission had succeeded — for the first time, it seems — in winning converts from the better educated and cultured circles".[93]

---

[89] Thus, I largely concur with the assessment of Stansbury ("Corinthian Honor", 463) and Chow (*Patronage*, 92-3) except that they only identify Erastus in this category.

[90] This is the contention of Fee (*First Epistle*, 80). The argument of Wire that women would not have been classed among the "few" of 1:26 because they were of generally low status, while most of the males who fit this category suffered a reduction of status on joining (*Women Prophets*, 64-6), is fatally flawed. For a start, she totally ignores wealth as a status category. Second, it is an argument from silence, since we do not know who the other members of the "few" were (although noble-women were frequently patrons of *collegia*), and there is no evidence to suggest that the status of either Erastus (who, *subsequent* to the writing of 1 Corinthians, was elected *aedilis*) or Gaius suffered by joining. In regards to the latter, she ignores the very real possibility that the church at Corinth itself had a strong social standing, something that would be inevitable given that some members of the ruling elite *were indeed members*.

[91] Dio Chrys. *Or.* 15.29-30.

[92] Paul never mentions any of his opponents or enemies by name, following a standard Greco-Roman rhetorical convention. See Augustus in *Res Gestae*; Plutarch *Aem.* 31.5; Cicero *Fam.* 1.9.20; Dio Chrys. *Or.* 46.6; cf. Marshall, *Enmity*, 344; Chow, *Patronage*, 88-91. This would suggest that certainly Gaius, and possibly Erastus, were not opposed to Paul.

[93] H. D. Betz, "The Problem of Rhetoric and Theology according to the Apostle Paul" in A. Vanhoye, ed., *L'Apôtre Paul: Personnalité, style et*

However, what 1:26 also suggests is that the bulk of the Corinthian Christians were not wealthy or elite. This is supported by Paul's request that they save so as to be able to contribute to the collection (1 Cor 16:2) — something that presupposes they did not have much surplus.[94] It is also implied in at least 11:22 that some of them were poor.[95] Furthermore, 7:21-2 clearly suggests that there were a number of slaves in the church.[96]

In other words, the church at Corinth seems to have included some from across the social spectrum. Clearly there were a few members of the elite, some of moderate means, some slaves and some who were quite poor. Given a predominantly Roman culture and a great desire for honor and status at Corinth, there is no doubt that the wealthy ones acted as both corporate and personal patrons and consequently were able to wield considerable influence within the Christian community.

3. Size

The difficulty of estimating the size of the Corinthian church is created by uncertainty regarding the manner in which they met together. It is generally assumed that this church met in the home of one of the elite Christians (normally Gaius, given the reference in Rom 16:23) and the size of the dining rooms in the luxury villas excavated at Corinth could have held no more than forty or fifty people. Consequently, it is argued, either the church did not meet as a whole very regularly or it was smaller than forty to fifty.[97] The nature and variety of the different factions and internal conflicts, which will be discussed below, suggest that we are dealing with a large group. Besides, if those named in relation to the Corinthian church, as well as those Paul does not name,

---

conception du ministère (BETL 73; Leuven: Leuven University Press, 1986) 24; cf. Witherington, *Conflict*, 115.

[94] See, for example, Chow, *Patronage*, 185.

[95] See Witherington, *Conflict*, 22.

[96] Theissen, *Social Setting*, 98. This would also be implied by, for example, the baptism and ministry of the οἰκία of Stephanas (1:16, 16:15). See chapter 1 of de Vos, "OIKOΣ"; cf. Witherington, *Conflict*, 115.

[97] See Fee, *First Epistle*, 683-4; Furnish, "Corinth", 27; Witherington, *Conflict*, 32, 91; Yeo, *Interaction*, 91; cf. also S. C. Barton "Paul's Sense of Place: An Anthropological Approach to Community Formation in Corinth" *NTS* 32 (1986) 225, who simply assumes that it follows a house-church model.

brought in the majority of their dependents, the usual estimate would be too low. Consequently, the church may have numbered in the order of one hundred, as many *collegia* did.[98]

Given such numbers, and if the Corinthians understood their church as a *collegium*,[99] it is quite possible that it met together monthly in a purpose-built "club-room" rather than a house. This could easily have been provided by Gaius — and hence the reference to him as "patron" to the whole church (ξένος) in Rom 16:23.[100] Indeed, such a scenario is feasible given the presence of a number of elite Christians. This also makes better sense of 1 Cor 14:23-4.[101] It is most

---

[98] In the case of both Stephanas (1 Cor 1:16) and Crispus (Acts 18:8) their households are also said to have been "converted". Assuming moderate numbers of slaves, and that the bulk of the households were included in the church, a number in the order of 12-15 is possible. Along with Chloe are "her people" — such a designation would surely refer to more than two. It is likely that Titius Iustus, Erastus and Gaius brought with them a number also. Given the status of the last two, that could involve a considerable number, say another 12-15. If Chloe and Iustus brought 3 each, the total is in the order of 30-6. In fact, Witherington argues there are 14 men named in association with Corinth who presumably had wives and children (not to mention slaves) this would equate with a group of about 40 (*Conflict*, 32, 243 n. 9). Although not all of their dependents may have joined the church, most would have. See also chapter 3 of de Vos, "OIKOΣ". At the same time, to this number must be added other individuals and household groups who are not mentioned but are "pro-Paul", and are presumable clients of those named. It is reasonable to assume that they numbered at least another 10-15. If "Paul's supporters" conservatively number 40-50, and the "anti-Paul" group are also considered, a number in the order of 100 is not unreasonable.

[99] See, for example, Chow, *Patronage*, 110; Witherington, *Conflict*, 30-1, 114-15.

[100] The term ξένος is normally used to refer to receiving or giving hospitality. It can also refer to someone who was a dinner guest and less frequently to a dinner-host (see, for example, Apollonius Rhodius 1.208; cf. LSJ sv "ξένος"). It need not indicate that Gaius is providing Paul with accommodation. For the term could also be used in the sense of a "friend", somewhat like the Roman idea of *amicus* (Xenophon *An*. 1.1.10f). As such, it may also be a polite term for "patron", especially given the corporate sense here. Indeed, in *IG* 10.2.1.255, a cognate is used to describe a certain Xenainetos acting as patron or benefactor for the *thiasos* of Isis and Sarapis in the home of Sosinike (ξενισμόν ἐν τᾶι οἰκίαι τᾶι Σωσινείκα); cf. *New Docs* 1.29-30.

[101] While *collegia* did meet in private homes, Witherington notes that it was normal for them to meet in temples or their own club-rooms

improbable that an outsider would simply drop into an elite house (and nothing in the text suggests that these potential visitors were invited guests), but conceivably would if there was a "club-room". The lack of archaeological evidence for churches meeting in such buildings in this period is not necessarily a difficulty, given the paucity of intact remains from Corinth and the potential uniqueness of the church in that city.

Therefore, in summary, the Corinthian church appears to have been a very large and mixed group. Its members came from Greek, Roman and Jewish backgrounds as well as the whole social spectrum, including some from Corinth's ruling elite. While the Christians may have met in smaller "house-groups" on a weekly basis, it is possible that they all met together like a *collegium* on a monthly basis in a purpose-built club-room.

III. CHURCH AND CIVIC COMMUNITY RELATIONS

Unlike 1 Thessalonians, there is no concentration of language related to suffering or external conflict found in 1 Corinthians.[102] Furthermore, when Paul describes his sufferings in 4:9-13 he specifically contrasts these with their apparent lack of suffering. In other words, unlike him and

---

(*Conflict*, 242 n. 6), but he does not take up this idea here. The donation of such a club-room by a patron is also paralleled in the case of the synagogue at Acmonia. See Trebilco, *Communities*, 83. This would also be appropriate if the Corinthian church was perceived by Greeks and Romans as a philosophical school, as Judge implies ("Scholastic Communities", 125, 135-6) and one that was "sponsored by local patrons to their social dependents" (ibid., 8). Although his argument should not be applied to the Pauline churches in general, it does seem to fit the situation of Corinth as the issues of 1 Cor 1-4 demonstrate. See section III.2 below.

[102] The only possible exceptions may be the reference to ἀνάγκη in 7:26, and the idea of "giving up one's body to be burnt" in 13:3. The former will be dealt with later in this chapter, but it would seem to relate to the eschatological woes and is introduced by Paul, not the Corinthians. In respect to the latter, the reference could not be to martyrdom as such methods had not yet been used at this time (*contra* Conzelmann, *1 Corinthians*, 222-3). In fact, the variant reading (καυχήσωμαι rather than καυθήσομαι) may make better sense. Fee suggests that since the case for either reading is indecisive, preference should be given "on the basis of intrinsic probability". The sense is of self-sacrifice not martyrdom (*First Epistle*, 629 n. 18, 633-4; cf. *TCGNT*, 497).

the other apostles, the Corinthian Christians did not experience slander, revulsion or persecution.[103]

1. Good Relations with Outsiders

In 1 Cor 5:1-11:1 Paul appears to deal with a number of issues that are related to the Christian community's relationship with the wider civic community. Some of the issues involve intermarriage, sexual relations with non-Christians, civil lawsuits, participation in Greek and Roman cults and receiving invitations to dinner (some of these also seem to be addressed in 2 Cor 6:14-7:1). A general impression from these issues is that the Corinthian Christians were on generally good terms with other Corinthians.

Yet, as it will be argued, most of these are really issues of the elite.[104] While the lack of conflict may exist because the elite Christians deliberately played down the more offensive aspects of their new faith,[105] the very fact of their position, wealth and power would have ensured this lack of conflict. And since there were some in powerful places, who presumably acted as patrons to the ordinary members of the church, the latter would also be protected (even if not all agreed with the position of the elite).

It is quite apparent in 7:12-16 that some Christians were married to non-Christians.[106] Nevertheless, in 7:39 Paul

---

[103] Barclay argues that Paul aims this at the whole church ("Contrasts", 57). But the contrast between them and Paul in respect to manual labor (4:12) suggests that he has mainly the elite members in mind. They are the ones who are most likely to have sought to retain good relations and thus their position in society (see Chow, *Patronage*, 101, 123; Witherington, *Conflict*, 113, 148-9). Yet there is no hint in 1 Corinthians that "ordinary" Christians experienced any conflict either.

[104] Plato, for example, argues that marital arrangements, legal cases, and cultic sacrifices were ways in which the elite enhanced and maintained their status, position and power (*Resp.* 362B-C; cf. Chow, *Patronage*, 123; Barclay, "Contrasts", 58). Meggitt simply assumes that the issues of 1 Corinthians are those of the "poor", and he ignores the possibility that issues such as dinner invitations, lawsuits, and divorce were more relevant for the elite (*Poverty*, 97-9).

[105] See Barclay, "Contrasts", 69.

[106] It is commonly argued that in this section the Corinthians were objecting to remaining in such marriages because they saw physical relations with non-Christians as polluting and an impediment to their relationship with God. See, for example, Barrett, *Commentary*, 165; Fee, *First Epistle*, 298-300, 307; W. Deming, *Paul on Marriage and Celibacy: The Hellenistic Background of 1 Corinthians 7* (SNTSMS 83; Cambridge:

Cambridge University Press, 1995), 139. Deming also links this with 5:9-13 to argue that "the Corinthians held a general aversion to establishing formal relations or even associating with non-Christians" (*Marriage*, 135-9; cf A. C. Thiselton, "Realized Eschatology at Corinth" *NTS* 24 [1978] 516). Deming's position involves a mis-reading of 5:9-13. Rather, as Barclay ("Contrasts", 59) and Chow (*Patronage*, 113) argue, this section shows that the majority of the Corinthian Christians had objected to what they perceived Paul to be asking of them, i.e. separation, when they saw no need for it. While there may have been a *small group* in the church with a separatist agenda, *this was not the position of the majority*. There is no good reason to lump all of the Christians together. Similarly, it is usually assumed that the slogan of 7:1 (καλὸν ἀνθρώπῳ γυναικὸς μὴ ἅπτεσθαι) refers to a gnostic tendency, or a form of asceticism, associated with the Hellenistic body/soul dualism. For example, Yeo links this slogan a proto-gnostic tendency and claims that to do otherwise is to down-play the spiritual radicalism of the Corinthians (*Interaction*, 120, 125). But, as mentioned earlier, there are no grounds for assuming any proto-gnostic thought and Yeo assumes what he seeks to prove. Some argue that this apparent asceticism in 1 Cor 7 may be related to a spiritual enthusiasm, under the belief that "receptivity to the divine was greatly improved where there was no interference from sexual activity" (Barclay, "Contrasts", 62). However, as Witherington points out, many elite Roman wives expected not to have sex with their husbands after they had produced children, because "sex in marriage was for procreation, not recreation" (*Conflict*, 178 n. 33; cf. Soranus, *Gyn.* 1.34; S. B. Pomeroy, *Goddesses, Whores, Wives, and Slaves: Women in Classical Antiquity* [New York: Schocken, 1975], 159-160; R. B. Ward, "Musonius and Paul on Marriage" *NTS* 36 [1990]: 286; S. M. Treggiari, *Roman Marriage: Iusti Coniuges from the Time of Cicero to the Time of Ulpian* [Oxford: Clarendon, 1991] 11, 264). This expectation may have been exacerbated by the Stoic teaching that sexual passion was incompatible with pursuit of the philosophical life. Indeed, the Roman Stoic Musonius taught that there should be no sexual pleasure between husband and wife (Ward, "Musonius", 285). Even the poet Ovid suggested that there should be no sexual pleasure between husband and wife because their relationship was a matter of duty (*Ars Amor.* 3.585-6; cf. Ward, "Musonius", 285; Martin, *Body*, 214-15). Since it is clear that the elite Christians had Stoic tendencies, given their use of a number of Stoic "slogans" (e.g., 4:8; 6:12; 8:1-4), the slogan of 7:1 (and the attitude behind it) should be seen as simply reflect the Stoic and "upper-class" values of the elite Corinthian Christians. In 7:25-35, however, Paul presents a "modified Cynic" marriage ethic as a response to their position. Although Stoics saw marriage as appropriate (Ward, "Musonius", 283-4), Cynics thought that it was a distraction from the pursuit of philosophy and that under adverse conditions and circumstances it should be avoided (Epictetus *Diss.* 3.22.67-71, 76; cf. M. Y. MacDonald, "Women Holy in Body and Spirit: The Social Setting of 1 Corinthians 7" *NTS* 36 (1990): 177; Deming, *Marriage*, 53-54, 60). Paul modifies this tradition via his eschatology: given the imminent return of Christ (7:29), they should relativize all their earthly attachments and loyalties, including marriage.

specifically argues against widows marrying non-Christians. This may be because he saw such a choice as unwise given that they have a different value-system. But the fact that he addresses it to widows, and does not include widowers, tends to rule this out.[107] Rather it may be, as Will Deming argues, that women "were particularly susceptible to apostasy once they had been incorporated into a non-Christian household in patriarchal Greco-Roman society".[108] However, the fact that Paul mentions the possibility of deliberate intermarriage suggests that some may have seriously considered it.

In 6:12-20 it seems that there may have been some men in the church who were still frequenting prostitutes. While Paul is vehemently opposed to such a practice, it is likely that many of the Corinthian Christians retained their traditional cultural norms that saw nothing wrong with (married) men having sexual relations with prostitutes and courtesans.[109] Such activity may even have been expected of members of the elite.[110]

It is also apparent that sexual relations were maintained with outsiders, given what Paul describes as a case of πορνεία in 5:1-5. The fact that he criticizes the man involved, a member of the Church, but not the woman, implies that she was not a Christian.[111] The man may have been a member of the elite and a major patron of their community since the church had not acted against him. As such, they could not afford to criticize him and therefore lose his patronage.[112] Yet, given that they did not criticize him, it

Although a number of scholars assume that the Corinthians (as a whole) have adopted a Cynic position of expediency, in light of the apocalyptic woes (Deming, *Marriage*, 110-112, 180-182; cf. Barrett, *Commentary*, 174-175; Conzelmann, *1 Corinthians*, 132; Fee, *First Epistle*, 330), it is clearly Paul who introduces this idea. As 1 Cor 15 will show, the perspective of those being addressed is, on the whole, a- or non-eschatological (cf. Martin, *Body*, 205).

[107] *Contra* Fee, *First Epistle*, 356.

[108] Deming, *Marriage*, 220. See also chapter 2 of de Vos, "OIKOΣ".

[109] See Pomeroy, *Goddesses*, 159; Treggiari, *Roman Marriage*, 264; Witherington, *Conflict*, 157.

[110] See Clarke, *Leadership*, 106. This does not even consider the norm that the *paterfamilias* was expected to have sexual relations with his slaves. See de Vos, "OIKOΣ", 16.

[111] See, for example, Chow, *Patronage*, 113-14; Clarke, *Leadership*, 73 n. 3; Witherington, *Conflict*, 158. See also de Vos, "Stepmothers, Concubines and the Case of Πορνεία in 1 Corinthians 5" *NTS* 44 (1998) 104-14.

[112] So Clarke, *Leadership*, 86.

is just as likely that they saw nothing particularly culpable in his actions, for according to Roman law he had done nothing wrong. At worst, his actions may have been "frowned upon" by his non-Christian peers.[113]

The fact that some Christians went to the normal civil courts to settle a dispute (6:1-6) suggests that the church was not held in disrepute. Indeed, the Roman legal system was anything but impartial. It was strongly biased towards the wealthy and elite, since it was they who controlled it via the elected offices of the city.[114] It was thought that unless one was well known in a particular city and quite wealthy it was impossible to get justice.[115] Given this bias, if the Corinthian Christians were despised or regarded as deviants they could not have expected to receive fair treatment.[116]

One of the major indications that the Corinthian church was on good terms with the wider community is that at least

---

[113] That the church does not disapprove of this action is suggested by 5:6-8 and fits the idea of "freedom" and πάντα μοι ἔξεστιν in 6:12f. But this need not be related to some notion of "theological libertinism" (Clarke, *Leadership*, 87), as ἔξεστιν may mean, quite literally, "lawful". In any case, πάντα μοι ἔξεστιν appears to be a standard Stoic idea. See T. Paige, "Stoicism, Ἐλευθερία and Community at Corinth" in M. J. Wilkins & T. Paige, eds., *Worship, Theology and Ministry in the Early Church* (JSNTSup 87; Sheffield: JSOT Press, 1992) 180-7; Martin, *Body*, 175; cf. Plutarch *De stoic. repug.* 1058B-C. Although Paul is critical of the relationship, this seems to reflect his Jewish ethical sensibilities, while their non-disapproval reflects the Roman norm of not criticizing a man for sexual relations *unless they were illegal*. But if, as I have argued elsewhere, the woman was actually his late father's concubine rather than his stepmother, the relationship would not have been illegal, even if it was somewhat unusual ("Stepmothers", 104-14).

[114] A. C. Mitchell, "1 Corinthians 6:1-11: Group Boundaries and the Courts of Corinth" (unpublished PhD dissertation, Yale University, 1986), 78, 95-6; Chow, *Patronage*, 78, 128-9; Clarke, *Leadership*, 27, 62; Nicolet, "Citizen", 21; Winter, *Seek*, 111-13; Horrell, *Social Ethos*, 70.

[115] Petronius *Sat.* 13-14; cf. Mitchell, "Group Boundaries", 75.

[116] Although P. Richardson suggests that the case in question may also involve a matter of *porneia*, given the structural and linguistic links between 1 Cor 5 & 6 ("Judgment in Sexual Matters in 1 Corinthians 6:1-11" *NTS* 25 [1983] 38, 53-5; cf. Mitchell, *Reconciliation*, 232-3), this is most unlikely. The term Paul uses, βιωτικά, implies that it was a commercial case (Mitchell, "Group Boundaries", 59; Fee, *First Epistle*, 228 n. 2, 241 n. 14; Chow, *Patronage*, 125; Clarke, *Leadership*, 59-60). If it involved a sexual matter it also would have been a criminal rather than a civil case, but it was clearly the latter, given the use of ἐλάχιστον (Witherington, *Conflict*, 107). At most, it may have involved a dispute over dowries (Chow, *Patronage*, 125-7; cf. Witherington, *Conflict*, 164).

some members continued to participate in cultic meals in temples. This is clearly Paul's concern in 8:1-12 and 10:14-22.[117] Indeed, it appears that the term εἰδωλόθυτα was only used to refer to food actually eaten in a temple, not to meat that had been previously sacrificed and then sold at the market.[118] Those who attended seem to have claimed this as their "right" (ἐξουσία — 8:9). As such, the setting may have been an important social or family occasion, such as a wedding or funeral.[119] Yet the context is more likely to be a religious festival.[120] The use of κύριοι in 8:5 may suggest a link to the Imperial cult, and a setting in association with the Greater Isthmian Games is possible, especially given the athletic imagery in 9:24-7.[121] Besides, during the games, the

---

[117] See G. D. Fee, "Εἰδωλόθυτα Once Again: An Interpretation of 1 Cor 8-10" *Bib* 61 (1980) 176-9; idem, *First Epistle*, 359-60; W. L. Willis, *Idol Meat in Corinth: The Pauline Argument in 1 Corinthians 8 and 10* (SBLDS 68; Chico: Scholars, 1985) 237; J. A. Davis, "The Interaction between Individual Ethical Conscience and Community Ethical Consciousness in 1 Corinthians" *HBT* 10.2 (1988) 11; Mitchell, *Reconciliation*, 240; Chow, *Patronage*, 141-2; Witherington, *Conflict*, 187; *contra* Gooch, *Dangerous Food*, 51-2. That some continued to participate in pagan cults is clearly implied by 2 Cor 6:16-17. See Witherington, *Conflict*, 405-6. Although 2 Cor 6:14-7:1 is often regarded as an interpolation, it is probably original. See Furnish, *II Corinthian*, 375-83. Contrary to the view of many scholars, Martin contends that both 1 Cor 8 and 10 are concerned with the one setting, i.e. the temple, rather than 1 Cor 8 and 10:14-22 being about meals in temples and 10:23-33 being about meals in private homes (*Body*, 182-3). In large part, this is based on the claim that there is no indication of a change of setting (ibid.). Yet there certainly does appear to be a change given Paul's repetition of the introductory slogan in 10:23, and that 10:25 refers to meat bought at market whereas 8:10 refers to meat eaten in a temple. Furthermore, Martin contends that to see the issue as one of setting is too modern, akin to a sacred vs secular distinction (ibid., 183). But it is clear that the issue in the first part is "if anyone sees you...at table in an idol's temple" (8:10) whereas later it is about meat from the market that originated in temple-worship, not meat eaten in a private gathering in a temple.

[118] See B. Witherington III, "Not So Idle Thoughts about *Eidolothuton*" *TynBul* 44 (1993) 239-42; cf. Fee, "Once Again", 178, 181-2.

[119] So Conzelmann, *1 Corinthians*, 148; Gooch, *Dangerous Food*, 37-8; Yeo, *Interaction*, 95. That ἐξουσία refers to a sense of "right" rather than "freedom" is quite clear from the way Paul uses the term about himself in 1 Cor 9. See Willis, *Idol Meat*, 84, 102-3; Mitchell, *Reconciliation*, 247-8; Chow, *Patronage*, 155; Winter, *Seek*, 167.

[120] See Chow, *Patronage*, 145-8.

[121] See Chow, *Patronage*, 146-8; Winter, *Seek*, 173-4.

agonothetes normally organized feasts for all the citizens of Corinth. For those who were citizens, it was their right and their duty to attend and there was a generally held expectation that they would.[122]

Attendance at such feasts was even more important for members of the elite. Indeed, it was their right to eat in the temple itself on the occasion of public festivals.[123] It was also vitally important for them to attend such occasions if they wished to maintain their standing in society and hope to be elected to office.[124] In fact, Erastus could not subsequently have been elected an *aedilis* if he had not participated in such activities. The fact that some of the elite Christians continued to participate in these cultic meals suggests that they may have regarded their relationships with their (elite) non-Christian peers as more important than those with other (lower-status) Christians.[125]

If some of the Corinthian Christians participated in cultic meals in temples, it seems that some also continued to receive invitations for dinner parties from their friends (10:27-30). Presumably some of them also continued to attend such functions, since shared meals and dinner parties were the main focus of social life. Indeed, it was held that a true friend was only someone with whom one had eaten and drunk.[126] It is also likely that this matter was a concern

---

[122] See, for example, Plutarch *Quaest. conv.* 723A; cf. Winter, *Seek*, 171-4. The setting cannot be the temple of Demeter and Kore given the archaeological finds mentioned above. A setting in the Asclepion is also unlikely, as feasts there were normally associated with healing and nothing in 1 Cor 8-10 suggests this. Nor would attendance be considered a "right". See Winter, *Seek*, 171; *contra* Gooch, *Dangerous Food*, 25-6.

[123] Chow, *Patronage*, 150-1; Winter, *Seek*, 166.

[124] See Theissen, *Social Setting*, 130-1; Chow, *Patronage*, 155-6; Clarke, *Leadership*, 34; Gooch, *Dangerous Food*, 40-3. As Gooch puts it, "you were whom you ate with" (*Dangerous Food*, 38).

[125] Barclay, "Contrasts", 60; cf. Witherington, *Conflict*, 196. The differences within the church on this matter will be discussed more below.

[126] Lucian *Paras.* 22: οὐδεὶς ἐχθρὸν ἢ ἀγνῶτα ἄνθρωπον ἀλλ' οὐδὲ συνήθη μετρίως ἐπὶ δεῖπνον καλεῖ, δεῖ πρότερον οἶμαι τοῦτον γενέσθαι φίλον, ἵνα κοινωνήσῃ σπονδῶν καὶ τραπέζης...ἐγὼ γοῦν πολλάκις ἤκουσά τινων λεγόντων, Ποταπὸς δὲ οὗτος φίλος ὅστις οὔτε βέβρωκεν οὔτε πέπωκεν μεθ' ἡμῶν, δῆλον ὅτι τὸν συμπίνοντα καὶ συνεσθίοντα μόνον πιστὸν φίλον ἡγουμένων. See also Lucian *Somn.* 11; Pliny *Ep.* 1.15; Plutarch *Quaest. conv.* 612D, 726E; cf. D. E. Smith, "Meals and Morality in Paul and His World" *SBLSP* (1981) 322; Gooch, *Dangerous Food*, 30-5, 43-4.

primarily for the elite Christians, since such dinner
invitations would have been common only for them. Indeed,
amongst the Roman elite, evening meals were normally eaten
with friends.[127] In the case of common people, if they wanted
to eat with their friends, they would have gone to a *popina*,
caupona or *taberna*. That members of the elite continued to
accept dinner invitations would seem to have been for the
same reason that they participated in cultic meals in temples
— the need to maintain their social contacts and their
position in society.[128]

In 10:28 Paul constructs a scenario at such a dinner-
party where τις ὑμῖν εἴπῃ· τοῦτο ἱερόθυτόν ἐστιν. The use of
this standard Greek term for meat that had previously been
offered in sacrifice, ἱερόθυτον, has led many scholars to
consider that the individual pointing out its origin must have
been a non-Christian.[129] While the use of the term alone is
ambiguous, the context suggests that this is the most likely
case. For a "weak" Christian, who had objections to eating
such food, would not have accepted an invitation.[130]

---

[127] Plutarch *Quaest. conv.* 726E; Martial *Epigr.* 5.47, 12.82.
Although dining was not restricted to the elite only, commoners probably
would not have received such invitations from friends, and invitations to
dine at their patron's house were quite infrequent. See, for example,
Juvenal *Sat.* 5.12-22. Besides, the context clearly suggests that Paul has
some elite Christians in mind. See Barclay, "Contrasts", 58; Gill, "Social
Élite", 336; Witherington, *Conflict*, 28; Horrell, *Social Ethos*, 107-8.
Furthermore, given the cramped conditions in which most of the common
people lived, they simply could not have entertained at home (*contra*
Meggitt, *Poverty*, 118-21).

[128] Theissen, *Social Setting*, 130-2; Willis, *Idol Food*, 236.

[129] See, for example, Conzelmann, *1 Corinthians*, 178; Fee, "Once
Again", 177; idem, *First Epistle*, 484; Theissen, *Social Setting*, 131;
Winter, *Seek*, 168; P. Borgen, "'Yes', 'No', 'How Far'?: The Participation of
Jews and Christians in Pagan Cults" in T. Engberg-Pedersen, ed., *Paul in
His Hellenistic Context* (Minneapolis: Fortress, 1995) 52; *contra* Willis,
Idol Meat, 261; Gooch, *Dangerous Food*, 85.

[130] Witherington objects that even a "weak" Christian would attend
because "eating meat was a luxury in antiquity which only a minority
could regularly afford" ("Idle Thoughts", 247). The matter of how often
ordinary people ate meat will be discussed in more detail below. Suffice to
say, it was much more common than Witherington allows. Furthermore,
if the scenario is a dinner party in the home of an elite non-Christian, as
the context suggests, this rules out his argument in any case. Barclay
contends that even members of the elite could experience "social
dislocation and significant resocialization" so that some of the "weak"
might be members of the elite and this would explain why they were at
the same dinner party ("Contrasts", 68). But this is self-defeating. If

The reason the other non-Christian guest points out the origin of the meat may be an attempt to embarrass the Christian.[131] But this is unlikely, for in response Paul speaks of considering the effect of eating on the non-Christian's conscience.[132] It is more likely, then, that the other guest is trying to be sensitive to Christian sensibilities, on the presumption that they were Jews and would see the eating of such food as a violation of their beliefs.[133] Another possibility is that Paul is concerned that the Christian guest might give the impression that Christianity was syncretistic.[134] In any case, both possibilities suggest that these Christians were on good terms with the wider community.

While most of the evidence for good relations between the church and the civic community involves the elite Christians, 14:23 seems to extend this to the whole church. The fact that non-Christians might at any time visit the gathered church suggests that it was held in good stead.[135] It also implies that the existence of the church, and its whereabouts, were well known.

If, as some scholars suggest, the "baptism for the dead" (15:29) was performed by some Christians on behalf of non-Christians, this would also show their concern for outsiders.[136] But what this rite actually involved is unclear since there are

---

they had undergone social dislocation and resocialization then they would not be at the dinner party in the first place, regardless of their social status.

[131] Willis, *Idol Meat*, 241-2. It is possible, of course, that the one pointing this out is the host.

[132] See Conzelmann, *1 Corinthians*, 178; Theissen, *Social Setting*, 131; Winter, *Seek*, 175-6. Barrett, however, claims that Paul would not be concerned with the conscience of non-Christians (*Commentary*, 241), but 10:32-3 clearly suggests that he does care (see Fee, *First Epistle*, 484). "Conscience" was understood by the Greeks and Romans as "awareness", not as some sort of moral guard-dog. See Willis, *Idol Meat*, 92; Borgen, "Participation", 49-50; Witherington, *Conflict*, 199. Its usage here, however, tends to suggest a meaning of "shame" or "reputation".

[133] So Willis, *Idol Meat*, 241; Fee, *First Epistle*, 484; Winter, *Seek*, 175-6; Witherington, *Conflict*, 227.

[134] Conzelmann, *1 Corinthians*, 178; Willis, *Idol Meat*, 241; Winter, *Seek*, 176; Borgen, "Participation", 53-4.

[135] So Barclay, "Contrasts", 58. Although Fee claims this is a purely hypothetical situation (*First Epistle*, 683) there is no reason to take it as such, given the other evidence for good relations and a high level of Christian integration in the civic community. Whether or not it did occur, Paul presents it as a distinct possibility and that alone suggests good relations.

[136] Chow, *Patronage*, 157.

no other examples known in early Christian texts.[137] It is quite possible that it was associated with Roman funerary rites that were thought to assist the difficult journey of the spirits of the dead through the underworld.[138] At the same time, however, such a rite may well have developed from the distinctly Roman religious mentality that emphasized practice over belief.[139]

Therefore, overall, the relationship between the church and the wider civic community at Corinth appears to have been very good. There is no evidence of any conflict. Although most of the matters that demonstrate this good relationship with outsiders concern the elite members of the church, it seems that the whole church was held in some esteem. The continued participation of the elite Christians in Corinthian society was probably a major factor in this, and it is likely that the rest of the church benefited from their power and influence.

2. Internal Conflict

While there is a lack of conflict between the church and outsiders there is also abundant evidence of conflict within the church. The rhetorical *propositio* of 1 Corinthians, ἵνα τὸ

---

[137] See Conzelmann, *1 Corinthians*, 275; Fee, *First Epistle*, 764-6; Chow, *Patronage*, 159.

[138] This connection has been argued most forcibly by R. E. DeMaris. He claims that the "pagan" cults at Corinth particularly focussed on deities associated with the underworld and had ritual acts to assist the dead "as they made the transition from life to death" ("Corinthian Religion and Baptism for the Dead [1 Corinthians 15:29]: Insights from Archaeology and Anthropology" *JBL* 114 [1995] 664-71; cf. Chow, *Patronage*, 160-1). If he is correct, whatever the baptismal rite practiced by the Corinthian Christians entailed, it would have been vicarious and most likely practiced by individuals for the benefit of their relatives (ibid., 674-5). Although DeMaris does not state explicitly that the "recipients" would have been outside the church, this would be a logical conclusion. Indeed, in a private communication, he has stated as much.

[139] If it was such a vicarious rite, that Paul does not argue against it suggests that it was practiced by a small group and that "he did not see this as a serious enough aberration to debate the point" (Witherington, *Conflict*, 305-6; cf. Barrett, *Commentary*, 363; Fee, *First Epistle*, 767). His argument here is with those who "denied" the resurrection. It is probably better to see the rite in the context of the Roman religious world-view (see section II.2 of chapter 2 herein) than to ascribe it to some sort of sacramentalism or magical view of the sacraments as these scholars suggest.

αὐτὸ λέγητε πάντες καὶ μὴ ᾖ ἐν ὑμῖν σχίσματα, ἦτε δὲ κατηρτισμένοι ἐν τῷ αὐτῷ νοΐ καὶ ἐν τῇ αὐτῇ γνώμῃ (1:10), suggests that the whole letter was a rhetorical argument against στάσις.[140] In fact, the letter is full of terms used in political speeches concerning factionalism, such as: σχίσματα (1:10; 11:18); ἔριδες (1:11); μερίζειν (1:13); ζῆλος (3:3; 13:4); συνεργοί (3:9); φυσιόω (4:6; 8:1; 13:4); συναναμίγνυσθαι (5:9, 11); συγκοινωνός (9:23); ἑδραῖοι, ἀμετακίνητοι (15:58); ἀνδρίζεσθε (16:13).[141]

There would appear to be several different groups within the church. The arguments in 1 Corinthians suggest there were differences related to Paul and his ministry (with some of the Christians being pro-Paul and others anti-Paul), or to life-style (with some Christians having ascetic or separatist tendencies and others "indulgent" tendencies). It may be that some of them were concerned with wisdom and knowledge while others were concerned with *charismata*.[142] Of course there was probably some overlap between the groups, since most of the issues reflect practices, beliefs and values that are consistent with those of the elite.[143] Yet there is also a growing consensus among scholars that except for the eschatology in 1 Cor 15,[144] the divisions within the

[140] See Stansbury, "Corinthian Honor", 20; Mitchell, *Reconciliation*, 60-3, 66; Welborn, "Concord", 3-4; cf. Martin, *Body*, 56.

[141] See Welborn, "Discord", 86-7; idem, "Concord", 25-9; Mitchell, *Reconciliation*, 67, 73-82, 86-7, 98-9, 107-8, 110-14, 135-6; cf. Dio Chrys. *Or.* 39.8.

[142] See Baird, "Intra-Church", 118, 131; Yeo, *Interaction*, 84; *contra* Fee, *First Epistle*, 5-6. It is probably inappropriate to label those who were particularly concerned with tongues as "spiritual enthusiasts". Indeed, it is more likely that this "enthusiasm" derives from a Greco-Roman syncretism that drew on mystery cult parallels. See H. W. House, "Tongues and Mystery Religions of Corinth" *BSac* 140 (1983) 142-5; Witherington, *Conflict*, 279; Yeo, *Interaction*, 108. In fact, as Martin notes, a preoccupation with such esoteric knowledge was particularly characteristic of those with high status in the Greco-Roman world. In other words, it was characteristic of the elite (*Body*, 88-92).

[143] See, Chow, *Patronage*, 94; Clarke, *Leadership*, 57; cf. Martin, *Slavery*, 147; Witherington, *Conflict*, 96, 157 n. 20.

[144] Those who "denied" the resurrection (15:12) may have simply rejected the need for a personal, bodily resurrection due to a Hellenistic body-soul dualism. See D. J. Doughty, "The Presence and the Future of Salvation in Corinth" *ZNW* 66 (1975) 74-5; Barclay, "Contrasts", 63; Kuck, *Judgment*, 255; Litfin, *Proclamation*, 180; Witherington, *Conflict*, 306-7. Others, however, assume that the problem was an overly-realized eschatology (Barrett, *Commentary*, 325; Conzelmann, *1 Corinthians*, 87

Corinthian church were social and ethical, rather than doctrinal.[145] It is also likely that part of the reason for these conflicts and the lack of cohesion is the strong ties that some

---

8; Thiselton, "Eschatology", 510-2; Meeks, *First Urban*, 178-9; idem, "Social Functions", 698-9; Fee, *First Epistle*, 12, 172-3; Stansbury, "Corinthian Honor", 423; A. T. Lincoln, *Paradise Now and Not Yet* [Grand Rapids: Baker, 1991] 33-5; Yeo, *Interaction*, 120). Most assume this based on 4:8, but this verse should not be interpreted eschatologically. Indeed, since the point of 4:8-13 as a whole is pride and social standing it is better to understand the claims of 4:8 in terms of Stoic notion of the "truly wise man" that uses just this terminology. See Paige, "Stoicism", 183-4, 187; Martin, *Body*, 65-6; cf. Plutarch *De stoic. repug.* 1058B-C; idem, *De cohib. ira* 472A; Cicero *Fin* 4.3. Besides, those who argue for a realized eschatology fail to account for it with respect to a (Greco-) Roman religious mentality. It is far more likely that the Corinthian deniers' world-view was *non-eschatological* (DeMaris, "Baptism", 678-9; Barclay, "Contrasts", 64). Since the relations between the church and the wider civic community appear to have been good, it is unlikely that Paul's apocalyptic eschatology would have made much sense to them (Barclay, "Contrasts", 68, 71; cf. Kuck, *Judgment*, 238). This would have been especially the case with the elite Christians, who may have also held to what Witherington describes as "Roman imperial eschatology", related to the idea of *pax Romana* and the Imperial cult, that there were special blessings for those who helped maintain the status quo (*Conflict*, 296-7). Yet, the non-eschatological perspective of many of the Corinthians may simply have arisen from the Roman perception of time. Recently, M. Bettini has shown that the Romans had a spatial sense of time and were little concerned with the future. Religiously speaking, time could be understood in a horizontal plane with the future at one's back and the past in front or going before. Particularly in relation to funerals, it could be perceived vertically such that the past is above. Therefore, apart from being a largely present experience, salvation "comes from the past, not from an...expectation of the future" (*Anthropology and Roman Culture: Kinship, Time, Images of the Soul* [Baltimore: Johns Hopkins University Press, 1991] 115, 122-8, 167-9, 176-7).

[145] See Welborn, "Discord", 88; Davis, "The Interaction", 2; Martin, *Slavery*, 146; H. O. Guenther, "Gnosticism in Corinth?" in B. H. McLean, ed., *Origins and Method: Towards a New Understanding of Judaism and Christianity* (JSNTSup 86; Sheffield: JSOT Press, 1993) 51, 77; Witherington, *Conflict*, 74; to some extent also Conzelmann, *1 Corinthians*, 32. However, T. Engberg-Pedersen argues that 1 Cor 1-4 was primarily a theological conflict, even if most of the other issues of 1 Cor were social ("The Gospel and Social Practice according to 1 Corinthians" *NTS* 33 [1987] 561). But this can be maintained only if by "theological" one means "concerning world-view" and "arising from social conditioning", as Engberg-Petersen's explanation implies (ibid., 562-3). There is no justification for W. Schmithals' claim that all the problems were due to "Gnostics" (*Gnosticism in Corinth* [Nashville: Abingdon, 1971], 221-5, 236-7). This will be discussed further below.

had with outsiders. Probably part of the reason was patronage ties within the church.

The main issue that Paul discusses in regard to factions in 1 Cor 1-4 is "wisdom" (σοφία). Wisdom and eloquence, as the pursuit of λόγος and σοφία, were greatly admired by the Greeks in general.[146] That they were especially esteemed by the Corinthians can be seen from the vast honors granted to the rhetors Favorinus, P. Aelius Sospinus and Antonius Sospis.[147] Although this obsession with rhetoric was found across the Corinthian population as a whole, it was especially characteristic of the elite, since rhetorical prowess was fundamental to their function in public office.[148] Personal attachment to various teachers is evident in the picture Dio Chrysostom paints of a large gathering of sophists around Poseidon's temple during the Games, arguing and abusing each other and their disciples.[149] This picture is particularly relevant for understanding 1 Cor 1-4. Indeed, in these chapters Paul seems to describe the various factions in terms of respect for various sophistic teachers.[150]

Despite the fact that Paul apparently identifies four factions in 1:12, he does not engage the beliefs of any of these "factions", nor does he correct any particular theological errors.[151] Nor is it possible to positively link these factions

---

[146] See, for example, Dio Chrys. *Or.* 37.27; Herodotus 4.77; cf. Judge, "Scholastic Community", 125-6; Litfin, *Proclamation*, 143.

[147] See Dio Chrys. *Or.* 37.8, 46; Plutarch *Quaest. conv.* 723A, 739E; cf. Stansbury, "Corinthian Honor", 353; Clarke, *Leadership*, 20-1; Litfin, *Proclamation*, 143-6; Witherington, *Conflict*, 100.

[148] See, for example, Dio Chrys. *Or.* 18.1-3; Petronius *Sat.* 48; Plutarch *Praec. rei. ger.* 801D-2E; cf. Theissen, *Social Setting*, 97; Chow, *Patronage*, 105; Clarke, *Leadership*, 36-9.

[149] Dio Chrys. *Or.* 8.9: Καὶ δὴ καὶ τότε ἦν περὶ τὸν νεὼν τοῦ κοδραιμόνων βοώντων καὶ λοιδορουμένων ἀλλήλοις, καὶ τῶν λεγομένων μαθητῶν ἄλλου ἄλλῳ μαχομένων.

[150] B. Fiore, "'Covert Allusion' in 1 Corinthians 1-4" *CBQ* 47 (1985) 96. Some claim that the Corinthian factions arose from an attachment to those who had baptized them after the pattern of mystery-cult initiations (Theissen, *Social Setting*, 54; Clarke, *Leadership*, 92; Yeo, *Interaction*, 114). But this is unlikely since there is no clear evidence that Peter ever visited Corinth, despite 1:13f (Fee, *First Epistle*, 57; Witherington, *Conflict*, 86), let alone baptized there, nor that Apollos baptized. Even the reference to Peter being accompanied by his wife (9:5) requires no more than that they have heard of Peter. Besides, the factions seem to be related to rhetorical ability, given the context.

[151] Paul never accuses them of faulty doctrine and he praises them in 1:4-9 — something he would not have done had there been doctrinal

with any of the other problems or issues discussed in 1 Cor 5-11.[152] Nevertheless, the focus of 1 Cor 1-4 certainly appears to be the pro-Apollos group. It may well be that Paul saw them as posing the greatest threat although, as a number of scholars have suggested, much of the problem seems to have been associated with a concomitant anti-Paul sentiment. In

---

problems if his letter to the Galatians is anything to go by (Clarke, *Leadership*, 89-91; Litfin, *Proclamation*, 178-80; Welborn, "Discord", 89-90). It is most likely that part of the problem was different philosophical tendencies, (see B. Fiore, "Passion in Paul and Plutarch: 1 Corinthians 5-6 and the Polemic against Epicureans" in D. L. Balch, E. Ferguson & W. A. Meeks, eds., *Greek, Romans and Christians* [Minneapolis: Fortress, 1990] 142-3; Stansbury, "Corinthian Honor", 423-4), especially since philosophy was chiefly concerned with ethics (Davis, "The Interaction", 7). Richard Horsley argues that the problem is a philonic-like Hellenistic-Jewish philosophy taught by Apollos ("Consciousness and Freedom among the Corinthians: 1 Corinthians 8-10" *CBQ* 40 [1978] 575-6; idem, "*Gnosis* in Corinth: 1 Corinthians 8:1-6" *NTS* 27 [1980] 32-9). But nothing suggests the problems stem from such a background, since Paul claims that it is *Greeks*, not Jews, who are concerned with wisdom. Such a reconstruction cannot explain many of the problems in Corinth and there is no compelling reason why the gentile Corinthians would adopt such a tradition when their own Greco-Roman philosophical tradition was closer at hand. See Fee, *First Epistle*, 13-14, 65; Chow, *Patronage*, 118-19; Litfin, *Proclamation*, 173, 231; Witherington, *Conflict*, 82. For a thorough critique of Horsley's position see Barclay, "Contrasts", 64-5 n. 29. Nor does anything in the text suggest a background in gnosticism or proto-gnosticism. This requires much to be read into the text, makes it an overtly theological issue, and assumes that *sophia* (which is not an overtly gnostic term) is to be equated with *gnosis* (although this term is only used in 1 Cor 8 in a decidedly non-gnostic way). See Guenther, "Gnosticism", 43-51; *contra* Schmithals, *Gnosticism*, 114-15, 143-4, 151; R. McL. Wilson, "Gnosis at Corinth" in M. D. Hooker & S. G. Wilson, eds., *Paul and Paulinism* (London: SPCK, 1982) 104-5; Georgi, *Theocracy*, 53-4; N. T. Wright, "One God, One Lord, One People: Incarnational Christology for a Church in a Pagan Environment" *Ex Auditu* 7 (1991) 52; Yeo, *Interaction*, 119, 125-6, 130-1. Besides, from 1:17 (οὐκ ἐν σοφίᾳ λόγου), 1:18-31 (especially the *hapax* συζητητής), 2:4-5, 3:10-17 it is clear that the main concern of 1 Cor 1-4 is rhetorical style. See Welborn, "Discord", 101-2; Litfin, *Proclamation*, 188-190, 202, 224; Martin, *Body*, 47. Although the content of the wisdom appears to be an issue in 2:6-13, the Greco-Roman rhetor began by "determining what results he wanted to achieve" then "shape[d] his message accordingly" using his "gifts, training, and experience" (Litfin, *Proclamation*, 207-8).

[152] Conzelmann, *1 Corinthians*, 34; V. P. Furnish, "Belonging to Christ: A Paradigm for Ethics in First Corinthians" *Int* 44 (1990) 151; Mitchell, *Reconciliation*, 67-8; Kuck, *Judgment*, 157-8; Clarke, *Leadership*, 91; Guenther, "Gnosticism", 47; Litfin, *Proclamation*, 181; Witherington, *Conflict*, 74.

real terms, then, it would appear that he is contending with a single opposition front.[153]

This opposition to Paul in 1 Cor 1-4 appears to be based on his refusal to preach in a rhetorical/sophistic style (especially 2:1-5).[154] Given the obsession with rhetorical skill, eloquence and sophism at Corinth, it is likely that for many Christians it was an embarrassment to have Paul seen as their teacher. It had the potential to affect severely the group's (and their individual) status.[155] Despite the fact that Gaius was probably on his side, many of those opposed to Paul would have been elite Christians, since their status in particular would have been damaged. Their preference for

---

[153] For example, Fee, *First Epistle*, 5-6, 9; Baird, "Intra-Church", 130; Chow, *Patronage*, 22, 87-8; Litfin, *Proclamation*, 184, 228-30; Witherington, *Conflict*, 84-5, 130; cf. Conzelmann, *1 Corinthians*, 72. However, the argument of Fee (*First Epistle*, 5-6, 56) and Guenther ("Gnosticism", 52) that it was the whole church versus Paul is most improbable, given that there is apparently a pro-Paul group in 1:12 and since Paul does not name his opponents it is most likely that Stephanas, Crispus, Gaius, Chloe and their supporters were pro-Paul. See Chow, *Patronage*, 88-91. Regarding a "Peter" party, it may be that some had heard of Peter and admired him, as there is no evidence that he ever visited Corinth and certainly no evidence of a Jewish-Christian or Judaizing philosophy: circumcision, Sabbath, table-fellowship and the Law are not issues (Fee, *First Epistle*, 57; Chow, *Patronage*, 87; Clarke, *Leadership*, 95; Guenther, "Gnosticism", 47; Witherington, *Conflict*, 87, 95, 130; *contra* Barrett, *Commentary*, 44; Schmithals, *Gnosticism*, 199-203). Michael Goulder, however, argues that the division is between Paul and Apollos vs Peter, based on reading 1 Cor 4:6 in light of 4:3 and 9:3 ("Σοφία in 1 Corinthians" *NTS* 37 [1991] 517). But this reads too much into the word εἰς, misconstrues the plain sense of the verse, and ignores the ὑπέρ in 4:6c. In light of his reading he tries to argue that σοφία refers to "Torah-wisdom" and he claims that the issue cannot be rhetoric or rhetorical style (ibid., 521-6). Not only does he inadequately explain why the majority of the Christians, who were from a non-Jewish background, would have heard σοφία in this way although this was a common idea in Greco-Roman rhetoric, he ignores the clear reference to rhetorical skill and style in 1 Cor 2:13. See also the criticisms by Litfin, *Proclamation*, 7 n. 20, 228; Witherington, *Conflict*, 84 n. 6.

[154] See Marshall, *Enmity*, 339-41; Chow, *Patronage*, 104-5; Clarke, *Leadership*, 104-5; Gill, "Social Élite", 331; Litfin, *Proclamation*, 153-5, 171, 188-3; Witherington, *Conflict*, 20.

[155] See Chow, *Patronage*, 102-4; Litfin, *Proclamation*, 162-3, 232-3; Savage, *Power*, 46-7; Witherington, *Conflict*, 103-4. Such concerns would also seem to underlie 2 Cor 3:1-3, 4:1-6:13, 10:1-12:13, where Paul's credentials are challenged and other, seemingly more gifted or qualified, teachers are preferred.

Apollos tends to suggest that he was rhetorically proficient and fitted the image of a sophist.[156] In support of this argument that elite Christians are behind the factions in 1 Cor 1-4 is Paul's use of "covert allusion" (the use of tools such as irony, hyperbole and metaphor in an effort to soften one's criticism), which was particularly used to rebuke members of the elite when one did not wish to offend them.[157]

The dense concentration of political language associated with στάσις in 1 Cor 1-4 suggests that this factionalism may have resembled the manner of ancient political contests. In other words, the factions within the church involve power struggles between members of the elite who are supported by their dependants and clients. Indeed, ancient political parties were formed according to personal alliances rather than specific policies. The campaigning was undertaken by the candidates' *liberti*, other clients, and the various *collegia* that they sponsored.[158]

Although Ben Witherington contends that the factions were centered on teachers and not political figures, he ignores the fact that none of the "authorities" to which the factions appealed in 1 Cor 1-4 were actually present in Corinth while the disputes were taking place. Nor did these "authorities" seem to play any part in initiating or promoting the factions. Rather, the leaders of the respective parties or factions would have been locals who probably appealed to respected figures within the church to increase their status

---

[156] This is most likely if, as most scholars assume, Luke's portrait of Apollos in Acts 18:24-5 is accurate. See Haenchen, *Acts*, 549-50; Marshall, *Acts*, 302-3; Chow, *Patronage*, 102-4; Johnson, *Acts*, 331-2; Clarke, *Leadership*, 104-5; Litfin, *Proclamation*, 162, 232-3; Witherington, *Conflict*, 20-1, 84, 103-4.

[157] See Fiore, "Covert Allusion", 94-5. Although Paul does make it apparent that he is using this technique, this is probably explained by his writing to them as their "father" (ibid., 95-7).

[158] See Welborn, "Discord", 89-92; idem, "Concord", 33-40; Stansbury, "Corinthian Honor", 20, 275-6, 424; Chow, *Patronage*, 7, 97; Clarke, *Leadership*, 91-4; Gill, "Social Élite", 337. Martin claims that since Paul uses so much language associated with status in 1 Cor 1-4, the split must be between the high-status and the low-status Christians (*Body*, 55-6, 69). None of the material he presents requires this, however, and is equally consistent with the view that the problem is one among the elite Christians only. He also ignores the evidence assembled by Welborn, Stansbury *et al* about the nature of ancient politics and factions.

and legitimacy.[159] The context for these factions would seem
to be the intense rivalries between members of the elite for
greater power and honor.[160] In Roman (Corinthian) society,
one way to gain greater honor and power was to patronize a
collegium.[161] Therefore, the elite Christians may have
competed for the privilege to patronize the church. Indeed, it
is highly likely that the church would become a battle-ground
for the competing rivalries among the elite Christians if the
church also comprised a number of household groups and
clientage networks.[162]

Rivalry among the elite is particularly evident in the
issue of lawsuits in 1 Corinthians 6. Indeed, such cases would
inevitably have been between members of the elite because
the Roman legal system was heavily biased towards those
with wealth and high status. This, together with the great
expense of legal fees, means that the Christians who went to
court would have been from the elite.[163] Given that such

---

[159] See Baird, "Intra-Church", 123; Welborn, "Concord", 52; Clarke,
Leadership, 107. Welborn identifies the "slogans" of 1:12 as actual
statements of political allegiance ("Discord", 92; "Concord", 34, 38; cf.
Horrell, *Social Ethos*, 115), but there are no real parallels to the form
found in 1:12. As Mitchell points out, "To say 'I support Marius for aedile'
is not the same thing as to say 'I belong to Marius'" (*Reconciliation*, 84).
Rather, Paul's language is that of servitude (ibid., 83-5). The λέγω δὲ
τοῦτο shows that Paul is not quoting them (ibid., 86; cf. Schüssler
Fiorenza, "Rhetorical Situation", 396), and so it is likely that he takes
their statements of socio-political allegiance and makes them
statements of servile dependence.

[160] As Marshall points out, the language of 1 Cor 1-4 comes from
arguments against ὕβρις — the self-indulgent way the elite used their
power, and their excessive behavior (Marshall, *Enmity*, 181-3, 187-9; cf.
Witherington, *Conflict*, 141). He also notes that appeals to ἐλευθερία
and πάντα ἔξεστιν were traditional with the elite to justify their behavior
and the status quo (*Enmity*, 284-5). Marshall's argument is also
compatible with the observation that these terms were standard Stoic
claims, as mentioned above (see Paige, "Stoicism", 180-7; cf. Martin,
Body, 175). Furthermore, Paul's refusal to accept the support of the
Corinthians in 1 Cor 9 may be because it came from one particular
faction and it came with "strings attached". See Marshall, *Enmity*, 231-
7; 397; Stansbury, "Corinthian Honor", 18-19.

[161] See Stansbury, "Corinthian Honor", 278, 283, 417-8; Chow,
Patronage, 66-8.

[162] Marshall, *Enmity*, 135; Stansbury, "Corinthian Honor", 417-18;
Chow, *Patronage*, 68-9; Witherington, *Conflict*, 32.

[163] See, for example, Theissen, *Social Setting*, 97; Mitchell, "Group
Boundaries", 78, 94, 211-12; Marshall, *Enmity*, 215; Barclay,
"Contrasts", 58; Chow, *Patronage*, 76, 127-9; Clarke, *Leadership*, 68; Gill,

cases would have involved rivalry among the elite Christians, presumably for more power and honor, the result would have an enhancement of the divisions within the church.[164] The fact that the lawsuits were pursued at all is further evidence that the elite Christians especially valued their standing in the civic community, sought to maintain it and, if possible, to increase it.

One of the most significant points of dispute within the Corinthian church appears to have been the issue of participation in Greco-Roman cults. There seems to have been two groups, the strict (or "weak") and the lenient. The former clearly come from a Greco-Roman cultic background (8:7) and were probably commoners. The latter were probably from the elite.[165] Theissen advocates such a "class" division, claiming

---

"Social Élite", 330; Winter, *Seek*, 108; Witherington, *Conflict*, 163; Horrell, *Social Ethos*, 110-11; *contra* Meeks, *First Urban*, 66. Fees for legal services were banned by Augustus (Dio Cassius 54.18), but Claudius permitted them and set a limit of 10,000 sesterces (Tacitus *Ann.* 11.5-6). Although the Senate abolished them again at the start of Nero's reign, it was not long before he reintroduced them (Tacitus *Ann.* 13.5; Suetonius *Ner.* 17). Meggitt ignores this information altogether, and all the evidence he cites in support of his contention that lawsuits were common among the plebs come from Egyptian papyri (*Poverty*, 122-5), which may not have been representative of other contexts, especially the wealthy city of Corinth. Martin contends that the issue here is the wealthy and elite taking poorer Christians to court, based on the assumption that the elite avoided lawsuits with one another (*Body*, 76-7). Yet he ignores the fact that lawsuits between the elite were very common and were used as a means to acquire greater status (see, for example, Winter, *Seek*, 108; Clarke, *Leadership*, 62-3). Indeed, this is a likely scenario given the game of challenge-response that was played out in Roman culture, which required the participants to be of similar status. See Malina, *World*, 34-7; Esler, "Making and Breaking", 289-90.

[164] So Mitchell, *Reconciliation*, 117; Clarke, *Leadership*, 68.

[165] See Theissen, *Social Setting*, 123; Borgen, "Participation", 47; Witherington, *Conflict*, 28. Gooch, however, claims there could have been no "weak" group and that it is a hypothetical construct since only the views of the "strong" or lenient are presented (*Dangerous Food*, 65-6). But this is not convincing. That Paul stresses this point so forcefully, and returns to it in 10:23, suggests he had some real group in mind. Furthermore, contrary to the opinion of Richardson ("Absence", 60, 69) and Baird ("Intra-Church", 121), 1 Cor 8-10 does not represent a conflict between Jewish and Gentile sensibilities for Paul assumes in 10:32 that both might take offence (Theissen, *Social Setting*, 123) and in 8:7 Paul *clearly* assumes they were not Jews. Nor can it be suggested that it was a case of Jews vs Gentiles on the assumption that εἰδωλόθυτα was a Jewish term for, as Witherington has convincingly shown, it was a term coined by the early Christians ("Idle Thoughts", 237-9). Davis argues

that the poor seldom ate meat except in religious contexts and thus associated it with idolatry.[166] But they regularly ate meat in *popinae, cauponae*, and the "take-away" food stalls at the baths. Furthermore, cured meats, such as ham and salted pork, have also been discovered in larders from relatively modest homes.[167]

Rather, it is more likely that there was a division between the elite and ordinary Christians because the latter were more superstitious.[168] Their problem is that they continue to perceive the sacrifices as truly offered to the gods and by participating they ran the risk of seeing Christianity syncretistically (8:9-11).[169] This is also linked to the idea of "conscience" (8:7) as "perception".[170] Given the difference in religious mentality, the division may also be between Romans and Greeks. In particular, the argument of the "strong" that separates belief from practice (8:4-6) may reflect a Roman religious mentality.[171] Ultimately, however, the rationale of

that the bulk of the church was opposed to the "strong"/lenient because of the influence of the Jewish-Christian members ("The Interaction", 9-10) but he wrongly assumes there was a monolithic Jewish response to pagan cults. See Borgen, "Participation", 32.

[166] Theissen, *Social Setting*, 125-8. His argument has been adopted with varying degrees of conviction by Meeks (*First Urban*, 69-70), Fee (*First Epistle*, 389 n. 68), Martin (*Body*, 75), Witherington ("Idle Thoughts", 243-4; *Conflict*, 189-90), and Yeo (*Interaction*, 92).

[167] See, for example, Stansbury, "Corinthian Honor", 234-5; Frayn, *Markets*, 72, 146; J. J. Meggitt, "Meat Consumption and Social Conflict in Corinth" *JTS* 45 (1994) 137-40; Horrell, *Social Ethos*, 107-8. It is surprising that Witherington, who is aware that the poor frequented *popinae* and *cauponae* and that such places served meat (*Conflict*, 192), just ignores this in relation to this issue. Gooch argues that nothing in 1 Cor 8-10 presupposes that the issue is meat, and hence Theissen's argument is meaningless (*Dangerous Food*, 53-5) but he does not adequately explain the specific reference to meat in 8:13.

[168] Even Theissen recognizes this (*Social Setting*, 137). See also Chow, *Patronage*, 153-4; Martin, *Body*, 185-6; Yeo, *Interaction*, 90. While Meggitt rightly critiques Theissen's argument that the conflict was based on patterns of meat consumption (*Poverty*, 107-18) he completely misses this point. Indeed, the use of Stoic theology in 8:4-6 is entirely consistent with the "strong" being members of the elite. As Sordi notes, Stoicism was "the philosophy of the ruling classes" at Rome (*Christians*, 159).

[169] See, for example, Fee, *First Epistle*, 372-3, 378-9; Gooch, *Dangerous Food*, 76-8; Borgen, "Participation", 50-1.

[170] See Willis, *Idol Meat*, 92; Borgen, "Participation", 49-50; Witherington, *Conflict*, 190, 199.

[171] See section II of chapter 2 herein. If the "strong" saw Christianity as another philosophy, they may have thought they could held that while engaging in cult activity, especially since their arguments

the "strong" is probably a convenient way of legitimizing the status quo. Since it was important for the elite, in particular, to continue to participate, such a form of legitimation would have been necessary. Apart from being more superstitious, ordinary Christians had less need to participate.

Paul also specifically identifies factions (σχίσματα) in the practice of the Lord's Supper (11:18). Generally, scholars contend that these divisions were along social lines, as a conflict between the "haves" and "have-nots", especially since Paul addresses those who seem to be home-owners.[172] Clearly, some of the elite treated the gathering as a normal social meal: they did not mix with their social inferiors, ate more and better food, and probably began before the others arrived after work.[173] Yet nowhere does Paul equate the factions with the different social classes. Instead, the factions seem to involve those who do what is right and those who do not, according to Paul's definition. It is just as likely that the conflict is among the more well-to-do concerning the manner of conducting the Eucharist. The scenario suggests that the elite "gluttons" were treating the poor in a manner customary for meals involving the different social strata. It is not at all clear that the poor themselves expected to be treated

---

may reflect a Stoic form of monotheism (cf. Paige, "Stoicism", 187-8). I assume, with Willis, that most of these verses make best sense as a quote from the "strong" (*Idol Meat*, 84-6; *contra* Fee, *First Epistle*, 371-2). But even if they are not *actual* quotes, they do sum up their position.

[172] See Theissen, *Social Setting*, 96, 146-50; Meeks, *First Urban*, 67-8; Fee, *First Epistle*, 543; Welborn, "Concord", 42; Stansbury, "Corinthian Honor", 470-1; Mitchell, *Reconciliation*, 264; Chow, *Patronage*, 94, 111; Gill, "Social Élite", 332; Witherington, *Conflict*, 29, 241; cf. Martin, *Body*, 73-4. Welborn claims that "virtually no one doubts that tensions between rich and poor were present in the church at Corinth" ("Discord", 94-5). The expression τοὺς μὴ ἔχοντας (11:22) is not a normal one for "the poor", as Meggitt points out (*Poverty*, 119-20), but this is its sense here since its direct object appears to be "houses in which to eat". The contrast is between those who have houses, and are therefore able to gorge themselves at home (οἰκίας...ἔχετε) and those who do not have houses. This is tentatively suggested by Barrett (*Commentary*, 263). Unfortunately, Meggitt ignores Barrett's suggestion in favor of his (unsubstantiated) idea of it relating to the elements of the Lord's Supper itself. But the earlier use of ἔχειν (11:22a), i.e. μὴ γὰρ οἰκίας οὐκ ἔχετε, is *clearly* concerned with *houses in which to eat*.

[173] Smith, "Meals", 327; Theissen, *Social Setting*, 149-56; Fee, *First Epistle*, 541-2; Mitchell, *Reconciliation*, 264; Baird, "Intra-Church", 128; Chow, *Patronage*, 111; Gill, "Social Élite", 332; Witherington, *Conflict*, 192-5, 248-9; Horrell, *Social Ethos*, 102-4; cf. Juvenal *Sat.* 5.

otherwise or considered that they were being maltreated.[174] Indeed, such a conflict may reflect the different attitudes to entertaining social inferiors among the elite.[175] It may also be the case that it is Paul who is creating an issue of it.

For many of these elite Christians, it would have been important for their public image that they function in the conventional way as patrons of *collegia*.[176] It is possible that they provided the food for the common meal, and may have done so as a means of gaining status (and of boasting).[177] If so, this would appear to be another case where the internal conflicts were due to the strong ties between the elite Christians and outsiders.

In summary, then, the relationship between the Christian and civic communities at Corinth appears to lacked conflict. Inter-marriage, sexual relations with outsiders, civil lawsuits, participation in Greco-Roman cults, dinner invitations and casual visitors to Christian worship gatherings are all evidence for this. Apart from the last, most of these concern the elite members of the church. While their continued participation in, and acceptance by, wider society seems to have saved the church from external conflict, it would appear to have contributed to the internal conflict. Much of this probably has arisen because the elite Christians were more concerned about their status or honor in the eyes of their peers than in those of their fellow-Christians.

---

[174] In fact, the examples Welborn gives of "class-conflict" ("Discord", 95-100) along this line, actually fit the idea of a failure of role-fulfilment better.

[175] Pliny, for example, ate the same simple food he served his clients (*Ep.* 2.6), while Martial (*Epigr.* 3.60) thought hosts should provide the lavish food for all guests. See, for example, Meeks, *First Urban*, 68; Fee, *First Epistle*, 544. Many of the elite Christians clearly followed the normal pattern of different food. Fee, however, seems to assume that Martial was not a member of the elite and that his position represents an argument "from below" (*First Epistle*, 544). Yet, despite his constant claims to poverty he did own a country villa (*Epigr.* 12.57). Of course, some probably did see it as other than a social meal.

[176] Members of the elite who joined or formed *collegia* were frequently elected as officials in the association, performed the cultic acts, received a greater share of the feasts and sat in the best places. See Chow, *Patronage*, 67-9; cf. *ILS* 7212.

[177] See Theissen, *Social Setting*, 148; Stansbury, "Corinthian Honor", 465-6; Chow, *Patronage*, 111. The perceived failure of the elite in this matter may be more pertinent if the context was a series of food shortages in Corinth. See Gill, "Social Élite", 333-5.

226 *Church and Community Conflicts*

IV. PAUL'S RESPONSE TO THE RELATIONSHIP

Paul's response to the relationship between the church and the wider civic community is reflected in the type of letter he wrote, as well as its content. The rhetorical genre of 1 Corinthians is generally accepted as deliberative.[178] In other words, its aim is to persuade its readers to consider what was expedient or in the common interest, and what was the honorable course of action.[179] The primary purpose of such a rhetorically structured letter is stated in its *propositio*. As mentioned above, this is found in 1:10, and it comprises a call to foster *homonoia* and to do away with factions.[180] In seeking to accomplish this goal, Paul uses a variety of means, including offering encouragement to the Corinthian Christians to strengthen the boundaries between the church and society, to work for unity, and to renounce their rights.

1. Strengthen Boundaries

Despite the differences in their respective world-views, one of the main ways that Paul attempts to reinforce the boundaries between the Christian and civic communities is by re-emphasizing his apocalyptic eschatology.[181] More specifically, he applies an apocalyptic dualism, deriding "this world" and "the present age" as doomed to destruction (1:18-2:8; 5:5; 6:1, 9-11; 7:31; 11:32; 15:24). Paul uses this dualism to relativize "this world" and the things pertaining to it, putting all worldly goods and pursuits into a heavenly perspective.[182] This is particularly evident in 7:29b-31.

---

[178] See, for example, Mitchell, *Reconciliation*, 64; Witherington, *Conflict*, 75; to some extent also Schüssler Fiorenza, "Rhetorical Situation", 393. Nevertheless, as was noted in the introduction to section IV of chapter 4 herein, the classical rhetorical genres may not necessarily fit the NT writings precisely, given their different settings.

[179] Schüssler Fiorenza, "Rhetorical Situation", 393; Witherington, *Conflict*, 75, 106.

[180] Schüssler Fiorenza, "Rhetorical Situation", 393; Mitchell, *Reconciliation*, 65-6; Witherington, *Conflict*, 75, 94.

[181] See Meeks, "Social Functions", 700; Kuck, *Judgment*, 237; Witherington, *Conflict*, 298.

[182] Conzelmann, *1 Corinthians*, 133; Doughty, "The Presence", 73; Mitchell, "Group Boundaries", 39-40; Engberg-Pedersen, "The Gospel", 581; Fee, *First Epistle*, 335; Barclay, "Contrasts", 59; Martin, *Body*, 175; Witherington, *Conflict*, 180.

His advice in handling lawsuits in 1 Cor 6 seems to fit this as well. It is generally assumed that in 6:7 Paul suggests that the Corinthian Christians should suffer injustice rather than have disputes.[183] Yet, as Alan Mitchell shows, the point of this verse is that they should suffer injustice rather than "receive judgments from pagans".[184] Indeed, while

> they persist in going before pagan judges they effectively deny the benefits of salvation because there is no real contrast between their behavior and the behavior of those who are outside.[185]

This argument explains Paul's emphasis on salvation and eschatology in this matter. In light of this, Paul advocates the formation of a judiciary process within the church — something that would strengthen the boundaries.[186] He also uses parenesis to strengthen the community's boundaries. In other words, he emphasises the need for them to be holy and disciplined (1:2; 3:16-17; 5:1-13; 6:15-20; 7:5b, 34; 10:6-14; 11:27-31). He argues that their way of life ought to go beyond the standard represented by traditional Greco-Roman norms and morals.[187]

Paul tries to strengthen the group boundaries by an emphasis on *koinonia*. This is most evident in 10:14-22. Wendell Willis notes that such an association of worship and *koinonia* is prevalent in the LXX and Philo in relation to the covenant. As such, Paul may be suggesting that by participating in the eucharist they constitute a covenant or "cultic community" and thus cannot participate in another.[188]

---

[183] So Barrett, *Commentary*, 135, 139; Conzelmann, *1 Corinthians*, 105-6; Fee, *First Epistle*, 234, 239-40.

[184] Mitchell, "Group Boundaries", 44. He points out that the "traditional" interpretation understands κρίματα ἔχετε as "to have lawsuits", when the more common usage in legal texts refers to "judgments" (ibid., 61-2).

[185] Ibid., 50; cf. Fee, *First Epistle*, 230.

[186] Mitchell argues that Paul advocates an informal, private arbitration process according to the Roman "extra-judicial procedure of private arbitration" ("Group Boundaries", 102-9; cf. Petronius *Sat.* 70). But the form does not matter in the context of Paul's argument.

[187] See Willis, *Idol Meat*, 221-2; Fee, *First Epistle*, 227, 463; Mitchell, *Reconciliation*, 228, 255-6; Kuck, *Judgment*, 242; Gooch, *Dangerous Food*, 84; Witherington, *Conflict*, 80, 160.

[188] See Willis, *Idol Meat*, 166-8, 175-7, 187-90; cf. Fee, *First Epistle*, 463. Yet, Willis contends that this sense of *koinonia* is purely between the worshippers/participants in the sacraments and does not involve

Indeed, if a covenantal sense is present, Paul may be developing an idea of the Christians as a "nation". In any case, his emphasis on the sacraments seems to strengthen the group boundaries by focussing their worship on shared traditions and rituals (11:2, 23-31).[189]

As with the case of 1 Thessalonians, there is also an abundant use of familial terms in 1 Corinthians. In fact, Paul uses ἀδελφός twenty-nine times in this letter, while he also describes himself as their "wet-nurse" (3:2) and their father (4:14-16). The use of such terms and expressions suggests that Paul was also trying to nurture a sense of (fictive) kinship within the Corinthian church, although in this case it was prompted by their circumstance of internal disunity, rather than by external conflict.[190]

2. Foster Unity

Consistent with his use of deliberative rhetoric, Paul exhorts them to be united on the basis of what was beneficial to the common good (6:12; 8:7-13; 9:19-22; 10:23-4).[191] This is particularly evident in his use of the standard metaphor of the "Body" to combat factionalism (12:12-26).[192] Usually this metaphor was employed to argue for unity and harmony on based on the traditional social hierarchy.[193] Paul, however, reverses its normal sense and uses it to argue *against* the traditional honor/status system of Greco-Roman society, and to relativize the self-importance of the elite members of the church. Indeed, he reverses the cultural expectation of what

---

Christ/God (*Idol Meat*, 200-4). But *koinonia* was normally understood as involving relationships on both the horizontal and vertical planes. See G. Panikulam, *Koinonia in the New Testament: A Dynamic Expression of Christian Life* (AnBib 85; Rome: Biblical Institute Press, 1979) 22-4; Fee, *First Epistle*, 467; Gooch, *Dangerous Food*, 57. Besides, Philo also seems to understand the Jewish sacrifices as involving a *koinonia* between worshippers *and* God, understood as host (*De spec.* 1.221).

[189] This was common in the ancient world. See, for example, Dio Chrys. *Or.* 38.22, 41.10; cf. Mitchell, *Reconciliation*, 141, 176.

[190] For a similar idea see Barclay, "Contrasts", 60.

[191] As Mitchell points out, a common *topos* in this sort of argument is compromise for the sake of the greater good (*Reconciliation*, 132, 143-5). See, for example, Dio Chrys. *Or.* 40.34; Plutarch *De vit.* 824E.

[192] For example, Aristotle *Pol.* 1302B35-3A2; Dion. Hal. *Ant. Rom.* 6.86.1-2; cf. Mitchell, *Reconciliation*, 157-61; Welborn, "Concord", 207.

[193] See, for example, Dion. Hal. *Ant. Rom.* 6.86.3-4; cf. Chow, *Patronage*, 175-9; Welborn, "Concord", 209.

was honorable and shameful.[194] In so doing, he expects an equality of care and respect for all Christians that would eliminate division (12:25), urging them to adopt ἀγάπη as an alternative unifying principle for the "Body" (12:31-14:1).[195]

3. Forgo Rights

Nowhere in 1 Corinthians does Paul explicitly exhort his readers (especially the elite) to renounce their rights as citizens. He does offer himself as a model for the renunciation of rights in 1 Cor 9, but he does not explicitly link this with a renunciation of the citizenship rights.[196] In 5:9 Paul also makes it clear that he does not want them to withdraw from the world, and in 10:27-30 he seems to have no qualms about them attending dinner-parties. But he does categorically ban participation in meals in temples (10:14-22). The consequences of this, especially for elite Christians, would have been severe, potentially preventing them from holding office or retaining their place in the social hierarchy.[197] Given

---

[194] Marshall, *Enmity*, 403; Furnish, "Belonging", 156; Stansbury, "Corinthian Honor", 426; Chow, *Patronage*, 178-9; Welborn, "Concord", 221; Witherington, *Conflict*, 29 n. 81, 259, 299. This relativization of the status of the elite Christians is also evident in Paul's expectation that *all* will contribute to the collection (16:2), not just the elite Christians who would thereby earn more status and honor. See Chow, *Patronage*, 185-6.

[195] Many of the things "love" is not (13:4b-6) are issues related to social status and honor. See Engberg-Pedersen, "The Gospel", 566-7, 572-4; Stansbury, "Corinthian Honor", 426, 433-4; Mitchell, *Reconciliation*, 165; Witherington, *Conflict*, 264-5; cf. Willis, *Idol Meat*, 113; Davis, "The Interaction", 13; Furnish, "Belonging", 157. In fact "love", in the form of ἔρως, was commonly used in arguments for *homonoia*. See, for example, Polybius 23.11.3; cf. Witherington, *Conflict*, 265. However, Theissen contends that Paul advocated a system of "love-patriarchalism", expecting the elite to continue to exercise authority and the church to reflect the hierarchical structure of society, but modified by a spirit of care and concern (Theissen, *Social Setting*, 139, 162-4; cf. Schüssler Fiorenza, "Rhetorical Structure", 397-9). This proposal, however, fails to consider some of Paul's more radical exhortations, such that the church be subject to the *household* of Stephanas. Theissen also misses some of the radical implications of Paul's renunciation of his rights in 1 Cor 9. See Engberg-Pedersen, "The Gospel", 575-7; Horrell, *Social Ethos*, 126-31, 195-8. He also fails to consider the way Paul has modified the traditional "Body" metaphor and its implications for the relationships between the elite and ordinary Christians.

[196] See, for example, Engberg-Pedersen, "The Gospel", 575-6; Gill, "Social Élite", 337.

[197] Gooch, *Dangerous Food*, 104-7; Witherington, *Conflict*, 175-6.

the belief that citizens should worship the gods of the city this would be, in fact, an implicit call to a renunciation of citizenship.

Paul's instructions, however, are ambiguous. He bans participation in temple-meals but not participation in other meals, although *all* socially-significant meals in the Greco-Roman world were overtly religious.[198] It is not possible to see some as purely religious and others as purely social.[199] Since Erastus appears to have been elected *aedilis* subsequently, and remained on good terms with Paul (Rom 16:23; cf. 2 Tim 4:20), Paul's position must have been more nuanced.[200] What did or did not constitute idolatry would have continued to be an issue for him.

In any case, he does not specifically call on the Corinthian Christians to renounce their citizenship. This may be because this church, unlike at Thessalonica, was in a very different position since it did not experience conflict with its wider society. Paul's modification of his position may also relate to the presence of members of the elite in the church.[201]

---

[198] See Fee, "Once Again", 183; idem, *First Epistle*, 361 n. 8; Gooch, *Dangerous Food*, 13, 38, 81-2; Martin, *Body*, 183; Witherington, "Idle Thoughts", 245; idem, *Conflict*, 188 n. 11, 222; cf. *New Docs* 1.5; Plutarch *Non posse* 1102A-B.

[199] Willis suggests that meals may be "sacramental" (worshippers eat the deity), "communal" (worshippers eat with the deity) or "social" (worshippers eat in the presence of the deity) (Willis, *Idol Meat*, 18-20). He rightly rejects the sacramental understanding as having no foundation in the Greco-Roman world (ibid., 23-9; cf. Fee, *First Epistle*, 361 n. 18; Mitchell, *Reconciliation*, 251; Witherington, *Conflict*, 225-6; *contra* Barrett, *Commentary*, 224; Schmithals, *Gnosticism*, 225; Conzelmann, *1 Corinthians*, 171-4 [who assumes a sacramental understanding based on Euripides' picture of the Dionysiac cult]; Yeo, *Interaction*, 117-18 [who misreads both Willis and Aristides and confuses the idea of "sacramental" and "communal"]). Willis opts for the social interpretation (*Idol Meat*, 20-1, 44-7; cf. Stansbury, "Corinthian Honor", 474). However many of the texts he cites in support of this (*Idol Meat*, 40-4, 172-3) actually show a communal understanding. See Witherington, "Idle Thoughts", 245. Willis' distinctions are also probably too modern and subtle.

[200] Wright argues that rather than seeking to define "how far can we go" in integrating into the wider society, Paul encourages them to "pursue a path of mission to the world" and to "seek to build shrines for the true god on ground at present occupied by paganism" ("One God", 51, 53). But this appears to reflect Wright's personal agenda since nothing in the text of 1 Corinthians itself suggests this.

[201] That is, he shows some socially-conditioned reserve when dealing with his social betters. His use of "covert allusion" (discussed above)

He seems to want them to be less integrated in civic society, but that would most likely lead to conflict with the civic community. Many of his arguments are particularly directed at the elite and could potentially undermine their values and norms, but he does not really draw out the radical implication of any of his exhortations in this letter.

V. CONCLUSION

In the first century CE Corinth was a large and busy city. Yet, it had the close and very public living characteristic of a community. Its planning, history and social structures suggest there was a reasonable association and interaction of different social groups. Corinth was most likely very cosmopolitan and there appears to have been a strong Jewish community. The city was a *colonia*, with a typical Roman political structure that was elitist and oligarchic. Yet patronal networks were very important. The religious pattern of Corinth was a mixture of Greek and Roman cults (the latter being especially prominent), and presumably a range of religious beliefs and mentalities.

The Corinthian church seems to have been a very large and mixed group. Greek, Roman and Jewish backgrounds are all present, and the full social spectrum seems to be represented, including some members of Corinth's ruling elite. While the Christians may have met in small house groups on a regular (weekly) basis, there is some evidence that points to them meeting together less frequently in a purpose-built club-room.

Relations between the Christian and civic community at Corinth apparently lacked conflict. Most of the evidence for this, however, involves members of the elite in the church. It is likely that their continued participation in, and acceptance by, wider society was a major factor in preventing conflict between the Christian and civic communities. Yet they also would have been a major factor in the development of internal conflict. Much of this probably arose because the

would support this. This may also be reflected in the ambiguity of his request to Philemon regarding Onesimus. J. M. G. Barclay notes the ambiguity of his request, and suggests Paul is being socially realistic, realizing that the wealthier Christians could not retain their social status if they manumitted their slaves and that Paul, in fact, relied on such people and their wealth and standing ("Paul, Philemon and the Dilemma of Christian Slave-Ownership" *NTS* 37 [1991] 183-4). But he ignores the role that status and/or class itself may have played in Paul's ambiguity.

elite Christians were more concerned about their relations with their peers, and their social standing, than with their fellow-Christians.

In response, Paul tries to strengthen the boundaries between the church and the wider society. To this end he uses an apocalyptic dualism to relativize their attachment to the world. He greatly emphasizes ethical living and the need to be holy, and he reminds them they are a *koinonia* with shared traditions. Paul tries to nurture a sense of (fictive) kinship, both to strengthen boundaries and prevent disunity. In this regard, he draws on the traditional image of the "Body", but uses it to relativize the self-importance of the elite Christians. He urges them to adopt ἀγάπη as an alternative unifying principle for the "Body", rather than honor and shame — as it was normally conceived.

Finally, Paul bans participation in Greco-Roman cults, and implicitly seems to encourage the Christians to renounce their citizenship, although he does not make that explicit. Nor does he ask them to withdraw from civic society entirely. Ultimately, his position is somewhat ambiguous. The differences between his instructions to the Corinthian Christians, compared to the Thessalonians, may result from the absence of conflict and the presence of members of the elite in the church.

Chapter Six

SOCIAL RELATIONS AT PHILIPPI

This chapter will proceed in a similar fashion to the previous two. It will seek to reconstruct the nature of Roman Philippi, the Philippian church, and the relationship between the church and civic community at Philippi. The reconstruction of the social context of the city will draw on the work of ancient writers, epigraphic evidence and other historical data, as well as the work of previous scholars and, where relevant, chapters two and three of this study. Reconstruction of the Philippian church and the relationship between it and the civic community will rely primarily on canonical Philippians and background material.[1]

---

[1] Along with the majority of scholars I accept the unity of the letter. For the extensive arguments in support of this see, in particular, V. P. Furnish, "The Place and Purpose of Philippians III" *NTS* 10 (1963) 80-8; R. Jewett, "The Epistolary Thanksgiving and the Integrity of Philippians" *NovT* 12 (1970) 40-53; D. E. Garland, "The Composition and Unity of Philippians: Some Neglected Literary Factors" *NovT* 27 (1985) 148-50, 154-9; D. F. Watson, "A Rhetorical Analysis of Philippians and Its Implications for the Unity Question" *NovT* 30 (1988) 57-88; P. T. O'Brien, *Commentary on Philippians* (NIGTC; Grand Rapids: Eerdmans, 1991) 348-9; D. A. Black, "The Discourse Structure of Philippians: A Study in Text-Linguistics" *NovT* 37 (1995) 101-3; *contra* Schmithals, *Paul*, 67-9; P. Perkins, "Philippians: Theology for the Heavenly Politeuma" in J. M. Bassler, ed., *Pauline Theology, Volume I* (Minneapolis: Fortress, 1991) 89; J. Reumann, "Contributions of the Philippian Community to Paul and to Earliest Christianity" *NTS* 39 (1993) 439. Wayne Meeks admits to having recently changed his mind and now accepts the letter's unity ("The Man from Heaven in Paul's Letter to the Philippians" in B. A. Pearson, ed., *The Future of Early Christianity* [Minneapolis: Fortress, 1991] 331 n. 6). It is quite clear that Philippians is a carefully constructed rhetorical argument. See Watson, "Rhetorical Analysis", 82-7; T. C. Geoffrion, *The Rhetorical Purpose and the Political and Military Character of Philippians: A Call to Stand Firm* (Lewiston, NY: Edwin Mellen, 1993) 193-4. Recently, however, D. J. Doughty has argued that Phil 3:2-21 is a deutero-Pauline interpolation

The reconstruction of the socio-historical context of Philippi is aided by the extensive and thorough excavation of the site, as is the case at Corinth, but many useful inscriptions have been unearthed and there is not the same problem of fragmentary remains as there is at Corinth. But, as will be noted, most of the material unearthed at Philippi comes from the second century CE or later, and the date of many of the inscriptions is uncertain. Therefore, as with all such endeavors which rely on fragmentary evidence, some of the data needed for this reconstruction must be extrapolated from other sources.

I. ROMAN PHILIPPI

The aim of reconstructing the nature of Roman Philippi is to provide material for analysis by the model in the next chapter. According to the model outlined in part one of this study, the incidence of conflict is determined by the particular set of norms, values and beliefs, the pattern of relational ties, and the distribution of political power. Therefore, material related to these factors will be considered in terms of Philippi's history, physical and demographic features, the nature of its social relations, its political features, and its religious profile. In so doing, this reconstruction of first-century Philippi will involve consideration of the same factors as the reconstructions of Roman Thessalonica and Corinth.

1. History

The town, variously known as Datum or Krenides early in its history, was settled by Greek colonists from the island of Thasos in 360 BCE. In 356 BCE the town was captured by Philip II of Macedon, who fortified it as a stronghold against the local Thracian tribes, enlarged it, and developed the local

---

("Citizens of Heaven: Philippians 3:2-21" *NTS* 41 [1995] 102-2). Unfortunately, he proceeds from the assumption of an interpolation and then proves what he assumes (ibid., 103 n. 4); he completely ignores the recent rhetorical arguments of Watson and Geoffrion and he seems to discount the possibility that the actual historical context of Philippi could have had any influence on Paul's language and message (ibid., 107-8, 114). He also fails to account for the common vocabulary and linguistic links between chapter 3 and the rest of the letter, especially between 3:20-1 and both 2:6-11 (cf. Lincoln, *Paradise*, 88) and 1:27-30.

gold mines. It was he who named the town "Philippi".[2] However, the gold did not last long and the population, and consequently the importance, of the town seems to have declined until the battle in 42 BCE.[3]

Following the battle between the Liberators (Brutus and Cassius) and the Triumvirs (specifically M. Antony and Octavian), the town was made a Roman colony. It was named *Colonia Victrix Philippensium*. A further settlement of colonists was made following Octavian's victory at Actium in 31 BCE, and the town's name was changed to *Colonia Iulia*

---

[2] See Diod. Sic. 16.3.7, 16.8.6; Appian *BCiv*.4.105; cf. Davies, "Macedonian Scene", 95; D. Lazarides, "Philippi (Krenides)" in R. Stilwell *et al.*, eds., *Princeton Encyclopaedia of Classical Sites* (Princeton, NJ: Princeton University Press, 1976) 704-5; L. Portefaix, *Sisters Rejoice: Paul's Letter to the Philippians and Luke-Acts as Seen by First-Century Philippian Women* (ConBNT 20; Stockholm: Almqvist & Wiksell, 1988) 60; H. L. Hendrix, "Philippi" *ABD* 5.314; Gill, "Macedonia", 411; P. Pilhofer, *Philippi, I: Die erste christliche Gemeinde Europas* (WUNT 87; Tübingen: J. C. B. Mohr, 1995) 86-7, 90.

[3] See Lazarides, "Philippi", 705; Portefaix, *Sisters Rejoice*, 60; L. Bormann, *Philippi: Stadt und Christengemeinde zur Zeit des Paulus* (NovTSup 78; Leiden: E. J. Brill, 1995), 19-20; Pilhofer, *Philippi*, 81. Strabo claims that Philippi was a κατοικία μικρά but ηὐξήθη...μετὰ τὴν περὶ Βροῦτον καὶ Κάσσιον ἧτταν (*Geog* 7 frag 41). Peter Oakes suggests that this reference was probably to the original settlement, but even if it was not, since Strabo gets details of geography wrong, his account cannot be trusted ("Philippians", 51-3). Furthermore, he contends that there would have been a large population prior to colonization given the fertility of the land (ibid., 67) and the existence of the Greek writer, Marsyas of Philippi (dated either first century BCE or CE), who was cited by Pliny and Athenaeus. He suggests that "either immediately pre-colonial Philippi could produce a substantial Greek writer, or the Greek community of colonial Philippi could" (ibid., 53). On the other hand, just because Strabo gets geographical data wrong does not mean he is necessarily wrong in other data. While the land was fertile, much of the population (who did not own or could not rent the land) would have moved on after the mines closed, leaving a small farming community. Also, much of the land that had once been royal land became *ager publicus* when the Romans defeated the Macedonians, so there need not have been a large population. This will be discussed more later in this chapter. Contrary to Oakes' claim, the presence of one prominent writer says nothing about the population (whereas if there had been several that would be significant). Marsyas probably dates from after colonization, since it is more likely that there would be the sort of patronage available then that would enable someone like him to pursue his art.

Augusta Philippensis.[4] Those settled in 42 BCE were predominantly Antony's veterans, including a number of his Praetorian guard (who would have received preferential treatment).[5] Although it is usually assumed that those settled at Philippi after Actium were Antony's veterans and supporters, it is more likely that they came from both sides.[6]

It is unclear how many veterans would have settled at Philippi. Some scholars suggest there were about 500 colonists in 42 BCE, and about the same number following Actium.[7] Most Caesarean and Triumviral colonies, however, received 2,000-3,000 colonists and there is no reason to

---

[4] P. Collart, *Philippes, villes de Macédoine depuis ses origines jusqu' à la fin de l'époque romaine* (Paris: de Boccard, 1937) 224-37; Larsen, "Greece", 448-9; Davies, "Macedonian Scene", 95; Lazarides, "Philippi", 705; Portefaix, *Sisters Rejoice*, 60; Bormann, *Philippi*, 35; L. M. White, "Visualizing the 'Real' World of Acts 16: Toward Construction of a Social Index" in L. M. White & O. L. Yarbrough, eds., *The Social World of the First Christians* (Minneapolis: Fortress, 1995) 241; cf. Pliny *NH* 4.42; Strabo *Geog.* 7 frag 41; *ILS* 2718; P. Collart, "Inscriptions de Philippes (1)" *BCH* 57 (1933) #6; idem, "Inscriptions de Philippes (2)" *BCH* 62 (1938) #1; cf Acts 16:12, Phil 4:15.

[5] Collart, "Inscriptions (1)", 358-9; Keppie, *Colonisation*, 60 n. 64; idem, *The Making*, 121; Bormann, *Philippi*, 14-15, 18; Pilhofer, *Philippi*, 87; cf. A. Salac, "Inscriptions du Pangée, de la Région Drama-Cavalla et de Philippes" *BCH* 47 (1923) #2.5.

[6] Dio Cassius claims that after Actium, Augustus' veterans received "an additional assignment of land" (γῆν προσκατένειμε) and that much of this had been confiscated from Antony's supporters in Italy. Many of those who were dispossessed supposedly settled in Dyrrachium and Philippi. Dio also suggests that many of those dispossessed were financially compensated for their loss (51.4.6; cf. Pilhofer, *Philippi*, 87). The latter is probably supported by Augustus' claim to have paid 260 million sesterces for land in the provinces for veterans (*Res Gestae* 16.1), although most of that presumably would have been used for the colonies he created in Spain and Gaul in 14 BCE. See Keppie, *Colonisation*, 76, 85. Indeed, given an average grant of 500 *iugera* per veteran-colonist and land prices of about 500 sesterces/ *iugerum*, that sum would cater for about 10,400 colonists (ibid., 76), of which the Philippian colonists would be only a small proportion. But Keppie notes that "epigraphic evidence from known Antonian colonies suggests that they remained on their estates". Besides, it would have been illogical for Octavian to engage in massive dispossession and deportation after the battle when he had gone to great lengths to win them over in the period leading up to Actium (ibid.). In any case, to create a pocket of Antonian support at Philippi would not have made great political sense.

[7] For example, Hendrix, "Philippi", 314; Bormann, *Philippi*, 21-2.

assume the same did not occur in this case.[8] It is also likely that the colony attracted some of the many Italian businessmen who were already resident in the province.[9] The colonists presumably would have also brought with them a large number of wives, children and slaves. Altogether, such an influx would have had a significant impact on the small town, and presumably encouraged its Romanization.[10]

2. Physical Features

Philippi lies on the *Via Egnatia*, about 13 kilometres to the northwest of the port of Neapolis. It is situated at the base of a steep hill, with woods to the north and marshes to the south, and very fertile plains, well watered with springs and rivers, to the west.[11] Given the nature of its colonization, the town was endowed with a very large *territorium*, covering about 1890 square kilometres.[12] The actual area within the town walls, however, was only 70 hectares.[13]

Unfortunately, the town plan is no longer visible. Nevertheless, it would have been laid out according to a standard Roman grid, with the *Via Egnatia* as the main east-west road. The streets that have been found are narrow, generally in the order of 2.0-3.0 metres wide.[14] Few remains of houses have been unearthed, but both villas and *insula* tenements appear to have been located near the forum. Living would have been quite close, and high-rise accommodation was probably common, given that the area

---

[8] See Brunt, *Man-Power*, 236, 261; cf. Oakes, "Philippians", 26.

[9] On Roman businessmen resident in Macedonia see Brunt, *Man-Power*, 244; Papazoglou, "Macedonia", 196; cf. Oakes, "Philippians", 92.

[10] In fact, Philippi is rather unique because it retained its thorough Romanness over a long period of time, unlike many other colonies in the east, which quickly became Hellenized. This is presumably related to the manner of colonisation. See Bormann, *Philippi*, 39-40, 63; Pilhofer, *Philippi*, 91-2.

[11] Appian, *BCiv.* 4.105; Strabo *Geog.* 7 frag 36; cf. Lazarides, "Philippi", 704; Oakes, "Philippians", 39; Pilhofer, *Philippi*, 78-81.

[12] Portefaix, *Sisters Rejoice*, 61; Bormann, *Philippi*, 27-8; Oakes, "Philippians", 40.

[13] Oakes, "Philippians", 40 n. 11.

[14] See Lazarides, "Philippi", 705; Pandermalis, "Monuments", 211; White, "Visualizing", 242. Indeed, even the *Via Egnatia* at Philippi is not much more than 2.0 metres wide.

available for building was limited by the marshes and the steepness of the hill.[15]

Remains of the first century forum, beneath the Antonine one, include a number of shops to the north, right near temples, and not far from the theatre. It is also likely that the two temples at the eastern and western corners of the later forum had first century precursors, and there was an early Bacchus shrine just to the south of the forum. Shops and houses have also been found near the *macellum*, which adjoined the southern edge of the forum. Although these structures date from the second century, this arrangement is consistent with what is known in other *coloniae*.[16]

It is clear from this arrangement of space in the town that there was a close connection between the commercial, religious, political, social and residential aspects of life. Indeed, the narrowness of the roads, the limited building space, the large size of the first century forum, and the mix of building types, suggest that, like Thessalonica and Corinth, Philippi's life was very communal and that it functioned as a *Gemeinschaft*-type community. Given the small size of the actual *urbs* this sense of "community" may have been particularly strong.

3. Demographic Features

While the area within the town walls appears to have been about 70 hectares, only about 45 hectares of that could have been built on, given the steepness of the terrain. Based on the population density used in the previous two chapters (200-250 per hectare), the population of the *urbs* would have

---

[15] See, for example, Portefaix, *Sisters Rejoice*, 63-4; Oakes, "Philippians", 40. Nevertheless, Portefaix's assumption that the tenements follow the Ostia pattern is not warranted. See section I of chapter 3 herein.

[16] See Collart, *Philippes*, 367; Davies, "Macedonian Scene", 96-7; Lazarides, "Philippi", 705; Pandermalis, "Monuments", 211; H. W. Catling, "Archaeology in Greece" *Arch Rep* 31 (1985) 49; Portefaix, *Sisters Rejoice*, 62-3, 72; McRay, *Archaeology*, 285; Gill, "Macedonia", 412; Oakes, "Philippians", 62; Bormann, *Philippi*, 41, 52. An indication of the integration of life in Philippian society is the inscription dedicated to the *genius* of the *macellum* (P. Lemerle, "Inscriptions latines et greques de Philippi" *BCH* 58 [1934] #45). There is also a well-preserved 42-seat public latrine just south of the forum.

been about 9,000-11,500.[17] Despite the size of its *territorium*, the township itself was relatively small.

The population of the town was mixed, with Romans, Thracians, Macedonians and other Greeks.[18] According to Luke's account in Acts 16, there was a Jewish community in the town, yet even he alludes to it being very small and insignificant. For Paul and his companions were not certain where the Jews met (16:13), indicating they were not staying with Jews, and Luke records that Paul and his companions spoke only to some women. Indeed, ταῖς συνελθούσαις γυναιξίν (16:13b) implies that the gathering consisted only of women.[19] Furthermore, there is a complete lack of supporting evidence for a Jewish presence in the first century.[20] Luke's introduction of a Jewish community may well follow his standard motif of having Paul begin his ministry among the Jews.[21] But his account does not follow his usual pattern, even if it does retain certain typical elements.

An important demographic feature is the degree of ethnic integration in Philippian society. To a large extent the pattern of ethnic integration is dependent on the process of colonization and the changes it brought about. Initially, it is

---

[17] Oakes suggests a population of about 10,000 for the *urbs* based on the data for Pompeii ("Philippians", 73). He also assumes there would have been a further 5,000 in the "suburbs", and a population for the *territorium* of 21,000 based on the figure for Italy of 24 persons per square kilometre (ibid., 73). However, few of these would have had much impact on the town's life.

[18] See Collart, *Philippes*, 389-486; Davies, "Macedonian Scene", 95; Portefaix, *Sisters Rejoice*, 67; V. A. Abrahamsen, *Women and Worship at Philippi: Diana/Artemis and Other Cults in the Early Christian Era* (Portland, ME: Astarte Shell, 1995) 11. Although Pilhofer suggests, based on the inscriptional evidence, that the Thracians predominantly lived in the villages of the *territorium* and few lived in the *urbs* itself (*Philippi*, 88-9).

[19] Haenchen, *Acts*, 499; Marshall, *Acts*, 266-7; Portefaix, *Sisters Rejoice*, 73; Abrahamsen, *Women*, 23 n. 34; D. Peterlin, *Paul's Letter to the Philippians in the Light of Disunity in the Church* (NovTSup 79; Leiden: E. J. Brill, 1995) 165-6. Johnson suggests that the encounter with the women occurred *on the way* to the synagogue (*Acts*, 292), but συνελθούσαις seems to rule that out.

[20] See Peterlin, *Paul's Letter*, 165-6; Oakes, "Philippians", 45; White, "Visualizing", 246-9; cf R. R. Brewer, "The Meaning of *Politeuesthe* in Philippians 1:27" *JBL* 73 (1954) 81. There is only one late inscription concerning a synagogue, as yet unpublished (Oakes, "Philippians", 45 n. 33).

[21] White, "Visualizing", 246.

likely that the colonists lived in the township itself, or in its suburbs (and hence were effectively part of the township), especially given a history of Thracian raids early in the colony's life.[22]

On the other hand, it is also clear that significant numbers of Romans settled in villages in the *territorium* and lived alongside the natives.[23] The presence of significant numbers of monumental epitaphs on estates in the *territorium* may suggest that many colonists did settle on their plots and worked them themselves.[24] While some may have lived there, the presence of tombstones is somewhat ambiguous. They could function as markers of ownership where there were disputes.[25] It is also clear in other colonies that many lived in the town and had tenants farm their land.[26] Indeed, there is evidence of tenants and absentee landlords at Philippi, for several inscriptions refer to *actores*, or agents, involved in managing tenancies.[27]

The elite would have generally lived in the town, along with many of the Romans, although some of them did live in the villages in the *territorium*.[28] The *territorium*, however, seems to have been predominantly populated by native Thracians and Macedonians, given the use of Greek units of measurement and the persistence of Thracian cults there. Some Thracian towns are also known.[29]

---

[22] Oakes, "Philippians", 57.

[23] See, for example, Salac, "Inscriptions", ##1.4-5, 8, 14-15, 17, 23, 28-30, 32-3, 36, 40-1; 2.7, 26, 30; *CIL* 3.656; cf Collart, *Philippes*, 285-8, 412; H. W. Catling, "Archaeology in Greece" *Arch Rep* 34 (1988) 54; McRay, *Archaeology*, 287; Oakes, "Philippians", 60.

[24] See Collart, *Philippes*, 285-8; Hendrix, "Philippi", 315; Oakes, "Philippians", 62.

[25] See Keppie, *Colonisation*, 126-7.

[26] See, for example, Vergil *Ecl.* 9.9; Juvenal *Sat.* 2.2; Keppie, *Colonisation*, 125-6; cf. Portefaix, *Sisters Rejoice*, 68; Peterlin, *Paul's Letter*, 139. As suggested in section II of chapter 3 herein, the average grant of 50 *iugera* was sufficient for a veteran to live very comfortably if he tenanted his property and lived in town.

[27] For example, Salac, "Inscriptions", #2.7; cf Oakes, "Philippians", 60-1. Pilhofer also discusses an inscription from one village dealing with land leasing arrangements (*Philippi*, 80).

[28] See Collart, *Philippes*, 266-7, 472; Oakes, "Philippians", 62; cf. Stambaugh, "Social Relations", 80; Papazoglou, "Macedonia", 201; Bormann, *Philippi*, 24.

[29] See Portefaix, *Sisters Rejoice*, 69-70, 73, 104; Oakes, "Philippians", 57, 59-60; Pilhofer, *Philippi*, 88-9; cf. White, "Visualizing", 242.

Peter Oakes, however, claims that the process of colonization at Philippi resulted in a widespread dispossession of the native Thracians, Macedonians and Greeks. The bulk of these, he suggests, moved to the town and sought alternative employment in the service and manufacturing industries, along with migrants from Asia Minor.[30] Consequently, he proposes a model for the population of the township itself of 40% Roman and 60% "Greek", of whom 3% were elite, 20% were colonist farmers, 37% were in service groups, 20% were slaves and 20% were poor/destitute.[31]

Oakes also suggests the town was predominantly Greek, since those who built the forum used Greek letters as alignment markers, and the majority of inscriptions to the Egyptian gods (60%) are in Greek. He dismisses the significance of the Latin inscriptions, claiming they are found in very "Roman" areas and reflect the wealth and power of the Romans, not necessarily their numerical superiority.[32] Furthermore, he contends that the predominance of Greeks is also seen in the numbers of inscriptions in Greek that name priests (seven), compared to those in Latin (five).[33]

There are, however, serious problems with Oakes' approach. His argument presupposes a large population in the town and its *territorium* at the time of colonization. This is most unlikely, as has already been discussed. In fact, there was probably a considerable depopulation during the campaigns at Philippi.[34] He also ignores the fact that there was a large amount of *ager publicus* that was available for

---

[30] Oakes, "Philippians", 42, 49, 55-6, 61-2, 67, 76; cf. Pilhofer, *Philippi*, 86.

[31] Oakes, "Philippians", 75-7.

[32] Oakes, "Philippians", 65. On the alignment marks see Collart, *Philippes*, 305; Pilhofer, *Philippi*, 82, 85. On the Egyptian cult inscriptions see also Portefaix, *Sisters Rejoice*, 69, 115; Collart, *Philippes*, 303.

[33] Oakes, "Philippians", 65.

[34] At the battle of Philippi, Brutus actually had two legions consisting of Macedonians whom he had enlisted and trained, as well as Thracian cavalry in support. See Appian, *BCiv.* 3.79, 4.75; Cicero *Phil.* 10.13, 11.27; Plutarch *Brut.* 24; cf. Papazoglou, "Macedonia", 195; Brunt, *Man-Power*, 240, 252, 485; Peterlin, *Paul's Letter*, 160. It is likely that many of them were from Philippi, and through death and capture (and presumably subsequent slavery) there would have been a significant local depopulation. Bormann may also be right in suggesting that a number would have fled the area before (or during) the campaigns (*Philippi*, 19-20).

colonization.[35] Besides, if we assume there were 3,000 colonists (the upper limit), who would have received on average 50 *iugera* each, the total area they would have occupied was about 37,500 ha or 375 km^2.[36] This represents less than 20% of the *territorium*, and it is too small a proportion to argue for massive dispossession, especially given the substantial area of *ager publicus*. For a smaller number of colonists this is even less likely.

The presence of Greek letters as alignment markers is meaningless, since the builders were probably slaves. Besides, since these buildings are dated to the mid-second century, they may not be significant for understanding Philippi in the mid-first century. While there was a predominance of Greek inscriptions in association with the Isis cult, this simply suggests that it was popular among the predominantly Greek-speaking community and actually proves nothing regarding their numbers. He also too readily dismisses the fact that the extant inscriptions are overwhelmingly in Latin, and not all of them come from Romans. Indeed, there are twenty six inscriptions in Latin that come from people with Thracian names.[37]

The number of inscriptions that mention priests does not really prove anything. On the other hand, when the number of priests named in inscriptions is compared, the numbers are much closer — six of them have Roman names and seven have Greek names. Oakes does not take into account the fact that many of those he assumes are "Greek" are actually *liberti*, and in most cases they appear to have been strongly Romanized. Indeed, in most Roman *coloniae* the majority of those engaged in crafts and trade are *liberti*.[38]

---

[35] See Cicero, *Leg. Agr.* 2.51; Larsen, "Greece", 313; Papazoglou, "Macedonia", 196; Brunt, *Man-Power*, 246.

[36] On these figures see the discussion in section II of chapter 3 herein.

[37] See Collart, *Philippes*, 301 n. 5; Portefaix, *Sisters Rejoice*, 68 n. 89, 69 n. 110; cf. Meeks, *First Urban*, 45; Hemer, *Book*, 113 n. 30; Gill, "Macedonia", 413. However, Portefaix's argument that the Latin inscriptions by Thracians were an attempt to flatter the ruling Romans in the hope of gaining citizenship (*Sisters Rejoice*, 68) seems to lack an awareness of the process of enfranchisement and assumes a more calculating attitude that is necessary. The inscriptions simply indicate a high level of ethnic integration.

[38] See Papazoglou, "Macedonia", 200; section II of chapter 3 herein. Pilhofer *assumes* that the artisans and merchants were Thracians or Greeks (*Philippi*, 85-6). Like Oakes, he ignores the likelihood that they

Consequently, the proportion of Romans in the *urbs*, including *liberti*, would have been much higher than Oakes' model allows.[39]

There have already been some hints that there was a considerable degree of ethnic integration. Such a scenario is suggested by the number of Latin inscriptions by Thracians, the dominance of Latin, and the mix of Romans and "Greeks" in the various cults, especially the Isis cult. Furthermore, the extant inscriptions also suggest that there was considerable ethnic integration at Philippi.[40] For example, although most of the members of the Silvanus *collegium* have Roman tripartite names, their *cognomina* suggest that they come from a variety of backgrounds. A large number have *cognomina* that are Greek or indicate a servile origin, while a

---

were slaves and *liberti* and, in most cases, would have been strongly romanised. In fact, a number of *liberti* are known from inscriptions at Philippi (e.g. Lemerle, "Greques", ##1, 7, 11, 15, 17, 25) and the names of many others suggest a servile origin (see, for example, the inscription cited in Collart, *Philippes*, 414 n.1; *CIL* 3.633.2). Joshel has calculated that *liberti* make up 35.3% of artisans mentioned in Roman inscriptions and slaves make up 32.6% — that is, 67.9% come from servile origins. A further 30.6% are uncertain and could be either *liberti* or freeborn ("The Occupations", 201-2). Furthermore, Oakes' contention that there would have been a large population of migrant artisans and merchants is most implausible. The town was small and generally rural in nature, it was not a provincial capital (nor even the capital of one of the divisions of Macedonia), this stretch of the *Via Egnatia* was in a poor state of repair during the first half of the first century CE, and very little construction work was undertaken prior to the town's patronage by the Antonines. See Portefaix, *Sisters Rejoice*, 66; Bormann, *Philippi*, 27; White, "Visualizing", 49. Although some scholars claim that silver was probably still mined in the area, given the large number of silver coins minted by the first division of Macedonia (Larsen, "Greece", 324; Papazoglou, "Macedonia", 195), this may simply reflect the wealth of the first division, not the fact that silver was still mined there, nor that Philippi itself was wealthy. In other words, because first century Philippi was not politically and economically significant, it would not have attracted many migrant artisans and merchants seeking economic prosperity.

[39] Besides, the account of Paul before the magistrates at Philippi suggests that the majority of the crowd were Roman citizens. See Acts 16:21-2.

[40] For example, there is an inscription (*CIL* 3.703) found on the acropolis of a *thiasos* to *Liber Pater*, the Roman form of Dionysus, from Bithus of Tauzigis, Zipacenthus of Tauzigis, Bithicenthus of Cerzula (3 Thracians), Rufus, and Sabinus Dioscuter (2 Romans); cf Salac, "Inscriptions" #2.9. There are also eight inscriptions to Diana found on the acropolis, of which two appear to come from Thracians (Bernas, Galgestia Primilla). See Abrahamsen, *Women*, 32.

few may have come from Africa and Gaul.[41] Even more significantly, inscriptions from the villages in Philippi's *territorium* show that many people with Thracian names worshipped distinctly Roman gods and took part in *collegia* dedicated to them.[42] Overall, therefore, there appears to have been some ethnic diversity, as well as significant ethnic integration at Philippi.

---

[41] There are 65 members named in *CIL* 3.633.2. Of these, 8 are slaves (including 4 public slaves), 24 have Greek *cognomina* and/or common servile *cognomina* strongly suggesting they come from a servile background, especially since many have the same praenomina and nomina (i.e. C. Abellius Agathopus, C. Abellius Anteros, M. Alfensus Aspasius, L. Atiarius Moschos, L.Atiarius Suavis, L. Atiarius Successus, L. Atiarius Thamyrus, L. Domitius Callistus, L. Domitius Icario, L. Domitius Ikarus, L. Domitius Primigenius, L. Domitius Venerianus, T. Flavius Clymenus, M. Herennius Helenus, P. Herennius Venustus, P. Hostilius Philadelphus, L. Laelius Felix, C. Paccius Mercuriales C. l., C. Paccius Trophimus, M. Plotius Gelos, M. Publicius Primigenius, M. Varinius Chresimus, A. Velleius Onesimus, P. Vettius Aristobulus), and 17 have cognomina suggesting they were freeborn (i.e. L. Atiarius Firmus, C. Atilius Niger, _. Canuleius Crescens, T. Claudius Magnus, _. Domitius Peregrinus, C. Flavius Pudens, _. Fonteius Capito, M. Glitius Carus, _. Iulius Candidus, M. Minucius Ianuarius, L. Nutrius Valens iun., M. Plotius Valens M. f., M. Publicius Valens, P. Trosius Geminus, C. Valerius Firmus, _. Valerius Clemens, L. Volattius Firmus). Although there are 11 about whom nothing can be sure, C. Velleius Rixa appears to have a Celtic cognomen, there are two by the name of L. Volattius Urbanus — and nearly half of all those with this cognomen came from the province of Africa, and C. Decimius Germanus, who could come from either Germany, Spain or Africa. On the origin of names see Kajanto, *Cognomina* and the index of *ILS*. A few of these same members are listed in *CIL* 3.633.1, while *CIL* 3.633.3 lists some of them plus a few others. However the mix is similar. Abrahamsen's assumption that the members were all *liberti* or slaves is clearly wrong (*Women*, 37; cf Collart, *Philippes*, 405-8). She also suggests that inscriptions 1-3 come from the second century CE (*Women*, 37), but she offers no justification. In fact, some of the names suggest a mid-first century CE date and, in any case, the Silvanus sanctuary where the inscriptions are located probably dates from the Augustan or Tiberian period. See Davies, "Macedonian Scene", 101; Portefaix, *Sisters Rejoice*, 72 n. 134; Hendrix, "Philippi", 315. A similar mix is found in the list in Collart, "Inscriptions (1)" #28.

[42] For example, an inscription to Diana Minerva in one village is dedicated by people with a mix of Greek, Thracian and Roman names (Salac, "Inscriptions" #1.24); there is also an inscription to Jupiter Fulmen (a Gallic god), Mercury and Myndrytus from two or three Thracians, written in Latin (ibid., #1.25).

4. Social Relations

Given the nature of its colonization, it is unlikely that first century Philippi was an egalitarian society. As suggested in the previous chapter, in planning a colony the commissioners sought to create a stable oligarchic community and generally designated the colony's first magistrates (and hence the basis of its future elite). Since Philippi was a veteran colony, its social structures would have reflected a military pattern. So at the time of colonization, there would have been a clear social stratification of army officers (who were presumably chosen as magistrates and decurions), Praetorians, other soldiers and colonists, some *liberti*, non-enfranchised natives and slaves. With successive generations a standard Roman stratification would have evolved, with an elite (presumably the descendants of the colonists), other Romans, *liberti*, and natives. As in other colonies, it is likely that the elite created strong social boundaries to restrict access to their group.[43]

Since Philippi was a Roman *colonia*, formal patronage ties would have been very important. As already noted, the inscriptions refer to a significant number of *liberti*, many of whom probably had former masters (now patrons) within the colony itself, and there is some evidence of tenancy arrangements.[44] The fact that P. Hostilius Philadelphus, who appears to be a *libertus*, managed to be elected *aedile* also suggests that he was well connected, and is further evidence of strong patronal ties within the colony.[45]

---

[43] See sections III.2 of chapter 3 and I.4 of chapter 5 herein. As Pilhofer notes, all of those who served as *duum viri* or *decuriones* in the first century were Romans (*Philippi*, 91).

[44] For example, C. Paccius Mercuriales and C. Paccius Mercuriales C.l. (*CIL* 3.633.2), C. Firmius Pater, C. Firmius, Sex. Firmius & L. Firmius Eros L.l. erected a funerary inscription for their patron (Salac, "Inscriptions" #1.17). Two of the women who belonged to the Bacchus *collegium*, Pomponia Hilara and Marronia Eutychia, have *cognomina* suggesting they were of servile origin and *nomina* that are quite common at Philippi — cf. a P. Marronius Narcissus who was aedile (Collart, *Philippes*, 414 n. 1; *CIL* 3.654-5; Salac, "Inscriptions" #2.8; cf. also Kajanto, *Cognomina*; Mora, *Prosopographia Isiaca* ##1173-6).

[45] See *CIL* 3.633.1-2. Several inscriptions attest to the presence at Philippi of *seviri Augustales*, the Imperial cult positions filled by *liberti* (*CIL* 3.655, 657, 7341, 7344; cf. Salac, "Inscriptions", 73-4; Collart, "Inscriptions (2)", 412; Bormann, *Philippi*, 45-6). It is likely that to be elected to such a position, a *libertus* would also need to be well-connected.

The Silvanus *collegium* is a good example of the way that people across the social spectrum interacted at Philippi. In the first inscription from this *collegium* there are seven members named (also named in the second inscription), who are probably group patrons, although L. Domitius Primigenius and P. Hostilius Philadelphus seem to be *liberti*. There are also three others in the main list whose names strongly suggest they were from the freeborn elite, and at least two appear to be freeborn plebeians.[46] As noted above, there were a large number of *liberti* in the *collegium* as well as four public slaves and four slaves belonging to members of the *collegium*.[47] This suggests a considerable interaction between members of the various social strata at Philippi.

5. Political Features

Philippi was one of only four *coloniae* in Macedonia that received the extra privilege of the grant of *ius Italicum*.[48] This probably contributed to the strong Romanness of the town, and the citizens' pride in their Romanness. In light of this, few of the native Macedonians and Thracians, if any, would have been enfranchised.[49] Unlike Corinth and Thessalonica, however, the town was not the provincial capital, nor even the leading city of the first district.[50]

As a *colonia*, Philippi had a standard Roman administration with *duoviri, aediles, quaestores*, an *ordo*

---

[46] In *CIL* 3.633.2, M. Glitius Carus, T. Claudius Magnus, and _. Fonteius Capito have common elite *cognomina*, while _. Canuleius Crescens and _. Valerius Clemens have common plebeian ones (Kajanto, *Cognomina*, 234-5, 261, 263, 284; Peterlin, *Paul's Letter*, 168); cf. *CIL* 3.633.1.

[47] The public slaves are Orinus Coloniae, Phoebus Coloniae, Phoibus Coloniae and Tharsa Coloniae; the other slaves are Crescens Abelli (belonging to one of the three C. Abellii listed), Hermeros Metrodori (master not listed) and Chrysio Pacci (belonging to one of the three C. Paccii listed). See *CIL* 3.633.2.

[48] The others were Cassandreum, Dium and Dyrrachium, while the only other Triumviral *coloniae* in Macedonia were Byllis and Pella. See McRay, *Archaeology*, 283-4; White, "Visualizing", 242.

[49] See section III.2 of chapter 3 herein.

[50] This is despite Luke's claim that Philippi was πρώτη[ς] μερίδος τῆς Μακεδονίας πόλις (Acts 16:12). As most scholars suggest, this is probably a reference to its being a city of the first division of Macedonia. See Sherwin-White, *Roman Law*, 93; Haenchen, *Acts*, 494; Marshall, *Acts*, 266; Hemer, *Book*, 113; Johnson, *Acts*, 292; cf *TCGNT*, 393-5.

decurionum and a number of official priests.[51] There is evidence of one *libertus* who was elected to office but, unlike Corinth where the colonists were predominantly *liberti*, the fact that the colonists were predominantly veterans tends to suggest that such a practice was not common here. Like other Roman *coloniae*, the average citizen would have had limited political power given the strongly hierarchical and oligarchic system. Patronage ties would have been politically important.

6. Religious Profile

The religious profile of Philippi is mixed, with both Roman and Thracian strands (the gods and cults of the Greek residents appear to have been subsumed under their Roman equivalents after colonization).[52] From inscriptions, shrines, rock reliefs and coins, the Roman gods worshipped included Jupiter, Juno, Minerva, Diana, Mercury, Silvanus, Bacchus/ Liber Pater with Libera and Hercules, Venus, Cupid, and Mars. A range of "abstract" gods were also worshipped including Fortuna, Victoria and various *genii*, including the *Genius* of the Colony.[53] The prominent Thracian gods were

---

[51] See Portefaix, *Sisters Rejoice*, 65; Abrahamsen, *Women*, 11.

[52] See Collart, *Philippes*, 392; Portefaix, *Sisters Rejoice*, 70, 98; Bormann, *Philippi*, 64; Abrahamsen, *Women*, 15; cf. Papazoglou, "Macedonia", 204. Portefaix argues that south of the Via Egnatia the gods were generally Roman, while to the north of the Via they were predominantly Thracian or Greek (*Sisters Rejoice*, 71). But she ignores the sanctuary of Silvanus to the north of the road. Although she notes that the rock reliefs on the acropolis predominantly depict Diana, and ones depicting Minerva and Jupiter have also been found, she fails to take this into consideration (ibid., 72). There was also a meeting place for an Isis *collegium* in the town center, and a shrine of Apollo Komaios and Artemis found just to the south east of the forum. See Collart, *Philippes*, 446-7; A. H. B Megaw, "Archaeology in Greece" *JHS Sup* (1963) 24.

[53] See, for example, *CIL* 3.633, 686; Salac, "Inscriptions", #1.33; Collart, "Inscriptions (1)", #6; Lemerle, "Greques", ##4, 7, 45; idem, "Nouvelles inscriptions latines de Philippi" *BCH* 61 (1937) #7; Burnett, *Roman Provincial Coins* #1.1651; Megaw, "Archaeology" 24; H. W. Catling, "Archaeology in Greece" *Arch Rep* 32 (1986) 70; R. A. Tomlinson, "Archaeology in Greece" *Arch Rep* 41 (1995) 48; Collart, *Philippes*, 414 n. 1; Lazarides, "Philippi", 705; Portefaix, *Sisters Rejoice*, 71, 98-101; Abrahamsen, *Women*, 13-18; Bormann, *Philippi*, 6. Most of the 17 inscriptions found have been to Liber Pater (not Dionysus) and in most cases he is associated with Libera and Hercules. A sanctuary to the three has been found south of the forum, underneath the second century baths. See Abrahamsen, *Women*, 13.

Dionysus, Bendis, and the Thracian Horsemen. These gods tend to be found chiefly in the *territorium*.[54] A number of Oriental gods were also found, especially Isis, Magna Mater and Cybele.[55]

Healing gods appear to have been particularly important in the town. Isis, Serapis and Diana all appear to have been worshipped as such, given the finds of terracotta body parts dedicated to them. An Asclepion has also been found in one of the villages, dated from the fourth century BCE, but with evidence of Roman use.[56] The Macedonian interest in the "cult of the dead" also appears to have been strong in the villages of Philippi's *territorium*.[57]

Nevertheless, Diana appears to have been one of the most popular gods at Philippi, given inscriptions and especially the large number of rock reliefs depicting her. Valerie Abrahamsen suggests that the quality of the reliefs probably indicate that they were made by the lower classes and that she was primarily their god.[58] However, since most of the reliefs probably date from the second century CE,[59] too

---

[54] Portefaix, *Sisters Rejoice*, 70-3, 98; Hendrix, "Philippi", 314; Abrahamsen, *Women*, 15; cf. Papazoglou, "Macedonia", 204; Lemerle, "Nouvelles inscriptions" #10. There was also an oracle of Thracian Dionysus on Mount Pangaion, to the south (Herodotus 7.111; cf Hendrix, "Philippi", 314), but whether this was still in existence in the first century CE cannot be known. Bormann claims that there was no religious pluralism in the town in the first century CE, arguing that the Isis sanctuary should be dated to either the second or third centuries (*Philippi*, 64-5; cf. Abrahamsen, *Women*, 25). But, as Oakes suggests, Bormann's argument for "a lack of oriental cults in the first century seems an argument from a rather dubious silence", since coins from the Claudian period were found in the sanctuary, suggesting at least a first century dating ("Philippians", 235). Besides, it is likely that the Egyptian cults were brought to the town by the Thasian settlers, since an Isis sanctuary has been found there (ibid., 237).

[55] Collart, *Philippes*, 444-7; Lazarides, "Philippi", 705; Pandermalis, "Monuments", 212; Portefaix, *Sisters Rejoice*, 71, 115, 118-19; Abrahamsen, *Women*, 15-18, 34; cf. Papazoglou, "Macedonia", 207; Bormann, *Philippi*, 55.

[56] See H. W. Catling, "Archaeology in Greece" *Arch Rep* 22 (1976) 22; Portefaix, *Sisters Rejoice*, 81-2, 118-19; Abrahamsen, *Women*, 34.

[57] Particularly prominent was the rite of *parakausis* performed on the *Rosalia* (the day of the roses), when tombs were decorated with roses, and offerings were made. See Collart, *Philippes*, 474-85; Larsen, "Greece", 491; Papazoglou, "Macedonia", 205-6.

[58] Abrahamsen, *Women*, 25-6.

[59] See Portefaix, *Sisters Rejoice*, 72; Abrahamsen, *Women*, 25-6; Bormann, *Philippi*, 66.

much cannot be read into this regarding the worship of Diana in Paul's time. By the same token, the Silvanus cult at Philippi appears to have attracted people from across the social spectrum, although Silvanus was particularly popular with *liberti* and was predominantly an agricultural god, the patron of shepherds and woodcutters.[60]

Probably the most important cult, on the evidence of inscriptions and coins, was the Imperial cult. Numerous inscriptions attest to a range of cult personnel: *flamines, seviri,* priests of *divus Augustus,* and priestesses of *diva Augusta* (Livia). Indeed, the two sanctuaries at the east and west ends of the forum were probably both dedicated to the Imperial cult.[61] Furthermore, it is possible that many other gods were connected with the Imperial cult, especially foreign ones such as the Egyptian gods and Cybele.[62]

While the *territorium* may have been predominantly Thracian in its worship practices, it is likely that there was a predominantly Roman religious mentality within the township itself. Admittedly, the bulk of the Isis inscriptions are in Greek, but there is no evidence for a mystery cult associated with it. It was largely a healing cult.[63] This may reflect a more Roman approach. However, the other gods and cults found there are strongly Roman or Romanized, not least by being linked to the Imperial cult. Furthermore, the *liberti* in the town (who were probably a significant proportion of the population of the township) overwhelmingly seem to have been strongly Romanized and to have adopted Roman gods.

In summary, therefore, in the first century CE Philippi was a small rural town with a large *territorium*. It was very

---

[60] See Dyson, *Community,* 128-9.

[61] See *CIL* 3.386, 650-1, 655, 660; Salac, "Inscriptions" #2.29; Collart, "Inscriptions (1)" ##13a, 27; idem, "Inscriptions (2) #9; Lemerle, "Greques" #6; idem, "Nouvelles inscriptions" #3; Burnett, *Roman Provincial Coins* ##1.1650, 1653; cf. M. Sève & P. Weber, "Un Monument honorifique au forum de Philippes" *BCH* 112 (1988) 468-70; Bormann, *Philippi,* 41-4.

[62] See Bormann, *Philippi,* 55-9. This is suggested by the reference to a M. Velleius as a *dendrophorus* and an *Augustalis* — the link of these two is known elsewhere. See Lemerle, "Greques", 466-71 and inscription #7. There is also a dedication to Isis on behalf of the Imperial household. See P. Collart, "Le sanctuaire des dieux égyptiens à Philippes" *BCH* 53 (1929) 83-7. However, even Roman gods were specifically linked to the Imperial cult, such as one dedication to Mercury Augustus (Lemerle, "Greques" #4).

[63] See Bormann, *Philippi,* 57-8

much a community, with close and very public living and a strong integration of the various aspects of city life. The town's planning and the epigraphic evidence suggest that there was a reasonable association and interaction of different social and ethnic groups. Patronal ties were probably very important in this.

Although there was probably a modest ethnic diversity, there is no evidence of any significant Jewish presence in the town. The population of the township itself was probably comprised of Romans and *liberti*, possibly some of the native Thracians and Macedonians, and maybe some Greek immigrants. Given the town's overall insignificance, the number of these migrants would have been quite small. The town was a *colonia iuris Italici*, and hence had a typical Roman pattern of government: elitist and oligarchic. Nevertheless, the Roman-style patronage system would have meant that there were relational ties between the elite and the ordinary residents.

There is a degree of religious diversity at Philippi. Various Macedonian and Thracian gods and religious practices probably dominated the *territorium*, although there is some evidence of Roman cults there. But in the township itself, the gods and the cults appear to be very Roman, along with a few oriental cults (that were also popular among Romans elsewhere). The latter may well have been linked to the Imperial cult, which appears to have been dominant in the town. Overall, there was probably a strong Roman religious mentality, since the *liberti* seem to have been strongly Romanized and worshipped Roman gods, and those Thracians in the town seem to have done likewise. Healing cults are also particularly prominent.

II. THE CHRISTIAN COMMUNITY AT PHILIPPI

The Christian community at Philippi will be examined according to the three characteristics used in the previous two chapters to reconstruct the natures of the Thessalonian and Corinthian churches. That is, the characteristics that will be considered are the ethnic composition, the social profile, and the size of the church. These three aspects will be examined because they are the most important for understanding the relationship between the Christian and civic communities and the development of conflict at Philippi.

1. Ethnic Composition

In Philippians 1:1, Paul addresses the letter πᾶσιν τοῖς ἁγίοις ἐν Χριστῷ Ἰησοῦ τοῖς οὖσιν ἐν Φιλίπποις. This uses a locative expression that gives no clue as to the composition of the church. Although Paul does refer to them as Φιλιππήσιοι in 4:15, Oakes suggests this does not necessarily mean that they were citizens of the town. He contends that the term may have been used generally for its residents by the mid first-century CE since it appeared on the coins.[64] But this is unlikely. Given the town's history, the citizens would have taken great pride in their citizenship. Rather, Davorin Peterlin may be correct that in using Φιλιππήσιοι, "Paul had in mind earliest Philippian Christians of ethnic Roman extraction for whom precisely the Latin form of the name of their city carried particular significance".[65]

Nevertheless, it may be that, as in the case of his use of Κορίνθοι (2 Cor 6:11) and Γαλάται (Gal 3:1), Paul is moved by emotion and is not careful about his language.[66] While that is very likely, there are hints in the letter that the church did include people who were Roman citizens and residents of the town (whether freeborn or freed), and who did fit this title. Specifically, the deliberate contrast that Paul draws between Christ and the Emperor, and between the Roman Empire and the "Kingdom of God", strongly suggests that the recipients of the letter are largely Roman citizens.[67]

---

[64] Oakes, "Philippians", 83-4.

[65] Peterlin, *Paul's Letter*, 167. If, as it will be argued later, the church was comprised of freeborn Romans, *liberti*, and some slaves, Paul's reference to them as Φιλιππήσιοι fits all but the last group. But the context in which it is used in 4:15 suggests it refers only to those of free status. It is doubtful that few ordinary slaves could have contributed to Paul's support. On the other hand, those who were members of the *familia Caesaris* at Philippi may have had sufficient funds to contribute and they could conceivably be included in the term Φιλιππήσιοι since they were regarded as being owned by the colony. For example, in the Silvanus inscription such slaves are named as ____ *coloniae*.

[66] See section II.1 of chapter 4 herein.

[67] Something similar is suggested by B. Witherington III, *Friendship and Finances in Philippi: The Letter of Paul to the Philippians* (Valley Forge, PA: TPI, 1994) 23; G. D. Fee, *Paul's Letter to the Philippians* (NICNT; Grand Rapids: Eerdmans, 1995) 162.

This contrast is most evident in Paul's use of πολιτεύεσθε (1:27) and πολίτευμα (3:20).[68]

A few scholars have suggested that Paul's reference to the *familia Caesaris* (οἱ ἐκ τῆς Καίσαρος οἰκίας) in 4:22 implies that this group was represented in the church.[69] While Paul may have singled out greetings from Christians of this group in Rome to make a specific point (namely, that despite conflict and oppression there had been success right "under the Emperor's nose"), the fact that he chose them is surely more than coincidental. Rather, it is likely that by referring to Christians from the *familia Caesaris* Paul wants to pass on greetings from one group of people to another who knew each other.[70]

All of those named in Paul's letter, and in association with the Philippian church in Acts (Clement, Epaphroditus, Euodia, Syntyche, Lydia and the jailer), have Greek or Roman names and associations. But the actual Greek names of the Christians tend to suggest they come from a servile origin.[71] Those with Greek names were probably *liberti*, since Paul normally moved among the artisan class and most of them would have been *liberti* at Philippi.

There is little to suggest that there were Jews within the church. As noted above, it is not clear whether there was

---

[68] Oakes claims these terms can be explained by the Romanness of the Philippian *context* ("Philippians", 83-4), but his argument is based on his model of few Romans in the town and plays down the extent of the contrast with the Empire. Although the terms πολίτευμα and πολιτεύεσθε will be discussed in more detail in section IV.3 below, his attempt to play down the sense of "citizenship" in the latter term is without justification. Besides, for the contrast to be meaningful in terms of competing for their allegiance, most needed to have been citizens.

[69] See Brewer, "The Meaning", 81; Witherington, *Friendship*, 26, 137; Peterlin, *Paul's Letter*, 150-1. Witherington includes (*Friendship*, 137) Lydia in this, but this is unlikely as will be discussed below. If Luke's account of the conversion of the gaoler in Acts 16:30-4 is to be trusted, then it is clear that some members of the *familia Caesaris* were in the Philippian church. See my, "The Significance of the Change from Οἶκος to Οἰκία in Luke's Account of the Philippian Gaoler (Acts 16.30-4)" *NTS* 41 (1995) 293, 296; cf. Peterlin, *Paul's Letter*, 143.

[70] Peterlin, *Paul's Letter*, 150-1.

[71] See Witherington, *Friendship*, 107-8; Abrahamsen, *Women*, 84; Peterlin, *Paul's Letter*, 167-9; *contra* Portefaix who suggests the church was probably mainly Greek in origin (*Sisters Rejoice*, 137). Even Oakes admits that Syntyche is probably a servile name ("Philippians", 82). That the Christians were *liberti* and artisans will be discussed in more detail in the next section of this chapter.

a Jewish community at Philippi in Paul's time, and Luke does not suggest that Paul converted any Jews. Lydia, his only convert from the "synagogue", is really presented as a "God-fearer" (σεβομένη τὸν θεόν — Acts 16:14). Furthermore, nothing in the letter itself suggests a Jewish presence. There is little that is Jewish in content or tone, Paul does not cite from the OT, nor does he use midrashic arguments (as he does in Romans, 1 Corinthians and Galatians).[72]

Indeed, Paul scarcely even alludes to the OT. The majority of scholars claim that there is an allusion to the suffering servant of Isaiah (Isa 45, 52-3) in the "hymn" of Phil 2:6-11.[73] But the "hymn" is thoroughly Greek in nature and content.[74] Elsewhere, Paul does not draw on Isaiah's

---

[72] See Portefaix, *Sisters Rejoice*, 137; L. M. White, "Morality between Two Worlds: A Paradigm of Friendship in Philippians" in D. L. Balch *et al.*, eds., *Greeks, Romans and Christians* (Minneapolis: Fortress, 1990) 205-6.

[73] See, for example, F. W. Beare, *A Commentary on the Epistle to the Philippians* (BNTC; 3rd ed.; London: A. & C. Black, 1973) 86-7; S. E. Fowl, *The Story of Christ in the Ethics of Paul: An Analysis of the Function of the Hymnic Material in the Pauline Corpus* (JSNTSup 36; Sheffield: JSOT Press, 1990) 61, 67; P. S. Minear, "Singing and Suffering in Philippi", in R. T. Fortna & B. R. Gaventa, eds., *The Conversation Continues* (Nashville: Abingdon, 1990) 213; L. G. Bloomquist, *The Function of Suffering in Philippians* (JSNTSup 78; Sheffield: JSOT Press, 1993) 162-3; Reumann, "Contributions", 444; Witherington, *Friendship*, 68.

[74] See C. J. Robbins, "Rhetorical Structure of Philippians 2:6-11" *CBQ* 42 (1980) 82; White, "Morality", 205-6. Some scholars have argued for a Semitic original or precursor for the "hymn". See, especially, J. A. Fitzmyer, "The Aramaic Background of Philippians 2:6-11" *CBQ* 50 (1988) 470-83. But if so, we would expect different vocabulary (see White, "Morality", 208), and the phrase οὐχ ἁρπαγμὸν ἡγήσατο in 2:6 is "a precisely nuanced idiom" used in a "characteristically Hellenistic way". See N. T. Wright, *The Climax of the Covenant: Christ and Law in Pauline Theology* (Minneapolis: Fortress, 1991), 97-8. According to C. Basevi and J. Chapa, "the presence of Greek rhythmical clauses at the end of the sentences and the strong rhythmical structure of the text makes it very implausible to regard this text as a translation", especially since other known Greek translations of Hebrew poetry, such as the Psalms and Canticles, tried to keep the Hebrew rhythm ("Philippians 2.6-11: The Rhetorical Function of a Pauline 'Hymn'" in S. E. Porter & T. H. Olbricht, eds., *Rhetoric and the New Testament* [JSNTSup 90; Sheffield: JSOT Press, 1993] 342). Besides, the "hymn" fits the present context too well to consider it as a separate composition. See Wright, *Climax*, 98; Basevi & Chapa, "Rhetorical Function", 342-3; *contra* Reumann, who suggests that the "hymn" originated in the Philippian church ("Contributions", 453-5).

Servant for his christology, and given the way in which Isa 52-3 served as a proof text in the early church, if Paul had this in mind the linguistic links between them would have been stronger than they are. As Pobee argues, "where there appear to be similarities and coincidences, they are not in regard to the main and obvious characteristics of the Servant".[75] Paul may allude to Job 13:16 in Phil 1:19, to Deut 32:5 in Phil 2:15, and to Israel's grumbling in the Wilderness (Ex 15-17, Num 14-17) in Phil 2:14.[76] But it is not at all clear that, even if these were intended, the Philippians understood them as such. In other words, Paul's OT allusions here are consistent with what we would expect *from* someone like Paul, and not what we would necessarily expect if there were Jews in the church.

Consequently, it is likely that the church at Philippi was entirely non-Jewish in make-up. Furthermore, some of the terminology Paul uses, and the intentional contrast he makes between being a Christian and being a Roman citizen, suggest the Christians were predominantly Roman citizens together with public slaves who had a significant sense of allegiance to Rome. The bulk of those named have Greek names, but this probably suggests the church was largely comprised of *liberti*, and as suggested above, in most cases Philippian *liberti* were well Romanized.

2. Social Profile

A social profile of the Philippian church can be constructed using two pieces of data. The first is the people Paul names in his letter and those associated with the church according to Acts, and the second is the clues Paul provides in the letter itself.[77] Both of these will be examined in turn.

---

[75] Pobee, *Persecution*, 51.

[76] See, for example, G. F. Hawthorne, *Philippians* (WBC; Waco, TX: Word, 1983) 101; O'Brien, *Commentary*, 290, 294; Bloomquist, *Suffering*, 154; Witherington, *Friendship*, 72; Fee, *Philippians*, 243, 245.

[77] Admittedly, we do need to be careful about relying on those named in Acts, as has been suggested in the previous two chapters (cf. Meeks, *First Urban*, 61; Portefaix, *Sisters Rejoice*, 135). Support for the Acts 16 narrative is strong, apart from the account of the earthquake at the gaol (e.g. Haenchen, *Acts*, 500-1; J.-F. Collange, *The Epistle of Saint Paul to the Philippians* [London: Epworth, 1979] 1-2; Oakes, "Philippians", 45; and to some extent White, "Visualizing", 236-7). Abrahamsen claims that since Lydia is not mentioned in Paul's letter, "this story must be viewed critically and Lydia placed in the category of

Of those cited in the letter, only Clement (4:3) has a Roman name. We know nothing about him except that he has some sort of leadership role in the church. This may suggest that he was reasonably well-to-do. But it is an unwarranted assumption, for the name Clement (*Clemens*) was one that was usually given to freeborn plebeians.[78] Peterlin suggests that he may have been of "military stock",[79] but there is nothing to support this, and it is unlikely that there were any in the church who were descendants of the original colonists. Certainly nothing remotely hints at his being a member of the ruling elite.

Some scholars suggest that Euodia and Syntyche (4:2) were among the merchants and artisans who had migrated from Asia Minor. They also contend that since these women are named as Paul's co-workers, and appear to be leaders in the church, they must have had a degree of independence and wealth.[80] Their names, however, appear to reflect a

fiction or symbolism" (*Women*, 19). But this is probably going too far. White suggests that while the outline is factual the detail cannot be substantiated ("Real World", 236-7). However, there is nothing in the account of Lydia that makes it at all improbable, unlike the account of the earthquake at the gaol.

[78] See the listing in Kajanto, *Cognomina*, 263; cf. Peterlin, *Paul's Letter*, 168. This *cognomen* is also found in the list of the Silvanus *collegium* (*CIL* 3.633.2).

[79] Peterlin, *Paul's Letter*, 168-9; cf. N. A. Dahl, "Euodia and Syntyche and Paul's Letter to the Philippians" in L. M. White & O. L. Yarbrough, eds., *The Social World of the First Christians* (Minneapolis: Fortress, 1995) 3. While there is a centurion by the name of Clement during Tiberius' reign (Tacitus *Ann.* 1.28), there is nothing to suggest it was a common name among those of military stock. In fact, the derivation of the name, and its connotations, make this most improbable.

[80] See, for example, Meeks, *First Urban*, 57; Garland, "Composition", 172; Portefaix, *Sisters Rejoice*, 137 n. 11; Witherington, *Friendship*, 108; Dahl, "Euodia and Syntyche", 4; Peterlin, *Paul's Letter*, 123-4. There is no reason for assuming that the two women were the leaders of different house churches (*contra* Peterlin, *Paul's Letter*, 127; Witherington, *Friendship*, 108) since nothing in the letter suggests there were the sort of problems here as in the Corinthian church. Witherington claims that "in Greek and Roman oratory it was common not to mention women by name, unless they were either very notable or very notorious. One would suspect that this too indicates that Euodia and Syntyche were women of status and of great importance for the congregation in Philippi" (*Friendship*, 108). His first observation is correct, but he has chosen the "notable" interpretation, ignoring the "notorious". Given Paul's argument, especially in the context of the letter (to be discussed in more detail below), the second is preferable. He names them because

servile origin, and not many *libertae* at Philippi would have been very wealthy.[81] Besides, Paul's description of them as "fellow soldiers" (συνήθλησαν) means they assisted Paul in his mission, presumably as preachers, but it does not necessarily prove that they were designated leaders within the church.[82] The same could be said of Epaphroditus. His name is consistent with his being a *libertus*, for although it was not a particularly common name, those so named were commonly of servile origin.[83] The jailer (Acts 16:27-34) was most likely a public slave. It is doubtful that he was very wealthy, although he appears to be the warden.[84]

It is generally assumed that Lydia was a wealthy merchant who had migrated from Asia Minor. This is based on her being a dealer in "purple" (πορφυρόπωλις — Acts 16:14), and the assumption that she had a large house since it would have been socially inappropriate for a single woman to host male guests otherwise.[85] She is generally thought to be single, presumably widowed, since her husband is not

their behavior is reprehensible and he shames them as an example to others. The claim that σύζυγε (4:3) is a personal name is unconvincing. See Fee, *Philippians*, 392-3; *contra* Peterlin, *Paul's Letter*, 120.

[81] There are only four known occurrences of the name Euodia. Two of those are *liberta*, and a third is married to a Jew at Rome (and hence presumably of low, if not servile, status also). See *New Docs.* 4.178-9; *IG* 5.2.277; *CIJ* 1.391. Although the name Syntyche is otherwise unknown (which is in itself suggestive), as Oakes notes, it "sounds like various slave names" ("Philippians", 82). Even Witherington admits that they are both probably *libertae* (*Friendship*, 107-8).

[82] Pfitzner, *Agon Motif*, 161. That theyn are portrayed as preachers need not imply that the church at Philippi as a whole was engaged in proclamation (*contra* I. H. Marshall, "The Theology of Philippians" in K. P. Donfried & I. H. Marshall, *The Theology of the Shorter Pauline Letters* [Cambridge: Cambridge University Press, 1993] 157).

[83] See the indices of *ILS* and *SIGLM*.

[84] See de Vos, "The Significance", 293-5; cf. Peterlin, *Paul's Letter*, 143. Oakes, however, claims he was a *libertus* since Luke implies he "owns" his own house, and because of the use of πάσιν in 16:32 ("Philippians", 82). But as a public slave, and especially as a minor official such as the prison warden, he would have had his own residence — the phrase need not imply he *owned* the house, and it is doubtful that many *liberti* would have owned their own homes. Oakes has also ignored my argument that πάσιν here does not refer to the gaoler's own household.

[85] See, for example, Haenchen, *Acts*, 491, 499; Meeks, *First Urban*, 61; Portefaix, *Sisters Rejoice*, 137 n. 12; Johnson, *Acts*, 292-3, 297; Abrahamsen, *Women*, 94; Oakes, "Philippians", 82; Peterlin, *Paul's Letter*, 158-9.

mentioned and it is said to be ὁ οἶκος αὐτῆς (Acts 16:15).[86]
While she may well have been a widow, nothing in the text
gives any clue as to the sort of house she had.[87] It is possible
that the missionaries slept with the few slaves who worked in
the business, or that they slept in the workshop part of the
house itself. In any case, if it was inappropriate for a single
woman to host men (although it is doubtful that hosting four
men was seen in the same light as hosting only one man), it
would not matter what size her house was.

The assumption that Lydia was wealthy is based on the
presumption that she dealt in *murex* or marine purple. This is
most unlikely, since this industry, being an Imperial
monopoly,[88] would not have been organized in an insignificant town like Philippi that was not actually on the
coast. Rather, she would have dealt in garments dyed with
the madder root, the so-called "Turkey Red", an industry that
is well known in association with Thyatira. Unlike *murex*-
dyeing, this did not require much capital investment and the
returns were also considerably lower.[89]

It is most likely that she too was a *liberta*. Most of those
described as πορφυρόπωλεις or *purpurariae* are known to be
liberti.[90] Many were public slaves engaged in the *murex*
trade. Yet it is still likely that Lydia was a freedwoman for
geographical names, like Λυδία, were usually given to slaves
and the fact that her occupation is recorded suggests she was
not well-to-do.[91] Even if she was above average, compared to
other artisans and merchants in Philippi, she need not have

---

[86] Marshall, *Acts*, 268; Oakes, "Philippians", 82; Abrahamsen, *Women*, 84.

[87] See White, "Visualizing", 245.

[88] See *New Docs* 2#3 and the discussion on pp. 26-8 therein. I will
use # to refer to texts cited in *New Docs* and page numbers to refer to
commentary on those texts.

[89] See *New Docs* 3.53; Homer *Il.* 4.141-2; Strabo *Geog.* 12.8.16; cf.
Hemer, *Book*, 114-15; Peterlin, *Paul's Letter*, 156; White, "Visualizing",
244.

[90] See, for example, *CIL* 6.4.3; *IGRR* 4.107; *New Docs.* 2.27. See
also Joshel, "The Occupations", 165-6.

[91] Hemer contends that while it is an appropriate name for
someone from a servile origin, there are two inscriptions where it is the
cognomen of well-to-do women, e.g. Iulia Lydia from Sardis and Iulia
Lydia Laternae from Ephesus (*Book*, 114; cf. *New Docs* 3.54; *SEG*
28.869, 928). In both cases, however, the women appear to be from
servile stock given their *nomina*. However, the specific reference to the
occupation of the Lydia in Acts 16 strongly suggest that she is a *liberta*.

been very wealthy. Nothing suggests she was a member of the elite.[92]

Thus, none of those mentioned in either Philippians or Acts appears to be a member of the elite, and it is doubtful that any were very wealthy. Apart from Clement, who was most likely a freeborn commoner, and the gaoler, who was a public slave, the others all seem to be *liberti*. This is consistent with the sort of people Paul would have contacted at Philippi. Generally, he would not have met many living in the *territorium*, but he would have preached to the artisans and merchants working near the forum. Such a pattern is known elsewhere.[93] It would also make sense for him to concentrate his mission on those with whom he had most in common. Furthermore, the amount of commercial language that Paul uses in 4:10-20, which he assumes they will understand, supports this idea.[94]

---

[92] Similarly, Peterlin, *Paul's Letter*, 159-60.

[93] See Oakes, "Philippians", 25, 44-5; Peterlin, *Paul's Letter*, 138-9, 160, 169; cf. Hock, *Social Context*. Although there is nothing to suggest that he did work here, as his did at Thessalonica and Corinth, if he did stay with Lydia then he would have still been mixing in artisan circles.

[94] See Meeks, *First Urban*, 67; Peterlin, *Paul's Letter*, 153. J. P. Sampley suggests that this language in 4:10-20 shows that Paul and the Philippian Christians had entered into a formal business contract, known as *societas*, whereby he preached and they met his financial needs (*Pauline Partnership in Christ: Christian Community and Commitment in Light of Roman Law* [Philadelphia: Fortress, 1980] 51-3). He is followed by P. Perkins ("Christology, Friendship and Status: The Rhetoric of Philippians" *SBLSP* [1987] 515-16) and, with some modification, by B. J. Capper ("Paul's Dispute with Philippi: Understanding Paul's Argument in Phil 1-2 from His Thanks in 4:10-20" *TZ* 49 [1993] 193-203). There are, however, serious flaws in the theory. It is not at all clear that κοινωνία actually was the equivalent of *societas*. Besides, the κοινωνία in Philippians includes God (1:5-6), not just Paul and the Philippians. See White, "Morality", 212; Geoffrion, *Rhetorical Purpose*, 87; Reumann, "Contributions", 441 n. 14; Witherington, *Friendship*, 118-19. The plural in 2 Cor 11:8-9 also suggests Paul did not accept support from just the Philippian church, as Sampley's model presupposes. See B. Holmberg, *Paul and Power: The Structure of Authority in the Primitive Church as Reflected in the Pauline Epistles* (ConBNT 11; Lund: C. W. K. Gleerup, 1978) 94; cf. Reumann, "Contributions", 440-1; Witherington, *Friendship*, 124. The explanation of this language in terms of Greco-Roman ideas of "friendship", as advocated by White ("Morality", 210-11) and S. K. Stowers ("Friends and Enemies in the Politics of Heaven: Reading Theology in Philippians" in J. M. Bassler, ed., *Pauline Theology, Volume I* [Minneapolis: Fortress, 1991] 107-8), is better in accounting for the relationship between them. Nevertheless, the association of the

At the same time, it is most unlikely that there were any members of the elite, nor even any really wealthy members of the church. He would not have had access to them since he did not come with any recommendations.[95] Nor are there the sorts of problems associated with elite and wealthy members as in Corinth. Indeed, the fact that he openly accepts their support, especially given the Roman context of Philippi and the importance of patronage ties in Roman culture, suggests they were not in a position to regard any gifts to him as if they were his patron.[96] In other words, Paul and they would have been of the same general status-level: subsistence-level artisans.

Paul's reference to the poverty of the Macedonian Christians (2 Cor 8:1-2), which presumably included the Philippians, suggests that they were not, on the whole, wealthy. While this text is ambiguous regarding the profile of the Philippian church, if poverty refers to a loss of one's position, it tends to suggest the church had not secured any substantial patronage. For protection from difficult times was the very essence of patronage.[97] Furthermore, the fact that the Christians at Philippi were probably not wealthy is also implied by Paul's use of ἠκαιρεῖσθε in Phil 4:10b.[98] This "lack of opportunity" could well refer to their financial situation, especially if they had been generous contributors to the collection as 2 Cor 8:2 affirms. In any case, the amount of money that they gave to support Paul need not have been very much since, for an itinerant missionary like Paul who

---

commercial language with the idea of friendship does not negate the argument that Paul's usage suggests they were from the artisan class (his use is metaphorical in any case), and he presumes they understand.

[95] See Oakes, "Philippians", 44, 77; Peterlin, *Paul's Letter*, 165. It is not necessary to assume the presence of elite members on the presumption that a large *villa* was needed for the church to meet in. See sections II.2-3 of chapter 4 herein; cf. Peterlin, *Paul's Letter*, 165 n. 175.

[96] Witherington also argues that Paul's refusal of support at Corinth was probably related to patronage offers but he does not explain why it was not an issue at Philippi (*Conflict*, 209, 229 n. 39; *Friendship*, 126). In fact, it is likely that Paul's refusal to accept support from the Corinthians was unusual (Holmberg, *Paul and Power*, 94), and reinforces the idea of the uniqueness of that church in regard to its social profile.

[97] See section I of chapter 3 and section II.2 of chapter 4 herein.

[98] See Beare, *Commentary*, 151-2; Marshall, *Enmity*, 234. Since Paul does not spell out what occasioned the lack of opportunity, most commentators consider financial hardship to be at least one of the likely possibilities. See, for example, Hawthorne, *Philippians*, 197; O'Brien, *Commentary*, 519; Witherington, *Friendship*, 128.

was accustomed to quite a frugal lifestyle, even a little extra would make a significant difference.[99]

Overall, therefore, it would appear that the Philippian church was comprised of people who belonged to the artisan classes. It is highly unlikely, however, that there were any Christians who belonged to the ruling elite. At the same time, the majority were probably *liberti*, although there seems to have been some who were freeborn plebeians, and there were probably some public slaves, that is, members of the *familia Caesaris* at Philippi.[100] While there were no members of the ruling elite, those who belonged to the *familia Caesaris* would have had some degree of status and influence within the political system of the town, even if it was limited.[101]

3. Size

There is too little information to estimate accurately the size of the Philippian church. Some scholars claim that it would have comprised in excess of one hundred members since there is evidence of considerable organization, such as the appointing of officials — ἐπισκόποις καὶ διακόνοις (1:2).[102] This argument is weak, however, since all *collegia*, regardless of size, had a number of office bearers. Given that the Philippian Christians were most probably artisans, they

---

[99] Oakes, "Philippians", 86; cf. Collins, *The Birth*, 13.

[100] Oakes constructs a model of the Philippian church that parallels his model of the general Philippian population. Although he makes allowances, he assume that the profile of the church was generally that of the population: 36% Roman, 64% Greek, with 1% elite, 15% colonist farmers, 16% slaves, 25% poor and 43% service industry ("Philippians", 78). Apart from the unwarranted starting premise, he again makes the mistake of ignoring *liberti*, presumes that those named were largely migrants, and he overestimates the level of wealth. As noted above, his attempt to argue against the Christians being citizens is also a failure.

[101] Imperial slaves and *liberti* at Rome could have considerable wealth, status, influence and power, depending on their position. See MacMullen, *Social Relations*, 92; Alföldy, *Social History*, 132; Garnsey & Saller, *Roman Empire*, 24-5. As Alföldy notes, however, despite their power and wealth few actually joined the elite (*Social History*, 132). It is even less likely to occur in an insignificant town like Philippi. Nevertheless, the Imperial slaves and *liberti* there would have had some influence in local affairs.

[102] Portefaix, *Sisters Rejoice*, 137; Oakes, "Philippians", 77.

would have met in a small house or an *insula* workshop.
Consequently, there may have been about thirty members.[103]

In summary, therefore, the Christian community at
Philippi would have been a fairly small group, mainly
comprised of *liberti*, with some freeborn, and some slaves. As
such, the great majority would have been Roman citizens and
they were probably artisans and merchants. However it is
unlikely that any of them were particularly wealthy or that
they were able to acquire any significant group patron.
Consequently, they probably met together in an *insula*-
workshop or a small house .

III. CHURCH AND CIVIC COMMUNITY RELATIONS

In Philippians 1:29-30 Paul asserts that ὑμῖν ἐχαρίσθη...
πάσχειν, τὸν αὐτὸν ἀγῶνα ἔχοντες, οἷον εἴδετε ἐν ἐμοὶ καὶ
νῦν ἀκούετε ἐν ἐμοί. This clearly indicates that the
Philippian Christians are experiencing conflict at the time
that he writes. Paul also understands this conflict in the same
terms as that which he himself had confronted at Philippi
and that he is experiencing at that particular time.[104] It is

---

[103] Peterlin gives no actual figure but he claims there were several
house-churches based on the assumption of at least four extended
households (*Paul's Letter*, 169-70). He admits that there were probably
few slaves in the church, since most who joined the church belonged to
households that joined, and few of the Christians' households there would
have had many slaves (ibid., 139-40). If Clement, Lydia, Epaphroditus,
Syntyche, Euodia and the gaoler all had "average" size families
(husband, wife, two children) and a couple of slaves and all of their
dependants joined, that would be a total of thirty-three. Yet it is doubtful
that all of the dependants would have joined, not least the husbands of
women converts. On the size of Greco-Roman families see de Vos,
"ΟΙΚΟΣ", 9-10, 19-20.

[104] See Brewer, "The Meaning", 82; Perkins, "Christology", 512;
Bloomquist, *Suffering*, 157-8; Geoffrion, *Rhetorical Purpose*, 181; M.
Tellbe, "The Sociological Factors behind Philippians 3.1-11 and the
Conflict at Philippi" *JSNT* 55 (1994) 106-7; Fee, *Philippians*, 172-3;
Oakes, "Philippians", 99-102. Pfitzner suggests that the term in 1:29
refers to both Paul's suffering in prison and his striving for the gospel
(*Agon Motif*, 118-20), but that does not rule out the fact that he is
experiencing actual conflict and suffering. Witherington, however, doubts
that there was any real conflict or that Paul was actually suffering,
claiming that it is not clear whether he was actually in prison (or simply
under house arrest) at the time he writes (*Friendship*, 18-20, 31-2). Yet
this is not possible given Paul's repeated reference to his δεσμοί (1:7, 13,
17). Witherington also plays down the strength of Paul's expression in

also suggested by the way Paul connects his own suffering to theirs throughout the letter, especially in 1:12-30, 2:12-18, and possibly also in the use of συμμιμηταί in 3:17.

1. Conflict/Repression

According to the narrative in Acts 16:20-4, Paul was brought before the *duoviri*, beaten with rods by their *lictores*, and thrown into prison. The charge(s) against him almost certainly had a religio-political motivation.[105] Leaving aside some of the details of that narrative, which may be of dubious value (such as the earthquake in gaol), the reference to Paul's having been beaten and imprisoned is probably accurate. Indeed, it fits well with Paul's reference in 1 Thess 2:2 to προπαθόντες καὶ ὑβρισθέντες...ἐν Φιλίπποις and his claim to having been beaten by rods in 2 Cor 11:25.[106]

Consequently, by connecting their experience of conflict and suffering to his, Paul indicates that the "opponents" would have been people outside the church. This is also implied by his reference to them being destined for destruction (1:28b). Presumably, those involved are residents or citizens of Philippi. That the local authorities are involved is suggested by the fact that ἀγῶνα...οἷον...νῦν ἀκούετε ἐν ἐμοί can, in its context, only refer to his imprisonment by the

---

1:30 by taking εἴδετε as a present tense and ἐν ἐμοί in the sense of something internal (ibid., 51), i.e. something like "the mental anguish which you see I am having". But the verb is clearly an aorist referring to what they saw (once) when he was with them.

[105] See Tellbe, "Sociological Factors", 108. It is usually suggested that Paul was charged both with disturbing the peace and introducing an "illicit" foreign cult (e.g. Sherwin-White, *Roman Law*, 77; Haenchen, *Acts*, 496; Marshall, *Acts*, 270; Tellbe, "Sociological Factors", 107-8). The second charge is unlikely given the general Roman attitude to Judaism and the fact that the Philippians did permit foreign cults. D. R. Schwartz claims that he was accused of not truly following his ancestral customs as a Jew ("The Accusation and Accusers at Philippi [Acts 16,20-21]" *Bib* 65 [1984] 361). It is more likely, however, that he was charged with illicit magic (see my "Finding a Charge that Fits: The Accusation against Paul and Silas at Philippi [Acts 16.19-21]" *JSNT* forthcoming). It does not matter, for the charge arose from the exercise of his ministry, and each of these three possible charges was certainly political, not least due to the interplay between religion and politics in first century society.

[106] See Pfitzner, *Agon Motif*, 114; Haenchen, *Acts*, 496, 504; Marshall, *Acts*, 271; Hemer, *Book*, 186; Johnson, *Acts*, 296; Geoffrion, *Rhetorical Purpose*, 78; Fee, *Philippians*, 173; Oakes, "Philippians", 162.

Roman government and this is the *same* as the ἀγῶνα...οἷον εἴδετε ἐν ἐμοί.[107]

Some scholars assume that the opposition Paul mentions in Phil 1:27-30 comes from the same opponents that he will discuss in 3:2-11 (or 3:2-21).[108] But this fails to explain the clear reference in 1:30 to Paul's experience in Philippi. Indeed, there is no record of any Jewish or Jewish-Christian opposition that troubled Paul during his initial visit, nor any reason Luke would have failed to mention this, given that he consistently refers to Jewish opposition to Paul's preaching (Acts 9:23-5; 13:50; 14:2-6, 19; 15:1-5; 17:5-9, 13; 18:12-16).

The instigators are ordinary residents of Philippi (non-Christians) as suggested by Paul's call for the Christians to be "blameless and innocent" μέσον γενεᾶς σκολιᾶς καὶ διεστραμμένης, ἐν οἷς φαίνεσθε (Phil 2:15). This may draw on language from the LXX for disobedient Israel, but those among whom the Philippian Christians lived were "pagans", and the phrase is an appropriate pejorative description of those who are oppressing the Christians. Indeed, the most likely context for such polemic is where a minority feels threatened or is actually suffering.[109] The reference to the

---

[107] See Brewer, "The Meaning", 82; Beare, *Commentary*, 70; Reumann, "Theologies", 527; Geoffrion, *Rhetorical Purpose*, 181; Fee, *Philippians*, 173. It is most likely that Paul's imprisonment was at Rome since the reference to the *praetorium* in Phil 1:13 clearly refers to *people*, not a barracks nor a provincial governor's headquarters, and this could only be said of the Praetorian Guard at Rome. See Brewer, "Meaning", 81; Witherington, *Friendship*, 25-6; H. W. Tajra, *The Martyrdom of St. Paul* (WUNT 2.67; Tübingen: J. C. B. Mohr, 1994) 59-61; Fee, *Philippians*, 459. For further arguments in support of a Roman imprisonment as the setting for the letter see Hemer, *Book*, 273-5; Marshall, "Theology", 121-2; Peterlin, *Paul's Letter*, 11; Witherington, *Friendship*, 24-6.

[108] For example, Collange, *Epistle*, 56-7, 75; Hawthorne, *Philippians*, 56-8; Marshall, "Theology", 125; cf. A. F. J. Klijn, "Paul's Opponents in Philippians iii" *NovT* 7 (1964) 278-84. While Collange and Marshall presuppose that the opposition comes from the "Judaizers" Paul discusses in Phil 3, Hawthorne claims the problem is Jewish missionaries from Thessalonica. Apart from the fact that this does not sit with 1:30, it is hardly plausible. As mentioned in chapter 2 herein, there is no clear evidence for Jewish missionaries. For further arguments against Hawthorne's reconstruction see Oakes, "Philippians", 110-13.

[109] Compare, for example, Tellbe, "Sociological Factors", 105; Fee, *Philippians*, 245-6; Oakes, "Philippians", 104.

destruction of their oppressors in 1:28b also supports the idea that the conflict was external.[110]

This conflict would have been precipitated by the Christians' withdrawal from the traditional Greco-Roman cults, especially from the Imperial cult. Such behavior would have been considered subversive.[111] Indeed, given a dominant Roman religious mentality it would also be seen as a threat to the *pax deorum*, and hence to the well-being of the whole community. At the same time, once some Christians had been labelled as troublemakers because of this, others would have been so labelled merely by association.[112]

Oakes suggests that some locals took offence, there was some disturbance so the *duoviri* became involved, the Christians were labelled as trouble-makers, and punished. Those initiating the process were probably the associates of the Christians.[113] He claims the conflict probably involved oppressive measures such as economic sanctions, strained social relations, even sporadic violence. He doubts, however, that it involved "mass arrests, long-term imprisonment or executions" since nothing suggests the measures were taken in a formal legal sense.[114] Oakes is correct that such opposition would not have been carried out by formal edict at this time, unlike the later "persecutions", and that the whole

---

[110] Furthermore, the reference to στήκετε in 1:27 strongly suggests that Paul is referring to a context involving external conflict. As K. P. Donfried notes, this term is "part of a well-formed tradition of teaching in the context of persecution" ("The Theology of 2 Thessalonians", in K. P. Donfried & I. H. Marshall, *The Theology of the Shorter Pauline Letters* [Cambridge: Cambridge University Press, 1993] 88).

[111] See Perkins, "Theology", 93; Oakes, "Philippians", 114-15.

[112] Oakes, "Philippians", 114-18; cf. Perkins, "Theology", 91, 93. Oakes also suggests that the conflict may have been prompted by the evangelistic preaching of the Christians ("Philippians", 120). But this is unlikely. Indeed, it is not at all clear that the Philippian Christians were engaged in proclamation (see Geoffrion, *Rhetorical Purpose*, 167 n. 24). Even less likely is Bormann's claim that the opposition arose because the church had a patron other than the Emperor and its organization was outside the control of the town authorities (*Philippi*, 223-4). Rather, the church's structure would not have been greatly different from any of the other *collegia* in the town, and other *collegia* (e.g. the Silvanus *collegium*) had patrons other than the emperor. Instead, what would have caused offence was their withdrawal from the traditional cults and the Imperial cult (see Oakes, "Philippians", 248; cf. my discussion of the conflict at Thessalonica in section III.1 in chapter 4 herein).

[113] Oakes, "Philippians", 121-2.

[114] Ibid., 106-7, 125.

church was not in prison as Paul was, but that does not rule out a significant involvement of the magistrates. What he ignores is the possibility of an oath of allegiance at Philippi such as probably occurred at Thessalonica. Therefore, while the actions were probably sporadic and only infrequently violent, the involvement of the local authorities is likely.[115]

2. The Response of the Philippian Church

Since conflict and suffering (1:29-30) appear to be the reason for Paul's call to unity and steadfastness in 1:27-8, and also the call to unity in 2:1-5, the response of the Philippian Christians to the conflict would appear to be disunity.[116] Oakes suggests that this disunity may have been caused by a tension between economic interests and belief. For example, the Christians' withdrawal from the traditional cults may have harmed their employment prospects since it would also have involved withdrawal from cults associated with the particular patron deities of their trade. Consequently, it is possible that those who were employed may have suffered more than those who owned their own businesses.[117] There is

---

[115] Something similar is hinted at by Perkins, "Christology", 512; Fee, *Philippians*, 172. See also section III.1 of chapter 4 herein.

[116] Compare, for example, Geoffrion, *Rhetorical Purpose*, 32, 55-7; E. M. Krentz, "Military Language and Metaphors in Philippians" in B. H. McLean, ed., *Origins and Method: Towards a New Understanding of Judaism and Christianity* (JSNTSup 86; Sheffield: JSOT Press, 1993) 113; Tellbe, "Sociological Factors", 120 n. 84; Fee, *Philippians*, 366. Oakes claims that Geoffrion plays down the issue of disunity ("Philippians", 194) but, given the structure of the letter (especially the parallels between 1:28-30 and 4:1, 9), Geoffrion is probably right to argue that the theme of disunity is subordinate, although related, to that of conflict (*Rhetorical Purpose*, 105-6). Some scholars, however, claim that disunity is the primary focus of the letter, even that the dispute between Euodia and Syntyche is the main reason Paul wrote (e.g. Garland, "Composition", 172; Winter, *Seek*, 99-101; Black, "Structure", 16-17, 30-1, 44-5; Dahl, "Euodia", 8-9; Peterlin, *Paul's Letter*, 12-15, 102-3). As Oakes points out, however, the rhetorical structure and the prominence of the theme of suffering make this unlikely ("Philippians", 150). Indeed, as Geoffrion notes, "if 4:2 flows from 4:1, then the specific exhortation, which follows immediately, appears to be a specific case of application" of the call to stand firm (*Rhetorical Purpose*, 115-16).

[117] Oakes, "Philippians", 5, 127. He also claims, on the basis of 2:2-4, that it is likely that some who suffered little, due to greater wealth and status, were failing to help financially those who were poorer and of lower status (ibid., 220; cf. Peterlin, *Paul's Letter*, 64). In support, he takes

nothing in the text of Philippians, however, that clearly supports his conjecture.

It is rather more likely that the disunity within the church would have arisen because of differing opinions about how to deal with the conflict.[118] In particular, it appears that there was a tendency to try to avoid or minimize this conflict on the part of many of the Philippian Christians.[119] This is suggested by Paul's reference to them being afraid of their opponents (1:28), by his assertion that their suffering was granted by Christ (1:29), by his emphasis in the "hymn" on Christ's death on the cross (2:8), and by his stress on the importance of sharing the sufferings of Christ (3:10-11).[120] Consequently, although it is seldom recognized by scholars, the problem of the opponents in Phil 3:2-21 should be understood within the context of this conflict with the wider

ἐριθεία (2:2) as "being concerned with one's own social advantage" and κενοδοξία as "pride in one's high (social) position" (Oakes, "Philippians", 205; cf. Witherington, *Friendship*, 63). But he assumes that status is simply equivalent to wealth, when it could refer to many other things. Indeed, it is just as likely that the difference is between those in the church who are citizens and those who are not, and that those who were, may have used this to their advantage. Nevertheless, the issue in 2:2f is certainly not "spiritual pride" as R. Jewett ("Conflicting Movements in the Early Church as Reflected in Philippians" *NovT* 12 [1970] 373-4), Beare (*Commentary*, 73) and Collange (*Epistle*, 80) suppose. See Peterlin, *Paul's Letter*, 63.

[118] So Fee, *Philippians*, 366.

[119] Jewett contends that this tendency to avoid suffering is indicative of a group with "divine-man" tendencies, who saw imprisonment and suffering as incompatible with the gospel ("Movements", 367-368). But Paul's rivals in 1:15-17 cannot be "divine-man missionaries" since the implication in 1:14 is that Paul's imprisonment made them bolder to preach (O'Brien, *Commentary*, 104), nor has it been proved that such people actually existed in the Greco-Roman world (Bloomquist, *Suffering*, 200), nor is there evidence that these rivals preached a gospel of miracles (C. L. Mearns, "The Identity of Paul's Opponents at Philippi" *NTS* 33 [1987] 201). It is much more likely that he is dealing with some who had tendencies towards "voluntary martyrdom", for φθόνος (1:15) does not just imply "rivalry" but the intent to do actual harm. Hence, they may have done something to harm his case when he came to trial (Tajra, *Martyrdom*, 63-4; Winter, *Seek*, 94). Although they are clearly presented as Paul's rivals at the place of his imprisonment, Peterlin claims that it is difficult to image some preaching for selfish reasons and not being rebuked, so what Paul says must be addressed primarily to the Philippians (*Paul's Letter*, 38-40). Since it is not at all clear that Paul is rebuking the Philippians, Peterlin's argument is self-defeating.

[120] Compare, for example, Minear, "Singing", 208.

civic community.[121] More specifically, this conflict and suffering has left them afraid (1:28) and hence vulnerable to the arguments of these adversaries.[122]

It has been widely recognized that the opponents described in Phil 3:2-11 are some sort of Judaizing Christians.[123] Paul's insults in 3:2 clearly show that they had

---

[121] This is recognized by Perkins, "Theology", 94; Geoffrion, *Rhetorical Purpose*, 26-7; Tellbe, "Sociological Factors", 116-18; Fee, *Philippians*, 289. Jewett, however, assumes that the opponents' message appealed to a Philippian tendency toward "spiritual enthusiasm" ("Movements", 386). It is clear from the letter's structure, especially its rhetorical structure, that these adversaries must be seen in relation to this wider conflict. Although the rhetorical structure will be discussed more below, 1:27-30 constitutes the *narratio* or the statement of the proposition to be argued. The argument in support of this proposition (*probatio*) is found in 2:1-3:21 and consists of a number of examples, both positive and negative, of what it means to stand firm in the face of suffering. In this context, these opponents are important precisely because of the danger they pose in the face of external conflict. Fee also notes that most attempts to explain the opponents of Phil 3 ignore the fact that the text ends with the letter's chief theme, namely, "standing firm" (*Philippians*, 341). Indeed, both 4:1 and 4:9 pick up the language of 1:27-30.

[122] Compare, for example, Minear, "Singing", 212.

[123] For example, Jewett, "Movements", 382-3; Mearns, "The Identity", 197-202; Geoffrion, *Rhetorical Purpose*, 152; Marshall, "Theology", 123; O'Brien, *Commentary*, 368, 418; Fee, *Philippians*, 290, 295-6. But A. B. du Toit points out that care must be taken with mirror-reading polemic language for it cannot be assumed that there is a "one to one relationship between the depiction of the encoded adversaries in our documents and their real-life counterparts. An element of distortion must certainly be accepted" ("Vilification as a Pragmatic Device in Early Christian Epistolography" *Bib* 75 [1994] 411-2). Excessive "mirror-reading" is a problem with many attempts to identify these opponents. Schmithals argues that these adversaries are Jewish-Christian-Gnostic-libertines (*Paul*, 82-83; cf. C. R. Holladay, "Paul's Opponents in Philippians 3" *ResQ* 12 [1969] 78), and H. Koester claims they are Jewish-Christian-Gnostic-perfectionists ("The Purpose of the Polemic of a Pauline Fragment [Philippians III]" *NTS* 8 [1962] 331). But a gnostic identification is improbable since many of the features of these adversaries are not unique to Gnostics, while the concern with circumcision and the Law are decidedly non-gnostic. See Mearns, "The Identity", 200-1; Perkins, "Christology", 510 n. 7. Holladay argues for Gnostics by reading the context of the Pastorals back into Philippians ("Opponents", 81). It is commonly suggested that the problem is Gnostics because of the τελει-language in 3:12-16 (so Jewett, "Movements", 373; Schmithals, *Paul*, 91-2, 99-101; J. B. Tyson, "Paul's Opponents at Philippi" *PRS* 3 [1976] 86). Others claim that this language refers to a group of Jewish-Christians with an overly-realized

some connection to Jewish beliefs and/or practices. For example, the verbal form of κατατομή is used in the LXX of a pagan ritual mutilation that was expressly forbidden (Lev 21:5; 3 Kgs 18:28; Hos 7:14; Isa 15:2).[124] Therefore, his use of this term here seems to parody their devotion to circumcision (περιτομή) as no better than a pagan mutilation. But it is seldom explained how such a group would be relevant to the Philippian Christians in their particular situation.

---

eschatology, based on the assumption that this is dealing with the same problem as 1 Corinthians (e.g. Holladay, "Opponents", 78, 83; Tyson, "Opponents", 85; Lincoln, *Paradise*, 92-3; J. Reumann, "Philippians 3.20-21 — a Hymnic Fragment?" *NTS* 30 [1984] 604; "Mearns, "The Identity", 195). But, as I argued in the previous chapter, there is no evidence for Gnostics in 1 Corinthians, and the Corinthians have an non-eschatological rather than an overly-realized eschatology. In any case, to interpret this τελει-language in relation to 1 Corinthians or the Pastorals is both an unwarranted and inappropriate imposition on the text. Rather, this language is clearly part of the athletic metaphor running throughout 3:12-16 (Perkins, "Theology", 100). As Oakes suggests this argument "is so suitable to a call to perseverance of any kind, particularly in the face of suffering, that it seems not really to need to be addressing the issue of perfectionism" and hence is not aimed at any opponents at all ("Philippians", 146). In short, nothing in 3:2-11 suggests a gnostic or overly-realized group, nor are such groups needed to explain the situation.

[124] See O'Brien, *Commentary*, 357; Witherington, *Friendship*, 89; *TDNT* 8.110. Fee observes that each of the insults in 3:2 represents a reversal of fundamental Jewish concerns: "dogs", and hence impurity, in contrast to "purity", "evil works" in contrast to "good works", and "mutilation" in contrast to "circumcision" (*Philippians*, 295-6). Kenneth Grayston, however, claims that the so-called "reversed-insult theory" (on the assumption that "dogs" was a Jewish insult for pagans — here applied to Jews) fails "in the same way that an Australian cannot refer to another Australian as a 'pommie bastard'". Hence, he argues that this insult and the idea of "mutilation" must refer to Gentiles who are advocating circumcision as some sort of pagan initiation rite ("The Opponents in Philippians 3" *ExpTim* 97 [1986] 171). But he does not adequately explain Paul's emphasis on his Jewish credentials, nor the statement that "we are the true circumcision" (3:3). See also Fee, *Philippians*, 341. Furthermore, Grayston's theory is suspect, as is the "reversed-insult theory", because "dog" was a much more general insult than is usually recognized, and there is no evidence that it was racially specific. For example, it is found in the LXX as a term of self-deprecation by Israelites (e.g. 2 Kgs 9:8, 16:9; 4 Kgs 8:13). Such a sense can also be found in the wider Greek and Hellenistic world. See, for example, Homer *Il.* 6.354-5; idem, *Od.* 19.91-2; Hesiod *Op.* 373-4; Callimachus *Dian.* 63; idem, *Aet.* frag 191.83. I am indebted to Alan Cadwallader for bringing these references to my attention.

Furthermore, the real issue in Phil 3:2-11 does not appear to be circumcision and the Law. There is not the sort of argument we find in either Galatians or Romans, and the very brevity of Paul's treatment of these issues here suggests they are not the focus. Nor does the presence of "standard" Judaizers explain the abrupt shift from the Law in 3:9 to the issue of suffering in 3:10. Rather the issue appears to be confidence in human status.[125] Also, Paul's reference to the Christians being *the* circumcision (ἡμεῖς γάρ ἐσμεν ἡ περιτομή) in 3:3 suggests that the issue concerns who are "the people of God".[126]

As suggested above, however, the appeal of these opponents must be seen in relation to the conflict between the Christians and their wider civic community. Therefore, the emphases in Phil 3:2-11 (circumcision and Jewish identity) would be attractive as a way of avoiding conflict. In other words, by being seen as "proper" Jews, who abided by their ancestral customs, they would be afforded a measure of acceptance and recognition. It would be a legitimate way of gaining exemption from the expectation to participate in the traditional cults, and especially the Imperial cult.[127]

---

[125] Perkins, "Theology", 91, 99; Bloomquist, *Suffering*, 200; Oakes, "Philippians", 145; Dahl, "Euodia", 12; *contra* Jewett, "Movements", 383; Mearns, "The Identity", 201-2; O'Brien, *Commentary*, 368, 418. Besides, "to decide that Philippi faces, say, 'Judaizers' does not mean that the Judaizers must share characteristics other than Judaizing with those in Galatia nor that other aspects of the Galatian situation must be present in Philippi" (Oakes, "Philippians", 3; cf. W. Cotter, "Our *Politeuma* is in Heaven: The Meaning of 3:17-21" in B. H. McLean, ed., *Origins and Method: Towards a New Understanding of Judaism and Christianity* [JSNTSup 86; Sheffield: JSOT Press, 1993] 94).

[126] Tellbe, "Sociological Factors", 101; Fee, *Philippians*, 298.

[127] See Perkins, "Theology", 92-4; Tellbe, "Sociological Factors", 103-4, 116-18; Fee, *Philippians*, 289; see also section II.3.iii of chapter 2 herein. It is unfortunate that Tellbe relies on the non-existent idea of *religio licita*, although he recognizes its non-existence ("Sociological Factors", 107 n. 46). Oakes claims that "the trouble that the Philippians faced seems unlikely to have been of a kind that would be alleviated by such a move" and does not take this argument seriously ("Philippians", 118 n. 72). But Oakes assumes a widespread Roman animosity towards Jews that, as demonstrated in chapter 2 herein, did not exist. He also assumes there was no official action against the Christians as there was no edict. If there were oaths of allegiance to the emperor at Philippi (cf. section III.1 of chapter 4 herein), however, this is just the sort of "move" that would have alleviated the conflict. The issue is one of *appearing to be Jews* to outsiders. I am not suggesting that the Christians were seeking

Some scholars claim that these opponents cannot have been present in Philippi at the time that Paul writes and hence they do not pose an immediate threat. For example, Jewett contends that "one doesn't say 'look out for the dogs' to someone presently being attacked by them, but rather to someone potentially in danger of being so attacked".[128] But this is a little too pedantic and pushes the metaphor too far. Rather, it is just as likely that βλέπετε τοὺς κύνας refers to a present danger.

The idea that these opponents may not be present is also implicit in the argument that ἐργάται (3:2) was a technical term for itinerant missionaries.[129] But no other text offered in support of this has the term ἐργάται qualified (as here), except for ἐργάται δόλιοι in 2 Cor 11:13. Therefore, only this text is a true parallel and we cannot be certain that Paul implies the same thing in both cases. Besides, those who argue it refers to itinerant missionaries ignore parallels in the LXX. For example, in 1 Macc 3:6 apostate Jews are called οἱ ἐργάται τῆς ἀνομίας.[130] In light of this, it is just as likely, if

to become Jews *per se*. Indeed, the fact that Paul does not use any scriptural arguments against these opponents strongly suggests that they were not Jews or Jewish-Christians in the true sense, and lends weight to my argument that the issue is one of *perception and status*.

[128] Jewett, "Movement", 382-3; cf. Witherington, *Friendship*, 29; Perkins, "Theology", 90-1. Many argue that βλέπετε in 3:2 cannot mean "beware" as it is not followed by μή + aorist subjunctive or ἀπό (Hawthorne, *Philippians*, 124; Garland, "Composition", 165-6; Stowers, "Friends", 116). But such an argument ignores the strength of the three-fold repetition that clearly indicates considerable urgency and passion (see Collange, *Epistle*, 124 n. 1; O'Brien, *Commentary*, 353-4; J. T. South, *Disciplinary Practices in Pauline Texts* [Lewiston, NY: Edwin Mellen, 1992] 150; Geoffrion, *Rhetorical Purpose*, 196-7; Tellbe, "Sociological Factors", 100 n. 14; Witherington, *Friendship*, 29).

[129] See Jewett, "Movements", 382; Schmithals, *Paul*, 85; Beare, *Commentary*, 104; Collange, *Epistle*, 114; cf. Lincoln, *Paradise*, 90; Grayston, "Opponents", 171; Marshall, "Theology", 123. The texts cited in support of this are 1 Cor 3:9-15; 2 Cor 11:13; Mt 9:37-8, 10:10, 20:2-8; Lk 10:2-7, 13:27; 1 Tim 5:18; 2 Tim 2:15. See Jewett, "Movements", 382 n. 1. In 1 Cor 3:9-15 Paul uses συνεργοί, which is a quite different term, and it simply refers to "ministers" in general. While the synoptic texts may refer to missionaries, it is also used in a metaphorical way, and we cannot simply assume Paul understood terms in the same way that the synoptic writers did. What is ignored is the fact that in 1 Tim 5:18 it actually refers to church *elders* not missionaries!

[130] Fee notes that οἱ ἐργαζόμενοι τὴν ἀνομίαν is common in the Psalms, e.g. 5:5; 6:8; 13:4; 35:12; 52:4; 58:2-5; 91:7-9; 93:4, where it is also used for apostate Israelites (*Philippians*, 296 n. 47).

not more so given the context, that κακοὺς ἐργάτας applies to locals who had been draw in by the "Jewish option", whom Paul now regards as apostates. Overall, the strength of Paul's warning suggests there is a real and present threat and that some had been taken in by it.[131]

It is also frequently assumed that Paul is dealing with the same "Judaizing" adversaries in 3:18-21.[132] This assumes that ὁ θεὸς ἡ κοιλία refers to a concern with Jewish food laws and ἡ δόξα ἐν τῇ αἰσχύνῃ αὐτῶν to a concern with circumcision.[133] But neither phrase can be understood that way. In the LXX κοιλία never refers to the penis or circumcision, whereas κοιλίας ὄρεξις occurs as a reference to gluttony and lust (Sir 23:6).[134] Furthermore, in Greek literature κοιλία commonly refers to the stomach as the seat of hunger or desire.[135] Indeed, ὁ θεὸς ἡ κοιλία is similar to expressions that were used to criticize promiscuous and decadent people. For example, Philo claims that a Jew who

---

[131] Indeed, Paul's call for imitation in 3:17 (συμμιμηταί μου γίνεσθε) suggests that not all of them were imitating him in relation to dealing with conflict with the wider community, given his statement in 1 Thess 1:6 that the Thessalonian Christians μιμηταί ἡμῶν ἐγενήθητε specifically in relation to "receiving the word in much affliction".

[132] See, for example, Lincoln, *Paradise*, 95; Reumann, "Theologies", 527-8; Perkins, "Christology", 510 n. 7; Watson, "Rhetorical Analysis", 75; Fowl, *Story*, 100 n. 4; South, *Disciplinary Practices*, 151; Marshall, "Theology", 123; Witherington, *Friendship*, 28. It is implied by Collange, *Epistle*, 137-8; Stowers, "Friends", 116-18.

[133] So Koester, "The Purpose", 331; Lincoln, *Paradise*, 96; Hawthorne, *Philippians*, 166; Fowl, *Story*, 100 n. 4; Marshall, "Theology", 123; Witherington, *Friendship*, 89-90. Mearns takes both κοιλία and αἰσχύνη as euphemisms for the penis and hence circumcision ("The Identity", 198-9).

[134] See Fee, *Philippians*, 371 n. 36. Even Mearns recognizes the sense of the term in Sir 23:6, but he fails to take it into account.

[135] Jewett, "Movements", 380; Fee, *Philippians*, 372; Oakes, "Philippians", 147. Koester admits that κοιλία has the sense of "carnal appetite in Greco-Roman literature" but he denies this here claiming that no NT writer so uses it. Thus it must refer to Jewish dietary observance ("The Purpose", 331; cf. Lincoln, *Paradise*, 96; Hawthorne, *Philippians*, 166; Fowl, *Story*, 100 n. 4; Witherington, *Friendship*, 89). But this *is* the sense in which it occurs in Rom 16:18. Besides his argument is self-defeating for no NT writer uses it in the sense of purity or circumcision (not even Mt 15:17//Mk7:18-23 comes close). Also it is used 13 times for "womb" (Mt 12:40, 19:12; Lk 1:15, 41, 42, 44, 2:21, 11:27, 23:29; Jn 3:4; Acts 3:3, 14:8; Gal 1:15). As will be seen, Koester also ignores the connotations of the next phrase in Phil 3:19.

joins a θίασος has "made a god of the body (θεοπλαστεῖν μὲν
τὸ σῶμα)", something he links to the story of the Golden Calf
(Ex 32).¹³⁶ Similarly, in Athenaeus a certain Cynic insults
someone with whom he is arguing by calling him "you
glutton, whose god is your belly (κοιλιόδαιμον)". Euripides
has one character claim that he sacrifices to the greatest of
gods, his stomach (τῇ μεγίστῃ γαστρὶ...δαιμόνων).¹³⁷

Likewise, αἰσχύνη cannot refer to "shameful member"
and hence circumcision. Paul never refers to circumcision as
shameful, simply irrelevant, and there is a complete lack of
parallels for taking it in this way.¹³⁸ On the other hand,
whenever αἰσχύνη and δόξα occur in the same context in
Greek literature they refer to "shame" and "honor", where
shame is the dishonor (ἀδοξία) that accrues to misdeeds.¹³⁹
The term αἰσχύνη was also heavily loaded with sexual
connotations. Indeed, one of the major causes of shame was
licentiousness or illicit sexual relations.¹⁴⁰ Proverbs 26:11a
(LXX), following a statement about the man who returns to
his sin, claims that ἔστιν...αἰσχύνη ἐπάγουσα ἁμαρτίαν, καὶ
ἔστιν αἰσχύνη δόξα καὶ χάρις. In this context, the "negative"

---

¹³⁶ Philo *Ebr.* 95.

¹³⁷ Athenaeus 97c; Euripides *Cyc.* 335; cf. Xenophon, who uses the
idea of δουλεύειν γαρτρί (*Mem.* 1.6.8); cf. Jewett, "Movements", 380.
Cicero also claims that Metrodorus, Epicurus' colleague, criticized his
brother "for hesitating to measure every element of happiness by the
standard of the belly" (*Quod dubitet omnia quae ad beatam vitam
pertineant ventre metiri* — *Nat D.* 1.113). This is, of course, intended by
Cicero as a criticism of the Epicurean philosophy. Indeed, such a
criticism as "their god is their belly" fits Epicureanism well.

¹³⁸ See Jewett, "Movements", 381; Schmithals, *Paul*, 110; Beare,
Commentary, 133; Fee, *Philippians*, 373 n. 46; cf. *TDNT* sv "αἰσχύνη",
1.189-90.

¹³⁹ See, for example, Aristotle *Rh.* 1383B.2-4A.14; Diog. Laer. *Zeno*
112; Dio Cassius 38.25.5; Diod. Sic. 23.15.4; Philo *Vit. Mos.* 1.293;
Josephus *AJ* 7.168. This usage is clear evidence that the NT world was
very much an honor-shame society. See Malina, *World*, 28-60.

¹⁴⁰ See, for example, Aristotle *Rh.* 1384B.13-14; Philo *De spec.*
1.280-1; cf. Cotter, "*Politeuma*", 93; *TDNT* sv "αἰσχύνη", 1.189-90.
Koester also recognizes this point, but again argues it cannot have that
sense here as no other NT writer so uses it ("The Purpose", 326), while
Lincoln simply dismisses the possibility without justification (*Paradise*,
96; cf. Hawthorne, *Philippians*, 165; Fowl, *Story*, 100 n. 4; O'Brien,
Commentary, 457). Again, this argument is self-defeating, for no NT
writer uses it in the sense of circumcision. Besides, even Paul should
have been aware that the term was so loaded and those in the church
would have heard it in that sense (Cotter, "*Politeuma*", 93).

sense of αἰσχύνη (which Paul's use of the term in Phil 3:19 must be, since it is intended as an insult) refers to a shameful act or, more specifically, to wilful sin. The term αἰσχύνη is also found in the LXX as a euphemism for idols (for example, Hos 9:10; Jer 3:24-25) and even as a reference to Ba'al (3 Kgs 18:19, 25).[141]

Hence, the criticisms Paul levels against the opponents in 3:18-21 appear to combine ideas of idolatry, gluttony and illicit sexual activity. Such a combination is not dissimilar to his charge to the Corinthians to "flee idolatry", when he quotes from the Golden Calf narrative (1 Cor 10:7). A likely setting for such practices was the *collegium* or θίασος. Indeed, these were often criticized for this sort of indulgent behavior.[142] Sexuality, as both symbolism and actual re-enactments, was very prominent in mystery rites and these were often associated with *collegia*. However, even if actual sexual acts did not occur in all, such acts were thought by many to have been involved and this was a common means of criticizing them.[143] Paul's reference to his tears for them, in combination with his use of the term περιπατοῦσιν for their conduct, suggests they are former Christians — or at least that Paul regards them as apostates.[144]

---

[141] Compare, for example, Oakes, "Philippians", 147.

[142] See, for example, Varro *Rust.* 3.2.16; Philo *Ebr.* 22-5, 29, 95; idem *De spec.* 1.323, 2.44. A good example is Philo's claim that *thiasoi* are based on "strong liquor and drunkenness and sottish carousing and their offspring, wantonness" (ἄκρατος καὶ μέθη καὶ παροινίαι καὶ ἡ τούτων ἔκγονος ὕβρις — *In Flacc.* 136). See also MacMullen, *Social Relations*, 77; Borgen, "Participation", 45.

[143] See Burkert, *Ancient*, 104-8. There is an inscription from Prusa that suggests that initiation into the Isis cult there may have involved some sort of sexual re-enactment of the Isis-Osiris myth (*SEG* 28.1585). Josephus' account of the Paulina case tends to support this (*AJ* 18.73). Furthermore, in his account of initiation into the Bacchic mysteries Livy suggests initiands were raped (*cum per vim stuprum inferatur* — 39.10.7).

[144] Geoffrion, *Rhetorical Purpose*, 153-4. Cotter claims that the reference to tears in 3:18 does not show this, but should be seen as a rhetorical tool, such that Paul appears as a "man of *humanitas*" by showing sensitivity to those whom the Philippians know and care about ("*Politeuma*", 96). But this is most unlikely given that he describes them as "destined for destruction" and is anything but gracious towards them in the rest of 3:19. Oakes suggests that "the πολλοί makes me cautious about taking the ἐχθροί as apostates. Perhaps one could take them as being people in the general population who were tempting the Christians away from the way of faithful suffering" ("Philippians", 147). But this

Given that the problem of the opponents in Phil 3:2-21 lies in the options they offer for avoiding conflict with the wider civic community, it is most likely that in 3:18-21 Paul refers to people who sought to persuade the Christians to return to their traditional cult practices.[145] A major focus of this would appear to be the Imperial cult. Especially in 3:20 there is an unambiguous contrast drawn between Christ and the Emperor.[146] In fact, Christ is described as both σωτήρ and κύριος, something that is unique among Paul's writings.[147] Structurally, this contrast is presented as Paul's direct

---

would not fit with his grief over their destiny. Also, as Geoffrion notes, the term ἐχθροί was often used for alienated φιλοί. The reference to "many" may suggest he is referring to a wider group that just those apostates at Philippi. See Fee, *Philippians*, 368-9. That the issue at stake is discipleship, rather than doctrine, is suggested by Paul's description of what makes them "enemies", namely, περιπατοῦσιν. This would exclude the possibility that these opponents were some sort of Gnostics (*contra* Jewett, "Movements", 378-80; Beare, *Commentary*, 133-4; Schmithals, *Paul*, 108).

[145] Further support for my contention that 3:20-1 deals with participation in Greco-Roman cults, and not Judaism, is found in some parallels to these verses in Philo. In *De spec.* 1.323 he contends that evil people, including those who belong to *collegia* or *thiasoi* and are initiated into the mysteries, should "be banished from the confines of any state or constitution in which morality and truth are honored for their own sakes" (φυγαδευέσθωσαν πόλεως καὶ καταστάσεως, ἐν ᾗ τὸ καλὸν καὶ ἡ ἀλήθεια δι' αὐτὰ τιμᾶται). Earlier, Philo argues that Moses did not permit people who belonged to the Jewish "commonwealth" (πολιτεία) to take part in mystery initiations (*De spec.* 1.319).

[146] See Perkins, "Theology", 93-4; Tellbe, *Rhetorical Purpose*, 112; Oakes, "Philippians", 158. Unfortunately, few scholars recognize or take this comparison and contrast seriously in their interpretation. Witherington, for example, notes that this is the only occurrence of σωτήρ in the genuine Paulines, and is a term loaded with Imperial connotations (*Friendship*, 100; *Conflict*, 297). But he does not allow this to influence his interpretation, opting still to see the opponents in 3:18-21 as the same group of Judaizers from 3:2-11. But Paul's response does not make sense if the opponents he has in mind are some sort of Judaizers.

[147] Compare, for example, Tellbe, "Sociological Factors", 113; Fee, *Philippians*, 251; Oakes, "Philippians" 158, 169-71. Terms such as σωτήρ, κύριος, θεός were prominent in the Imperial cult in the mid-first century, and certainly in relation to Claudius. See, for example, *IGRR* 4.12, 584; *SIG*[3] 814; Tacitus *Ann.* 4.37-8; cf. Jones, "Christianity", 1030-1; Pobee, *Martyrdom*, 80; Oakes, "Philippians", 162; Witherington, *Friendship*, 47. The link of power (3:21) and salvation (3:20) was also a stock image in Imperial ideology (Oakes, "Philippians", 164).

response to the temptation of the cults.[148] Hence, it is likely that Paul is deliberately warning them not to join *collegia* that offered worship to the Emperor. Since other gods and cults were connected with the worship of the Emperor at Philippi they may also have been involved.

Presumably many of the Philippian Christians, who had a Roman religious mentality that separated belief from practice, would have been particularly attracted to this last option. That is, if they understood Christianity as a new "philosophy" or system of belief, that did not necessarily mean it had to affect their religious, and especially their cultic, practice. Indeed, they may not have seen any particular conflict between adhering to Christian beliefs while engaging in *collegia* and other traditional cults.[149]

Overall, therefore, the Philippian Christians encountered conflict and oppressive measures because of their withdrawal from their traditional cult practices. This conflict left them afraid and at odds over how they should deal with it, with a significant group who sought to alleviate or avoid the conflict. Some of them were tempted to be circumcised to assume the status of Jews who followed their ancestral practices. Others, because of a Roman religious mentality, were tempted to maintain their traditional religious practices, worship the Emperor, and join *collegia*. There were probably some who had already taken these options, whom Paul regarded as apostates, and who were trying to persuade the Philippian Christians to follow them in order to avoid the conflict they were experiencing.

IV. PAUL'S RESPONSE TO THE RELATIONSHIP

Paul's response to the relationship between the Christian and civic communities is indicated by the type of letter he wrote and its contents. Most scholars agree that the rhetorical genre of the letter is primarily deliberative.[150] As such, it is intended

---

[148] Oakes, however, claims that these terms may refer to the Emperor without relating to the Imperial cult ("Philippians", 159-60). But this is most unlikely. It is doubtful that the two were at all separate in people's minds, and the way the terms and imagery are used in 3:20-1 as a direct response to the opponents of 3:18-19 suggests otherwise.

[149] See section II of chapter 2 herein, and the discussion of "idol food" in section III.2 of the previous chapter.

[150] See, for example, Watson, "Rhetorical Analysis", 59; Bloomquist, *Suffering*, 120; Black, "Structure", 16; Geoffrion, *Rhetorical*

to persuade the readers/hearers to take the course of action that the author advocates, rather than that of any opponents, and in support of which significant use is made of examples.[151] Overall, Paul's response to the Philippians' fear,

Purpose, 30; Witherington, *Friendship*, 19. Based on the "hymn" of 2:6-11 Basevi & Chapa claim that the letter is primarily epideictic. As such, it constitutes a praise of Christ ("Rhetorical Function", 348-50). While this may be true of the "hymn" (although it is doubtful even there since the "hymn" functions primarily as an *example*), it does not fit the letter as a whole. Bloomquist may be correct that the letter actually contains mixed genres (*Suffering*, 120), especially since none of Paul's letters exactly correspond to the classical rhetorical genres as was noted in the introduction to section IV of chapter 4 herein (cf. J. T. Fitzgerald, "Philippians in the Light of Some Ancient Discussions of Friendship" in idem, ed., *Friendship, Flattery, and Frankness of Speech* [NovTSup 82; Leiden: E. J. Brill, 1996] 142-3). The rhetorical structure of the letter is best understood such that 1:3-26 is the *exordium* (establishment of ethos), 1:27-30 is the *narratio* (containing the statement of the proposition to be developed), 2:1-3:21 is the *probatio* (the various arguments developing the proposition) and 4:1-20 is the *peroratio* (summary and final appeal). See Watson, "Rhetorical Analysis", 61, 65, 67, 76-7; Geoffrion, *Rhetorical Purpose*, 22-5, 160-1. Witherington takes 1:3-11 as the *exordium*, 1:12-30 as the *narratio*, and 2:1-4:3 as the *peroratio* (*Friendship*, 18-19, 104). But this breaks the flow of the argument and stretches the categories. It is quite clear that 1:12-26 is an attempt to establish ethos, not a part of the actual problem, and, as argued above, the case of Euodia and Syntyche appears to be a special application of the argument, not part of the argument summary, especially since it is clear from 4:1 that Paul is beginning his summary. Bloomquist incomprehensibly suggests that 1:12-14 is the *narratio* (*Suffering*, 121-4). Not only is there no statement of an argument that is defended throughout the rest of the letter, the structure of the letter and the flow of the argument (including the intensity of some of the polemic) do not fit his suggestion. See, for example, Krentz, "Military Language", 113; Oakes, "Philippians", 139. Black dismisses such analyses, claiming they are too subjective since Watson and Bloomquist reach vastly different arrangements using the "same" method ("Structure", 21 n. 19). But their methods are hardly identical, especially since Bloomquist proceeds from a faulty presupposition. In any case, such an argument could be levelled against the whole historical-critical method! Furthermore, Black's own analysis (ibid., 46-8) is itself subjective, it lacks ancient rhetorical parallels, and it cuts across the flow of the argument.

[151] See Watson, "Rhetorical Analysis", 59-60, 67; Geoffrion, *Rhetorical Purpose*, 30, 127; Witherington, *Friendship*, 19-20; cf. Aristotle *Rh.* 1394A9-11. Although the absence of an *indignatio* component (reiteration of the case against the opponents) to the *peroratio* in this letter may suggest the opponents were not "firmly entrenched", it is more likely that "its absence is in line with the needs of deliberative rhetoric to be persuasive rather than invective where opposition is concerned" (cf. Watson, "Rhetorical Analysis", 78).

disunity and tendency to avoid conflict is in the form of exhortation, rather than practical advice.

1. Be Good Soldiers for Christ

Paul's response here follows that of the other two letters examined in seeking to strengthen group boundaries and encourage unity. This can be seen in his use of familial-language to nurture a sense of (fictive) kinship. For example, he calls them ἀδελφοί on six occasions (1:12, 3:1, 3:13, 3:17, 4:1, 4:8) — most of which occur in the context of his discussion of disunity. Similarly, he stresses that they are his partners (μοι ἐκκλησία ἐκοινώνησεν — 4:15), and that God is their father (θεῷ καὶ πατρὶ ἡμῶν — 4:19). Paul also seeks to strengthen the boundaries via apocalyptic dualism. This is evident in his description of their oppressors as "destined for destruction" (αὐτοῖς ἔνδειξις ἀπωλείας — 1:28) and "a crooked and perverse generation" (γενεᾶς σκολιᾶς καὶ διεστραμμένης — 2:15).

His response in this letter, however, is quite unique in that his arguments for unity are strongly couched in military language and imagery.[152] Unity was vitally important for the Roman military system since it relied on numbers, not individual skill. This is particularly evident in the Roman *testudo*, where a group of soldiers stood in a rectangle and arranged their shields to cover the group as a whole (hence the name "tortoise"). Paul's language in 1:27, μιᾷ ψυχῇ

---

[152] This usage is only recognized by Geoffrion (*Rhetorical Purpose*) and Krentz ("Military Language"). The appropriateness of such language here is not surprising, not only because of Philippi's history, but because the most important topic of deliberative speeches was war, peace and the defence of one's country (e.g. Aristotle *Rh.* 1359B19-23; cf. Geoffrion, *Rhetorical Purpose*, 36 n. 3). In so doing, Paul may be following a philosophical tradition which described the philosophical or ethical life in terms of the faithful soldier. See, for example, Epictetus *Diss.* 1.14.15-16, 3.24.95-9; Seneca *Ep.* 59.7-8, 96.5, 102.9-10; Plato *Ap.* 28D-E; cf. Pfitzner, *Agon Motif*, 157; Geoffrion, *Rhetorical Purpose*, 38-42, 59; Krentz, "Military Language", 105-7. Witherington, however, claims that the primary issue the *narratio* addresses is that of *concordia* (*Friendship*, 18). But he fails to note the prevalence and importance of this military language which suggests otherwise. Unlike the situation in 1 Corinthians, where *concordia* is Paul's prime concern and the chief problem, here the issue of unity is important not in its own right but, as 1:29-30 makes clear, due to the context of conflict or (to use the imagery of the *narratio*) because they are at war.

συναθλοῦντες, is particularly reminiscent of the standard battle line, where each soldier had an allotted place and was expected to keep it at all times. Indeed, if any individual soldier broke ranks and allowed the enemy through, the whole company could be lost.[153]

Throughout the letter Paul uses military language and imagery related to fulfilling one's duty as a soldier. Indeed, this language, and the way in which he makes use of it, shows many similarities to the speeches that were given by generals to encourage their troops prior to battle.[154] This is most apparent in the statement of the proposition in 1:27-30.[155] Specifically, Paul calls upon the Philippian Christians to fulfil their duty as citizens (ἀξίως... πολιτεύεσθε), to stand firm (στήκετε), to have a single purpose and attitude (μιᾷ ψυχῇ), to fight side by side (συναθλοῦντες), and not to be intimidated by the enemy forces (μὴ πτυρόμενοι...ὑπὸ τῶν ἀντικειμένων).[156]

Examples of great military deeds were also commonly used in Greek and Roman education.[157] In his letter to the Philippians, Paul presents himself (1:2-26), Timothy (2:19-24) and Epaphroditus (2:25-30) as models of faithful soldiers and citizens. He emphasizes the steadfast commitment of each to God.[158] By implication, this is what he expects from the Philippian Christians as well. In other words, they should

---

[153] Watson, *Roman Soldier*, 70-1; cf. Krentz, "Military Language", 119-24.

[154] Geoffrion, *Rhetorical Purpose*, 54-69; Krentz, "Military Language", 113-15.

[155] Military language and metaphors are, however, found throughout the letter. For example, he describes Epaphroditus as συστρατιώτην μου (2:25), and Euodia and Syntyche as συνήθλησάν μοι (4:2). Although Watson claims that the problem addressed by the *narratio* is a rival gospel ("Rhetorical Analysis", 58-9), there is no evidence for this, and he misses the prominence of the military language/imagery in the letter.

[156] Krentz notes that "fear" was seen as the "great enemy of unity of purpose in war" and was swiftly dealt with by generals ("Military Language", 124).

[157] See Geoffrion, *Rhetorical Purpose*, 125-6; cf. Lucian *Anach.* 20-2.

[158] See Geoffrion, *Rhetorical Purpose*, 76-8, 128, 145; cf. Garland, "Composition", 163; A. B. Luter & M. V. Lee, "Philippians as Chiasmus: Key to the Structure, Unity and Theme Questions" *NTS* 41 (1995) 98; C. S. Wansink, *Chained in Christ: The Experience and Rhetoric of Paul's Imprisonment* (JSNTSup 130; Sheffield: Sheffield Academic Press, 1996) 117-18.

show steadfast commitment to God as disciplined and faithful soldiers, be united in purpose, stand their ground and not break ranks, and not be afraid of their opposition despite their strength.

2. Accept Suffering

Paul also calls upon them to accept their suffering, and not to try to avoid it. This is particularly evident in his affirmation that ὑμῖν ἐχαρίσθη τὸ ὑπὲρ Χριστοῦ...πάσχειν (1:29), and in the example he presents of his own approach to conflict. Indeed, Paul portrays himself as a martyr and in so doing presents himself as an example for the Philippians to imitate. This is suggested by the way he speaks of his own death (1:20-3), which governs his calls to them in the *narratio* (1:27-30), and by his attitude of joy in the face of suffering (2:17-18; 3:1; 4:4-9), which is a common martyrological theme.[159] It is also possible that the language of "perfection"

---

[159] See, for example, 3 Macc 4:1; 4 Macc 1:18-23, 10:20-1; Josephus *AJ* 2.299; cf. Pobee, *Martyrdom*, 98-103. Hawthorne doubts that 2:17, and especially the idea of being poured out as a libation, has a martyrological inference. He claims that the term σπένδομαι does not normally refer to killing and it is a present here, not a future, as a martyrological interpretation would require (*Philippians*, 106). But since the term does refer to his sufferings for the gospel, it is not possible to rule out such a motif. Yet the element that perhaps most suggests martyrdom here is not the idea of libation but of joy in the face of suffering, a point he misses. Besides, Hawthorne does not adequately explain the ἀλλὰ εἰ καί of 2:17, which does suggest Paul considered his death a real possibility. In other words, Paul expresses his *willingness* to be martyred on their behalf (O'Brien, *Commentary*, 305-6). Paul's language in 1:21ff. also draws on Greco-Roman ideas of "noble suicide", where death was understood as a "gain" because "the burdensome travails of this earthly life are left behind" (T. F. Dailey, "To Live or Die: Paul's Eschatological Dilemma in Philippians 1:19-26" *Int* 44 [1990] 24; cf. D. W. Palmer, "'To Die is Gain' [Philippians 1:21]" *NovT* 17 [1975] 208-16; A. J. Droge, "*Mori Lucrum*: Paul and Ancient Theories of Suicide" *NovT* 30 [1988] 264-73, 280-1; J. L. Jaquette, "A Not-so-noble Death: Figured Speech, Friendship and Suicide in Philippians 1:21-26" *Neot* 28 [1994] 178-9, 182-3; Wansink, *Chained*, 120-2). However, he rejects this option in his context of conflict and suffering for the sake of the readers (1:24-6). Jaquette contends that Paul raised the possibility of his suicide to scare the Philippian Christians into ending their disunity ("Not-so-noble", 182-3) but he fails to adequately explain Paul's rationale and, as has been argued, the main focus of the letter is not disunity but dealing with conflict and suffering. It is more likely that Paul is offering himself as a model of how to deal with conflict for those who were afraid and may

in 3:12-15 may come from a martyrological tradition. For example, a group of zealous Jewish martyrs claimed that "after our death (μετὰ τὴν τελευτήν) we shall enjoy greater felicity (πλειόνων ἀγαθῶν)".[160]

The foremost example of martyrdom that Paul offers is Christ, as can be seen in the "hymn".[161] That Christ is portrayed as a martyr seems to be the plain sense of 2:8, and

---

have opted to commit suicide to spare their families from shame.

[160] Josephus *BJ* 1.653, cf. 1.650. See also 4 Macc 7:15; Wisd 4:7, 13; Philo *Leg. All.* 3.74; cf. Pfitzner, *Agon Motif*, 147. Pfitzner ultimately rejects a martyrological motif in these verses in favor of the idea that Paul was taking up and countering catchwords of the opponents of 3:2-11 (ibid., 151). But the idea that these terms relate to some gnostic or enthusiast opponents has already been ruled out. Consequently, given Paul's emphasis on his (and their) participation in the sufferings of Christ in 3:10, a martyrological motif in 3:12-15 is indeed quite likely.

[161] Pobee, *Martyrdom*, 53; Stowers, "Friends", 119. However, from its context it is clear that Christ is presented as an example in 2:6-11. See L. W. Hurtado, "Jesus as Lordly Example in Philippians 2:5-11" in P. Richardson & J. C. Hurd, eds., *From Jesus to Paul* (Waterloo, Ont.: Wilfred Laurier University Press, 1984) 116, 123-6; Fowl, *Story*, 77, 80-2; Meeks, "Man from Heaven", 331; Wright, *Climax*, 97. This is clear from Paul's statement of intent in 2:5 (Watson, "Rhetorical Analysis", 70; Witherington, *Friendship*, 60). R. T. Fortna, however, claims that "to suggest that he intends the Philippians to be more orderly and considerate because of Jesus' death is simply absurd. Rather, what this unique christology of the "hymn" fits and fits precisely is Paul's situation, not the Philippians" ("Philippians: Paul's Most Egocentric Letter" in R. T. Fortna & B. R. Gaventa, eds., *The Conversation Continues* [Nashville: Abingdon, 1990] 224). But this argument, and indeed his contention that the letter as a whole concerns Paul and his situation and does not relate to that of the Philippians, is misguided. He ignores how Paul also presents himself and others as models, following the model of Christ. For example, the linguistic links between 2:19-30 and 2:4-11 strongly suggest that Paul "has chosen to emphasize in Timothy's and Epaphroditus's behavior the same qualities he extolled in Christ" (Geoffrion, *Rhetorical Purpose*, 145; cf. Garland, "Composition", 163). It is also likely that Paul's call συμμιμηταί μου γίνεσθε (3:17) is a call for them to join together in imitating Paul, in which is also implied "as I imitate Christ" (Fee, *Philippians*, 365; cf. Hawthorne, *Philippians*, 160; O'Brien, *Commentary*, 445; Geoffrion, *Rhetorical Purpose*, 131). Fee is probably correct that, "by failing to recognize Philippians as a letter of friendship", Fortna is "quite insensitive both to the formal aspects of the letter and to its character. The result is a caricature of Paul that is based more on Western psychologizing than on the text itself" (*Philippians*, 183 n. 50). On Philippians as a "letter of friendship" see White, "Morality"; Stowers, "Friends"; Fitzgerald, "Friendship", 141-60. But their attempt to interpret the letter as *simply* a "letter of friendship" is flawed because it ignores the content and context of Paul's message to the Philippians.

especially 2:9-11, where his obedient death is vindicated by God.[162] While 2:9-11 describes something the Philippian Christians cannot emulate, it is still an example to them of God's vindication of the faithful.[163] It is possible that the image of the martyr may not have been one that they could relate to, given their non-Jewish background, but suffering on behalf of one's state and ruler was inherent in one's pledge of loyalty. For example, in the oath of allegiance sworn to Augustus as Emperor at Paphlagonia the residents promise that for the sake of Augustus and his descendants διαφερόντων μήτε σώματος φείσεσθαι μήτε ψυχῆς μήτε βίου μήτε τέκνων, ἀλλὰ παντὶ τρόπῳ ὑπὲρ τῶν ἐκείνοις ἀνηκόντων πάντα κίνδυνον ὑπομενεῖν.[164]

Therefore, Paul encourages the Philippian Christians to be loyal to their ruler and willing to suffer anything for his sake. In the face of suffering and oppression, they should not seek to avoid it but to accept it as Christ did during his life on earth (2:8) and as Paul is now doing (2:17, 3:10-15), even if that meant being martyred. At the same time, through the "hymn" (2:9-11), he assures them of God's vindication if they remain faithful. He also assures them that God will strengthen, support and equip them (4:11-12, 19).[165]

3. Reject Status and Change Political Loyalties

Consequently, to seek to avoid the conflict by continuing to take pride in their status as Roman citizens and by worshipping the Emperor (and to a lesser extent by seeking refuge in Jewish status), is disloyalty to Christ their new "Emperor". That is, Paul calls on them to change their political loyalties. This is most evident in his motif of

---

[162] See Fowl, *Story*, 64; cf. Perkins, "Theology", 96; Geoffrion, *Rhetorical Purpose*, 133; Marshall, "Theology", 136.

[163] Hurtado, "Example", 123; Fowl, *Story*, 66, 95; Geoffrion, *Rhetorical Purpose*, 138. As Hurtado acknowledges, "it is not strictly *imitatio* but rather *conformites*" ("Example", 125; cf. White, "Morality", 210).

[164] *ILS* 8781. See also Thucydides 2.41.22-4, 2.64.4-2.65.1; cf. Geoffrion, *Rhetorical Purpose*, 71, 76.

[165] Oakes rightly suggests that "to see 4:11-13 as a model for the Philippians of Christ's ability to sustain the sufferer, under whatever conditions might arise, makes much more sense of the place of the passage in the context of the development of the argument of the letter as a whole" ("Philippians", 153; cf. Geoffrion, *Rhetorical Purpose*, 214-15).

"heavenly citizenship", where πολιτεύεσθε (1:27) refers to the behavior that was appropriate for the heavenly πολίτευμα (3:20) to which they now belong.[166]

Oakes, however, claims that πολιτεύεσθε would not initially have been heard as "live as citizens of heaven" even if it was on subsequent hearings.[167] But his objection is weak because there was a strong philosophical tradition concerning

---

[166] Perkins, "Theology", 102; Geoffrion, *Rhetorical Purpose*, 24-5; cf. Fowl, *Story*, 86; O'Brien, *Commentary*, 145; Witherington, *Friendship*, 51. Brewer, however, claims Paul uses πολιτεύεσθε to call the Philippian Christians to "discharge your obligations as citizens and residents of Philippi faithfully and as a Christian should" ("The Meaning", 83; cf. Winter, *Seek*, 82-4, 104; T. Engberg-Pedersen, "Stoicism in Philippians" in idem, ed., *Paul in His Hellenistic Context* [Minneapolis: Fortress, 1995] 263 n. 12). But, as Geoffrion notes, there is no other instruction given that was aimed at increasing their respectability and lessening the conflict with the wider community (*Rhetorical Purpose*, 47), such as in 1 Thess 4:11-12, 5:14-15. Indeed, Paul's call to perseverance, steadfastness and acceptance of suffering suggests otherwise. Rather, "he urges them to think in terms of what it means to be good citizens in the civil context and then apply that construct to their identity as Christians" (Geoffrion, *Rhetorical Purpose*, 48; cf. Fowl, *Story*, 86; Fee, *Philippians*, 161-2). On the other hand, E. C. Miller suggests that rather than a Greco-Roman context, the use of πολιτεύεσθε should be seen in a Jewish context. For example, he notes that in the Maccabean literature, for example, it "refers to the Jews living faithfully in fidelity to Torah as God's chosen people", or that it refers to being "a member of Israel, the Jewish nation, in good standing". Consequently, he claims *politeuma* cannot mean "commonwealth" but is more akin to the Biblical idea of "the remnant" ("Πολιτεύεσθε in Philippians 1.27: Some Philological and Thematic Observations" *JSNT* 15 [1982] 86, 89-91; cf. Peterlin, *Paul's Letter*, 55). But this is highly improbable. The (Gentile) Philippian Christians would not have heard it in those terms (see Oakes, "Philippians", 200; Engberg-Pedersen, "Stoicism", 263 n. 12) and Miller ignores the deliberate Imperial-cult language Paul uses in 3:20 in conjunction with *politeuma* that suggest it was deliberately intended to be understood in its Greco-Roman context.

[167] Oakes, "Philippians", 199. His contention also stems from his earlier argument that the Philippian church was not primarily composed of citizens, but this has already been rejected as unsatisfactory. Furthermore, in that context, Oakes suggests that πολιτεύεσθε refers more generally to conduct within the whole public sphere, rather than referring to "live as citizens" (ibid.). In support he cites Winter (*Seek*, 82). But he misrepresents Winter, who actually considers it "'to live as citizens' (πολιτεύεσθε) in the world of *politeia* in a way that is worthy of the gospel". Indeed, on at least two other occasions Winter specifically speaks in terms of "citizenship" (ibid., 102, 104). Nor does Oakes offer any primary sources to support his contention.

the heavenly or ideal "state".[168] For example, Philo claims that for the "wise" the heavenly regions, where their citizenship is (τὸν οὐράνιον χῶρον ἐν ᾧ πολιτεύονται), is their "native land", while they are sojourners (παροικοῦντες) on earth.[169] Oakes also ignores the fact that there are occurrences where the verb πολιτεύομαι was used in a spiritual sense. For example, Heraclitus contends that after his death πολιτεύσομαι οὐκ ἐν ἀνθρώποις, ἀλλ' ἐν θεοῖς.[170]

Paul's expression ἡμῶν...τὸ πολίτευμα ἐν οὐρανοῖς, suggests that he has something like this philosophical notion in mind. There are, however, considerable differences.[171] What Paul refers to is not simply some sort of platonic ideal, but to a reality that is as a direct competitor to, and contrast with, the Roman Empire. Hence, the sense of πολίτευμα here is of "commonwealth" or "state", in the same sense in which writers speak of τὸ Ῥωμαίων πολίτευμα.[172] Timothy Geoffrion asserts that "in a spiritual sense, their citizenship derives

---

[168] See, for example, Plato *Resp.* 597B; Cicero *Rep.* 6.13-29; Dio Chrys. *Or.* 30.26; Plutarch *Cleom.* 9; Alexarchus in Athenaeus 98D; Marcus Aurelius 3.11; cf. J. Ferguson, *Utopias of the Classical World* (London: Thames & Hudson, 1975) 68-9, 108-9, 120; Portefaix, *Sisters Rejoice*, 153; Stowers, "Friends", 111-12. It should also be noted that the terms πολιτεύεσθε and πολίτευμα form an *inclusio* around the body of the argument, something that Oakes also misses. See Black, "Structure", 34.

[169] Philo *Confus.* 77-8; cf. *Agr.* 81; *Confus.* 107-9; *Ios.* 69-71.

[170] Heraclitus *Ep.* 5. Similarly, Menander Rhetor asserts that a certain man who has died "is sharing the community of the gods" (πολιτεύεται γὰρ μετὰ τῶν θεῶν — Επιδ. 421.15).

[171] For example, Paul does not follow Philo in portraying heaven as their "homeland" or the Christians as "sojourners", i.e. he uses πολίτευμα, not πάτρα or πατρίς. See also Lincoln, *Paradise*, 108; cf. Stowers, "Friends", 112; Witherington, *Friendship*, 52. Cotter, however, claims that Paul's contrast is not between heaven and Rome "because the home city of the Philippians is Philippi" (*"Politeuma"*,104). But she assumes that Paul's conception follows that of Philo's heavenly homeland, and she understands *politeuma* in terms of a traditional Greek πόλις, rather than the relationship between a Roman *colonia* and Rome.

[172] See, for example, Polybius 6.56.6. Indeed this term is commonly used by both Polybius and Dionysius of Halicarnassus for the Roman state. See also Lincoln, *Paradise*, 99. The context in which Paul uses it rules out the idea that it means "a colony of heaven", as Reumann suggests ("Hymnic Fragment", 600). Nor can it be understood as a reference to the supposed idea of the Jewish *politeuma* as a political entity within Diaspora cities. See section II.3.iii of chapter 2 herein; *contra* Perkins, "Christology", 516-17.

from heaven, just as their earthly citizenship, deriving from Philippi's status as a Roman colony, is tied to Rome", and "Paul emphasizes their identity in terms of their relationship to their fellow citizens of heaven".[173] He is wrong, however, to limit this to "a spiritual sense", since life in the ancient world was non-compartmentalized. Rather, as citizens of this new "state" they are to reflect its laws and values, rather than those of the Roman Empire, in the full context of their lives.

Witherington, however, claims that Paul is not trying to incite a revolution against the empire since his emphasis in 3:21 is on Christ accomplishing this on his return. Rather, he promotes a relativization of, and detachment from, Roman citizenship.[174] But Witherington ignores the highly subversive nature of this relativization in the context of conflict with the wider civic community. To ascribe loyalty to someone other than the Emperor was treasonous.

Furthermore, Paul also calls on the Philippian Christians to renounce their status, something that is also socially and politically subversive. This call is chiefly found in his account of Christ in the "hymn".[175] The reference to Christ as τὸ εἶναι ἴσα θεῷ (2:6c) suggests that he sees the equality in terms of status or position. This is confirmed by the "position" to which he goes, namely, "taking the form of a slave". Indeed, going from equality with God to being a slave represents the widest possible change in status imaginable.[176]

---

[173] Geoffrion, *Rhetorical Purpose*, 28; cf. Lincoln, *Paradise*, 100; Portefaix, *Sisters Rejoice*, 139. Polybius uses two Greek phrases to describe the Roman state: τὸ Ῥωμαίων πολίτευμα and τὰ Ῥωμαίων πράματα (6.56.6-7). Given the way he uses these two, it is likely that the former corresponds to the Latin idea of *Senatus Populusque Romanus* (SPQR) and the latter to *res publica*. If so, the former emphasis is on the state as a group of citizens, the latter on the more formal and legal institution. This distinction is supported by the fact that most nouns ending in -ευμα appear to be collective nouns, e.g. ἱεράτευμα (1 Pet 2:5, 9), στράτευμα (Mt 22:7; Acts 23:10; Rev 19:14). Therefore, the fact that Paul has specifically chosen the term πολίτευμα may support Geoffrion's assertion at this point.

[174] Witherington, *Friendship*, 100; cf. idem, *Conflict*, 298.

[175] See, for example, Perkins, "Theology", 103-4; Wright, *Climax*, 87; Cotter, *"Politeuma"*, 97-8; Marshall, "Theology", 136. Paul also presents himself as a model for the renunciation of status for the sake of the gospel in his rejection of his Jewish status in 3:2-11. Indeed, in this passage Paul parallels Christ's renunciation of his status in the "hymn". See Cotter, *"Politeuma"*, 97-8.

[176] See Oakes, "Philippians", 218.

The idea of renunciation of status is inherent in the term ἁρπαγμός (2:6b), which means "something to take advantage of'", and the idea that Christ "did not consider being equal with God something to be taken advantage of".[177] In other words, the temptation for Christ was to cling to his status and rights and opt out of what was expected of him.[178]

The political nature of this example is most evident in the phrase θανάτου δὲ σταυροῦ (2:8). Regardless of whether this line was added to the "hymn" or was an original part, it is clear from the structure and the argument that it is the crux or the key to the text.[179] For a church in such a Roman setting as Philippi, the very mention of the word "cross" would have been unpleasant. It was a highly offensive and shameful symbol.[180] As a punishment it was largely restricted to the lower classes, provincials and slaves and nearly always was associated with rebellion and high treason.[181]

Therefore, to affirm that the one whom they now regarded as their new Lord had been convicted and executed as a traitor, a rebel and a slave is more than a relativization of, or detachment from, their allegiance to Rome. It constitutes a massive paradigm shift. To affirm this did not just involve a change in attitude or thinking but a completely new way of relating and living within the wider civic community. It was tantamount to a complete rejection of their

---

[177] See Wright, *Climax*, 57-97. I accept the growing consensus that Wright is correct. See also Fowl, *Story*, 56; O'Brien, *Commentary*, 212; Marshall, "Theology", 132-3; Witherington, *Friendship*, 66; Fee, *Philippians*, 206 n. 56; Oakes, "Philippians", 219.

[178] Wright, *Climax*, 92.

[179] For arguments that the phrase was an addition see Beare, *Commentary*, 85; Robbins, "Rhetorical Structure", 73; Hurtado, "Example", 123; Reumann, "Theologies", 529. For arguments that it was an original part see Collange, *Epistle*, 104; Minear, "Singing", 206; O'Brien, *Commentary*, 230; Basevi & Chapa, "Rhetorical Function", 346; Fee, *Philippians*, 217. The latter is probably more likely if the passage as a whole has a chiastic structure as Black contends ("Structure", 37). In any case, there is little doubt about the importance of the phrase in the passage.

[180] See M. Hengel, *Crucifixion in the Ancient World and the Folly of the Message of the Cross* (Philadelphia: Fortress, 1977) 22, 32, 37-8.

[181] See, for example, Appian *BCiv.* 4.20; Cicero *Phil.* 13.21; idem, *Rab. Post.* 9-17; idem, *Verr.* 2.12, 5.169; Dion. Hal. *Ant. Rom.* 7.69.1, 15.51.3; Josephus *BJ* 2.75, 5.449-51; Livy 30.43.13; Petronius *Sat.* 53.3; Strabo *Geog.* 4.18; Tacitus *Hist.* 2.72, 4.11; cf. Hengel, *Crucifixion*, 29-30, 34, 39-41, 46-7, 51-3, 59.

rights and status as Roman citizens.[182] So Paul is calling on those Philippian Christians who were Roman citizens to renounce their citizenship and consider themselves as slaves — without rights or privileges — within the realm of the Roman Empire.

In his instructions and injunctions Paul does not offer any practical advice about minimizing or avoiding the conflict with the wider civic community. To the contrary, he reinforces attitudes that would sustain or escalate that conflict. In this his exhortation is vastly different from that in 1 Thessalonians, although there is also a call to renounce their citizenship. Yet his approach to this in Philippians has the potential to exacerbate the conflict since, rather than being a simple renunciation of citizenship, it involves a direct challenge to the authority of the "state".

V. CONCLUSION

In the first century CE Philippi was a small rural town and very much a community. Its planning and its epigraphic evidence suggest there was a reasonable association and interaction of different ethnic groups. There was some ethnic diversity, with Romans, *liberti*, some native Thracians and Macedonians, and maybe a few Greek immigrants. But there was no significant Jewish presence. The town was a *colonia iuris Italici*, and hence had a typically elitist and oligarchic pattern of government. Nevertheless, the patronage system meant that there were ties between the elite and the ordinary residents. The religious pattern at Philippi was diverse. Various Macedonian or Thracian gods and cults probably dominated the *territorium*, while in the township itself the gods and cults appear to be very Roman. The non-Roman gods there may have been linked to the Imperial cult, which appears to have been dominant. Overall, there was probably a strong Roman religious mentality in the town.

The Philippian church appears to have been a relatively small group, comprising some freeborn, a few slaves, and a large number of *liberti*. Most would have been

---

[182] Consequently, it is probably better to take the language of "status" and "humility" in 2:3-5 in terms of "political" or "civic" status rather than some sort of "economic" status as most commentators assume (e.g. Oakes, "Philippians", 206-8).

Roman citizens, and probably artisans and merchants. It is unlikely that any of them were very wealthy or that the church had acquired any significant group patron. Consequently, they probably met together in a small house or an *insula*-workshop.

Relations between the Christian and civic communities at Philippi involved quite serious conflict and oppressive measures because of withdrawal from the traditional cult practices. This conflict had left the Christians afraid and at odds over how to deal with it. A significant group within the church tried to alleviate or avoid the conflict. Some were tempted to be circumcized and gain the protection afforded to Jews who followed their ancestral practices. Others, because of a Roman religious mentality, were tempted to offer worship to the Emperor and/or join *collegia*. There were probably some who had already followed these options, whom Paul regards as apostates, and who tried to persuade the Philippian Christians to follow them.

In response, Paul exhorts them by offering various examples of the sort of behavior that is appropriate. He calls on them to think of themselves as soldiers for Christ and exhorts them to remain steadfast in their commitment to Christ, to be united in purpose, not to break ranks, and not to be afraid of their opposition. Paul also calls on them to accept their suffering on behalf of Christ, following Christ's example of martyrdom, in a manner that was expected of citizens on behalf of their state and ruler. At the same time, he assures them of God's vindication if they remain faithful.

Finally, he urges them to consider themselves citizens of a new empire, τὸ πολίτευμα ἐν οὐρανοῖς, and to renounce the rights, status and values of the Roman Empire. In so doing, Paul offers advice that will lead to a further exacerbation of the conflict. Although he calls on them to renounce their citizenship, as he does with the Thessalonian Christians, here this does not simply involve becoming as *metics* and peacefully withdrawing from public life. Rather, Paul encourages them to see themselves as citizens and soldiers of another "Empire" at war with the one in which they live.

Chapter Seven

DIFFERENT CITIES, DIFFERENT
RELATIONSHIPS

The previous three chapters have sought to reconstruct the civic and Christian communities of Thessalonica, Corinth and Philippi and to explore the relationships between the communities for each city. In this chapter I will formally compare and contrast the church-city relationships. This comparison will proceed, firstly, by drawing together the material from the previous three chapters concerning the relationships and the response of the churches to those relationships. Following that, the model that was outlined in the conclusion to part one of this study will be used to explain the differences in these relationships.

I. A COMPARISON OF THE THREE CITIES & CHURCHES

On the most simple level, it is clear that the Thessalonian and Philippian churches both experienced conflict with their wider civic communities. The Corinthian church, however, did not. It was suggested in chapters four and six that when such conflict did arise it was due to the Christians' withdrawal from their traditional cultic practices — an action that would have had political, social, and religious implications. Such a withdrawal would have been a serious issue given the way in which these aspects of life were integrated in the first century.

At both Thessalonica and Philippi the response of the
civic community to this withdrawal would have involved
predominantly strained social relations. This could have been
manifest as social ostracism, insults/abuse, discrimination,
financial sanctions, even sporadic violence. Yet, it is also
likely that some legal actions were taken, even if there was
no edict or ban on Christianity at this stage. Such actions
may have related to breeching the oath of allegiance to the
Emperor, which could have been met with a variety of
responses such as beatings, imprisonment or possibly even
death. At Thessalonica, however, the Christians also would
have been labelled as "atheists" — a serious crime in a
"Greek" community.[1] The same charge would not have been
levelled at Philippi.

Furthermore, it is clear that the conflict at Thessalonica
had been present from the very beginning. In other words, it
was provoked by the Christians' conversion *per se*. This link
of conflict with conversion does not appear to have been the
case in other towns in Macedonia and Achaia, as 1 Thess 1:6-
9 implies. Nothing in Paul's letter to the Philippians suggests
that the conflict they were experiencing at the time he wrote
was one *they* had experienced from the moment of their
conversion. Indeed Phil 1:30 implies that the conflict at
Philippi is only a recent phenomenon. In other words, once
begun the conflict might have been of a similar magnitude in
both towns, but the incidence of conflict was higher (or the
conflict-threshold was lower) at Thessalonica.

The Corinthian church, on the other hand, did not
experience conflict with its wider community. Indeed, there is
much in 1 Corinthians to suggest that the relationship
between the civic and Christian communities was generally
very good, even if most of this evidence (intermarriage,
sexual relations, lawsuits, participation in cultic celebrations,
dinner invitations) relates to the few elite Christians.
Nevertheless, the recognition that outsiders could drop in "off
the street" (1 Cor 14:23-4) is indicative of a lack of conflict.

While there are some similarities between Thessalonica
and Philippi in terms of their church-city relationships, the
churches' responses to those relationships were quite

---

[1] As throughout this study, the terms "Greek" or "Greeks" are used
to refer to communities and people who share norms, values and beliefs
that may be broadly defined as Greek or Hellenistic, but who may come
from diverse geographical regions, e.g. Greece itself, Macedonia, Asia
Minor, Greek Islands.

different. The Thessalonian Christians generally held separatist tendencies. This was exacerbated by the apocalyptic eschatology they had adopted from Paul, which helped to explain their situation. They also retaliated against the treatment they received. This possibly involved civil disturbance and disobedience, including strikes, protests, and disruptions to the meetings of the *demos*. Some, however, were losing heart and may have been tempted to return to their traditional religious practices. But none of them appear to have lapsed.

On the other hand, within the Philippian church many sought to avoid the conflict they were experiencing. Indeed, fear of repercussions and oppressive measures had already led some to become "apostates" and others were being tempted either to take refuge in Jewish status, by appearing to follow Jewish ancestral customs, or to return to their traditional cults and *collegia*. There was also a significant element of disunity within the church concerning the appropriate response. Such disunity does not appear to have been significant in the Thessalonian church, given the style of the letter Paul wrote and his argument (compared to Philippians or 1 Corinthians).

The Corinthian church was plagued by internal conflict, to a much greater extent than the Philippian church. Indeed, Paul's chief concern in 1 Corinthians appears to be factionalism and struggles for status and power within the church, especially on the part of the elite Christians. In this regard, it was suggested in chapter five that the elite Christians may have been more concerned about the opinions of their non-Christian peers or equals than their fellow Christians. They do not appear to have adopted Paul's apocalyptic eschatology, and may have misunderstood his teaching on idolatry.

Paul's response to conflict is to encourage a strengthening of the boundaries between the Christian and civic communities. This involves his fostering a strong sense of (fictive) kinship, and reaffirming an apocalyptic dualism and the adoption of a moral code that clearly separates them from those outside the church. It also involves a call to renounce their rights and status as citizens. The difference in his response from the Thessalonian to the Philippian churches, however, could indicate a hardening of his position. For example, there is nothing in his letter to the Philippians that is specifically aimed at reducing the conflict, unlike his injunctions in 1 Thess 4:11-12. There could be a number of explanations for this apparent hardening, such as the length of time between the two letters, while Paul's changed eschatological expectations may have contributed. But it is more likely that the divergence is due to the different contexts and the different responses of the churches.

This can be seen in Paul's call for a similar withdrawal at Corinth, although the Corinthian Christians did not experience this sort of conflict. In 1 Corinthians, however, his more radical concerns are veiled in some ambiguity. This probably reflects the status of those he is addressing. In other words, he shows some socially-conditioned reserve when dealing with his social betters at Corinth, who serve a protective role, and his reserve appears even to result in some ambiguity and some compromise. This reserve probably also reflects the difficulty of his relationship with the Corinthians. Nevertheless, 2 Cor 6:14-7:1 suggests that his efforts to foster greater unity within the church and to strengthen the boundaries between the church and its wider community failed, and these efforts may have contributed to the further worsening of their relationship.[2]

Overall, then, there are considerable differences between the three churches and their relationships to their wider civic communities. On a scale from a very high incidence of conflict to a very low incidence, Thessalonica and Corinth would appear to be at the respective extremes, with Philippi somewhere in the middle (although more on the high conflict side).

II. EXPLAINING THE DIFFERENCES

It was argued in the introduction to this study that explanation — the answering of "why" questions — requires the use of theories and models. Hence, a specific model was developed in part one of this study for the purpose of explaining differences in conflict response between different societies. Before the propositions of that model are discussed

---

[2] The issue of Paul's response to the relationship between the Christian and civic communities, and especially an evaluation of the adequacy of his response, is a study in its own right. The same could be said regarding the issue of how and why these various churches differently appropriated Paul's gospel. Both are clearly beyond the scope of this current study.

and applied to these three churches, it would be helpful to briefly recall some of the theory on which they are based.

According to the "Culture of Conflict" theory, the incidence of conflict varies according to a society's particular world-view and social institutions, such that societies can be classified as high or low conflict cultures. A high conflict culture is one where primary socialization is harsh, relational ties are reinforcing,[3] there is a pattern of ethnic homogeneity or segregation of ethnic groups, and there is a concentration of political power in the hands of a few (or egalitarianism with reinforcing ties). In most cases, however, the particular pattern of norms, values and beliefs is more important than the manner of socialization.

It was also argued in part one of this study that perhaps the most important factor in determining the incidence of conflict was the pattern of relational ties. Indeed, in a society where the pattern of ties is more cross-cutting, the incidence of conflict will be reduced because both sides of a potential conflict are connected to each other and to a large number of other parties. Consequently, it is in everyone's best interest to avoid any conflict.

While first century Mediterranean society was a high conflict culture, not least because harsh socialization was a common feature, at a lower level of abstraction there appear to be variations. Indeed, there are considerable differences between Greek and Roman communities in some of the factors mentioned above. Specifically, there are differences in the pattern of norms, values and beliefs, the pattern of relational ties, and the type of political system.

1. Norms, Values and Beliefs

The first proposition of the model outlined in the conclusion to part one contends that *conflicts between a Christian community and its wider civic community would center on the particular norms, values and beliefs of the civic community, especially those related to being a citizen or resident.* It is apparent from the previous three chapters that

---

[3] A pattern of reinforcing ties occurs when an individual's kin and neighborhood ties, and ties associated with social groups and political affiliations, overlap such that the same people are involved in each case and there is only one main difference between groups. In contrast, a pattern of cross-cutting ties occurs when an individual's various ties are shared by a variety of people.

the various religious and political norms, values and beliefs associated with being a citizen or resident were points of contention. And given that each of the cities functioned as a *Gemeinschaft*-type community, its particular combination of norms, values and beliefs would have been firmly held by each city.

Thessalonica was a *civitas libera* and, as such, a Greek city. This is quite evident in its political structures and the gods its people worshipped. Consequently, it was suggested that the dominant religious mentality would also have been Greek, and hence that there would have been a high value placed on congruity between religious belief and practice. It is for this reason that the charge of "atheism" would have been a pertinent one in the city. The Thessalonian church itself seems to have retained this religious perspective, since there is a clear congruity between its Christian belief and practice. This is especially seen in its separatist tendencies.

Although the Thessalonian Christians maintained this value, the very congruity of their Christian belief and practice would have been a major issue in initiating conflict, for the content of their belief and practice was a direct threat to the rest of Thessalonian society. This is even more significant if, as was argued in chapter four, the Thessalonian church was comprised of native Thessalonians. Indeed, a deviant definition of reality is less tolerated when it involves defectors from the plausibility structure of the dominant group. This may help to explain the lack of a trigger for the development of conflict in that city.[4]

The city's political vulnerability may also have played a significant role. Indeed, the privilege of *civitas libera* was one that could be, and often was, revoked. Consequently, there would have been a greater concern at Thessalonica with maintaining peace and order, and avoiding anything that hinted at subversion or rebellion. Besides, since it was a Greek community, there would have been a particularly high value placed on *homonoia* and against *stasis*. Consequently, there would be little tolerance towards a small, but vocal, minority group. A continuing commitment to Greek city-state principles would also have been important in the city.

---

[4] As will become clearer over the course of this chapter, Thessalonian society was a high conflict culture. Consequently, this apparent lack of a trigger is consistent with the low threshold for the development of conflict we would expect in a high conflict culture.

Therefore, the refusal of the Christians to worship the city's gods would have been interpreted as disloyalty, and taken as an insult by the city's citizens.

Corinth, by its very nature would have been more "tolerant". The city's origins were recent and its population came from varied backgrounds. Indeed, there would have been a mixture of Greek and Roman religious mentalities, although the latter would have been more prevalent among the elite and citizens. Evidence also suggests that philosophy, especially Stoicism, was important in the town. A similar mix of religious mentalities and philosophical influences is also evident in the church. It is perhaps significant that Corinth is the only one of the three cities and churches where Jews were prominent. Their presence suggests that there was a considerable diversity of religious norms, values and beliefs. Such a variety means that the incidence of conflict between the church and the civic community would be much less at Corinth, since there would not be a united front against the Christians. It would always be possible to play one group off against another.

The religious mentality at Philippi, on the other hand, would have been strongly Roman — at least in the township itself. As such, there would have been a great emphasis on the right conduct of cultic practices, and little concern with what people believed as individuals. The response of the Philippian Christians is also consistent with such a mentality, in that many were tempted to avoid the conflict by maintaining their traditional religious practices while adhering to their Christian beliefs.

Hence, at Philippi, the conflict between the church and the civic community would have centered on their non-participation in the city's cults (although a strong sense of civic pride, due to the town's history, would also have been a factor). Withdrawal from the cults would have been viewed seriously because it threatened the *pax deorum / pax Romana*. As such it would have been seen as a threat to the town from the wrath of the gods. Therefore it is possible, given the prevalence of earthquakes in the area, that such a disaster may have been the trigger for the initiation of conflict proper, interpreted as the gods' punishment for "impiety".[5]

---

[5] A trigger such as this was probably required since Philippian society was only a moderately high conflict culture, as will become clearer in the course of this chapter. As such, its conflict threshold was probably significantly higher than was the threshold at Thessalonica.

This withdrawal of the Christians from the town's cults also constitutes a defection from the plausibility structure, as at Thessalonica. Thus, we would expect the conflict at Philippi to have been initiated by their conversion to Christianity, but this does not appear to be the case. Part of the difference may be that, as suggested in chapter two, the Romans were generally more tolerant toward foreigners and foreign cults than were the Greeks (although neither could be said to be tolerant *per se*).[6] When the Romans acted against foreign cults it was due to breaches of law and order. While this norm may go a little way towards explaining the difference in conflict incidence and response between Thessalonica and Philippi, it is still not completely clear why conflict appears to have taken some time to develop at Philippi. Clearly other factors are at work.

2. Relational Ties

The second proposition of the model asserts that *where there is a pattern of cross-cutting ties there will be lower incidence of conflict, especially when those ties include members of the ruling elite, while a pattern of reinforcing ties will have a higher incidence of conflict*. A pattern of cross-cutting ties results in a lower incidence of conflict since it prevents the development of a united front. This proposition appears to have significant potential for explaining the difference in conflict response in the three cities, since they had considerable differences in their patterns of relational ties.

There is little evidence of interaction between the different social strata at Thessalonica. Certainly, as a Greek city, there would have been no patronage system as there was at Corinth and Philippi. In chapter four it was argued that the Christians at Thessalonica were subsistence artisans, that there were no members of the ruling elite in the church, and probably no slaves or freedpersons (given a Greek rather than a Roman institution of slavery). In other words, the church was socially very homogeneous. Therefore, relational ties at Thessalonica, and especially those involving the Thessalonian Christians, were strongly reinforcing. The only distinction between them and the wider community is in

---

[6] Indeed, Sordi notes that action against Christians in the late first/ early second centuries was especially characteristic of the Greek cities of the eastern provinces (*The Christians*, 195-8).

religious allegiance — a single dominant cleavage. Such a pattern of strongly reinforcing ties helps to explain the high incidence of conflict in the city.

At Corinth, the opposite set of conditions existed. There was a strong interaction between the various social strata by means of the patronage system, as seen in the election of *liberti* to administrative and magisterial positions. The unique history of the city suggests that there was some social mobility, which was also facilitated by patronal ties. A full social spectrum is also present within the Corinthian church, including some members of the ruling elite (Gaius, Erastus, and some who are not named), artisans of modest wealth as well as many at subsistence level, and slaves. Consequently, the conditions suggest a strong pattern of cross-cutting ties. Indeed, this explains the lack of conflict between the church and the civic community, and it could even explain the weakness of the internal bonds and hence the high incidence of internal conflict.

The conditions at Philippi are somewhere in-between these two extremes. As a Roman town, the patronage system was strong and there was interaction between the various strata, as evidence from the *collegia* suggests. But there were no members of the elite in the Philippian church. Most of the Christians would have been subsistence artisans, with a few of modest wealth. Although the lack of significant group patronage probably made them more vulnerable to conflict, the presence of some members of the *familia Caesaris* would have contributed to the delay in the onset of the conflict since they had some status and influence. Thus, while there is a strong pattern of cross-cutting ties within Philippian society, the bonds between the Christians and the wider community were less so. This explains the moderate incidence of conflict between the church and city community and it could even explain the disunity within the church.

Related to the matter of relational ties is the third proposition of the model, which contends that *where there is a pattern of ethnic integration or assimilation there will be a lower incidence of conflict*. These two propositions are closely connected because the pattern of ethnic interactions also helps to determine whether the pattern of relational ties is cross-cutting or reinforcing. The discussion of the three cities has shown some difference at this point as well.

Thessalonica's population may have been fairly homogeneous. The pattern of ethnic integration, as suggested by the inscriptions (the Romans kept to themselves, there were ethnic groups such as the *Asiani*, and there may have been limited ethnic diversity within *thiasoi*), indicates that there was a reasonable degree of ethnic segregation. Consistent with this is the profile of the Thessalonian church. As has already been noted, this was comprised of native Thessalonians. Therefore, this pattern of ethnic segregation in the city and the church is consistent with and contributes to the pattern of reinforcing ties, and hence the high incidence of conflict between the church and the wider community. Such a pattern reinforces the single dominant cleavage between the two communities.

Corinth was a very cosmopolitan city. Although the evidence for ethnic interaction is sparse, what there is suggests that there was a reasonable level of integration and assimilation. The ethnic profile of the Corinthian church was also quite mixed, with Greeks, Romans and Jews. Therefore, this pattern of ethnic integration in the city and the church is consistent with and contributes to the pattern of cross-cutting ties, and hence the low incidence of conflict between the church and the wider community.

Philippi's population was also ethnically diverse with Romans, Thracians, Macedonians, some Greeks, and a large number of *liberti*. The inscriptions show that the Thracians were well integrated, readily adopting Latin and worshipping various Roman gods. Similarly, the *liberti* tended to be very Romanized. This pattern of ethnic integration and assimilation would have contributed to the strong cross-cutting ties within Philippian society. Within the church, however, there is less diversity with only freeborn Romans, *liberti*, and public slaves. Hence, the pattern of ethnic interaction in the Philippian church mirrors the pattern of its relational ties, namely, not as marked as in Philippian society generally. This would help to explain why the incidence of conflict between the church and civic community was higher than at Corinth but lower than at Thessalonica. It may also help to explain why the conflict within the Philippian church is also lower than within the Corinthian church.

3. Political Systems

The fourth proposition of the model contends that *where there is a hierarchical politico-legal system combined with strong cross-cutting ties that include the elite there will be a lower incidence of conflict than where there is an egalitarian system with reinforcing ties.* Specifically, in an egalitarian and especially in a democratic system, the decision-making process relies on numbers. Any individual or small group of individuals is relatively powerless. Within a hierarchical system, the decision-making process relies on influence and personal power, and hence connections.

Thus the democratic political system at Thessalonica worked against the Christians. Indeed, as a small group, they were relatively powerless and vulnerable to political and legal actions since they did not have force of numbers. Consequently, given that the Christians contravened the norms, values, beliefs *and* laws of the city, the distribution of political power at Thessalonica would have contributed to the conflict between the Christian and civic communities.

At Corinth, the combination of a strong patronage system, a hierarchical and oligarchic political system, and the presence of members of the ruling elite within the church would have contributed significantly to the lack of conflict between the Christian and civic communities. Indeed, under this set of conditions, conflict between the two communities is most unlikely. While the political system at Philippi was similar to that at Corinth, the church was in a very different situation. Indeed, the lack of a strong connection to the ruling elite would have been a significant factor in the development of conflict for it left the church politically and legally vulnerable. As mentioned, however, the Christians who were members of the *familia Caesaris* would have had some connection to those in power and hence may have helped delay the onset of conflict.

In summary, the model from part one has proven helpful in explaining the different incidence of conflict between the churches experienced in these three cities. There was a very high incidence of conflict at Thessalonica. This can be explained by that society's particular norms, values and beliefs that emphasized congruity and loyalty, by its pattern of relationships that permitted a unified front of opposition against defectors from its plausibility structure to form, and a democratic political system that effectively rendered the small Christian community powerless. In other words, there was a high incidence of conflict between the church and its wider civic community because Thessalonian society was a high conflict culture.

On the other hand, there was a very low incidence of conflict at Corinth. This low incidence can be attributed to more tolerant norms, values and beliefs, the diversity of Corinthian society, the level of integration and inter-connectedness of various social and ethnic groups, and the presence of some members of the ruling elite within the church. In other words, there was a low incidence of conflict between the church and its wider civic community because Corinthian society was a low conflict culture.

Some of these factors are clearly unique to Corinth itself. Indeed, at Philippi, which was also a Roman town, conflict between the Christian and civic communities did develop, although it took some time. This delay is explained by the dominant Roman values, especially a greater tolerance of diversity (compared to Greek communities, such as Thessalonica), the modest level of inter-connectedness of the Philippian Christians and the presence of some members of the *familia Caesaris*, who had some status and influence. The absence of any significant links to the ruling elite, and a lower level of ethnic and social diversity contributed to the development of conflict there. In other words, there was a moderately high incidence of conflict between the church and its wider civic community because Philippian society was a moderately high conflict culture.

CONCLUSION

This study began with the observation that the earliest Christians were subject to sporadic conflict with their wider civic communities. It is generally accepted that when such conflicts occurred they centered on the refusal of Christians to worship the traditional gods of those communities. To date, however, no one has attempted to explain why these conflicts were only sporadic. Therefore, in part one of this study, a specific social-scientific model was developed to explain why some of Paul's churches experienced conflict with their wider communities but others did not.

The preliminary model was largely based on the "Culture of Conflict" theory. According to this theory, the incidence of conflict varies according to a society's particular combination of psycho-cultural and social-structural factors. A high conflict culture is one where primary socialization is harsh, norms, values and beliefs are intolerant, relational ties are reinforcing, there is a pattern of ethnic homogeneity and/or segregation, resources are concentrated in the hands of a few and effective access to political power is very limited.

First century Mediterranean society was, generally speaking, a high conflict culture. However, when the preliminary model was tested against material from the first century Greco-Roman world, it was apparent that there was significant diversity at a lower level of abstraction. That is, individual "Greek" and Roman communities could be classed as high and low conflict cultures since there were significant differences in their patterns of norms, values and beliefs, their patterns of relational ties and their political systems.

Consequently, some modifications were made to the preliminary model so that it could be used to explain the different incidence of conflict at this particular level of abstraction. These modifications included a greater emphasis on the pattern of norms, values and beliefs, the patterns of relational ties, and the link between relational ties and political structures.

Following this, the nature of the civic and Christian communities for Thessalonica, Corinth and Philippi, and the relationships between each civic and Christian community was reconstructed. When the model was applied to these reconstructions it was apparent that the incidence of conflict in each case did reflect the culture of conflict for each city. The high incidence of conflict at Thessalonica can be attributed to Thessalonian society being a high conflict culture. In other words, its pattern of norms, values and beliefs were intolerant, its pattern of relational ties permitted the development of a unified opposition to deviants, and its democratic political structures rendered a small group effectively powerless. The low incidence of conflict at Corinth can be attributed to Corinthian society being a low conflict culture. In other words, it had relatively tolerant norms, values and beliefs, considerable interaction between different social and ethnic groups, and there were members of the ruling elite in the church. Although conflict did occur at Philippi, it was delayed, something which is consistent with it having a moderately high culture of conflict. In other words, it had relatively tolerant norms, values and beliefs (like Corinth), but the relations between the church and the wider community were not as broad. There were some members from the *familia Caesaris* (who had some influence) but no members of the ruling elite.

Consequently, the model suggests that the sporadic nature of conflict between the earliest churches and their wider civic communities was a product of various local factors which determined the culture of conflict for that particular society. However, for this model to progress to an actual theory or social law, further testing would be necessary. In that regard, it would be worthwhile to analyse the church at Rome, and the seven churches in Asia Minor addressed in the book of Revelation (Rev 2-3). If the nature of other particular civic and Christian communities could be reconstructed (such as the contexts of 1 Peter, Hebrews, Matthew, or even Q), analysis of these by means of this model would prove useful.

In the course of this study, there was some discussion of Paul's response to the conflict for each of the churches explored. The adequacy of his response, however, has not been assessed at any length, nor has the reaction of the individual churches to his response. To do so would require a study in its own right, one that would employ its own social-scientific model, presumably based on theories of conflict management. Furthermore, many of the factors involved in determining whether or not conflict developed between a particular church and its wider civic community may have contributed to the different ways in which each church appropriated Paul's gospel. Indeed, these factors may also have contributed to the relationship of the churches to Paul himself. Again, such an hypothesis requires its own study. In any case, the model used in this study is not suited to exploring or explaining these phenomena.

Nevertheless, social-scientific models are evaluated in terms of whether or not they are useful in explaining the particular phenomenon in question.[1] The specific model that was constructed and used in this study has proven useful in its own right for explaining the different incidence of conflict between several of Paul's churches and their wider civic communities. Consequently, this study has made a valuable contribution to the understanding of Christian origins, not least by offering a new model with demonstrated usefulness. It has also made a contribution towards the larger on-going study of Paul, his churches, and their communities — a study that requires the use of a range of different models.

---

[1] See for example, Esler, *First Christians*, 13.

BIBLIOGRAPHY

Primary Sources

All ancient sources and translations are taken from Loeb Classical Library volumes except for the following:

Attridge, H. W. (ed.) *First-Century Cynicism in the Epistles of Heraclitus.* HTS 29. Missoula, MT: Scholars Press, 1976.

Brunt, P. A. & J. M. Moore (eds.) *Res Gestae Divi Augusti: The Achievements of the Divine Augustus.* Oxford: Oxford University Press, 1973.

Charlesworth, J. H. (ed.) *The Old Testament Pseudepigrapha.* vol. 2. Garden City, NY: Doubleday, 1985.

Levick, B. (ed.) *The Government of the Roman Empire: A Sourcebook.* London: Croom Helm, 1988.

Meijer, F. & O. van Nijf (eds.) *Trade, Transport and Society in the Ancient World: A Sourcebook.* London: Routledge, 1992.

Russell, D. A. & N. G. Wilson (eds.) *Menander Rhetor.* Oxford: Clarendon, 1981.

Shelton, J. (ed.) *As the Romans Did: A Sourcebook in Roman Social History.* New York: Oxford University Press, 1988.

Sherk, R. K. (ed.) *The Roman Empire: Augustus to Hadrian.* Cambridge: Cambridge University Press, 1988.

_____. (ed.) *Rome and the Greek East to the Death of Augustus.* Cambridge: Cambridge University Press, 1984.

Stern, M. (ed.) *Greek and Latin Authors on Jews and Judaism.* 3 vols. Jerusalem: Israel Academy of Sciences and Humanities, 1974-84.

Secondary Sources

Abbott, F. F & A. C. Johnson. *Municipal Administration in the Roman Empire.* New York: Russell & Russell, 1968.

Abrahamsen, V. A. *Women and Worship at Philippi: Diana / Artemis and Other Cults in the Early Christian Era.* Portland, ME: Astarte Shell, 1995.

Adams, B. N. "Interaction Theory and the Social Network". *Sociometry* 30 (1967): 64-78.

Alcock, S. E. *Graecia Capta: The Landscapes of Roman Greece.* Cambridge: Cambridge University Press, 1993.

Alföldy, G. *The Social History of Rome*. Baltimore: Johns Hopkins University, 1985.

Appelbaum, S. "The Legal Status of the Jewish Communities in the Diaspora". In *The Jewish People in the First Century*, edited by S. Safrai & M. Stern. 1:420-63. Assen: van Gorcum, 1974.

Attridge, H. W. "The Philosophical Critique of Religion under the Early Empire". *ANRW* 2.16.1 (1979): 45-78.

Baird, W. " 'One Against the Other': Intra-Church Conflict in 1 Corinthians". In *The Conversation Continues: Studies in Paul & John in Honor of J. Louis Martyn*, edited by R. T. Fortna & B. R. Gaventa, 116-36. Nashville: Abingdon, 1990.

Balsdon, J. P. V. D. *Life and Leisure in Ancient Rome*. London: Bodley Head, 1969.

_____. *Romans and Aliens*. London: Duckworth, 1979.

Bammel, E. "Preparation for the Perils of the Last Days: 1 Thessalonians 3.3". In *Suffering and Martyrdom in the New Testament*, edited by W. Horbury & B. McNeil, 91-100. Cambridge: Cambridge University Press, 1981.

Barclay, J. M. G. "Conflict in Thessalonica". *CBQ* 55 (1993): 512-30.

_____. "Deviance and Apostasy: Some Applications of Deviance Theory to First-Century Judaism and Christianity". In *Modelling Early Christianity: Social-Scientific Studies of the New Testament in its Context*, edited by P. F. Esler, 114-27. London: Routledge, 1995.

_____. *Jews in the Mediterranean Diaspora from Alexander to Trajan (323 BCE-117 CE)*. Edinburgh: T. & T. Clark, 1996.

_____. *Obeying the Truth: A Study of Paul's Ethics in Galatians*. SNTW. Edinburgh: T. & T. Clark, 1988.

_____. "Paul, Philemon and the Dilemma of Christian Slave-Ownership". *NTS* 37 (1991): 161-86.

_____. "Thessalonica and Corinth: Social Contrasts in Pauline Christianity". *JSNT* 47 (1992): 49-74.

Barker, G., J. Lloyd, & D. Webley. "A Classical Landscape in Molise". *PBSR* 46 (1978): 35-51.

Barraclough, R. "Romans 13:1-7: Application in Context". *Colloquium* 17 (1984): 16-22.

Barrett, C. K. *A Commentary on the First Epistle to the Corinthians*. BNTC. London: A. & C. Black, 1971.

Bartchy, S. S. *First Century Slavery and the Interpretation of 1 Corinthians 7:21*. SBLDS 11. Atlanta: Scholars Press, 1973.

Barton, S. C. "Paul's Sense of Place: An Anthropological Approach to Community Formation in Corinth". *NTS* 32 (1986): 225-46.

Basevi, C. & J. Chapa. "Philippians 2.6-11: The Rhetorical Function of a Pauline 'Hymn'". In *Rhetoric and the New Testament: Essays from the 1992 Heidelberg Conference*, edited by S. E. Porter & T. H. Olbricht, 338-56. JSNTSup 90. Sheffield: JSOT Press, 1993.

Beare, F. W. *A Commentary on the Epistle to the Philippians*. BNTC. 3rd ed. London: A. &C. Black, 1973.

Beker, J. C. "Recasting Pauline Theology: The Coherence-Contingency Scheme as Interpretive Model". In *Pauline Theology, Volume I*, edited by J. M. Bassler, 15-24. Minneapolis: Fortress, 1991.

Benko, S. *Pagan Rome and the Early Christians*. Bloomington: Indiana University, 1984.

Berger, P. L. *The Sacred Canopy: Elements of a Sociological Theory of Religion*. New York: Doubleday, 1967.

Berger, P. L. & T. Luckmann. *The Social Construction of Reality*. Harmondsworth: Penguin, 1966.

Best, E. *A Commentary on the First and Second Epistles to the Thessalonians*. BNTC. London: A. & C. Black, 1977.

Bettini, M. *Anthropology and Roman Culture: Kinship, Time, Images of the Soul*. Baltimore: Johns Hopkins University Press, 1991.

Betz, H. D. "The Problem of Rhetoric and Theology according to the Apostle Paul". In *L'Apôtre Paul: Personnalité, style et conception du ministère*, edited by A. Vanhoye, 16-48. BETL 73. Leuven: Leuven University Press, 1986.

Black, D. A. "The Discourse Structure of Philippians: A Study in Text-linguistics". *NovT* 37 (1995): 16-49.

Bloomquist, L. G. *The Function of Suffering in Philippians*. JSNTSup 78. Sheffield: JSOT Press, 1993.

Borgen, P. "'Yes', 'No', 'How Far?': The Participation of Jews and Christians in Pagan Cults". In *Paul in His Hellenistic Context*, edited by T. Engberg-Pedersen, 30-59. Minneapolis: Fortress, 1995.

Bormann, L. *Philippi: Stadt und Christengemeinde zur Zeit des Paulus*. NovTSup 78. Leiden: E. J. Brill, 1995.

Botha, J. *Subject to Whose Authority? Multiple Readings of Romans 13*. ESEC 4. Atlanta: Scholars Press, 1994.

Bowersock, G. W. *Martyrdom and Rome*. Cambridge: Cambridge University Press, 1995.

Brewer, R. R. "The Meaning of *Politeuesthe* in Philippians 1:27". *JBL* 73 (1954): 76-83.

Broneer, O. "Corinth: Center of Saint Paul's Missionary Work in Greece". *BA* 14 (1951): 78-96.

Brooten, B. J. *Women as Leaders in the Ancient Synagogue: Inscriptional Evidence and Background Issues.* BJS 36. Chico, CA: Scholars Press, 1982.

Bruce, F. F. *1 & 2 Thessalonians.* WBC. Waco, TX: Word, 1982.

Brunt, P. A. *Italian Man-Power 225 BC-AD 14.* 2nd ed. Oxford: Clarendon, 1987.

_____. "Laus Imperii". In *Imperialism in the Ancient World*, edited by P. D. A. Garnsey & C. R. Whittaker, 159-91. Cambridge: Cambridge University Press, 1978.

_____. *Roman Imperial Themes.* Oxford: Clarendon, 1990.

Burford, A. *Craftsmen in Greek and Roman Society.* London: Thames & Hudson, 1972.

Burkert, W. *Ancient Mystery Cults.* Cambridge, MA: Harvard University Press, 1987.

_____. "Craft Versus Sect: The Problem of Orphics and Pythagoreans", in *Jewish and Christian Self-Definition*, edited by B. F. Meyer & E. P. Sanders, 3:1-22. London: SCM, 1982.

Burnett, A. *et al. Roman Provincial Coins.* vol. 1. London: British Museum, 1992.

Capper, B. J. "Paul's Dispute with Philippi: Understanding Paul's Argument in Phil 1-2 from his Thanks in 4.10-20". *TZ* 49 (1993): 193-214.

Carney, T. F. *The Shape of the Past: Models and Antiquity.* Lawrence, KS: Coronado, 1975.

Carras, G. P. "Jewish Ethics and Gentile Converts: Remarks on 1 Thes 4,3-8". In *The Thessalonian Correspondence*, edited by R. F. Collins, 306-15.   BETL 87. Leuven: Leuven University Press, 1990.

Carrié, J.-M. "The Soldier". In *The Romans*, edited by A. Giardina, 100-37.   Chicago: University of Chicago Press, 1993.

Cary, M. *The Geographic Background of Greek and Roman History.* Oxford: Clarendon, 1949.

Cassidy, R. J. *Jesus, Politics, and Society: A Study of Luke's Gospel.* Maryknoll, NY: Orbis, 1978.

Casson, L. "The Role of the State in Rome's Grain Trade". In *The Seaborne Commerce of Ancient Rome: Studies in Archaeology and History*, edited by J. H. D'Arms & E. C. Kopff, 21-33. Rome: American Academy in Rome, 1980.

Catling, H. W. "Archaeology in Greece". *Arch Rep* 22 (1976): 22.

_____. "Archaeology in Greece". *Arch Rep* 31 (1985): 49.

_____. "Archaeology in Greece". *Arch Rep* 32 (1986): 70.

_____. "Archaeology in Greece". *Arch Rep* 34 (1988): 54.

Chandler, T. & G. Fox. *3000 Years of Urban Growth.* New York: Academic Press, 1974.

Chapa, J. "Is First Thessalonians a Letter of Consolation?". *NTS* 40 (1994): 150-60.

Chow, J. K. *Patronage and Power: A Study of Social Networks in Corinth.* JSNTSup 75. Sheffield: JSOT Press, 1992.

Clarke, A. D. "Another Erastus Inscription". *TynBul* 42 (1991): 146-51.

_____. *Secular and Christian Leadership in Corinth: A Socio-Historical and Exegetical Study of 1 Corinthians 1-6.* AGJU 18. Leiden: E. J. Brill, 1993.

Cohen, S. J. D. "Respect for Judaism by Gentiles According to Josephus". *HTR* 80 (1987): 409-30.

Collange, J.-F. *The Epistle of Saint Paul to the Philippians.* London: Epworth, 1979.

Collart, P. "Inscriptions de Philippes (1)". *BCH* 57 (1933): 313-79.

_____. "Inscriptions de Philippes (2)". *BCH* 62 (1938): 409-32.

_____. "Le sanctuaire des dieux égyptiens à Philippes". *BCH* 53 (1929): 70-100.

_____. *Philippes, villes de Macédoine depuis ses origines jusqu' à la fin de l'époque romaine.* Paris: de Boccard, 1937.

Collins, R. F. *The Birth of the New Testament: The Origin and Development of the First Christian Generation.* New York: Crossroad, 1993.

Conzelmann, H. *1 Corinthians.* Hermeneia. Philadelphia: Fortress, 1975.

_____. *Gentiles / Jews / Christians: Polemics and Apologetics in the Greco-Roman Era.* Minneapolis: Fortress, 1992.

Corbier, M. "City, Territory and Taxation". In *City and Country in the Ancient World,* edited by J. Rich & A. Wallace-Hadrill, 211-39. London: Routledge, 1991.

Cornell, T. "The End of Roman Imperial Expansion". In *War and Society in the Roman World,* edited by J. Rich & G. Shipley, 139-70. London: Routledge, 1993.

Coser, L. A. *The Functions of Social Conflict.* London: Routledge & Kegan Paul, 1956.

Cotter, W. "Our *Politeuma* is in Heaven: The Meaning of Philippians 3.17-21". In *Origins and Method: Towards a New Understanding of Judaism and Christianity,* edited by B. H. McLean, 92-104. JSNTSup 86. Sheffield: JSOT Press, 1993.

Crawford, M. H. "Rome and the Greek World: Economic Relationships". *EHR* 30 (1977): 42-52.

Cullmann, O. *The State in the New Testament.* New York: Scribners, 1956.

D'Arms, J. H. *Commerce and Social Standing in Ancient Rome.* Cambridge, MA: Harvard University Press, 1981.

Dahl, N. A. "Euodia and Syntyche and Paul's Letter to the Philippians", in *The Social World of the First Christians: Essays in Honor of Wayne A. Meeks,* edited by L. M. White & O. L. Yarbrough, 3-15. Minneapolis: Fortress, 1995.

Dailey, T. F. "To Live or Die: Paul's Eschatological Dilemma in Philippians 1:19-26". *Int* 44 (1990): 18-28.

Daniel, J. L. "Anti-Semitism in the Hellenistic-Roman Period". *JBL* 98 (1979): 45-65.

Davies, R. E. "The Macedonian Scene of Paul's Journeys". *BA* 26 (1963): 91-106.

Davis, J. A. "The Interaction between Individual Ethical Conscience and Community Ethical Consciousness in 1 Corinthians". *HBT* 10.2 (1988): 1-18.

de Blois, L. *The Roman Army and Politics in the First Century B. C.* Amsterdam: J. C. Gieben, 1987.

de Ste. Croix, G. E. M. *The Class Struggle in the Ancient Greek World from the Archaic Age to the Arab Conquests.* London: Duckworth, 1981.

_____. "Why Were the Early Christians Persecuted?". *Past & Present* 26 (1963): 6-31.

_____. "Why Were the Early Christians Persecuted? — A Rejoinder". *Past & Present* 27 (1964): 28-33.

de Vos, C. S. "'ΚΑΙ Ο ΟΙΚΟΣ...' The Nature and Religious Practices of Graeco-Roman Households as the Context for the Conversion and Baptism of Households in the Acts of the Apostles". Unpublished BTh(Honours) thesis, Flinders University of SA, 1993.

_____. "Finding a Charge that Fits: The Accusation against Paul and Silas at Philippi (Acts 16.19-21)". *JSNT* FORTHCOMING.

_____. "The Significance of the Change from Οἶκος to Οἰκία in Luke's Account of the Philippian Gaoler (Acts 16.30-4)". *NTS* 41 (1995): 292-6.

_____. "Stepmothers, Concubines and the Case of Πορνεία in 1 Corinthians 5". *NTS* 44 (1998): 104-14.

Delia, D. *Alexandrian Citizenship during the Roman Principate.* Atlanta: Scholars Press, 1991.

DeMaris, R. E. "Corinthian Religion and Baptism for the Dead (1 Corinthians 15:29): Insights from Archaeology and Anthropology". *JBL* 114 (1995): 661-82.

Deming, W. *Paul on Marriage and Celibacy: The Hellenistic Background of 1 Corinthians 7*. SNTSMS 83. Cambridge: Cambridge University Press, 1995.

Dixon, S. *The Roman Family*. Baltimore: Johns Hopkins University Press, 1992.

Donfried, K. P. "The Cults of Thessalonica and the Thessalonian Correspondence". *NTS* 31 (1985): 336-56.

_____. "The Theology of 1 Thessalonians". In *The Theology of the Shorter Pauline Letters*, edited by K. P. Donfried & I. H. Marshall, 1-79. Cambridge: Cambridge University Press, 1993.

_____. "The Theology of 1 Thessalonians as a Reflection of its Purpose", in *To Touch the Text: Biblical and Related Studies in Honor of Joseph A. Fitzmyer, SJ.*, edited by M. P. Horgan & P. J. Kobelski, 243-60. New York: Crossroad, 1989.

_____. "The Theology of 2 Thessalonians". In *The Theology of the Shorter Pauline Letters*, edited by K. P. Donfried & I. H. Marshall, 81-113. Cambridge: Cambridge University Press, 1993.

Doughty, D. J. "Citizens of Heaven: Philippians 3.2-21". *NTS* 41 (1995): 102-22.

_____. "The Presence and the Future of Salvation in Corinth". *ZNW* 66 (1975): 61-90.

Droge, A. J. "*Mori lucrum*: Paul and Ancient Theories of Suicide". *NovT* 30 (1988): 263-86.

du Toit, A. B. "Vilification as a Pragmatic Device in Early Christian Epistolography". *Bib* 75 (1994): 403-412.

Duncan-Jones, R. P. *The Economy of the Roman Empire: Quantitative Studies*. 2nd ed. Cambridge: Cambridge University Press, 1982.

_____. *Structure and Scale in the Roman Economy*. Cambridge: Cambridge University Press, 1990.

Dyson, S. L. *Community and Society in Roman Italy*. Baltimore: Johns Hopkins University Press, 1992.

Edson, C. "Cults of Thessalonica (Macedonica III)". *HTR* 41 (1948): 153-204.

_____. "Macedonica". *HSCP* 51 (1940): 125-36.

Edwards, K. M. *Corinth: Results of Excavations. Volume VI: Coins, 1896-1929*. Cambridge, MA: Harvard University Press, 1933.

Elias, J. W. "'Jesus Who Delivers Us from the Wrath to Come' (1 Thess 1:10): Apocalyptic and Peace in the Thessalonian Correspondence". *SBLSP* (1992): 121-32.

Elliott, J. H. *What is Social-Scientific Criticism?* GBS. Minneapolis: Fortress, 1993.

Engberg-Pedersen, T. "The Gospel and Social Practice According to 1 Corinthians". *NTS* 33 (1987): 557-84.

_____. "Stoicism in Philippians". In *Paul in His Hellenistic Context*, edited by T. Engberg-Pedersen, 256-90. Minneapolis: Fortress, 1995.

Engels, D. W. *Roman Corinth: An Alternative Model for the Classical City*. Chicago: University of Chicago Press, 1990.

Esler, P. F. *Community and Gospel in Luke-Acts: The Social and Political Motivations of Lukan Theology*. SNTSMS 57. Cambridge: Cambridge University Press, 1987.

_____. *The First Christians in their Social Worlds: Social-Scientific Approaches to New Testament Interpretation*. London: Routledge, 1994.

_____. "Group Boundaries and Intergroup Conflict in Galatians: A New Reading of Galatians 5:13-6:10". In *Ethnicity and the Bible*, edited by M. G. Brett, 215-40. BIS 19. Leiden: E. J. Brill, 1996.

_____. "Making and Breaking an Agreement Mediterranean Style: A New Reading of Galatians 2:1-14". *BibInt* 3 (1995): 285-314.

_____. "Introduction: Models, Context and Kerygma in New Testament Interpretation". In *Modelling Early Christianity*, edited by P. F. Esler, 1-20. London: Routledge, 1995.

Eyben, E. "Fathers and Sons". In *Marriage, Divorce, and Children in Ancient Rome*, edited by B. Rawson, 114-43. Oxford: Clarendon, 1991.

Fears, J. R. "The Cult of Jupiter and Roman Imperial Ideology". *ANRW* 2.17.1 (1981): 3-141.

_____. "The Cult of Virtues and Roman Imperial Ideology". *ANRW* 2.17.2 (1981): 827-948.

_____. "The Theology of Victory at Rome: Approaches and Problems". *ANRW* 2.17.2 (1981): 736-826.

Fee, G. D. "Εἰδωλόθυτα Once Again: An Interpretation of 1 Cor 8-10". *Bib* 61 (1980): 172-97.

_____. *The First Epistle to the Corinthians*. NICNT. Grand Rapids: Eerdmans, 1987.

_____. *Paul's Letter to the Philippians*. NICNT. Grand Rapids: Eerdmans, 1995.

Feldman, L. H. *Jew and Gentile in the Ancient World: Attitudes and Interactions from Alexander to Justinian*. Princeton, NJ: Princeton University, 1993.

Ferguson, E. *Backgrounds of Early Christianity*. 2nd ed. Grand Rapids: Eerdmans, 1993.

Ferguson, J. *The Religions of the Roman Empire*. London: Thames & Hudson, 1970.

_____. *Utopias of the Classical World*. London: Thames & Hudson, 1975.

Finley, M. I. "The Ancient City: From Fustel de Coulanges to Max Weber and Beyond". *CSSH* 18 (1977): 305-27.

_____. *Politics in the Ancient World*. Cambridge: Cambridge University Press, 1983.

Fiore, B. "'Covert Allusion' in 1 Corinthians 1-4". *CBQ* 47 (1985): 85-102.

_____. "Passion in Paul and Plutarch: 1 Corinthians 5-6 and the Polemic against Epicureans". In *Greeks, Romans and Christians: Essays in Honor of Abraham J. Malherbe*, edited by D. L. Balch, E. Ferguson, & W. A. Meeks, 135-43. Minneapolis: Fortress, 1990.

Fisher, N. R. E. *Slavery in Classical Greece*. London: Bristol Classical Press, 1993.

Fitzgerald, J. T. "Philippians in the Light of Some Ancient Discussions of Friendship". In *Friendship, Flattery, and Frankness of Speech: Studies in Friendship in the New Testament World*, edited by J. T. Fitzgerald, 141-60. NovTSup 82. Leiden: E. J. Brill, 1996.

Fitzmyer, J. A. "The Aramaic Background of Philippians 2.6-11". *CBQ* 50 (1988): 470-83.

Fortna, R. T. "Philippians: Paul's Most Egocentric Letter". In *The Conversation Continues*, edited by R. T. Fortna & B. R. Gaventa, 220-34. Nashville: Abingdon, 1990.

Fowl, S. E. *The Story of Christ in the Ethics of Paul: An Analysis of the Function of the Hymnic Material in the Pauline Corpus*. JSNTSup 36. Sheffield: JSOT Press, 1990.

Foxhall, L. "The Dependent Tenant: Land Leasing and Labour in Italy and Greece". *JRS* 80 (1990): 97-114.

Fraser, P. M. & E. Matthews. *A Lexicon of Greek Personal Names*. vol. 1. Oxford: Clarendon, 1987.

Frayn, J. M. *Markets and Fairs in Roman Italy: Their Social and Economic Importance from the Second Century BC to the Third Century AD*. Oxford: Clarendon, 1993.

_____. *Subsistence Farming in Roman Italy*. London: Centaur, 1979.

Frend, W. H. C. *Martyrdom and Persecution in the Early Church: A Study of a Conflict from the Maccabees to Donatus.* New York: New York University Press, 1967.

Frier, B. W. "Subsistence Annuities and Per Capita Income in the Early Roman Empire". *CPhil* 88 (1993): 222-30.

Furnish, V. P. "Belonging to Christ. A Paradigm for Ethics in First Corinthians". *Int* 44 (1990): 145-57.

_____. "Corinth in Paul's Time: What Can Archaeology Tell Us?". *BARev* 15.3 (1988): 14-27.

_____. "The Place and Purpose of Philippians III". *NTS* 10 (1963): 80-8.

_____. *II Corinthians.* AB. Garden City, NY: Doubleday, 1984.

Gager, J. G. *Kingdom and Community: The Social World of Early Christianity.* Engelwood-Cliffs, NJ: Prentice-Hall, 1975.

_____. *The Origins of Anti-Semitism: Attitudes toward Judaism in Pagan and Christian Antiquity.* New York: Oxford University Press, 1983.

Gardner, J. F. *Being a Roman Citizen.* London: Routledge, 1993.

Garland, D. E. "The Composition and Unity of Philippians: Some Neglected Literary Factors". *NovT* 27 (1985): 141-73.

Garnsey, P. D. A. & R. P. Saller. *The Early Principate: Augustus to Trajan.* Oxford: Clarendon, 1982.

_____. *The Roman Empire: Economy, Society and Culture.* Berkeley: University of California Press, 1987.

Garnsey, P. D. A. & G. Woolf. "Patronage and the Rural Poor in the Roman World". In *Patronage in Ancient Society*, edited by A. Wallace-Hadrill, 153-70. London: Routledge, 1989.

Gebhard, E. R. "The Isthmian Games and the Sanctuary of Poseidon in the Early Empire". In *The Corinthia in the Roman Period*, edited by T. E. Gregory, 78-94. JRASup 8. Ann Arbor: University of Michigan Press, 1994.

Geoffrion, T. C. *The Rhetorical Purpose and the Political and Military Character of Philippians: A Call to Stand Firm.* Lewiston, NY: Edwin Mellen, 1993.

Georgi, D. *Remembering the Poor: The History of Paul's Collection for Jerusalem.* Nashville: Abingdon, 1992.

_____. *Theocracy in Paul's Praxis and Theology.* Minneapolis: Fortress, 1991.

Giardina, A. "The Merchant". In *The Romans*, edited by A. Giardina, 245-71. Chicago: University of Chicago Press, 1993.

Gibbs, J. P. "Conceptions of Deviant Behavior: The Old and New". In *Deviant Behavior: A Text-Reader in the Sociology of Deviance*, edited by D. H. Kelly, 15-20. 3rd ed. New York: St. Martin's Press, 1989.

Gill, D. W. J. "Achaia". In *The Book of Acts in its Graeco-Roman Setting*, edited by D. W. J. Gill & C. H. Gempf, 433-53. BAFCS 2. Grand Rapids: Eerdmans, 1994.

_____. "Acts and Roman Religion: A. Religion in a Local Setting". In *The Book of Acts in its Graeco-Roman Setting*, edited by D. W. J. Gill & C. H. Gempf, 79-92. BAFCS 2. Grand Rapids: Eerdmans, 1994.

_____. "Corinth: A Roman Colony in Achaea". *BZ* 37 (1993): 259-64.

_____. "Erastus the Aedile". *TynBul* 40 (1989): 293-301.

_____. "Macedonia". In *The Book of Acts in its Graeco-Roman Setting*, edited by D. W. J. Gill & C. H. Gempf, 397-417. BAFCS 2. Grand Rapids: Eerdmans, 1994.

_____. "The Meat-market at Corinth (1 Corinthians 10:25)". *TynBul* 43 (1992): 389-93.

_____. "In Search of the Social Élite in the Corinthian Church". *TynBul* 44 (1993): 323-38.

Goddard, A. J. & S. A. Cummins. "Ill or Ill-Treated? Conflict and Persecution as the Context of Paul's Original Ministry in Galatia (Galatians 4. 12-20)". *JSNT* 52 (1993): 93-126.

Golden, M. *Children and Childhood in Classical Athens*. Baltimore: Johns Hopkins University Press, 1990.

Gooch, P. D. *Dangerous Food: 1 Corinthians 8-10 in its Context*. ESCJ 5. Waterloo, Ont.: Wilfred Laurier University Press, 1993.

Goodman, M. D. "Jewish Proselytizing in the First Century". In *The Jews Among Pagans and Christians in the Roman Empire*, edited by J. M. Lieu, J. North & T. Rajak, 53-78. rev. ed. London: Routledge, 1994.

_____. *The Ruling Class of Judaea: The Origins of the Jewish Revolt against Rome AD 66-70*. Cambridge: Cambridge University Press, 1987.

Goulder, M. D. "Σοφία in 1 Corinthians". *NTS* 37 (1991): 516-34.

Grayston, K. "The Opponents in Philippians 3". *ExpTim* 97 (1986): 170-2.

Guenther, H. O. "Gnosticism in Corinth?". In *Origins and Method*, edited by B. H. McLean, 44-81. JSNTSup 86. Sheffield: JSOT Press, 1993.

Gundry, R. H. "The Hellenization of Dominical Tradition and Christianization of the Jewish Tradition in the Eschatology of 1-2 Thessalonians". *NTS* 33 (1987): 161-78.

Haenchen, E. *The Acts of the Apostles*. Oxford: Blackwell, 1971.

Harris, J. M. "Coins Found at Corinth". *Hesp* 10 (1941): 143-62.

Hawthorne, G. F. *Philippians*. WBC. Waco, TX: Word, 1983.

Head, B. V. *A Catalogue of the Greek Coins in the British Museum. Macedonia Etc.* London: British Museum, 1879.

Helgeland, J. "Roman Army Religion". *ANRW* 2.16.2 (1978): 1470-505.

Hemer, C. J. *The Book of Acts in the Setting of Hellenistic History.* Edited by C. H. Gempf. Winona Lake, IN: Eisenbrauns, 1990.

Hendrix, H. L. "Archaeology and Eschatology at Thessalonica". In *The Future of Early Christianity: Essays in Honor of Helmut Koester,* edited by B. A. Pearson, 107-18. Minneapolis: Fortress, 1991.

_____. "Benefactor/Patron Networks in the Urban Environment: Evidence from Thessalonica". *Semeia* 56 (1992): 39-58.

_____. "Beyond 'Imperial Cult' and 'Cults of Magistrates'". *SBLSP* (1986): 301-8.

_____. "Philippi". *ABD* 5.313-17.

_____. "Thessalonicans Honor Romans". Unpublished ThD dissertation, Harvard University, 1984.

_____. "Thessalonica". *ABD* 6.523-527.

Hengel, M. *Crucifixion in the Ancient World and the Folly of the Message of the Cross.* Philadelphia: Fortress, 1977.

Heyob, S. K. *The Cult of Isis among Women in the Graeco-Roman World.* EPRO 51. Leiden: E. J. Brill, 1975.

Hill, J. L. "Establishing the Church in Thessalonica". Unpublished PhD dissertation, Duke University, 1990.

Hock, R. F. *The Social Context of Paul's Ministry: Tentmaking and Apostleship.* Philadelphia: Fortress, 1980.

Holladay, C. R. "Paul's Opponents in Philippians 3". *ResQ* 12 (1969): 77-90.

Holmberg, B. *Paul and Power: The Structure of Authority in the Primitive Church as Reflected in the Pauline Epistles.* ConBNT 11. Lund: C. W. K. Gleerup, 1978.

_____. *Sociology and the New Testament: An Appraisal.* Minneapolis: Fortress, 1990.

Holtz, T. *Der erste Brief an die Thessalonicher.* EKKNT 13. Zürich: Benziger, 1986.

Hopkins, K. "Economic Growth and Towns in Classical Antiquity". In *Towns in Societies,* edited by P. Abrams & E. A. Wrigley, 35-77. Cambridge: Cambridge University Press, 1978.

_____. "Taxes and Trade in the Roman Empire (200 BC-AD 400)". *JRS* 70 (1980): 101-125.

Horrell, D. G. *The Social Ethos of the Corinthian Correspondence: Interests and Ideology from 1 Corinthians to 1 Clement.* SNTW. Edinburgh: T. & T. Clark, 1996.

Horsley, G. H. R. "The Politarchs". In *The Book of Acts in its Graeco-Roman Setting*, edited by D. W. J. Gill & C. H. Gempf, 419-31. BAFCS 2. Grand Rapids: Eerdmans, 1994. .

Horsley, R. A. "Consciousness and Freedom among the Corinthians: 1 Corinthians 8-10". *CBQ* 40 (1978): 574-89.

_____. "*Gnosis* in Corinth: 1 Corinthians 8.1-6". *NTS* 27 (1980): 32-51.

House, H. W. "Tongues and Mystery Religions of Corinth". *BSac* 140 (1983): 134-50.

Hughes, F. W. "The Rhetoric of 1 Thessalonians". In *The Thessalonian Correspondence*, edited by R. F. Collins, 94-116. BETL 87. Leuven: Leuven University Press, 1990.

Hurtado, L. W. "Jesus as Lordly Example in Philippians 2:5-11". In *From Jesus to Paul: Studies in Honour of Francis Wright Beare*, edited by P. Richardson & J. C. Hurd, 113-26. Waterloo, Ont.: Wilfred Laurier University Press, 1984.

Jaquette, J. L. "A Not-so-noble Death: Figured Speech, Friendship and Suicide in Philippians 1:21-26". *Neot* 28 (1994): 177-92.

Jewett, R. "Conflicting Movements in the Early Church as Reflected in Philippians". *NovT* 12 (1970): 362-90.

_____. "The Epistolary Thanksgiving and the Integrity of Philippians". *NovT* 12 (1970): 40-53.

_____. "Tenement Churches and Communal Meals in the Early Church: The Implications of a Form-Critical Analysis of 2 Thessalonians 3:10". *BR* 38 (1993): 23-43.

_____. *The Thessalonian Correspondence: Pauline Rhetoric & Millenarian Piety.* Philadelphia: Fortress, 1986.

Johanson, B. C. *To All the Brethren: A Text-Linguistic and Rhetorical Approach to 1 Thessalonians.* ConBNT 16. Stockholm: Almqvist & Wiksell, 1987.

Johnson, L. T. *The Acts of the Apostles.* SP. Collegeville, MN: Michael Glazier, 1992.

_____. "The New Testament's Anti-Jewish Slander & the Conventions of Ancient Polemic". *JBL* 108 (1989): 419-41.

Johnson, T. & C. Dandeker. "Patronage: Relation and System". In *Patronage in Ancient Society*, edited by A. Wallace-Hadrill, 219-42. London: Routledge, 1989.

Jones, A. H. M. *The Roman Economy.* Oxford: Blackwell, 1974.

Jones, D. L. "Christianity and the Roman Imperial Cult". *ANRW* 2.23.2 (1980): 1023-54.

Jones, J. L. "The Roman Army". In *The Catacombs and the Colosseum*, edited by S. Benko & J. J. O'Rourke, 187-215. Valley Forge, PA: Judson, 1971.

Joshel, S. R. "The Occupations and Economic Roles of Freedmen in the Early Roman Empire: A Study in Roman Social and Economic Patterns". Unpublished PhD dissertation, Rutgers University, 1977.

Judge, E. A. "The Decrees of Caesar at Thessalonica". *RTR* 30 (1971): 1-7.

_____. "The Early Christians as a Scholastic Community: Part II". *JRH* 1 (1961): 125-37.

Kajanto, I. *The Latin Cognomina.* Helsinki: Societas Scientiarum Fennica, 1965.

Kanatsoulis, D. *Prosopographia Macedonica from 148 BC until the Time of Constantine the Great, edited by* A. N. Oikonomides. Chicago: Ares Publishers, 1979.

Kasher, A. *The Jews in Hellenistic and Roman Egypt: The Struggle for Equal Rights.* Tübingen: J. C. B. Mohr, 1985.

Kee, H. C. *Knowing the Truth: A Sociological Approach to New Testament Interpretation.* Minneapolis: Fortress, 1989.

Kelly, D. H. (ed.) *Deviant Behavior: A Text-Reader in the Sociology of Deviance.* 3rd ed. New York: St. Martin's Press, 1989.

Keppie, L. J. *Colonisation and Veteran Settlement in Italy 47-14 BC.* London: British School at Rome, 1983.

_____. *The Making of the Roman Army: From Republic to Empire.* London: Batsford, 1984.

Klijn, A. F. J. "Paul's Opponents in Philippians iii". *NovT* 7 (1964): 278-84.

Kloppenborg, J. S. "Φιλαδελφία, Θεοδίδακτος and the Dioscuri: Rhetorical Engagement in 1 Thessalonians" *NTS* 39 (1993): 265-89.

Koester, H. "From Paul's Eschatology to the Apocalyptic Schemata of 2 Thessalonians". In *The Thessalonian Correspondence*, edited by R. F. Collins, 441- 58. BETL 87. Leuven: Leuven University Press, 1990.

_____. "The Purpose of the Polemic of a Pauline Fragment (Philippians III)". *NTS* 8 (1962): 317-32.

Koukouli-Chrysanthaki, C. "Politarchs in a New Inscription from Amphipolis". In *Ancient Macedonian Studies in Honor of Charles F. Edson*, edited by H. J. Dell, 229-41. Thessaloniki: Institute for Balkan Studies, 1981.

Kraft, R. A. "Judaism on the World Scene". In *The Catacombs and the Colosseum*, edited by S. Benko & J. J. O'Rourke, 81-95. Valley Forge, PA: Judson, 1971.

Krentz, E. M. "Military Language and Metaphors in Philippians". In *Origins and Method*, edited by B. H. McLean, 105-27. JSNTSup 86. Sheffield: JSOT Press, 1993.

Krodel, G. "Persecution and Toleration of Christianity until Hadrian", edited by S. Benko & J. J. O'Rourke, 255-67. Valley Forge, PA: Judson, 1971.

Kuck, D. W. *Judgment and Community Conflict: Paul's Use of Apocalyptic Judgment Language in 1 Corinthians 3:5-4:5.* NovTSup 66. Leiden: E. J. Brill, 1992.

Lacey, W. K. "*Patria Potestas*". In *The Family in Ancient Rome*, edited by B. Rawson, 121-44. London: Routledge, 1992 [1986].

Landis, D. & J. Boucher. "Themes and Models of Conflict". In *Ethnic Conflict: International Perspectives*, edited by J. Boucher, D. Landis, & K. A. Clark, 18-31. Newbury Park, CA: SAGE, 1987.

Larsen, J. O. "Greece and Macedonia from Augustus to Gallienus". In *An Economic Survey of Ancient Rome*, edited by T. Frank, 4:259-498. Baltimore: Johns Hopkins University Press, 1938.

Laurence, R. *Roman Pompeii: Space and Society.* London: Routledge, 1994.

Lazarides, D. "Philippi (Krenides)". In *Princeton Encyclopaedia of Classical Sites*, edited by R. Stilwell *et al*, 704-5. Princeton, NJ: Princeton University Press, 1976.

Lee, C. L. "Social Unrest and Primitive Christianity". In *The Catacombs and the Colosseum*, edited by S. Benko & J. J. O'Rourke, 121-38. Valley Forge, PA: Judson, 1971.

Lemerle, P. "Inscriptions latines et greques de Philippi". *BCH* 58 (1934) 448-83.

_____. "Nouvelles inscriptions latines de Philippi". *BCH* 61 (1937): 410-20.

Lentz, J. C. JR. *Luke's Portrait of Paul.* SNTSMS 77. Cambridge: Cambridge University Press, 1993.

Levinskaya, I. *The Book of Acts in its Diaspora Setting.* BAFCS 5. Grand Rapids: Eerdmans, 1996.

Lincoln, A. T. *Paradise Now and Not Yet : Studies in the Role of the Heavenly Dimension in Paul's Thought with Special Reference to his Eschatology.* Grand Rapids: Baker, 1991 [1981].

Lintott, A. *Imperium Romanum: Politics and Administration.* London: Routledge, 1993.

_____. *Violence, Civil Strife and Revolution in the Classical City.* London: Croom Helm, 1982.

Litfin, D. *St. Paul's Theology of Proclamation: 1 Corinthians 1-4 and Greco-Roman Rhetoric.* SNTSMS 79. Cambridge: Cambridge University Press, 1994.

Loomis, J. W. "Cicero and Thessaloniki, Politics and Provinces". In *Ancient Macedonia II*, 169-88. Thessaloniki: Institute for Balkan Studies, 1977.

Luck, G. *Arcana Mundi: Magic and Occult in the Greek and Roman Worlds.* Baltimore: Johns Hopkins University Press, 1985.

Lüderitz, G. "What is the Politeuma?". In *Studies in Early Jewish Epigraphy*, edited by J. W. van Henten & P. W. van der Horst, 183-215. AGJU 21. Leiden: E. J. Brill, 1994.

Lührmann, D. "The Beginnings of the Church at Thessalonica". In *Greeks, Romans and Christians*, edited by D. L. Balch *et al*, 237-49. Minneapolis: Fortress, 1990.

Luter, A. B. & M. V. Lee. "Philippians as Chiasmus: Key to the Structure, Unity and Theme Questions". *NTS* 41 (1995): 89-101.

MacDonald, M. Y. "Women Holy in Body and Spirit: The Social Setting of 1 Corinthians 7". *NTS* 36 (1990): 161-81.

MacMullen, R. *Christianizing the Roman Empire AD 100-400.* New Haven, CT: Yale, 1984.

_____. *Enemies of the Roman Order: Treason, Unrest and Alienation in the Empire.* London: Routledge, 1992 [1966].

_____. "Market-days in the Roman Empire". *Phoenix* 24 (1970): 333-41.

_____. *Paganism in the Roman Empire.* New Haven, CT: Yale, 1981.

_____. "Peasants during the Principate". *ANRW* 2.1 (1974): 253-61.

_____. *Roman Social Relations 50 BC-AD 284.* New Haven, CT: Yale, 1974.

Malherbe, A. J. "God's New Family in Thessalonica". In *The Social World of the First Christians*, edited by L. M. White & O. L. Yarbrough, 116-25. Minneapolis: Fortress, 1995.

_____. " 'Pastoral Care' in the Thessalonian Church". *NTS* 36 (1990): 375-91.

_____. *Paul and the Thessalonians: The Philosophic Tradition of Pastoral Care.* Philadelphia: Fortress, 1987.

_____. "Self-Definition among Epicureans and Cynics". In *Jewish and Christian Self-Definition*, 3:46-59. edited by B. F. Meyer & E. P. Sanders. London: SCM, 1982.

Malina, B. J. *The New Testament World: Insights from Cultural Anthropology.* rev. ed. Louisville, KY: W/JK Press, 1993.

_____. "Normative Dissonance and Christian Origins". *Semeia* 35 (1986): 35-55.

Malina, B. J. & J. H. Neyrey, "Conflict in Luke-Acts: Labelling and Deviance Theory". In *The Social World of Luke-Acts: Models for Interpretation*, edited by J. H. Neyrey, 97-122. Peabody, MA: Hendrickson, 1991.

Mann, J. C. *Legionary Recruitment and Veteran Settlement during the Principate.* London: Institute of Archaeology, 1983.

Marshall, I. H. *Acts.* TNTC. Leicester: IVP, 1980.

_____. "The Theology of Philippians". In *The Theology of the Shorter Pauline Letters*, edited by K. P. Donfried & I. H. Marshall, 115-74. Cambridge: Cambridge University, 1993.

_____. *1 & 2 Thessalonians.* NCB. Grand Rapids: Eerdmans, 1983.

Marshall, P. *Enmity in Corinth: Social Conventions in Paul's Relations with the Corinthians.* WUNT 2.33. Tübingen: J. C. B. Mohr, 1987.

Martin, D. B. *The Corinthian Body.* New Haven, CT: Yale, 1995.

_____. *Slavery as Salvation: The Metaphor of Slavery in Pauline Christianity.* New Haven, CT: Yale, 1990.

Martin, L. H. *Hellenistic Religions: An Introduction.* New York: Oxford University Press, 1987.

Martin, T. R. "Inscriptions at Corinth". *Hesp* 46 (1977): 178-98.

Mason, H. J. *Greek Terms for Roman Institutions: A Lexicon and Analysis.* ASP 13. Toronto: Hakkert, 1974.

McKay, A. G. *Houses, Villas and Palaces in the Roman World.* London: Thames & Hudson, 1975.

McKnight, S. *A Light among the Gentiles: Jewish Missionary Activity in the Second Temple Period.* Minneapolis: Fortress, 1991.

McRay, J. *Archaeology and the New Testament.* Grand Rapids: Baker, 1991.

Mearns, C. L. "The Identity of Paul's Opponents at Philippi". *NTS* 33 (1987): 194-204.

Meeks, W. A. *The First Urban Christians: The Social World of the Apostle Paul.* New Haven, CT: Yale, 1983.

_____. "The Man from Heaven in Paul's Letter to the Philippians". In *The Future of Early Christianity*, edited by B. A. Pearson, 329-36. Minneapolis: Fortress, 1991.

_____. "The Social Functions of Apocalyptic Language in Pauline Christianity". In *Apocalypticism in the Mediterranean World and the Near East*, edited by D. Hellholm, 687-705. Tübingen: J. C. B. Mohr, 1983.

Megaw, A. H. B. "Archaeology in Greece". *JHS Sup* (1963): 24.

Meggitt, J. J. "Meat Consumption and Social Conflict in Corinth". *JTS* 45 (1994): 137-41.

_____. *Paul, Poverty and Survival*. SNTW. Edinburgh: T. & T. Clark, 1998.

Mellor, R. "The Goddess Roma". *ANRW* 2.17.2 (1981): 950-1030.

Millar, F. G. B. *The Emperor in the Roman World: 31 BC-317 AD*. London: Duckworth, 1977.

_____. "State and Subject: the Impact of Monarchy". In *Caesar Augustus: Seven Aspects*, edited by F. G. B. Millar & E. Segal, 37-60. Oxford: Clarendon, 1984.

Miller, E. C. "Πολιτεύεσθε in Philippians 1.27: Some Philological and Thematic Observations". *JSNT* 15 (1982): 86-96.

Millett, P. "Patronage and its Avoidance in Classical Athens". In *Patronage in Ancient Society*, edited by A. Wallace-Hadrill, 15-47. London: Routledge, 1989.

Minear, P. S. "Singing and Suffering in Philippi". In *The Conversation Continues*, edited by R. T. Fortna & B. R. Gaventa, 202-19. Nashville: Abingdon, 1990.

Mitchell, A. C. "1 Corinthians 6:1-11: Group Boundaries and the Courts of Corinth". Unpublished PhD dissertation, Yale University, 1986.

Mitchell, M. M. *Paul and the Rhetoric of Reconciliation: An Exegetical Investigation of the Language and Composition of 1 Corinthians*. Louisville, KY: W/JK Press, 1991.

Moehring, M. H. "The Persecution of the Jews and the Adherents of the Isis Cult at Rome". *NovT* 3 (1959): 293-304.

Mora, F. *Prosopografia Isiaca*. EPRO 113. 2 vols. Leiden: E. J. Brill, 1990.

Morel, J.-P. "The Craftsman". In *The Romans*, edited by A. Giardina. Chicago: University of Chicago Press, 1993, 214-44.

Morgan-Gillman, F. "Jason of Thessalonica (Acts 17,5-9)". In *The Thessalonian Correspondence*, edited by R. F. Collins, 39-49. BETL 87. Leuven: Leuven University Press, 1990.

Moxnes, H. "Patron-Client Relations and the New Community in Luke-Acts". In *The Social World of Luke-Acts*, edited by J. H. Neyrey, 241-68. Peabody, MA: Hendrickson, 1991.

Nanos, M. D. *The Mystery of Romans: The Jewish Context of Paul's Letter*. Minneapolis: Fortress, 1996.

Newbold, R. F. "Social Tension at Rome in the Early Years of Tiberius' Reign". *Athenaeum* 52 (1974): 110-43.

Nicolet, C. "The Citizen; Political Man". In *The Romans*, edited by A. Giardina, 16-54. Chicago: University of Chicago Press, 1993.

Nolland, J. L. "Proselytism or Politics in Horace *Satires* 1.4.138-143". *VC* 33 (1979): 347-55.

North, J. "Conservatism and Change in Roman Religion". *PBSR* 44 (1976): 1-12.

_____. "The Development of Religious Pluralism". In *The Jews Among Pagans and Christians in the Roman Empire*, edited by J. M. Lieu *et al*, 174-93. rev. ed. London: Routledge, 1994.

_____. "Religious Toleration in Republican Rome". *PCPS* 25 (1979): 85-103.

O'Brien, P. T. *Commentary on Philippians*. NIGTC. Grand Rapids: Eerdmans, 1991.

Oakes, P. "Philippians: From People to Letter". Unpublished DPhil dissertation, University of Oxford, 1995.

Ogilvie, R. M. *The Romans and Their Gods in the Age of Augustus*. London: Chatto & Windus, 1969.

Oikonomides, A. N. *The Acropolis of Athens*. Athens: N. Gouvoussis, 1995.

Olbricht, T. H. "An Aristotelian Rhetorical Analysis of 1 Thessalonians". In *Greeks, Romans and Christians*, edited by D. L. Balch *et al*, 216-36. Minneapolis: Fortress, 1990.

Oliver, J. H. "Civic Constitutions for Macedonian Communities". *CPhil* 58 (1963): 164-5.

Osborne, M. J. & S. G. Byrne, *A Lexicon of Greek Personal Names*. vol. 2. Oxford: Clarendon, 1994.

Owens, E. J. *The City in the Greek and Roman World*. London: Routledge, 1991.

Packer, J. E. "Housing and Population in Imperial Ostia and Rome". *JRS* 57 (1967): 80-95.

Pagels, E. "The Social History of Satan, Part II: Satan in the New Testament Gospels". *JAAR* 62 (1994): 17-59.

Paige, T. "Stoicism, Ἐλευθερία and Community at Corinth". In *Worship, Theology and Ministry in the Early Church. Essays in Honor of Ralph P. Martin*, edited by M. J. Wilkins & T. Paige, 180-93. JSNTSup 87. Sheffield: JSOT Press, 1992.

Palmer, D. W. "'To Die is Gain' (Philippians 1:21)". *NovT* 17 (1975): 203-18.

Pandermalis, D. "Monuments and Art in the Roman Period". In *Macedonia: 4000 Years of Greek History and Civilization*, edited by M. B. Sakellariou, 208-21. Athens: Ektodike Athenon, 1983.

Panikulam, G. *Koinonia in the New Testament: A Dynamic Expression of Christian Life*. AnBib 85. Rome: Pontifical Biblical Institute, 1979.

Papazoglou, F. "Macedonia under the Romans". In *Macedonia: 4000 Years of Greek History and Civilization*, edited by M. B. Sakellariou, 192-207. Athens: Ektodike Athenon, 1983.

Parkin, T. G. *Demography and Roman Society*. Baltimore: Johns Hopkins University, 1992.

Patterson, J. "Military Organization and Social Change in the Later Roman Republic". In *War and Society in the Roman World*. Edited by J. Rich & G. Shipley, 92-112. London: Routledge, 1993.

Pearson, B. A. "1 Thessalonians 2:13-16: A Deutero-Pauline Interpolation". *HTR* 64 (1971): 79-94.

Perkins, P. "Christology, Friendship and Status: The Rhetoric of Philippians". *SBLSP* (1987): 509-20.

_____. "Philippians: Theology for the Heavenly Politeuma". In *Pauline Theology, Volume I*, edited by J. M. Bassler, 89-104. Minneapolis: Fortress, 1991.

_____. "1 Thessalonians and Hellenistic Religious Practices". *To Touch the Text*, edited by M. P. Horgan & P. J. Kobelski, 325-34. New York: Crossroad, 1989.

Perring, D. "Spatial Organisation and Social Change in Roman Towns". In *City and Country in the Ancient World*, edited by J. Rich & A. Wallace-Hadrill, 273-93. London: Routledge, 1991.

Peterlin, D. *Paul's Letter to the Philippians in the Light of Disunity in the Church*. NovTSup 79. Leiden: E. J. Brill, 1995.

Pfitzner, V. C. *Paul and the Agon Motif: Traditional Athletic Imagery in the Pauline Literature*. NovTSup 16. Leiden: E. J. Brill, 1967.

Phillips, C. R. "The Sociology of Religious Knowledge in the Roman Empire to AD 284". *ANRW* 2.16.3 (1986): 2677-773.

Pilhofer, P. *Philippi, I: Die erste christliche Gemeinde Europas*. WUNT 87. Tübingen: J. C. B. Mohr, 1995.

Pleket, H. W. "An Aspect of the Emperor Cult: Imperial Mysteries". *HTR* 58 (1965): 331-47.

_____. "Urban Elites and Business in the Greek Part of the Roman Empire". In *Trade in the Ancient Economy*, edited by P. D. A. Garnsey, K. Hopkins, & C. R. Whittaker, 131-44. Berkeley: University of California Press, 1983.

Pobee, J. S. *Persecution and Martyrdom in the Theology of Paul.* JSNTSup 6. Sheffield: JSOT Press, 1985.

Pomeroy, S. B. *Goddesses, Whores, Wives, and Slaves: Women in Classical Antiquity.* New York: Schocken, 1975.

Portefaix, L. *Sisters Rejoice: Paul's Letter to the Philippians and Luke-Acts as Seen by First-Century Philippian Women.* ConBNT20. Stockholm: Almqvist & Wiksell, 1988.

Porter, J. N. & R. Taplin. *Conflict and Conflict Resolution.* Lanham, MD: University Press of America, 1987.

Price, S. R. F. "Gods and Emperors: The Greek Language of the Roman Imperial Cult". *JHS* 104 (1984): 79-95.

_____. *Rituals and Power: The Roman Imperial Cult in Asia Minor.* Cambridge: Cambridge University Press, 1984.

Rabello, A. M. "The Legal Condition of the Jews in the Roman Empire". *ANRW* 2.13 (1980): 662-762.

Rajak, T. "Was there a Roman Charter for the Jews?". *JRS* 74 (1984): 107-23.

Rajak, T. & D. Noy. "*Archisynagogoi*: Office, Title and Social Status in the Greco-Jewish Synagogue". *JRS* 83 (1993): 75-93.

Rawson, B. "Adult-Child Relationships in Roman Society". In *Marriage, Divorce, and Children in Ancient Rome*, edited by B. Rawson, 7-30. Oxford: Clarendon, 1991.

Reinhold, M. "Usurpation of Status and Status Symbols in the Roman Empire". *Historia* 20 (1971): 275-301.

Reumann, J. "Contributions of the Philippian Community to Paul and to Earliest Christianity". *NTS* 39 (1993): 438-57.

_____. "Philippians 3. 20-21 — a Hymnic Fragment?". *NTS* 30 (1984): 593-609.

_____. "The Theologies of 1 Thessalonians and Philippians: Contents, Comparison, and Composition". *SBLSP* (1987): 521-36.

Reynolds, J. M. "The Cities". In *The Administration of the Roman Empire 241 BC-AD 193*, edited by D. C. Braund, 15-51. Exeter: University of Exeter Press, 1988.

Rex, J. *Social Conflict: A Conceptual and Theoretical Analysis.* London: Longman, 1981.

Richard, E. "Early Pauline Thought: An Analysis of 1 Thessalonians". In *Pauline Theology, Volume I*, edited by J. M. Bassler, 39-51. Minneapolis: Fortress, 1991.

_____. *First and Second Thessalonians*. SP. Collegeville, MN: Michael Glazier, 1995.

Richardson, P. "Judgment in Sexual Matters in 1 Corinthians 6:1-11". *NovT* 25 (1983): 37-58.

_____. "On the Absence of 'Anti-Judaism' in 1 Corinthians". In *Anti-Judaism in Early Christianity, Vol. I*, edited by P. Richardson & D. Granskou, 59-74. ESCJ 2. Waterloo, Ont.: Wilfred Laurier University Press, 1986.

Robbins, C. J. "Rhetorical Structure of Philippians 2:6-11". *CBQ* 42 (1980): 73-82.

Robertson, I. *Sociology*. 3rd ed. New York: Worth, 1987.

Robinson, H. S. "Corinth". In *Princeton Encyclopaedia of Classical Sites*. Edited by R. Stilwell *et al*, 240-43. Princeton, NJ: Princeton University Press, 1976.

Roetzel, C. J. "*Theodidaktoi* and Handwork in Philo and 1 Thessalonians". In *L'Apôtre Paul*, edited by A. Vanhoye, 324-31. BETL 73. Leuven: Leuven University Press, 1986.

Rohrbaugh, R. L. "The Pre-Industrial City in Luke-Acts: Urban Social Relations". In *The Social World of Luke-Acts*, edited by J. H. Neyrey, 125-49. Peabody, MA: Hendrickson, 1991.

_____. "'Social Location of Thought' as a Heuristic Construct in New Testament Studies". *JSNT* 30 (1987): 103-19.

Romano, D. G. "Post 146 B.C. Land Use in Corinth, and Planning of the Roman Colony of 44 B.C." In *The Corinthia in the Roman Period*. Edited by T. E. Gregory, 9-30. JRASup 8. Ann Arbor: University of Michigan Press, 1994.

Ross, M. H. *The Culture of Conflict: Interpretations and Interests in Comparative Perspective*. New Haven, CT: Yale, 1993.

Russell, R. R. "The Idle in 2 Thess 3.6-12: An Eschatological or a Social Problem?". *NTS* 34 (1988): 105-19.

Salac, A. "Inscriptions du Pangée, de la Région Drama-Cavalla et de Philippes". *BCH* 47 (1923): 49-96.

Sallares, R. *The Ecology of the Ancient Greek World*. London: Duckworth, 1991.

Saller, R. P. *Patriarchy, Property and Death in the Roman Family*. Cambridge: Cambridge University Press, 1994.

_____. "Patronage and Friendship in Early Imperial Rome: Drawing the Distinction". In *Patronage in Ancient Society*, edited by A. Wallace-Hadrill, 49-62. London: Routledge, 1989.

Sampley, J. P. *Pauline Partnership in Christ: Christian Community and Commitment in Light of Roman Law*. Philadelphia: Fortress, 1980.

Savage, T. B. *Power through Weakness: Paul's Understanding of the Christian Ministry in 2 Corinthians*. SNTSMS 86. Cambridge: Cambridge University Press, 1996.

Scheid, J. "The Priest". In *The Romans*, edited by A. Giardina, 55-84. Chicago: University of Chicago Press, 1993.

Schlueter, C. J. *Filling up the Measure: Polemical Hyperbole in 1 Thessalonians 2.14-16*. JSNTSup 98. Sheffield: JSOT Press, 1994.

Schmidt, D. "1 Thess 2:13-16: Linguistic Evidence for an Interpolation". *JBL* 102 (1983): 269-79.

Schmithals, W. *Gnosticism in Corinth: An Investigation of the Letters to the Corinthians*. Nashville: Abingdon, 1971.

_____. *Paul and the Gnostics*. Nashville: Abingdon, 1972.

Schüssler Fiorenza, E. "Rhetorical Situation and Historical Reconstruction in I Corinthians". *NTS* 33 (1987): 386-403.

Schwartz, D. R. "The Accusation and Accusers at Philippi (Acts 16,20-21)". *Bib* 65 (1984): 357-63.

Sear, D. R. *Roman Coins and Their Values*. 4th ed. London: Seaby, 1988.

Segal, A. F. "The Costs of Proselytism and Conversion". *SBLSP* (1988): 336-69.

Sève, M. & P. Weber. "Un monument honorifique au forum de Philippes". *BCH* 112 (1988): 467-79.

Sevenster, J. N. *The Roots of Pagan Anti-Semitism in the Ancient World*. NovTSup 39. Leiden: E. J. Brill, 1975.

Sheppard, A. R. R. "*Homonoia* in the Greek Cities of the Roman Empire". *Ancient Society* 15-17 (1984-6): 229-52.

Sherwin-White, A. N. "The Early Persecutions and Roman Law Again". *JTS* 3 (1952): 199-213.

_____. *Racial Prejudice in Imperial Rome*. Cambridge: Cambridge University Press, 1967.

_____. *The Roman Citizenship*. 2nd ed. Oxford: Clarendon: 1973.

_____. "The Roman Citizenship. A Survey of its Development into a World Franchise". *ANRW* 1.2 (1972): 23-58.

_____. *Roman Law and Roman Society in the New Testament*. Grand Rapids: Baker, 1992 [1963].

_____. "Why Were the Early Christians Persecuted? — An Amendment". *Past & Present* 27 (1964): 23-27.

Shuler, C. "The Macedonian Politarchs". *CPhil* 55 (1960): 90-100.

Sjoberg, G. *The Preindustrial City: Past and Present.* New York: Free Press, 1960.

Smallwood, E. M. *The Jews under Roman Rule from Pompey to Diocletian.* SJLA 20. Leiden: E. J. Brill, 1976.

Smith, A. *Comfort One Another: Reconstructing the Rhetoric and Audience of 1 Thessalonians.* Louisville, KY: WJK Press, 1995.

Smith, D. E. "Meals and Morality in Paul and His World". *SBLSP* (1981): 319-40.

Sordi, M. *The Christians and the Roman Empire.* London: Routledge, 1994.

South, J. T. *Disciplinary Practices in Pauline Texts.* Lewiston, NY: Edwin Mellen, 1992.

Stambaugh, J. E. *The Ancient Roman City.* Baltimore: Johns Hopkins University Press, 1988.

_____. "The Functions of Roman Temples". *ANRW* 2.16.1 (1978): 554-608.

_____. "Graeco-Roman Cities". In *ABD* 1.1043-8.

_____. "Social Relations in the City of the Early Principate: State of Research". *SBLSP* (1980): 75-99.

Stambaugh, J. E. & D. L. Balch. *The Social World of the First Christians.* London: SPCK, 1986.

Stansbury, H. A. III. "Corinthian Honor, Corinthian Conflict: A Social History of Early Roman Corinth and its Pauline Community". Unpublished PhD dissertation, University of California at Irvine, 1990.

Stark, R. "Antioch as the Social Situation for Matthew's Gospel". In *Social History of the Matthean Community: Cross-Disciplinary Approaches*, edited by D. L. Balch, 189-210. Minneapolis: Fortress, 1991.

_____. "Christianizing the Urban Empire: An Analysis Based on 22 Greco-Roman Cities". *Soc An* 52 (1991): 77-88.

_____. "Jewish Conversion and the Rise of Christianity: Rethinking the Received Wisdom". *SBLSP* (1986): 314-28.

Staveley, E. S. *Greek and Roman Voting and Elections.* London: Thames & Hudson, 1972.

Still, T. D. "Θλîψις in Thessalonica: A Study of the Conflict Relations of Paul and the Thessalonian Christians with Outsiders". Unpublished PhD dissertation, University of Glasgow, 1996.

Stowers, S. K. "Friends and Enemies in the Politics of Heaven: Reading Theology in Philippians". In *Pauline Theology, Volume I*, edited by J. M. Bassler, 105-21. Minneapolis: Fortress, 1991.

Stroud, R. S. "The Sanctuary of Demeter on Acrocorinth in the Roman Period". In *The Corinthia in the Roman Period*, edited by T. E. Gregory, 65-73. JRASup 8. Ann Arbor: University of Michigan Press, 1994.

Tajra, H. W. *The Martyrdom of St. Paul: Historical and Judicial Context, Traditions and Legends*. WUNT 2.67. Tübingen: J. C. B. Mohr, 1994.

Taylor, N. H. "The Social Nature of Conversion in the Early Christian World". In *Modelling Early Christianity*, edited by P. F. Esler, 128-36. London: Routledge, 1995.

Tellbe, M. "The Sociological Factors behind Philippians 3.1-11 and the Conflict at Philippi". *JSNT* 55 (1994): 97-121.

Theissen, G. *Social Reality and the Early Christians: Theology, Ethics and the World of the New Testament*. Minneapolis: Fortress, 1992.

_____. *The Social Setting of Pauline Christianity: Essays on Corinth*. Philadelphia: Fortress, 1982.

Thiselton, A. C. "Realized Eschatology at Corinth". *NTS* 24 (1978): 510-26.

Tomlinson, R. A. "Archaeology in Greece". *Arch Rep* 41 (1995): 48

_____. *From Mycenae to Constantinople: The Evolution of the Ancient City*. London: Routledge, 1992.

Tönnies, F. *Community and Society: Gemeinschaft und Gesellschaft*. East Lansing: Michigan State University Press, 1957.

Trebilco, P. R. *Jewish Communities in Asia Minor*. SNTSMS 69. Cambridge: Cambridge University Press, 1991.

Treggiari, S. M. *Roman Marriage: Iusti Coniuges from the Time of Cicero to the Time of Ulpian*. Oxford: Clarendon, 1991.

Tyson, J. B. "Paul's Opponents at Philippi". *PRS* 3 (1976): 82-95.

Veyne, P. *Bread and Circuses: Historical Sociology and Political Pluralism*. London: Allen Lane, 1990.

Vickers, M. "Hellenistic Thessaloniki". *JHS* 92 (1972): 156-70.

_____. "Thessalonike". In *Princeton Encyclopaedia of Classical Sites*. Edited by R. Stilwell *et al*, 912-13. Princeton, NJ: Princeton University Press, 1976.

_____. "Toward Reconstruction of the Town Planning of Roman Thessaloniki". In *Ancient Macedonia*, edited by B. Laourdas & C. Makaronas, 239-51. Thessaloniki: Institute for Balkan Studies, 1970.

von Dobschütz, E. *Die Thessalonicher-Briefe*. 7th ed. Göttingen: Vandenhoeck & Ruprecht, 1909.

Wallace-Hadrill, A. "Elites and Trade in the Roman Town". In *City and Country in the Ancient World*, edited by J. Rich & A. Wallace-Hadrill, 241-72. London: Routledge, 1991.

_____. "Patronage in Roman Society: From Republic to Empire". In *Patronage in Ancient Society*, edited by A. Wallace-Hadrill, 63-87. London: Routledge, 1989.

Wanamaker, C. A. *A Commentary on 1 & 2 Thessalonians*. NIGTC. Grand Rapids: Eerdmans, 1990.

Wansink, C. S. *Chained in Christ: The Experience and Rhetoric of Paul's Imprisonment*. JSNTSup 130. Sheffield: Sheffield Academic Press, 1996.

Ward, R. B. "Musonius and Paul on Marriage". *NTS* 36 (1990): 281-9.

Ward-Perkins, J. B. *Cities of Ancient Greece and Italy: Planning in Classical Antiquity*. New York: George Braziller, 1974.

Wardman, A. *Religion and Statecraft among the Romans*. London: Granada, 1982.

Ware, J. "The Thessalonians as a Missionary Congregation: 1 Thessalonians 1,5-8". *ZNW* 83 (1992): 126-31.

Waters, M. & R. Crook. *Sociology One: Principles of Sociological Analysis for Australians*. 2nd ed. Melbourne: Longman Cheshire, 1990.

Watson, D. F. "A Rhetorical Analysis of Philippians and its Implications for the Unity Question". *NovT* 30 (1988): 57-88.

Watson, G. R. *The Roman Soldier*. London: Thames & Hudson, 1969.

Welborn, L. L. "On the Discord in Corinth: 1 Corinthians 1-4 and Ancient Politics". *JBL* 106 (1987): 85-111.

_____. "The Pursuit of Concord: A Political Ideal in Early Christianity". Unpublished PhD dissertation, Vanderbilt University, 1993.

Wengst, K. *Pax Romana and the Peace of Jesus Christ*. Philadelphia: Fortress, 1987.

Westermann, W. L. *The Slave Systems of Greek and Roman Antiquity*. Philadelphia: American Philosophical Society, 1955.

White, J. L. (ed.) *Light from Ancient Letters*. Philadelphia: Fortress, 1986.

White, L. M. "Finding the Ties that Bind: Issues from Social Description". *Semeia* 56 (1992): 3-22.

_____. "Morality Between Two Worlds: A Paradigm of Friendship in Philippians". In *Greeks, Romans and Christians*, edited by D. L. Balch *et al*, 201-15. Minneapolis: Fortress, 1990.

_____. "Shifting Sectarian Boundaries in Early Christianity". *BJRL* 70 (1988): 7-24.

_____. "Social Networks: Theoretical Orientation and Historical Applications". *Semeia* 56 (1992): 23-38.

_____. "Visualizing the 'Real' World of Acts 16: Toward Construction of a Social Index". In *The Social World of the First Christians*, edited by L. M. White & O. L. Yarbrough, 234-61. Minneapolis: Fortress, 1995.

Williams, C. K. II. "The Refounding of Corinth: Some Roman Religious Attitudes". In *Roman Architecture in the Greek World*, edited by S. MacReady & F. Thompson, 26-37. London: Society of Antiquities of London, 1987.

_____. "Roman Corinth as a Commercial Center". In *The Corinthia in the Roman Period*, edited by T. E. Gregory, 31-46. JRASup 8. Ann Arbor: University of Michigan Press, 1994.

Willis, W. L. "Corinthusne deletus est?". *BZ* 35 (1991): 233-41.

_____. *Idol Meat in Corinth: The Pauline Argument in 1 Corinthians 8 and 10*. SBLDS 68. Chico, CA: Scholars Press, 1985.

Wilson, A. "The Pragmatics of Politeness and Pauline Epistolography: A Case Study of the Letter to Philemon". *JSNT* 48 (1992): 107-19.

Wilson, R. McL. "Gnosis at Corinth". In *Paul and Paulinism: Essays in Honour of C. K. Barrett*, edited by M. D. Hooker & S. G. Wilson, 102-14. London: SPCK, 1982.

Winslow, D. "Religion and the Early Roman Empire". In *The Catacombs and the Colosseum*, edited by S. Benko & J. J. O'Rourke, 237-54. Valley Forge, PA: Judson, 1971.

Winter, B. W. "In Public and in Private: Early Christian Interactions with Religious Pluralism". In *One God, One Lord in a World of Religious Pluralism*, edited by A. D. Clarke & B. W. Winter, 112-34. Cambridge: Tyndale House, 1991.

_____. *Seek the Welfare of the City: Christians as Benefactors and Citizens*. Grand Rapids: Eerdmans, 1994.

Wire, A. C. *The Corinthian Women Prophets: A Reconstruction through Paul's Rhetoric*. Minneapolis: Fortress, 1990.

Wiseman, J. R. "Corinth and Rome I: 228 BC-AD 267". *ANRW* 2.7.1 (1981): 438-548.

Witherington, B. III. *Conflict and Community in Corinth: A Socio-Rhetorical Commentary on 1 and 2 Corinthians*. Grand Rapids: Eerdmans, 1995.

_____. *Friendship and Finances in Philippi: The Letter of Paul to the Philippians*. Valley Forge, PA: TPI, 1994.

_____. "Not So Idle Thoughts About EIDOLOTHUTON". *TynBul* 44 (1993): 237-54.

Witt, R. E. "The Kabeiroi in Ancient Macedonia". In *Ancient Macedonia II*, 67-80. Thessaloniki: Institute for Balkan Studies, 1977.

Wood, N. *Cicero's Social and Political Thought*. Berkeley: University of California Press, 1988.

Woodhead, A. G. "Conflict and Ancient Society". In *Conflict, Antithesis, and the Ancient Historian*, edited by J. W. Allison, 1-24. Columbus: Ohio State University Press, 1990.

Woolf, G. "Roman Peace". In *War and Society in the Roman World*. Edited by J. Rich & G. Shipley, 171-94. London: Routledge, 1993.

Wright, K. S. "A Tiberian Pottery Deposit from Corinth". *Hesp* 49 (1980): 135-77.

Wright, N. T. *The Climax of the Covenant: Christ and the Law in Pauline Theology*. Minneapolis: Fortress, 1991.

_____. "One God, One Lord, One People: Incarnational Christology for a Church in a Pagan Environment". *Ex Auditu* 7 (1991): 45-58.

Yarbro-Collins, A. *Crisis and Catharsis: The Power of the Apocalypse*. Philadelphia: Westminster, 1984.

Yavetz, Z. "Judeophobia in Classical Antiquity: A Different Approach". *JJS* 44 (1993): 1-22.

Yeo, K.-K. *Rhetorical Interaction in 1 Corinthians 8 and 10: A Formal Analysis with Preliminary Suggestions for a Chinese, Cross-Cultural Hermeneutic*. BIS 9. Leiden: E. J. Brill, 1995.

Zerbe, G. "Paul's Ethic of Nonretaliation and Peace". In *The Love of Enemy and Non-Retaliation in the New Testament*, edited by W. M. Swartley, 177-222. Louisville, KY: W/JK Press, 1992.

Zuckerman, C. "Hellenistic *Politeumata* and the Jews. A Reconsideration". *Scripta Classica Israelica* 8/9 (1988): 171-85.